Beginn

D1386146

WITHDRAWN
FROM STOCK

MANCHESTER
1824
Manchester University Press

Beginnings
Series editors: Peter Barry and Helen Carr

'**Beginnings**' is a series of books designed to give practical help to students beginning to tackle recent developments in English, Literary Studies and Cultural Studies. The books in the series will:

- demonstrate and encourage a questioning engagement with the new;
- give essential information about the context and history of each topic covered;
- show how to develop a practice which is up-to-date and informed by theory.

Each book focuses uncompromisingly upon the needs of its readers, who have the right to expect lucidity and clarity to be the distinctive feature of a book which includes the word 'beginning' in its title.

Each will aim to lay a firm foundation of well understood initial principles as a basis for further study and will be committed to explaining new aspects of the discipline without over-simplification, but in a manner appropriate to the needs of beginners.

Each book, finally, aims to be both an introduction and a contribution to the topic area it discusses.

Also in the series

Beginning theory (3rd edition)
Peter Barry

Beginning film studies
Andrew Dix

Beginning ethnic American literatures
Helena Grice, Candida Hepworth,
Maria Lauret and Martin Padget

Beginning Shakespeare
Lisa Hopkins

Beginning postcolonialism
John McLeod

Beginning postmodernism

Second edition

Tim Woods

Manchester University Press

Manchester and New York
distributed in the United States exclusively
by Palgrave Macmillan

First edition published 1999 by Manchester University Press

This edition published 2009 by
Manchester University Press
Oxford Road, Manchester M13 9NR, UK
and Room 400, 175 Fifth Avenue, New York, NY 10010, USA
www.manchesteruniversitypress.co.uk

Distributed in the United States exclusively by
Palgrave Macmillan, 175 Fifth Avenue, New York,
NY 10010, USA

Distributed in Canada exclusively by
UBC Press, University of British Columbia, 2029 West Mall,
Vancouver, BC, Canada V6T 1Z2

British Library Cataloguing-in-Publication Data
A catalogue record for this book is available from the British Library

Library of Congress Cataloging-in-Publication Data applied for

ISBN 978 0 7190 7996 2 paperback

Typeset
by Newgen Imaging Systems Pvt Ltd, Chennai, India

Printed in Great Britain
by Bell & Bain Ltd, Glasgow

for Helena

Contents

Figures

Every attempt has been made to obtain permission to reproduce copyright material/the figures illustrated in this book. If any proper acknowledgement has not been made, copyright holders are invited to inform the publisher.

Acknowledgements

A book like this does not emerge without considerable debts to various people for their aid with specialist information, bibliographical sources, concepts for debate, and anecdotes for possible use in discussions about contemporary culture. My single greatest debt is to Peter Barry, the series editor, for initially asking me to contribute to the series, and for his exacting, detailed and rigorous reading of the manuscript. His influence has undoubtedly made this a better book and he is an editor of the sort for which writers, I suspect, pray nightly. I would like to thank both Michelle O'Connell and Fiona Sewell, who offered invaluable aid at the editing stages. Several other people have read either the whole of or part of the manuscript in its various shapes and guises: Helena Grice has patiently read the book in several drafts and I thank her for her persistent reminders about the nature of my readership and her diligent corrections of my style; both Chris McNab and Matthew Jarvis offered helpful advice on Chapter 3; Tim Dunne has also offered unstinting advice about Chapter 8 and issues to do with international relations and the social sciences, as well as useful snippets of information and examples for the chapter on popular music. My colleagues in the Department of English – in particular, Robert Jones, Andrew Hadfield, Claire Jowitt and Martin Padget, who have suffered postmodernism in its *beginning*, middle and end – also deserve thanks for their help and discussion in various ways. Professor John Harvey of the School of Art at Aberystwyth University gave me last minute help on visual art matters. I would like to thank the Research Fund of Aberystwyth University and the Department of English for the sabbatical and research funding in 1997–98 during which part of this book was written. I would also like to thank Matthew Frost and Lauren McAllister at Manchester University Press for their help with the final stages of preparing the manuscript and obtaining permissions for the illustrations. Finally, I would like to thank all those students – undergraduate, Master's and doctoral – who have sat in on my seminars, lectures and discussions on 'Postmodern Fictions' over the years, and who have helped me work out my ideas and opinions concerning postmodernism. You know who you are. This book is for you, and the others who follow in your footsteps.

Preface to the second edition

When I set out to write *Beginning Postmodernism* in the late 1990s, the forensic signs of an *ending* were already evident. The intellectual world was still recovering from the furore caused by the hoax article written by Alan Sokal, published in a highly respected journal, that sought to reveal what he felt to be the intellectual poverty of postmodernist discourses. 'Transgressing the Boundaries: Towards a Transformative Hermeneutics of Quantum Gravity' (*Social Text*, 46/47 (1996): 217–52, reprinted in Alan Sokal and Jean Bricmont, *Intellectual Impostures: Postmodern Philosophers' Abuse of Science* (London, Profile Books, 1998), as Appendix A, pp. 199–240) purported to show how physical reality was merely 'a social and linguistic construct' (*Intellectual Impostures*, p. 200), yet the article was really aiming to show how gullible an academic readership could be when faced with scientific jargon. The scorn with which Sokal and Bricmont dismissed the scientific understanding of the leading postmodern philosophers (Lyotard, Kristeva, Virilio and Baudrillard are central targets), resulted from their belief that postmodern science was no better than intellectual fraud and charlatanism.

Since then, the death knell of postmodernism has been sounding a steady toll. Touching the prevailing sentiment that postmodernism was very *fin-de-siècle*, Simon Malpas felt able to hammer a nail into the coffin of postmodernism when he concluded that if the postmodern were a space for debate, then the debate had moved elsewhere in the 2000s (Malpas, *Postmodern Debates* (Basingstoke, Palgrave, 2001), p. 1). Linda Hutcheon hammered in another nail in the epilogue to the 2002 edition of her *Politics of Postmodernism*, where she states indisputably 'it's over' (p. 166), 'the postmodern moment has passed' (p. 181). Indeed, it would seem that whatever else may divide attention about postmodernism, there is nonetheless general agreement that the moment has passed. Steven Connor opens his introduction to *The Cambridge Companion to Postmodernism* by stating unequivocally that 'Surely, the first thing to be said about postmodernism, at this hour, after three decades of furious business and ringing tills, is that it must be nearly at an end' (*The Cambridge Companion to Postmodernism* (Cambridge, Cambridge University Press, 2004), p. 1). Taking his cue from Connor, writing in *The Year's Work in Critical and Cultural Theory* in 2006, Peter Boxall felt able to summarise the central assumption underlying the year's work in postmodernism of 2004, almost parodying *Monty Python's Flying Circus'* famous 'parrot sketch' with his repetitive use of euphemisms for death:

> Almost everybody that addresses the question of postmodernism in the books under review here does so with the end, the collapse, the exhaustion, the attenuation of the postmodern in mind. To write about the postmodern now, it seems, is to write about the dead, to write about something that is passing away or has already passed away. (A. Gasiorek and P. Boxall, 'Modernism and Postmodernism', *The Year's Work in Critical and Cultural Theory*, 14:1 (2006), pp. 64–88)

Yet while these public notices, obituaries and histories are being written, there have been several parallel efforts to read the runes of the future, asking what (if anything) comes after postmodernism. Jeremy Green has sought to characterise this period as 'late postmodernism' and convincingly points to latent metafictional developments in US fiction (see *Late Postmodernism* (Basingstoke, Palgrave, 2005)). Stephen Best and Douglas Kellner, two of our best intellectual guides to the uneven terrain of postmodernism, have urged the continued usefulness of understanding our contemporary era on the threshold of the third millennium as a 'postmodern adventure', as they investigate the developments in science, technology and culture. Even Steven Connor concedes that postmodernism is phoenix-like in its 'extraordinary capacity to renew itself in the conflagration of its demise' as it catches 'continuing success from [modernism's] surcease' (*Cambridge Companion to Postmodernism*, p. 1). More recently, Neil Brooks and Josh Tosh have placed the viability of postmodernism as a term of conceptual understanding on the table in *The Mourning After: Attending the Wake of Postmodernism* (Amsterdam and New York, Rodopi, 2007), a series of essays that address the 'death' of postmodernism yet at the same time continuing to negotiate a postmodern inheritance that still offers important ways of understanding contemporary culture.

It would seem, therefore, that the annunciation of the death of post-modernism comes a little too prematurely. For in preparing this second edition of *Beginning Postmodernism*, I have been struck by how varied the developments in postmodernism have been in the past decade since the book was first researched and written. In certain disciplines, such as literary theory, literature, or international relations, there has been little intellectual development, and new debates and intellectual trajec-tories have formed that have preoccupied those areas of cultural pro-duction. However, other fields have seen considerable developments: take theology, for example, where the debates started early (1960s) and have continued later than most, with major works being produced in the 2000s, as well as publications indicative of a discipline consolidating itself (see Chapter 2). In the field of serious music, the intellectual structures for understanding 'postmodern music' are still being worked out, and in some ways, the developments in music over the past ten years in postminimalist music have actually allowed these conceptual structures to be more sharply configured (see Chapter 6). Even in those areas where postmodernism might appear to have limped to a standstill, such as the field of art, there are sub-areas like installation art, perfor-mance art and new media art that continue to develop actively the intellectual ideas, theoretical avenues and potential structures opened up by postmodern debates. Furthermore, in disciplines where post-modernism was a vibrant issue, such as geography or architecture, contemporary trajectories and developments within them clearly owe a considerable debt to the issues raised by postmodernism. So debates about 'mobility' and 'globalisation' in geography, or 'new complexity' and 'ecology' in architecture, can be seen less as breaks with post-modernism and more as re-shapings and re-directions of existing debates (see Chapter 5).

All in all, postmodernism has seen a period of uneven development across the human and social sciences over the past ten years. There have been significant political and social occasions and major earth-shattering events that have continued to be regarded as archetypally postmodern. For instance, the voting fiasco and controversy that surrounded George W. Bush's election and his subsequent presidency have often been cast in the postmodern mould; the ghastly events of 9/11 and 7/7 have been seen both as the *consequences* of western postmodern consciousness, as well as being *interpreted* in postmodern terms; and the fast-paced emergence of the Chinese economy and the demands that it places upon rethinking global political, economic and

cultural issues, have been regarded in some quarters as symptomatic of
the creeping and insidious nature of postmodernism. On the other
hand, some see the events of 9/11 as *the* definitive moment at which
postmodernism (as a process of flattening history) came to an abrupt
end. Postmodernism's disdain for universal abstractions such as justice,
its denial that moral judgement or truth can exist objectively, suddenly
sounded terribly empty. Books such as Richard Wolin's *The Seduction
of Unreason: The Intellectual Romance with Fascism From Nietzsche
to Postmodernism* (Princeton NJ, Princeton University Press, 2004) and
Jonathan Clark's *Our Shadowed Present: Modernism, Postmodernism, and
History* (2003; Stanford CA, Stanford University Press, 2004) have
sought to reconstruct historical and philosophical edifices that, it is
claimed, have been weakened by the destructive relativism, nihilism
and subjectivism of postmodern thought. *The Seduction of Unreason*
attacks the investment of postmodern thought in the potential of
unreason and argues trenchantly for a return to humanist pragmatism,
which will allow for a traditional political response to the dangers and
promises of a post-Cold War, post-11 September global community.
The issues of 9/11 have resounded throughout cultural, political
and social debates since that September morning, and are picked up
particularly in disciplines like International Relations (see Chapter 8).

Yet despite these varying considerations, it is generally the case
that a weariness crept into cultural debates around the late 1990s, with
the term 'postmodernism'. It was not so much that the intellectual
agendas instituted by debates centring on postmodernism ceased to
be important. Rather, it was a recognition that a more precise, acute
and discriminating critical language and terminology needed to be
developed to diagnose and discuss the sociopolitical characteristics at
the turn of the millennium. Hence, commentators turned to areas
of study like 'mobility studies', 'ethics', 'globalisation', and 'transnationalism'; and in some areas, turned back to issues that appear to
be 'pre-postmodernist', like 'history', 'representation' and 'national
frontiers'. As I and others have sought to demonstrate in recent studies,
these areas of interest are in most cases not 'new': 'globalisation' has
been a major area of study since 1945 at least, whereas the study of
'ethics' certainly occurred in modernism, and goes back to classical
Greece! What is new though is a refocused interest in these areas
with a postmodern consciousness, as being crucial to understanding our
particular age.

Steven Connor feels we have reached a stage where a history of
postmodernism can be written, and in so doing, allows us to see the

trajectory of a concept that has had its heyday. Consequently, Connor posits four different phases in the development of postmodernism: (i) 'accumulation', in which 'the hypothesis of postmodernism was under development on a number of different fronts' (*Cambridge Companion to Postmodernism*, pp. 1–2), stretching through the 1970s and into the early 1980s; (ii) 'synthesis', from the mid-1980s into the 1990s, marks the second phase in which these separate accounts are gathered together and cogently theorised, such as in Jameson's essay 'Postmodernism, or the Cultural Logic of Late Capitalism'; (iii) 'autonomy', the third phase which saw an expansion of the theoretical discourse of postmodernism in which the languages constructed to diagnose postmodernism took on a self-sustaining legitimation of their own. Postmodernism moved from being a diagnostic cultural discourse to becoming an entire environment in which the 'post' achieved its own autonomy; and finally (iv) 'dissipation', the fourth phase in which postmodernism becomes so dispersed from specific disciplinary sites towards a generalised cultural category that it loses any analytical value in its evolution as an orthodoxy, a default position.

Whether one agrees with such a mapping or not – ironically a grand narrative of the history of postmodernism – the past ten years do seem to have altered the terms in which cultural debates are occurring. Among the key features of this shift in intellectual geography was Jacques Derrida's pronounced interest in politics, ethics and religion in his later writings, beginning with *Specters of Marx* (1994), and moving through *Politics of Friendship* (1997) and *Acts of Religion* (2002). Whether or not these works do indeed amount to a much-vaunted 'political turn' on Derrida's part need not detain us here; suffice it to say that these later writings clearly chimed with a growing late-1990s conviction that deconstruction needed to rise to the challenges that it had failed to offer any practical philosophical thought and ethical guidance on urgent political issues. Other features of this change were the increasing significance of Emmanuel Levinas, and his pressing ethical concerns, the escalating pressure of ecological imperatives, and (as I mentioned above) the factors associated with the 9/11 attacks. A new lexicon – globalisation, green politics, transnationalism, cyberterrorism, singularity, transdisciplinarity, gene therapy, biotechnology – dominates cultural discourses today; and while these clearly emerge from the concerns that certain strands of postmodernism initiated, 'postmodernism' in most disciplines is more likely to be met with yawns and groans than regarded enthusiastically as a descriptive or analytical term that has much cutting edge.

Despite this *ennui*, upon re-reading the 'Conclusion' to the first edition, although the optimism of the early Blair years in the UK now feels very distant, I was struck by the ways in which some of the cultural trends and characteristics identified therein have become more dominant and in some quarters fairly established. Consequently, I left it unaltered to stand as something of an historical document. It is my hope that this second edition of *Beginning Postmodernism*, with its additional sections and updatings, will continue to provide interested parties with a solid and thorough guide to the areas in which post-modernism was such a major force, and to indicate the new directions and trajectories that are beginning to open up across the humanities and social sciences as the tide of postmodernism gradually ebbs. So whilst the book is bound by the series title of 'Beginning', one might nevertheless construe the debates in this second edition as occurring under the title 'Ongoing', 'Continuing' …

1

Introduction: the naming of parts

What is/are/was/were postmodernism(s)?

> From the modernism you choose you get the postmodernism you deserve. (David Antin, 'Modernism and Postmodernism', *Boundary* 2: 1 (1972))

What connects the Duchess of York, Batman, the new MI6 Building, Bill Clinton and Blur? Well, they are all apparently postmodern. For among the tally of 'isms', the new password is 'postmodernism'. To adapt Wordsworth, we may say that the postmodern is too much with us; late and soon, getting and spending, we lay waste our lives before it. Books proliferate on the subject; newspaper journalists write articles on the phenomenon; it is bandied about on radio; few self-respecting English departments ignore it; in a recent magazine multiple-choice questionnaire to measure one's 'hipness', one of the questions asked which of the following people is regarded as the founder of the term: (1) F.R. Leavis, (2) Fredric Jameson, (3) Prince Charles, (4) Jean Baudrillard, (5) Charles Jencks. I am pleased to say that I chose the correct response (Charles Jencks, according to the magazine), although I shall not disclose what my overall 'hip' rating was. The term gets everywhere, but no one can quite explain what it is. In the midst of all this terminological mayhem, Harry Enfield recently mused as to whether there is a First Class Postmodernism and a Second Class Postmodernism, and whether it is all delivered by Post(modernist-)man Pat.

But even if there is a postman involved, does he deliver anything at all? Does postmodernism amount to much and, if so, what
importance has it for our lives? Is it a *concept* or a *practice*; a matter
of local style, or a whole new period or economic phase? What are its
forms, effects and place? How are we to recognise its advent? Are we
truly beyond the modern, truly in (say) a postindustrial age?

This spectre – the spectre of postmodernism – haunts our
society at every turn. As Dick Hebdige's exaggerated and excessive
parodic list of definitions of postmodernism in *Hiding in the
Light* makes clear, postmodernism is ubiquitous and yet highly
contradictory:

> It becomes more and more difficult as the 1980s wear on to specify
> exactly what it is that 'postmodernism' is supposed to refer to as
> the term gets stretched in all directions across different debates,
> different disciplinary and discursive boundaries, as different factions
> seek to make it their own, using it to designate a plethora of incom-
> mensurable objects, tendencies, emergencies. When it becomes
> possible for people to describe as 'postmodern' the decor of a room,
> the design of a building, the diagesis [narrative] of a film, the con-
> struction of a record, or a 'scratch' video, a television commercial,
> or an arts documentary, or the 'intertextual' relations between them,
> the layout of a page in a fashion magazine or critical journal, an anti-
> teleological [possessing no overall design or universal plan] tendency
> within epistemology [the science of knowledge], the attack on the
> 'metaphysics of presence' [a self-certifying or absolute structure or
> foundation which lies beyond the operation of language], a general
> attenuation of feeling, the collective chagrin and morbid projections
> of a post-War generation of baby boomers confronting disillusioned
> middle age, the 'predicament' of reflexivity, a group of rhetorical
> tropes, a proliferation of surfaces, a new phase in commodity fetish-
> ism, a fascination for images, codes and styles, a process of cultural,
> political or existential fragmentation and/or crisis, the 'de-centring'
> of the subject, an 'incredulity towards metanarratives', the replace-
> ment of unitary power axes by a plurality of power/discourse
> formations, the 'implosion of meaning', the collapse of cultural
> hierarchies, the dread engendered by the threat of nuclear self-
> destruction, the decline of the university, the functioning and effects
> of the new miniaturised technologies, broad societal and economic
> shifts into a 'media', 'consumer' or 'multinational' phase, a sense
> (depending on who you read) of 'placelessness' or the abandonment

of placelessness ('critical regionalism') or (even) a generalised substitution of spatial for temporal co-ordinates – when it becomes
possible to describe all these things as 'postmodern' (or more
simply, using a current abbreviation, as 'post' or 'very post'), then it's
clear we are in the presence of a buzzword. (Dick Hebdige, *Hiding
in the Light: On Images and Things* (London, Routledge, 1988),
pp. 181–2)

As a current 'buzzword', postmodernism increasingly appears
in virtually every sphere of our culture and media. There are
academic journals dedicated to the subject, such as *Sub-Stance,
Diacritics, Enclitic* and the on-line *Postmodern Culture* (World Wide
Web address <http://muse.jhu.edu/journals/postmodern_culture>)
and *Ctheory* (World Wide Web address <http://www. ctheory.
com/>); references abound to it in a knowing and sometimes ironic
way in films, magazines and newspapers and on the television; and
although it is treated with disdainful scepticism by many scientists
themselves, it has seeped into subjects like speculative physics and
non-linear dynamics (often popularly referred to as chaos theory)
(for example, see Ilya Prigogine and Isabelle Stengers, *Order Out
of Chaos* (London, Heinemann, 1984), or N. Katherine Hayles'
book, *Chaos and Order: Complex Dynamics in Literature and Science*
(Chicago, University of Chicago Press, 1991)). Although the term
takes on very specific cultural significations within particular discourses, in its wider popular reception it appears to be a rather
vague, nebulous, *portmanteau* word for everything that is more
modern than modern. Books, articles and discussions have prolifer-
ated at an exceptional rate, as people have sought to identify and
locate the term in relation to their specific fields of interest. The
origins of postmodernism appear to be completely confused and
underdetermined; and perhaps appropriately so, since postmodernism denies the idea of knowable origins. Postmodernism has acquired
a semantic instability or a shifting meaning that shadows and echoes
its notes of indeterminacy and insecurity. The establishment of its
relativistic cultural politics as a new orthodoxy, coupled with the
complexity of grasping all the philosophical discourses and terminology, means it has the potential for discursive ambiguity and
metaphoric appropriation (for example, being used in another discipline with completely different associations and reference points).

STOP and THINK

Where did you first come across the term 'postmodernism'? What was being described, and what did you understand about the word from the context of the description?

- Was the word associated with any particular person or subject?
- Was it used positively or negatively?
- Is it a word used in casual conversation by you or your friends?
- Is it used in the lectures or seminars you attend?
- Have you come across any of the ways in which Dick Hebdige describes its use? Are there concepts, phrases or words used by Hebdige which you have not come across before, or which appear to have a special usage?

As a quick exercise, try to match the following nine terms with the nine definitions.

Terms
(a) incommensurable, (b) anti-teleological, (c) metanarrative, (d) intertextual, (e) reflexivity, (f) metaphysics of presence, (g) decentring of the subject, (h) a plurality of power/discourse formations, (i) implosion of meaning.

Definitions
1. Possessing no overall design or universal plan; resistant to totalisation or universalisation.
2. The existence of a variety of structures of language generated by specific configurations of power, all seeking precedence and the imposition of particular rules and hierarchies.
3. The way in which linguistic structures or discourses maintain a radical difference from one another.
4. An overarching explanation of a state of affairs, like those offered, for example, by Marxism, the Enlightenment or Christianity.
5. A self-certifying or absolute structure or foundation which lies beyond the operation of language.

6. The collapse of signification as a set of discernible and discrete units of meaning.
7. An identity, consciousness or ego which is deferred, displaced, fragmented or marginalised within a structure.
8. The relationship texts have with other texts or discourses, whether on a conscious or unconscious level.
9. Self-conscious incorporation of the processes of production, construction or composition.

These terms are difficult to use at an early stage. However, it would be useful for you to familiarise yourself with them, since they are significant within the debate about postmodernism, and will recur throughout this book. (Answers are supplied at the end of the chapter.)

Debates have raged with intensity in some of these fields for several years now, most prominently in architecture, visual art, literature and cultural theory, while in some areas the term is only just beginning to gain currency, as in various social sciences and law. As a result, individual subject areas have thrown up varying bodies of work on postmodernism and a particular subject, and very little effort has been made to compare (a) the different or comparable uses of the term in differing disciplines, and (b) the nature of its impact on different areas of knowledge, its specialised terminology, or its interrelationship with different subjects. This book seeks to fulfil these aims, establishing in one volume a guide to the various fields in which postmodernism is emerging as a cultural concept, with chapters embracing significant figures, terminologies, developments, works and events in the 'history' of this notion. The book aims to consider the important debates, to introduce the work of significant figures, to acquaint the reader with the significant texts or cultural works, and to investigate important areas of contemporary cultural production, as well as providing a useful annotated bibliography for new students. The book is not intended to be polemical, and it is designed for the reader who wishes to probe the 'mystique' that surrounds the concept and use of postmodernism.

The growth of postmodernism has been, in the words of one of the major theorists of architecture, Charles Jencks, 'a sinuous, even tortuous, path. Twisting to the left and then to the right, branching down the middle, it resembles the natural form of a spreading root, or a meandering river that divides, changes course, doubles back on itself and takes off in a new direction' (Jencks, *What is Post-Modernism?* (London, Academy Editions, 1986), p. 2). Gilles Deleuze and Felix Guattari, two gurus of contemporary social analysis, have described postmodernism using the metaphor of the 'rhizome'. This is the lateral root structure of certain plants, and the metaphor describes how all social and cultural activities in postmodernism are dispersed, divergent and acentred systems or structures. This contrasts with the organised, hierarchical, 'trunk-and-branch' structure of modernism. Others talk about the 'doubleness' of postmodernism, meaning its ironic, self-reflexive or parodic, imitative action. In all definitions, postmodernism has proved to be a snake-like concept whose twists and coils are difficult to pin down. From the inception of the term in Arnold Toynbee's *A Study of History* (written in 1934, and published in 1947), the term has accumulated contradictory meanings.

How then is one to understand the term 'postmodern'? One can easily have the feeling of drowning when dealing with the term and its manifestations. The prefix 'post' suggests that any postmodernism is inextricably bound up with modernism, either as a replacement of modernism or as chronologically after modernism. Indeed, with *post*modernism, *post*feminism, *post*colonialism and *post*industrialism, the 'post' can be seen to suggest a critical engagement with modernism, rather than claiming the end of modernism, or it can seem that modernism has been overturned, superseded or replaced. The relationship is something more akin to a continuous engagement, which implies that postmodernism needs modernism to survive, so that they exist in something more like a host–parasite relationship. Therefore, it is quite crucial to realise that any definition of *postmodernism* will depend upon one's prior definition of *modernism.* Modernism was generally the name given to the earthquake in European culture in the first half of the twentieth century, which undermined many aesthetic tenets and principles throughout the arts. Its geographical force was broad – affecting Berlin, Paris, Vienna, Rome, London, New York and Zurich – and the cultural force was deep – affecting all areas, like architecture, music, visual art, philosophy and literature. From about 1910 until about the beginning of the Second World War, artists as diverse as T.S. Eliot, James Joyce, Virginia Woolf, Ezra Pound, Marcel Proust, Stephen Mallarmé, Bertolt Brecht, Franz Kafka and Tristan Tzara in literature, Arnold Schoenberg, Anton Weber, Igor Stravinsky, Charles Ives and Benjamin Britten in music, Marcel Duchamp, Pablo Picasso and Wassily Kandinsky in art, and movements like Futurism, Dadaism, Surrealism, Cubism, Constructivism and Imagism ushered in experimental and innovative modes of representation. We might catalogue some of the characteristics of modernism as follows:

1. A commitment to finding new forms to explore *how* we see the world rather than *what* we see in it (e.g. the break with realist modes of narrative in favour of a stream of consciousness; in visual art, the emergence of Cubism, which represents objects as a series of discontinuous, fractured planes, all equidistant from the viewer, rather than using light and perspective to suggest pictorial depth containing solid, three-dimensional objects; in music, the abandonment of harmony in favour of tone).

2. A new faith in quasi-scientific modes of conceptualisation and organisation, for instance using basic geometric shapes like cubes and cylinders in the tower blocks of modernist architecture, as the expression of a rationalist, progressive society.

3. An ideologically inspired use of fragmented forms, like collage structures in art, and deliberately discontinuous narratives in literature to suggest the fragmentation and break-up of formerly accepted systems of thought and belief.

4. Aesthetic self-reflexivity, in which artefacts explore their own constitution, construction and shape (e.g. novels in which narrators comment on narrative forms, or paintings in which an image is left unfinished, with 'roughed-in' or blank sections on the canvas).

5. A clear demarcation between popular and elite forms of culture (e.g. intellectual distinctions made between atonal electronic music like Karlheinz Stockhausen's and modern jazz, or between modern jazz and rock, or between rock and 'pop', etc.).

6.   A gradual growth of interest in non-western forms of culture,
     albeit as a way to reinvigorate tired traditional aesthetics (e.g.
     the interest that avant-garde photographers at the turn of the
     century took in Japanese prints; or the widespread interest
     of artists such as Picasso and Georges Braque in 'primitive'
     African masks).

This outline of modernism is necessarily painted with broad
brushstrokes. To what extent does postmodernism emerge out of
this, or react to it? At first glance, the 'post' suggests a cultural era
'after' modernism, indicating some form of linear periodisation,
though this quickly becomes highly problematic, since the conceptual appears then to be conflated with the historical. In many
respects, postmodernism dovetails with many of these tendencies,
often practising *exactly the same aesthetic characteristics*. So the relationship between the two is clearly more complex than a simple linear model of historical development – first modernism, then
postmodernism – would suggest. Theorists like Jürgen Habermas
and Alex Callinicos argue that postmodernism is no different from
modernism in certain formal respects, and that the definition of a
different cultural practice rests upon a neo-conservatism which
seeks to negate the critical edge of modernist aesthetics as a formalist cul-de-sac. Despite the prefix 'post' suggesting that postmodernism emerges *after* modernism, as a chronologically later
period in social and cultural history, there are many theorists who
argue that postmodernism is *not* a chronological period, but more of
a way of thinking and doing. Zygmunt Bauman, one of the foremost
social theorists, regards postmodernity as 'modernity conscious of
its true nature' (*Intimations of Postmodernity* (London, Routledge,
1991), p. 187): in other words, it is a social and intellectual self-
reflexive mood within modernity. In a moment of parodic insight,
Todd Gitlin acutely lampoons the relationship by stating that
'Modernism tore up unity and postmodernism has been enjoying
the shreds' (Gitlin, 'Postmodernism: Roots and Politics', in Ian Angus
and Sut Jhally (eds), *Cultural Politics in Contemporary America*
(London, Routledge, 1989), pp. 347–60; p. 351). Postmodernism is
a *knowing* modernism, a *self-reflexive* modernism, a modernism that
does not agonise about itself. Postmodernism does what modernism
does, only in a celebratory rather than repentant way. Thus, instead

of lamenting the loss of the past, the fragmentation of existence and the collapse of selfhood, postmodernism embraces these characteristics as a new form of social existence and behaviour. The difference between modernism and postmodernism is therefore best seen as a difference in *mood* or *attitude*, rather than a chronological difference, or a different set of aesthetic practices.

One issue which is at the centre of this debate between post-modernism and modernism is the extent to which the legacy of Enlightenment values is still a valuable source for social and cultural analysis. Whereas philosophers such as Jean-Jacques Rousseau, Immanuel Kant and G.W.F. Hegel at the beginning of the Enlightenment placed a great deal of faith in a human's ability to reason as a means of ensuring and preserving humanity's freedom, many twentieth-century philosophers – especially those living through and after the Holocaust – have come to feel that such faith in reason is misplaced, since the exercise of human reason and logic can just as probably lead to an Auschwitz or Belsen as it can to liberty, equality and fraternity. Such questioning suspicion of the Enlightenment is principally associated with the work of Jean-François Lyotard, for whom postmodernism is an attack on reason. As Sabina Lovibond puts it:

> The Enlightenment pictured the human race as engaged in an effort towards universal moral and intellectual self-realisation, and so as the subject of a universal historical experience; it also postulated a universal human *reason* in terms of which social and political tendencies could be assessed as 'progressive' or otherwise (the goal of politics being defined as the realisation of reason in practice). Postmodernism rejects this picture: that is to say, it rejects the doctrine of the unity of reason. It refuses to conceive of humanity as a unitary subject striving towards the goal of perfect coherence (in its common stock of beliefs) or of perfect cohesion and stability (in its political practice). ('Feminism and Postmodernism', *New Left Review*, 178 (1989): 6)

Postmodernism pits *reasons* in the plural – fragmented and incommensurable – against the universality of modernism and the long-standing conception of the human self as a subject with a single, unified reason. The subject is the space demarcated by the 'I', understood as a sense of identity, a selfhood which is coherent, stable, rational and unified. Based upon this sense of individuality

('individuus' is the Latin word for 'undivided'), it is believed that
people possess agency and can use their capacities to alter, shape
and change the world in which they live. Postmodern theory is
suspicious of the notion of humans possessing an undivided and
coherent self which acts as the standard of rationality, and guaran-
tees all knowledge claims irrespective of time and place. It no longer
believes that reasoning subjects act as vehicles for historically
progressive change.

It is perhaps useful to distinguish between *postmodernity* and
postmodernism. The first is a concept which describes our socio-
economic, political and cultural condition. For example, in the West
we live in increasingly postindustrial, 'service-oriented' economies,
while our dealings with mundane tasks like, for instance, shopping,
are ever more mediated through the computer interface, as we communicate with each other by e-mail, voice-mail, fax, tele-conference
on videolink, accessing the wider world via the net, and choosing
for entertainment the high-speed image bombardment of the pop
video or the tongue-in-chic thriller anti-narratives of *The X Files*.
Such conditions of living are often referred to as 'postmodernity'.
Postmodernism on the other hand describes the broad aesthetic
and intellectual projects in our society, on the plane of theory. Thus,
for instance, people refer to minimalist art which combats notions
of art as ego-centred self-expressions of the 'inner self', or to literary works which take pleasure in 'playing' with language for its own
sake rather than with a moralistic or realistic purpose. Or they refer
to poststructuralist philosophy's claim that ideas which maintain
that there are centres of truth which escape or stand outside the
logic of language are merely convenient or ideologically motivated
illusions – all these might be referred to as *postmodernism*.

Nonetheless, despite this attempt at a simplified explication,
there is a variety of competing definitions of postmodernism. It is a
term used roughly since the 1960s about cultural forms that display
certain characteristics, among which are:

1. the undercutting of an all-encompassing rationality;
2. an incredulity towards metanarratives and a challenge to total-
    ising discourses, which is a suspicion of any discursive attempts
    to offer a global or universalist account of existence;
3. a rejection of modernism.

In all this, postmodernism represents a decline of faith in the keystones of the Enlightenment – belief in the infinite progress of knowledge, belief in infinite moral and social advancement, belief in teleology – and its rigorous definition of the standards of intelligibility, coherence and legitimacy. Consequently, postmodernism seeks local or provisional, rather than universal and absolute, forms of legitimation. The chapters in this book aim to explain the significance of these arguments in relation to various subject areas.

In recent times, many articles have appeared across the disciplines which begin by decrying their loss of direction, a crisis in their field, or a disruption in their disciplines or areas of thought. They then frequently go on to perceive and explain the postmodern/deconstructionist opening as a signpost pointing the way out of the cultural and epistemological cul-de-sac. It is also the case that postmodernism seems to appeal to societies in which the demise of their former economic, cultural and political superiority has led to a responsiveness to nostalgia and frustration. As a result, there has been an increasingly large influence of philosophy and textual interpretation in many disciplines. *Beginning Postmodernism* embraces the works, ideas and concepts from these disciplines both within and outside the humanities, where the impact of 'postmodernism' has manifested itself and influenced the discourse of these subjects. These cover such subjects as literature, film, visual and plastic art, 'classical' and popular music, cultural theory, sociology, law, anthropology, psychology, feminism, architecture and geography, as well as including references to important individual works which formulate notions of postmodernism and put forward significant terminologies. As such, it collects together in a *single text* a whole cross-section of information on 'postmodernism'. It is intended that this multi-disciplinary approach is part of the book's strength, since it tries to make *Beginning Postmodernism* available to a readership which is not simply humanities-oriented. It encourages some cross-referencing between disciplines to begin, and hopefully to indicate how different disciplines are using each other's ideas, texts and concepts. At this introductory level, it is also hoped that people from one discipline may investigate how their discipline touches upon, or has contact with, other disciplines. In this way, it is envisaged that *Beginning Postmodernism* might also prove to be a useful initial text to spark further *rapprochement* between different disciplines.

The term 'postmodernism' is not understood in the same way in all disciplines, and indeed, as its impact has been variable, its usefulness as a descriptive term varies from subject to subject: in fact, the same words sometimes lead to almost mutually exclusive concepts in different fields of thought. There are also different dates for the emergent postmodernisms in different disciplines – the late 1950s for art, the late 1960s for architecture, the early 1980s for cultural theory, the late 1980s for many social sciences. These distinctions and differences are made clear, while the comparable concepts are brought together. *Beginning Postmodernism* tries to show how postmodernism has permeated such scientific and aesthetic enterprises as sources of money, models of government, literary experimentation, commercial possibilities, physical movements of the body, and urban developments. Many of these areas of study are concerned with the way their disciplines are affected by language. It shapes even as it articulates. An impressive body of work exploring how metaphors, narrative patterns, rhetorical structures, syntax and semantic fields affect scientific discourse and thought is building up: for example, Donald McCloskey's *The Rhetoric of Economics* (Brighton, Wheatsheaf, 1986), Charles Bazerman's *Shaping Written Knowledge* (Madison, University of Wisconsin Press, 1988), Bruno Latour's *Science in Action* (Milton Keynes, Open University Press, 1987) and Thomas Kuhn's *The Structure of Scientific Revolutions* (Chicago, University of Chicago Press, 1970). This argument about the active nature of the engagement of language with 'reality' has deep affinities with the articulations that have emerged from the postmodern context.

There are many exponents and many different points of reference for postmodernism, which has not surprisingly led to a variety of reactions to the value of postmodernism as a cultural definition. One of the principal problems which has caused widespread disagreement about the value of postmodernism results from its relationship to the dominant culture. For however critical the subversion, there remains a troubling complicity with the hegemonic or dominant culture which cannot be denied. For example, when a multinational company like Benetton advertises its clothes by modelling them on a multiethnic basis, it may appear to be a simple subversion of the dominance of Caucasians in western advertising; but it carries with it an attempt to sell more of its clothing by cashing in on a high-profile racial issue. In the light of this 'political ambidextrousness', to stress only the radical or the reactionary side of postmodernism is to reduce the complexity of the cultural debate. Describing a society which lacks firm belief systems and long-term political commitments, which is given over to hedonism, playfulness, individualism and living for the moment, and yet which also promotes the marginalised and hidden and purports to be anti-essentialist, anti-elitist and anti-hierarchical, the political and ethical implications of postmodernism are not easy to distinguish. This is also one of the principal reasons for disagreement about the value of postmodernism's 'problematisation' of history, representation, subjectivity and ideology. For although postmodernism makes a virtue of its politics of the demystification of structures like patriarchy, imperialism and humanism, as we shall see, these concerns interconnect with those of Marxism, feminism and poststructuralist analysis. However, they should not be conflated with one another: Marxism and feminism bear theories of political action and agency that often appear insufficient or absent in postmodernism. Another vexed and contradictory issue appears in the sexual politics of postmodernism: for all its noise about representing the hitherto repressed voices, from bop to pop, from funk to punk, it remains dominated by the masculine in many areas. For example, apart from the notable exception of the Iraqi architect Zaha Hadid, there is a dearth of high-profile women architects; and the spheres of music, politics and philosophy are still dominated by men. Finally, postmodern theorists have often been criticised for confusing the collapse of certain *ideologies* of the real and the social with the collapse of reality and society. This clearly goes to the heart of the matter, for it is upon one's conviction about whether this distinction is blurred or confused that a politics of culture stands.

Beginning Postmodernism hinges upon the chapters on the relevant disciplines. In each chapter, examples from the principal primary works, the secondary critical material and, where appropriate, critical readings of these works are presented. The chapters branch out from these central figures and works, and range from relatively brief discussions of individual minor but influential figures to much longer discussions, which provide broader overviews of the contributions and influences of prominent individuals and the explanation of major terms and characteristics in those fields. The emphasis is always on the relevance of the subject matter of each chapter to the overarching context of postmodernism. Indeed, since most versions of this cultural tendency are against reducing things to 'bare essentials', it seems symptomatic of post-modernism's character that there is a lack of short, pithy definition. Postmodernism's obsession with fragments or fractures is a resistance to the totalising system which seeks to explain everything under a single rubric; postmodernism thus offers a rationale for a guide with chapters with discrete sections, rather than a clear, totalising essay. Postmodern knowledge is provisional and dependent upon the context of inquiry. In this context, *Beginning Postmodernism* can maintain something of a 'postmodern' style by providing a variety of chapters and subsections on various disciplines without giving precedence to any particular discipline or definition, while at the same time exemplifying aesthetic, sociological, ideological and scientific manifestations of the cultural concept.

There is, though, something of a 'terminological lag' in the various cultural disciplines within postmodernism. In some cases, the book concentrates on fields in which the concept of postmodernism has only recently been adopted as a topic of inquiry (as in musicology, history or some of the social sciences), and where the debates, authors and methods remain in a nascent state. Hence, it is necessary to maintain some looseness of definition in the term 'postmodernism' to allow for new developments in these emergent discourses and arguments. However, the approach to postmodernism that informs this book is not interested in forging a unified vision of the 'mature' postmodern phenomenon. Rather, it is the intention to acquaint the reader with as many different concretisations of postmodern discourse as space permits. Michel Foucault is often understood to be one of the principal theorists of discourse. 'Discourse' is a slippery word, but it is often understood as the institutionalised practice through which signification and value are imposed, sanctioned and exchanged. In other words, discourses are the variety of different linguistic structures in which we engage in dynamic interchanges of beliefs, attitudes, sentiments and other expressions of consciousness, underpinned as they are by specific configurations of historical, social and cultural power. 'Postmodernism' is therefore treated as a 'discursive event' embracing a whole range of disciplines, while I recognise that in some fields, agreements over the importance of issues, texts and authors are better developed and more advanced than in others. Hence, chapters inevitably vary in length according to the cultural significance accorded to ideas of the 'postmodern' within a particular discipline.

Beginning Postmodernism positions the cultural concept precisely as a *cultural* concept, a notion that pervades a whole swathe of subjects, and not simply as an esoteric word debated by ivory-tower academics; it is a vibrant concept provoking a wide range of analogous albeit not coterminous developments. A volume such as *Beginning Postmodernism* does run the risk of establishing a 'canon' of postmodernisms and postmodernists, delimiting who is *in* and who is *out*. It also runs the risk of becoming a *modernist* survey of *postmodernist* culture: the cataloguing approach is inimical to postmodernity's desire for fluidity of boundaries, a free play of information systems, and a suspicion of any form of reductionist tabulation. However, considering the very nature of the anti-canonicity and destabilisation of the strategies of postmodernism, this is most definitely not the book's aim. Selection of the material covered within each chapter discipline is based on such criteria as typicality, general consensus and prominent characteristics, and where a subject is contentious and debate is central to the material, this is incorporated within the discussion. *Beginning Postmodernism* tries to position a concept within the specific manifestations of that discourse, be it in literature, architecture, music, politics, law, sociology, geography, or business and management systems. Such definitions can place people, works and events within specific concrete existences, rather than delimiting them as specifically one thing or another, and thus balancing them within the sum total of a wide variety of cultural explorations, cognitive experiences, historical tensions, scientific structures or aesthetic forms. The concept of 'postmodernism' can itself exist, so to speak, as a tension within *Beginning Postmodernism*, between various chapters and subsections, in which no one chapter provides the definitive explanation of the concept.

Beginning Postmodernism brings together in a single volume a selection of the principal figures and terms in the particularly

important literary and cultural disciplines; yet it also seeks to connect these areas with analogous areas and issues from right across
the spectrum of knowledge, creating a beginner's guide to a field in
which competence for a person in one area may overlap with limited
knowledge in another. It is hoped that that gap is partially redres-
sed by this volume, which, through a series of inflected chapters
and suggested cross-references, provides a guide to analogous and
parallel areas of interest in other disciplines. To that end, a series
of thematic issues recurs throughout the book:

1. the function of history and the representation of the past in
   contemporary culture;
2. the nature of the everyday in contemporary existence;
3. the political role of aesthetic adornment or ornament;
4. the representation of the body and the emergence of new
   concepts of the human or self;
5. the insistence on metaphors of space in contemporary social
   experience;
6. the 'textualism' of modern knowledge and life.

The issues listed here recur persistently throughout debates about
postmodernism, and they form the nuts and bolts of the postmodernist scaffolding. Each chapter concludes with an annotated
Selected Reading list which indicates further reading in all the
disciplines. It is hoped that one of the benefits of this volume will
thus be that it can act as an impetus for initiating the expansion
of the horizons of what might be accomplished in any one field,
opening the way for parallel explorations of cultural theory in a
cross-disciplinary fashion.

Beginning Postmodernism is primarily intended to function as an
introductory guide to students and teachers of cultural theory,
modernism and postmodernism in various intellectual disciplines
in secondary, further and higher education, whose interests mainly
lie in the fields of literary and cultural studies. Although postmodernism manifests a relentless interdisciplinarity, its proportional
impact on various subject areas has been uneven. Consequently, the
text reflects this variability of impact by focusing principally on
the thrust of postmodernism in the fields of literature, cultural
theory, the 'human arts', sociology, and those people interested in

continental philosophy (and other arts disciplines), albeit taking into account and acknowledging some of those areas where explicit influence has been less marked.

The text is conceived of principally as an accessible introductory book which will provide a central resource for students and teachers alike. The 'Stop and Think' sections are designed to prompt dialogue, self-interrogation and self-reflection about the text and the positions which are adopted here. *Beginning Postmodernism* should provide students and teachers with a book that goes beyond the numerous books on the market which address the issue of 'postmodernism' in its various guises. For many of these are either highly academic in their orientation, like Peter Beilharz, Gillian Robinson and John Rundell (eds), *Between Totalitarianism and Postmodernity* (Cambridge MA, MIT Press, 1992); or written with a specifically polemical argument in mind, like Alex Callinicos' *Against Postmodernism* (Cambridge, Polity Press, 1989); or, like Malcolm Bradbury and Richard Ruland (eds), *From Puritanism to Postmodernism* (New York, Viking, 1991), quite strictly focused on specific nationalities, specific disciplines, or specific areas of knowledge (postmodern literature, postmodern law, postmodern art, postmodern architecture; e.g. Steinar Kvale's *Psychology and Postmodernism* (London, Sage, 1992), Costas Douzinas, Ronnie Warrington and Shaun McVeigh's *Postmodern Jurisprudence* (London, Routledge, 1991) or Edmund Smyth's *Postmodernism and Contemporary Fiction* (London, Batsford, 1991)). *Beginning Postmodernism* aims not to replace these texts, but to do something quite different. It aims to bring together all the principal exponents from different disciplines and different nationalities under one cover. It is hoped that through scrutinising a variety of disciplines and the way postmodernism has had an impact upon them, through the different accounts of different postmodernisms, readers can gradually build up a picture which cross-references and interlinks with others, and reinforces the knowledge gained from one discipline. Often the debates from one discipline throw new light on another. The book is also designed to alert readers to the multiplicity of postmodern debates, and open up doors through which interested readers might be able to pass to further inquiry. And the answers to those earlier questions are: (a) 3, (b) 1, (c) 4, (d) 8, (e) 9, (f) 5, (g) 7, (h) 2, (i) 6.

2

Postmodernism: philosophy, cultural theory and theology

Debates about postmodernism in philosophy and cultural theory have been extensive and varied since the late 1960s, often involving serious argument and vitriolic passion. Charge and counter-charge about the political, social and cultural value of postmodernism, postmodernity and postmodern culture have been flung left, right and centre. One famous example in the 'theory wars' occurred in 1986, when Paul de Man's pro-fascist, collaborationist wartime writings were unearthed and made public. This led to a number of Marxist 'I told you so' critiques of poststructuralism, opportunistically taking the event to discredit poststructuralism further by pointing to what they felt to be its inherent right-wing conservatism (see Werner Hamacher, Neil Hertz and Thomas Keenan (eds), *Responses: On Paul de Man's Wartime Journalism* (Lincoln NE, University of Nebraska Press, 1989) for a documentation of this scandal). Having to take account of the philosophical influences of Marxism, structuralism, poststructuralism, psychoanalysis, phenomenology and more, the cultural effects of various modernist art movements, and the social thought of at least the past four hundred years frequently creates the feeling that one has to do an intensive course in the history of all forms of western thought and culture before one can come to grips with postmodern ideas. There are several additional complexities to this picture:

- Jacques Derrida's theories of deconstruction and grammatology, which seek to disrupt the illusion of priority which tends to collect around one term in any binary opposition, e.g. the priority given to the former terms in the following

pairings: male/female, masculine/feminine, father/mother, sun/moon, white/black, centre/margin;
- Jacques Lacan's notions of desire, which replace the Enlightenment's faith in reason as the motor for historical change, arguing that the self is split between conscious and unconscious minds, and that as the self knows that what it knows is not all that it is (that there is a gap between consciousness and being), the desire for that *other* becomes a constituting part of the subject, which in turn drives history;
- Michel Foucault's 'genealogical' theory of history, which seeks to replace the conventional 'linear' model of knowledge with a more diverse, pluralistic model.

One can begin to feel that these debates are impenetrable. And if that were not enough, the omniverousness of postmodernism constantly finds new theoretical food for its diet, as in the work of Michel de Certeau, Emmanuel Levinas, Guy Debord, Paul Virilio, and more recently, the critiques of Gianni Vattimo and Slavoj Žižek. Reading through all these debates can sometimes feel like walking through a tunnel with little or no light at the end.

So how can we chart a path through the quicksands of contemporary philosophical debate about postmodernism? Who are the key figures to consider? What are the fundamental issues beneath all this argument? From what do they arise? This chapter will focus upon the key philosophical theorists of postmodernism, both its advocates and its challengers, and offer insights into how their ideas have shaped the specific debate about the philosophical effects and theoretical impact of postmodernism. It will then consider how these ideas have also developed within theological debates. A useful supplement to poststructuralist philosophical ideas might be found, for example, in Peter Barry's *Beginning Theory* (1996; 3rd edition, Manchester, Manchester University Press, 2008).

Philosophical champions of postmodernism

French double-acts – the two Jeans

Arguably the philosopher who put the first postmodern cat among the modernist pigeons was Jean-François Lyotard. *The Postmodern Condition: A Report on Knowledge* (1979; Manchester, Manchester

University Press, 1984) stands prominently among a number of
books which develop attacks on modernity. Commissioned as a
report on the state of modern knowledge by the government of
Quebec, *The Postmodern Condition* paved the way for contemporary
debate. It opens with the grand assertion that 'Our working hypothesis is that the status of knowledge is altered as societies enter
what is known as the postindustrial age and cultures enter what is
known as the postmodern age' (*Postmodern Condition*, p. 3). Dating
the advent of this postmodern age as the end of the 1950s, 'the completion of the reconstruction of Europe', the main argument is that
the era is marked by the demise of *'grandes histoires'* or an 'incredulity towards metanarratives' (*Postmodern Condition*, p. xxiv) and the
emergence of *'petites histoires'* or 'micronarratives' in their place. In
other words, there is a disillusionment with ambitious 'total explanations' of reality, such as those offered by science, or religion, or
political programmes like Communism; instead there is a growing
preference for smaller-scale, single-issue preoccupations, so that
people devote their time to saving the whale, or opposing a proposed
local by-pass road. These might exemplify Lyotard's *'petites histoires'*; the 'metanarratives' would be appeals to the emancipation of
the working classes or saving the global environment. Lyotard's
book is in fact a highly polemical attack on the discourses of modernity. Contrary to modern science, which Lyotard describes as any
science that 'legitimates itself with reference to a metadiscourse . . .
making an explicit appeal to some general grand narrative, such
as . . . the emancipation of the rational or working subject [Marxism],
or the creation of wealth [capitalism]', postmodern science concerns
itself with 'undecidables, the limits of precise control, conflicts
characterised by incomplete information, *"fracta"* [portions], catas-
trophes, and pragmatic paradoxes' (*Postmodern Condition*, p. 60). In
other words, knowledge in the postmodern era can no longer be
legitimated or sanctioned according to the great 'narratives' that
have shaped western knowledge to date, like the notion of progress
embedded in the Enlightenment, or the notion of social liberation
through history embedded in Marxism, or the release from unconscious trauma harboured by Freudian theory. Indeed, Lyotard
regards such narratives as violent and tyrannical in their imposition
of a 'totalising' pattern and a false universality on actions, events

and things. Instead, all one can do is utilise local narratives to explain things; hence, knowledge can only be partial, fragmented and incomplete. This is regarded as a radically new form of epistemological freedom, resisting the dominance of overarching patterns which appear to ignore the details and experiences of differences in their effort to construct patterns which make sense of the world on a grand scale.

In *The Postmodern Condition*, Lyotard argues (like Derrida) for a rejection of the search for logically consistent, self-evidently 'true' grounds for philosophical discourse, and the substitution of *ad hoc* tactical manoeuvres as justification for what are quite often eccentric lines of argument. It is essentially a strategic practice concerned with undermining the philosophical establishment and its commitment to foundationalist principles. Ultimately, Lyotard is suspicious of all claims to proof or truth: 'Scientists, technicians, and instruments are purchased not to find truth, but to augment power' (*Postmodern Condition*, p. 46). Beneath apparent objectivity then, lies a buried and dominant discourse of *Realpolitik:* 'the exercise of terror' (*Postmodern Condition*, p. 64) as Lyotard calls it. Thus, legitimation of any sort is always an issue of power; and it is the connection of power and the rhetoric of truth and value which preoccupies Lyotard's study.

Lyotard's target of attack is 'metanarratives' (the grand ideologies that control the individual); metanarratives are foundational and thus to be avoided, since they work to limit the abuse of language power. Lyotard argues that there must be an attempt to recoup the power of the individual to tell his or her narrative; that is, antifoundationalism in this guise becomes the access to the control of one's own politics. However, not everyone who can string together a narrative is politically desirable, after all. The principal tenor of Lyotard's argument in this book is the 'delegitimation' of 'grand narratives' in modern times (such as Marxism) and he states that:

> We no longer have recourse to the grand narratives – we can resort neither to the dialectic of Spirit nor even to the emancipation of humanity as a validation for post-modern scientific discourse. But as we have just seen, the little narrative [*petit récit*] remains the quintessential form of imaginative invention, most particularly in science. (*Postmodern Condition*, p. 60)

Lyotard identifies what he calls 'an equation between wealth, efficiency, and truth', and argues that it is continually a question of: 'No money, no proof – and that means no verification of statements and no truth. The games of scientific language become the games of the rich, in which whoever is wealthiest has the best chance of being right' (*Postmodern Condition*, p. 45). Lyotard is most acute at moments like this, where he pursues the misuse of power by institutions which monopolise the privilege of legitimation. He also demonstrates how utilitarianism is pervasive in institutions:

> The question (overt or implied) now asked by the professionalist student, the State, or institutions of higher education is no longer 'Is it true?' but 'What use is it?' In the context of the mercantilization of knowledge, more often than not this question is equivalent to: 'Is it saleable?' And in the context of power-growth: 'Is it efficient?' … What no longer makes the grade is competence as defined by other criteria true/false, just/unjust, etc. (*Postmodern Condition*, p. 51)

However, Lyotard gradually develops a narrative of the difference between modernist and postmodernist aesthetics which moves away from an historical period. This difference is that postmodernism is characterised by a new concept of the sublime, which attempts to put 'forward the unpresentable in presentations itself'. In the appendix to the English translation, an essay from 1982 entitled 'Answering the Question: What is Postmodernism?', Lyotard makes the paradoxical claim that 'A work can become modern only if it is first postmodern. Postmodernism thus understood is not modernism at its end but in the nascent state, and this state is constant' (*Postmodern Condition*, p. 79). He argues that modernism is:

> an aesthetic of the sublime, though a nostalgic one. It allows the unpresentable to be put forward only as the missing contents; but the form, because of its recognizable consistency, continues to offer to the reader or viewer matter for solace or pleasure. Yet these sentiments do not constitute the real sublime sentiment, which is an intrinsic combination of pleasure and pain: the pleasure that reason should exceed all presentation, the pain that imagination or sensibility should not be equal to the concept.
>
> The postmodern would be that which, in the modern, puts forward the unpresentable in presentation itself; that which denies

itself the solace of good forms, the consensus of a taste which would make it possible to share collectively the nostalgia for the attainable; that which searches for new presentations, not in order to enjoy them but in order to impart a stronger sense of the unpresentable. (*Postmodern Condition*, p. 81)

From this lengthy extract, it is clear that Lyotard's concept of the postmodern is *aesthetic* rather than *historical*. His emphasis falls on the postmodern as a particular form rather than as a particular epoch, regarding postmodernism less as a period of *time* (for example, the late 1950s onwards, late capitalism, postindustrialism) than as *a set of strategies* undertaken by artists to infuse a new sense of the sublime. For Lyotard, postmodernity is an attitude, an 'incredulity towards metanarratives'. This means that 'postmodernity' need not necessarily come after modernity: it means not modernity at its end, but in its nascent state, which is constant. This formalist approach to contemporary culture has caused a great deal of controversy in past decades for what has been regarded as Lyotard's lack of attention to material practices and what consequently appears to amount to an attack on Marxist ideas of history.

Lyotard has published several other influential books which develop these and similar theories. In particular, *The Differend* (Manchester, Manchester University Press, 1988) addresses the problems of judgement and incommensurability, or the manner in which different paradigms or models of knowledge remain irreducibly unlike one another, the principal target being foundationalism once again. We can summarise Lyotard's most important conceptualisations of postmodernism in the following way:

1. It is first and foremost 'an incredulity towards metanarratives' and an anti-foundationalism.
2. Although it presents the unpresentable, it does not do so nostalgically, nor does it seek to offer solace in so doing.
3. It contains pleasure and pain, in a reintroduction of the sublime.
4. It does not seek to give reality but to invent allusions to the conceivable which cannot be presented. In this respect, there is something theological in his concept of representational art.
5. It actively searches out heterogeneity, pluralism, constant innovation.

6. It is to be thought of not as an historical epoch, but rather as an aesthetic practice.
7. It challenges the legitimation of positivist science.

STOP and THINK

- As a result of eschewing macro-theories, Lyotard is unable to analyse the relations between technology, capital and social development adequately. The world economy is increasingly 'global' – a ripple of unease in Tokyo's financial circles can rapidly build into a tidal wave sweeping through all the world's money markets. Likewise, a localised conflict can quickly draw in major powers and threaten world political stability. But if you eschew macro-theories, 'overarching' explanations and so on, surely you will disempower the intellect and prevent yourself ever understanding such things. Is this a serious weakness in his argument?

- When Lyotard announces that he intends 'to wage war on totality', how can one be sure that the correct 'targets' will be defeated? Furthermore, in arguing that metanarratives no longer work, and that they have been replaced by local narratives, does he implicitly inscribe a new historical metanarrative of fragmentation and heterogeneity?

- Lyotard rejects totalising theories, which he describes as master narratives which impose simplistic models on discourses and reduce difference in cultural and social experience. Yet in arguing that there is a 'postmodern condition', does Lyotard himself presuppose a master narrative about a radical break with modernity as the emergence of a new society from an old one? Does the very term 'postmodern' imply some periodising thought, which in turn suggests some master narrative, precisely the homogenising and universalising perspective that Lyotard criticises in others?

- Furthermore, does Lyotard class jointly a variety of large narratives, thus imposing a violence on the diversity of narratives in our culture? Is it possible or necessary to distinguish between different types of master narrative: for example, between empowering and disabling narratives; between those which seek to subsume everything into one totalising theory (like some versions of Marxism, or Fascism) and those which seek to tell a large story such as the rise of capital, the establishment of patriarchy, or the consolidation of the colonial subject?

- Similarly, might one want to distinguish between a *synchronic* narrative, which tells a story about a specific society at a given point in history, and a *diachronic* narrative, which highlights discontinuities, ruptures and upheavals through history? Finally, in his prohibition on master narratives and their illegitimate claims for privileged authority, does Lyotard subvert his own call for a plurality of discourses in which everything is relativised?

If Jean-François Lyotard was the founder of this new French 'religion' of postmodernism, then Jean Baudrillard might be regarded as its high priest. Between them, the two Jeans have been the prime movers in this field of cultural debate, Baudrillard often making outrageous iconoclastic statements about contemporary society and technology in the course of his analyses, which have veered increasingly towards a full-blown postmodernism frequently considered deeply nihilistic. Baudrillard's views emerge as a conglomeration of ideas derived from Marxism, cybernetics, social theory, psychoanalysis, communications theory and semiotics. Following in the anti-foundationalist line of Derrida and Lyotard, his work develops a narrative about the end of modernity as an era dominated by production, industrial capitalism and 'a political economy of the sign'. Just as Marx's critique of political economy sought an analysis of the operation of exchange based in the commodity form, so Baudrillard argues that because signs are produced as commodities, semiology (the way signs are produced and understood) also needs the same radical critique that Marx developed in his political economy. The advent of postmodernity is further characterised for Baudrillard by 'simulations' and new forms of technology, culture

and society. Focusing on the technology of contemporary communication, Baudrillard argues that whereas earlier cultures depended
on either face-to-face symbolic communication or, later, print, contemporary culture is dominated by images from the electronic mass
media. These new global electronic media foreshadow a world of
simulacra, of models, codes and digitalised reality. Increasingly, our
lives are being shaped by simulated events and opportunities on
television, computer and video: like home shopping over the television, computer shopping at 'virtual stores', potential election-voting
by internet, or 'witnessing' the 'trial' of the president of the United
States by being able to read the transcripts of the United States
Senate committee's judicial investigation into Bill Clinton's alleged
perjury.

Baudrillard's conception of postmodernity is founded upon
three principal ideas – simulation, implosion and hyperreality. Like
Lyotard, Baudrillard claims we have entered a new postmodern era
of simulations which is governed by information and signs and a
new cybernetic technology. In a society where simulations have
become dominant, these models structure experience and erode
distinctions between the model and reality. Simulation is where the
image or the model becomes more real than the real: as for instance,
a television soap-opera actor receiving hate mail for his role in the
show. Consequently, Baudrillard argues that the demarcation
between image or simulation and reality implodes, and along with
this collapse, the very experience of the real world disappears. Simulation is the central concept in Baudrillard's conception of history,
which has moved through three stages: (a) the 'counterfeit', the
dominant structure of the 'classical' period, from the Renaissance to
the industrial revolution, where signs reflected and then distorted
reality; (b) 'production', the principal structure of the industrial
age, where signs disguised the absence of a basic reality; (c) 'simulation', the reigning social model for the current era, where signs no
longer bear any relationship to reality.

With simulation, there is a 'generation by models of a real without origin or reality: a hyperreal' (Baudrillard, *Simulations* (New
York, Semiotext(e), 1983), p. 2). Where the distinctions between
the real and the unreal become so blurred, the word 'hyperreal' is
used to signify *more than real*, where the real has been produced

by the model. Hyperreality is the state where distinctions between objects and their representations are dissolved, and one is left with only simulacra. Media messages are prime examples: self-referential signs lose contact with the things they signify, leaving us witness to an unprecedented destruction of meaning. For example, advertisements – frequently set to the brash confidence of 'New York, New York' sung by Frank Sinatra – represent the megalopolis with images of the glamorous, glitzy, neon-flashing, wealth-inspiring, skyscraping city of the 'Big Apple', the financial centre of the world and home to the world's leading media corporations. Yet this disregards the fact that New York is also the site of terrible poverty, homelessness, mass unemployment and a horrendous drug problem. The images of sparkle and light casually erase the urgent socioeconomic problems. TV is the principal embodiment of these aesthetic transformations, where the implosion of meaning and the media result in 'the dissolution of TV into life, the dissolution of life into TV (*Simulations*, p. 55). The principal locus for these observations in Baudrillard's work is the United States, especially in his books *America* (London, Verso, 1988), *Cool Memories I* (London, Verso, 1990) and *Cool Memories II* (Durham NC, Duke University Press, 1996). For example, he argues that in Disneyland, the models of scenes and figures from the United States are hyperreal, more real than their real instantiations in the social world. Other examples of where the model substitutes for the real are in ideal home exhibitions, the human figures of fashion models, or a computer simulation of how to handle a particular scenario. In all of these instances, the model determines the real, and hyperreality increasingly erases everyday life. Not only does it become ever more difficult to distinguish the simulation from real life, but the reality of the simulation becomes the benchmark for the real itself. The world becomes a universe of simulacra without referents.

Baudrillard regards this state of affairs as something to celebrate, because it marks the transcendence of alienated sensibilities:

> We leave history to enter simulation. … This is by no means a despairing hypothesis, unless we regard simulation as a higher form of alienation – which I certainly do not. It is precisely in history that we are alienated, and if we leave history we also leave alienation. (Baudrillard, 'The Year 2000', in E. Grosz *et al.* (eds),

Futur°Fall: Excursions into Postmodernity (Sydney, Power Institute, 1987), p. 23).

'Alienation' is a key term in Marxist theories of the self, describing the condition in capitalism of being severed from one's own productive activity and the consequent experience of loss of power or agency in the world which faces one. Baudrillard's cavalier disregard for the problems of alienation has caused severe criticism from Marxists, who regard alienation as something that needs to be worked out *in* history. What Baudrillard implies is that there is no possibility for social change, and that we are all inevitably locked on a course towards 'the end of history': 'everything happens as if we were continuing to manufacture history, whereas in accumulating signs of the social, signs of the political, signs of progress and change, we only *contribute to the end of history* ('The Year 2000', p. 27).

Contrary to the explosion of the modern industrial world, with the expansion of manufactured products, science and technology, and capital, Baudrillard argues that the postmodern world has 'imploded', that there is a collapse of social boundaries, including an implosion of meaning in the media. 'Only signs without referents, empty, senseless, absurd and elliptical signs, absorb us', claims Baudrillard (Baudrillard, *Seduction* (New York, St. Martin's Press, 1990), p. 74).

Baudrillard has become a byword for what many perceive to be the excesses of postmodern theory. Many, like Christopher Norris, berate Baudrillard for his overstated irrationalism and his philosophical muddles, and argue that his ideas need not be treated too seriously. His writing does tend to be hyperbolic and declarative, often lacking sustained, systematic analysis when it is required; he totalises his insights, ignoring differences and specificities. He could also be accused of extrapolating his rather bleak view of the world from a rather narrow base of experience. However, his supporters can make his failings into virtues, and his lack of philosophical rigour is often considered to be the sign of a tactical postmodern refusal to play by the theoretical 'rules'. In his favour, one might argue that he has provided new perspectives on everyday life in post-Second World War social orders, organised around consumption, display and the use of consumer goods.

STOP and THINK

- In Baudrillard's analysis of electronic media, does the fact that modern media may help to form as well as mirror realities necessarily mean that sign or image is everything? Does Baudrillard underestimate the extent to which TV audiences have a knowledge of how to decode TV, allowing them to resist being quite as passively drugged and stupefied by TV's fragmented narratives as he implies? In relation to such questions, you might like to consider Baudrillard's essay 'The Ecstasy of Communication', in Hal Foster (ed.), *Postmodern Culture* (London, Pluto Press, 1985), pp. 126–33.

- With regard to Baudrillard's lament over the loss of the real in a sea of simulacra, does this not prompt the question as to when was the real? Was it before the advent of electronic simulation, i.e. pre-cinema and TV? But Walter Benjamin argues that there was mechanical reproduction before photography and film. Before this, it has been frequently argued that language was the first 'technology' by which humans reproduced and controlled their environment. Does this suggest that the 'real' has always lacked a distinct referent, and that Baudrillard's dilemma is not simply characteristic of a new postmodern age?

- Christopher Norris has been especially critical about the more excessive aspects of postmodernist theory. In particular, he was quite outspoken about Baudrillard's arguments about the spectacle of information and its impact on the Gulf War (see Baudrillard, 'The Gulf War Did Not Take Place', *Guardian,* 11 January 1991). More broadly, Norris has been critical of the relativism, or the denial of the possibility of rational debate between competing traditions, that so many of the postmodern theorists espouse, which he perceives as particularly damaging to the ability to make truth-claims in the world (see Norris's rejoinder in *Uncritical Theory: Postmodernism, Intellectuals and the Gulf War* (London, Lawrence and Wishart, 1992)). Consider this debate and examine the consequences of Baudrillard's

argument about a simulated war for politics and social life.
(See Chapter 7 for a further discussion of this issue.)

Schizoanalysis: Deleuze and Guattari

Gilles Deleuze and Felix Guattari are also exponents of French
poststructuralist philosophical ideas. Although they have individu-
ally published many works under their own names, it is their two
joint works, *Anti-Oedipus* (Paris, Editions de Minuit, 1972; English
trans. London, Athlone Press, 1984) and *A Thousand Plateaus: Capitalism and Schizophrenia* (Paris, Editions de Minuit, 1980; English
trans. London, Athlone Press, 1988), that have achieved most noto-
riety. For their project has been a concentrated attack on what they
regard as the repressive mechanisms and discourses of modernity,
in an idiosyncratic blend of psychoanalytic ideas, a poststructuralist
attack on representation and the subject, and a critique of the state
and party idolatry of Marxism, which has earned them the outspoken hostility of many on the left. Deleuze and Guattari regard
modernity as an unparalleled historical stage of domination based
upon the proliferation of discourses and institutions which seek to
legitimate and normalise existing structures and states of affairs.
Their critique of the capitalist era is partly based upon a rebellion
against Freudian psychoanalysis, since they regard the Freudian
unconscious as a capitalist construction, a result of repression
produced by capitalism in the family. The tyrannical state and the
Oedipalised individual have been fostered by political and psychiat-
ric institutions, to the detriment of the human as a body of varied
and unorganised desires. Like Lyotard, they enthusiastically espouse
a micro-politics that seeks to precipitate radical change through a
liberation of desire. Postmodern existence occurs where individuals
are able to surmount repressive modern forms of identity and stasis
to become desiring nomads in a constant process of becoming and
transformation.

   Anti-Oedipus formed the first volume of *Capitalism and Schizophrenia*, in which they developed their notion of 'schizoanalysis'.
This approach articulated a new mode of postmodern self organised
around concepts of plural and multiple identities and decentred or
displaced consciousnesses. They start from the basis that desire is
itself revolutionary and radically subversive. Hence, society has

needed to repress and control desire, to 'territorialise' it within demarcated areas and delimited structures: 'To code desire is the business of the socius' (*Anti-Oedipus*, p. 139). In this view, the 'socius' or communal structure within which we live is a repressive regime: it organises social harmony not through *enabling* collective action to result from rational debate, but by *preventing* individual and collective desires from being allowed their freedom.

Anti-Oedipus is a historical analysis of the ways in which desire is channelled and controlled by different social regimes. Deleuze and Guattari theorise desire as a dynamic machine which constantly produces new connections and productions. Perceiving the libido as still fluid and as a flow prior to representation and production, 'schizoanalysis' opposes all those discourses and mechanisms which block the flow of the unconscious. For example, the family structure is one site where individual desires are 'controlled' or 'dammed up', as certain social structures are produced and reproduced through parental roles, sibling rivalries and the imposition of gendered identities. Contrary to conventional psychoanalysis, Deleuze and Guattari understand desire to be essential, and contend that it does not signify a lack, a subject in search of a lost object. Bodies are construed as 'desiring-machines' because machines arrange and connect flows. This 'deterritorialised' body is called the 'body-without-organs' – a body without organisation, a body that casts off its socially articulated, regularised and subjectified circumstances. In this respect, schizoanalysis has various tasks that can be considered postmodern:

1. It attempts a decentred and fragmented analysis of the unconscious, aiming to recapture pre-linguistic experiences, unconscious investments of sounds and sights which liberate desire.
2. It seeks to release the libidinal flow and to create 'new' (postmodern) desiring subjects.
3. Contrary to the processes of psychoanalysis, which neuroticises the subject, it 're-eroticises' the body by freeing it for libidinal pursuits.

A Thousand Plateaus is the second volume of *Capitalism and Schizophrenia*, and continues this project of 'deterritorialising' the body. This book reinforces Deleuze and Guattari's theory of 'non-totalisable multiplicity' based upon the concept of the 'rhizome',

their new term for 'deterritorialised' movement. They argue that
hitherto knowledge has been organised by systematic and hierarchical principles, as the metaphor 'tree of knowledge' indicates. In
opposition to these structural metaphors of arborescence and trees,
they pose the models of roots and rhizomes. In their concern to
uproot these philosophical trees and to remove their foundations,
the rhizome becomes a model of non-hierarchical lines that connect
with others in random, unregulated relationships. Rhizomes flow in
myriad directions constituting a network of multiplicities. Hence,
'rhizomatics' is a form of 'nomadic thought' opposed to the thought
which attempts to discipline and control rhizomatic movement.
Deleuze and Guattari's brand of postmodern thought seeks to liberate differences and intensities from the grip of state machines. The
schizo, rhizome and nomad are all models for Deleuze and Guattari's postmodern theme of breaking with repressive, representational
identity and producing a fragmented, liberated, libidinal body. They
represent emancipated, non-authoritarian modes of existence which
refuse social regulation.

To sum up: in theorising the micro-structures of domination,
Deleuze and Guattari's ideas institute a postmodern logic of difference, perspectives and fragments. Their ideas focus upon the following issues:

1. the institutional appropriation, taming and neutralising of
    desire;
2. championing the liberation of the body and desire;
3. the pursuit of a 'schizoanalytic' destruction of the ego and
    superego in favour of a dynamic unconscious;
4. the rejection of the modernist notion of the unified, rational
    and expressive subject and the substitution of a postmodern
    subjectivity which is decentred, liberated from fixed identities,
    and free to become dispersed and multiple.

Gianni Vattimo and 'weak thought'

One of Italy's foremost contemporary philosophers, Gianni
Vattimo, who has considered the relationship between nihilism and
the postmodern extensively, has emerged in the 1990s and early
2000s as a major voice in the philosophical debates about the

characterisation of postmodernism, through a series of key publications: *The End of Modernity* (1985; English trans. J. Snyder, Baltimore, Johns Hopkins University Press, 1988); *The Transparent Society* (1989; English trans. D. Webb, Baltimore, Johns Hopkins University Press, 1992); *The Adventure of Difference* (1989; English trans. C. Blamires, Baltimore, Johns Hopkins University Press, 1993); and *Beyond Interpretation* (1994; English trans. D. Webb, Stanford CA, Stanford University Press, 1997). Living as we do in an era when mass media and information technology have made people increasingly aware that there are multiple histories rather than just one, Vattimo shares Lyotard's view that postmodernism is a rejection of the foundational certainties of modernity and the fragmentation of society into multiple, incommensurable forms of life in which fragmentation means that no single 'metanarrative' (to use Lyotard's well-known term) can explain social reality as a whole. In this respect, he agrees that 'if (postmodernity) has a meaning at all, it has to be described in terms of the end of history' (Vattimo, 'The End of (Hi)story', *Chicago Review* 30:4: 20–30, p. 22). Vattimo regards the 'end of history' as the end of the *unilinear* version of history that underpins the concepts of progress or emancipation. Yet Vattimo's understanding of the postmodern is not Lyotard's atemporal version, but rather refers to a particular moment of Western thought, namely, the 'end of modernity as "the epoch in which simply being modern became a decisive value in itself"' (*The Transparent Society*, p. 1). Deriving his ideas from hermeneutics (the philosophy of interpretation), Gianni Vattimo formulates a postmodern hermeneutics in his influential book *The End of Modernity*, where he distinguishes himself from his Parisian counterparts by posing the question of postmodernity as a matter for ontological hermeneutics. In other words, instead of arguing for experimentation with counter-strategies and functional structures, Vattimo regards our experiences of heterogeneity and diversity in the world as hermeneutical problems to be solved by developing a sense of continuity between the present and the past. This continuity is a unity of meaning rather than the repetition of structures, and the meaning is ontological. In this respect, Vattimo's project is an extension of Heidegger's inquiries into the meaning of being. However, where Heidegger argues that Nietzsche is trapped within the limits of metaphysics, Vattimo links Heidegger's ontological hermeneutics with Nietzsche's attempt to go beyond nihilism and historicism with his concept of 'eternal return'. Interpreting Heidegger and Nietzsche through one another (*The End of Modernity*, p. 176) marks a significant point of difference between Vattimo and the French postmodernists, who read Nietzsche against Heidegger, and preferred Nietzsche's textual strategies over Heidegger's pursuit of the meaning of being. Endeavouring to rethink the philosophical tradition of modernity without seeking to transcend it, he draws on Nietzsche and Heidegger, and he introduces the concept of 'weak thought' as a distinctive discourse of a condition of knowledge that resists reinstating the dominance of the ontological structures, while not trying radically to break with them. As one commentator has put it, 'Vattimo wants to preserve the identity and operational value of philosophy instead of reducing it to textual "discourse" or to a free play of signifiers, and aims at a coherent conceptualization of the postmodern, adopting analytical tools that the postmodern seems to diagnose as in crisis, or even discard as obsolete' (Nicoletta Pireddu, 'Gianni Vattimo', in Hans Bertens and Joseph Natoli (eds), *Postmodernism: The Key Figures* (Oxford, Blackwell, 2002), p. 302).

The core argument of *The End of Modernity* is that the diverse theories of postmodernism can only be clarified by positioning them in juxtaposition to the philosophies of Nietzsche and Heidegger, particularly the nihilistic aspects of their thought. Since modernity is regarded as a process of a rejection of the old, a development away from and an overcoming of the traditional, Vattimo accepts Nietzsche's abandonment of the category of overcoming as an inherently modernist concept that ultimately seeks a vanished 'original ground'. Insisting on the nihilistic consequences of hermeneutics, this nihilistic reading of history involves a particular attitude towards modernity whereby modernity is dissolved 'through a radicalization of its own innate tendencies' (*The End of Modernity*, p. 166), dispersed immanently through a twisting, distorting radicalisation of modernity's premises. Vattimo uses Heidegger's term *Verwindung* to capture this postmodern recovery from modernity, in the sense of a twisting or distorting modernity itself, rather than an *Überwindung* or progression beyond it. This dissolution includes the production of 'the new' as a value and the drive for critical overcoming in the sense of appropriating foundations and origins. In this respect, Nietzsche shows that modernity results in nihilism: all values, including 'truth' and 'the new', collapse under critical appropriation. For Vattimo, this means a 'weakening' (Vattimo also uses the terms 'secularisation' and 'disenchantment') of structures, and the philosophical injunction is to embrace nihilism, rather than seeing it as a challenge to the legitimacy of one's theories and values.

STOP and THINK

- List some of the similarities and differences between Lyotard's and Vattimo's conceptions of postmodernism.
- Consider the different roles played by Nietzsche's philosophy in cultural and philosophical debates about postmodernism. Consider why some postmodernists may wish to affirm nihilism rather than take the accusation that postmodernism is nihilistic as a charge that must be refuted.
- While acknowledging the force of Nietzsche's 'God is dead', how does Vattimo's philosophy of *pensiero debole* or 'weak thinking' show that moral values can continue to exist without being guaranteed by an external authority; and is it still possible to speak of moral imperatives, individual rights, and political freedom?

Adversaries of postmodernism

Postmodern theory has not met with unequivocal acclaim, and there have been many who are critical of its stances and ideologies. The oppositional voices are not homogeneous though. Their critiques often stem from fundamentally differing positions, and therefore use differing discourses and different historical assumptions. Perhaps the most vociferous critics have emerged from the Marxist left, like the German philosopher Jürgen Habermas, the American cultural critic Fredric Jameson, the British literary critic Terry Eagleton (*The Illusions of Postmodernism* (Oxford, Blackwell, 1996)), the British geographer David Harvey (*The Condition of*

Postmodernity (Oxford, Blackwell 1989) and the British social philosopher Alex Callinicos (*Against Postmodernism* (Cambridge, Polity Press, 1989)), who have argued that postmodern theory ignores history, installs a reactionary conception of subjectivity, misconstrues the mechanisms of representation, and, despite its supporters' protestations to the contrary, has generally acted as a surrogate discourse for the vested power interests of late capitalism. More recently, the maverick Slovenian philosopher Slavoj Žižek has stridently weighed into debates about postmodern society with an idiosyncratic hybrid of Marxism and Lacanian theories. Others, like the British philosophers Christopher Norris, Stuart Sim (*Beyond Aesthetics* (Brighton, Harvester Wheatsheaf, 1992)), Kate Soper (*Humanism and Anti-humanism* (London, Hutchinson, 1986)) and Peter Dews (*Logics of Disintegration* (London, Verso, 1987) and *The Limits of Disenchantment: Essays on Contemporary European Philosophy* (London Verso, 1995)) have criticised postmodern theory for its philosophical contradictions and its crude misconception of Enlightenment reason. In a series of recent books, like *The Truth About Postmodernism* (Oxford, Blackwell, 1993) and *New Idols of the Cave* (Manchester, Manchester University Press, 1997), Norris argues that Enlightenment reason is not a unitary, monolithic move-ment which inevitably led to narrow authoritarianism and false progress. Like Habermas, Norris wants to adhere to the notions of progress, truth and the possibility of criticising ideology associated with the Enlightenment, and criticises what he terms the 'anti-realist' position of the postmodernist theorists. While there have been fem-inist advocates of postmodernist ideas like Hélène Cixous, Luce Irigaray and those who perceive postmodernism as opening a door for previously marginalised gender narratives, other feminist theo-rists like Linda Nicholson, Jane Flax and Susan Hekman have questioned the relevance for feminist theory of a set of ideas which undermines metanarratives of emancipation. The rest of this chapter will look at some of the vital issues raised in these debates.

Jürgen Habermas

One of the most outspoken critics of postmodern theory has been the German philosopher Jürgen Habermas. Reacting specifically to the argument about a legitimation crisis (the collapse of our grand

narratives) in Lyotard's philosophical critique of the Enlightenment, Habermas's most frequently cited critique of postmodernism,
'Modernity – An Incomplete Project' (widely anthologised and
reprinted in Thomas Docherty (ed.), *Postmodernism: A Reader*
(Brighton, Harvester Wheatsheaf, 1993)), initiates one of the most
prominent debates about the politics of postmodernism. Lyotard's
The Postmodern Condition directly challenges the two great Hegelian
metanarratives allegedly underlying the philosophical position of
Habermas: namely, the goal of the ultimate emancipation of humanity and the speculative aim of achieving a unity of knowledge.
Lyotard's assault on the concept of 'totality' and the notion of
sovereignty, which underpins the autonomous, rational subject,
confronts Habermas's notion of a rational society modelled on com-
municational processes. Habermas urges a 'universal pragmatics',
through which he aims to identify and reconstruct the universal
conditions of possible understanding in the context of specific validity
claims like comprehensibility, truthfulness and rightness. Searching
for the general conditions of communication between two or more
people, this model offers a deep structure embedded in all societies
and is known as the 'theory of communicative action'. Habermas
responds to Lyotard's charges by focusing on the alleged conservatism of the poststructuralist position. His initial lecture in 1980,
'Modernity versus Postmodernity' (*New German Critique*, 22 (1981):
3–22), is deliberately framed within a binary opposition which is
the hallmark of classical reason. Habermas defines himself as the
defender of the 'project of modernity' against the 'anti-modern'
sentiments of a line of French poststructuralist thinkers running
'from Bataille to Derrida by way of Foucault'. Habermas's argument is that modernity has yet to be fulfilled as a social and political
enterprise, and that to proclaim its demise is actually a neo-conser-
vative reactionary argument which ignores modernity's democratic
and liberatory potential. He takes the 'modern' to be akin to the
Enlightenment, and hence seeks to defend many of those principles
which perceive individual freedom emerging from shared communicative rationality and aesthetic creativity between several people.
Habermas is critical of the relativism of deconstructionist theories
in so far as they undermine the socially agreed and normal status of
social values. Deconstruction understands language as a series of

signs which create a set of relations which we mistakenly take to be putative things, but which is in fact nothing more than a chain of infinite references to other signs, thus forestalling the possibility of a definite interpretation of a text. Habermas on the contrary develops a theory based on rational consensus which opposes the positivist position (truth based upon scientific, empirical, objective observation), but which does not resort to the radical textuality of postmodernism (where the text is understood as an open-ended, infinite *process* of disruptive signification). Discourse for Habermas is not simply the interplay of signifiers with no touchstone for making truth-claims. Habermas has sought to defend many of the same principles, while making a more detailed critique of the ideas of postmodernist theorists in *The Philosophical Discourse of Modernity* (Cambridge MA, MIT Press, 1987).

Fredric Jameson

Like that of Habermas, Jameson's critique of postmodernism emerges from a left perspective. In a tremendously influential article entitled 'Postmodernism, or the Cultural Logic of Late Capitalism' (*New Left Review*, 146 (July–August 1984): 53–92, reprinted extensively, but available in extract in Docherty (ed.), *Postmodernism: A Reader*, and in expanded book form in Jameson's *Postmodernism, or the Cultural Logic of Late Capitalism* (London, Verso, 1991)), Jameson argued that postmodernism ought to be thought of as the apologetic or justificatory cultural discourse of the third stage of capitalism, namely, late or multinational capitalism. Borrowing from the work of the Marxist economist Ernest Mandel in his book *Late Capitalism* (1972; English edition, London, Verso, 1975), Jameson periodises capitalism in this way, suggesting that the first two phases are classical capitalism and high capitalism. Each new phase of capitalism has brought with it a concomitant distancing of the social. In postmodernism, people are most removed from the economic system of production which they serve. Postmodernism in Jameson's view ought to be understood as a 'cultural dominant' rather than a single style, as modes rather than a genre. Jameson uses the term 'cultural dominant' to ensure that his historical period is not understood as an enormous, single, bounded entity, but as the presence and coexistence of a variety of alternative, competing features.

In other words, not everything is postmodern, but post-modernity acts as 'the force field in which very different kinds of cultural impulses ... must make their way' ('Postmodernism', p. 57). According to Jameson, the principal characteristics of this discourse are:

1. 'a new kind of flatness or depthlessness, a new kind of superficiality in the most literal sense – perhaps the supreme formal feature of all the postmodernisms' ('Postmodernism', p. 60);

2. a waning of affect, or feeling, linked to the alleged loss of a separate and unique individual identity or self ('Postmodernism', p. 61);

3. the replacement of affect (particularly alienated *Angst*) by a 'peculiar kind of euphoria' coupled with a loss of memory;

4. the effacement of a personal, unique style and a sense of history itself, and their replacement by *pastiche* (not parody, but the rewriting or transcoding of typical modernist idioms into jargon, badges and other ˙decorative codes) and nostalgia, thereby instituting a celebration of surfaces which denies the hermeneutics of depth ('Postmodernism', pp. 64–5);

5. the fragmentation of artistic texts after the model of schizophrenic *écriture*, which specifically takes the form of collage governed by a logic of 'differentiation rather than unification' ('Postmodernism', pp. 71–6). This is an attempt to resist the obliteration of differences, the effort to make unlike things the same, and the imposition of an overall identity on radically dissimilar concepts, ideas, or persons;

6. the 'hysterical sublime', a theme developed by Lyotard, in which the 'other' of human life, what lies beyond our powers of understanding, surpasses our power to represent it and pitches us into a sort of Gothic rapture ('Postmodernism', pp. 76ff). This 'hallucinatory exhilaration' or 'glossy skin' of experience in postmodernist culture presents one with new challenges in representing that euphoria or those intensities, akin to the limits of figuration and depiction presented by the Romantic concept of the sublime, although now without its sense of the revelation of truth.

In order to combat this cultural deterioration, Jameson proposes, in a sonorous phrase, 'an aesthetic of cognitive mapping' as a remedy.

'Cognitive mapping' is a reorientation of our experience of time and space in an era where the opportunity to place ourselves into a definable time–space location (*viz. a place* with a unique, individual identity) has become systematically challenged by the culture of global capitalism, which, for example, replicates the same chain stores, fast-food outlets, theme pubs and shopping malls in every High Street across the land. This is Jameson's 'cure' for the fragmented alienation of subjects in postmodern culture. Yet in the final analysis, although Jameson utilises modernist Marxism to combat what he feels to be the alienating and debilitating effects of postmodernist logic, he appears to harbour a grudging penchant for many of the cultural artefacts of postmodern culture.

STOP and THINK

- Jameson's account of postmodern culture has been very influential, but it has also been very controversial. What are Jameson's weaknesses?
- He argues that modernist authors had unmistakable styles (like D.H. Lawrence's nature imagery or William Faulkner's long sentence), whereas with the disappearance of the individual self in postmodernity, there has been a disappearance of an individual *style*. Thus, postmodernist authors can no longer be imitated, since theirs is a collage of other people's styles: 'Modernist styles thereby become postmodernist codes.' Are you able to distinguish, for example, a difference in *style* between writers like Angela Carter, Thomas Pynchon, Salman Rushdie or Kathy Acker (all writers who have been considered as postmodernist)? How does one account for the blankness of style in the work of a *modernist* author like James Joyce? Consider whether there are differences of style in Joyce's novels *Portrait of an Artist as a Young Man*, *Ulysses* and *Finnegans Wake*.
- Should we conclude that authors can be *modernist* and *postmodernist?* Jameson describes pastiche as 'blank parody', 'speech in a dead language … but without any of parody's ulterior motives, amputated of the satiric impulse'.

Do you agree with his distinction between modernist parody and postmodernist pastiche? Can you find examples where this distinction breaks down?

- Is Jameson's model of history and capitalism one with which you would agree? To what extent does Jameson fall victim to the story that Marxism is just as the celebrants of postmodernity paint it, namely a *'grande histoire'* of social emancipation, and then has to play on their own ground? Is Marxism a pernicious, authoritarian metanarrative?

The Žižek effect

With his dizzyingly prolific rate of publication (about fifty books during the past fifteen years), the Slovenian philosopher Slavoj Žižek has whirled into English-speaking debates about postmodernism like a tumultuous tornado. Through his unique blend of Lacanian psychoanalysis, Marxism, and critique of popular culture, Žižek aims to reveal the invisible workings of ideology across an omnivorous range of such diverse topics as the Iraq War, fundamentalism, capitalism, tolerance, political correctness, globalisation, subjectivity, human rights, Lenin, myth, cyberspace, postmodernism, multiculturalism, post-Marxism, David Lynch and Alfred Hitchcock. It was with the publication of his first book written in English, *The Sublime Object of Ideology* (London, Verso, 1989), that Žižek achieved international recognition as a major social theorist. Since then, he has maintained his status as an intellectual outsider and confrontational maverick, often courting controversy, such as he did in one of his most widely discussed books, *The Ticklish Subject* (London, Verso, 1999), which explicitly positioned itself against Deconstructionists, Heideggerians, Habermasians, cognitive scientists, feminists and what Žižek describes as New Age 'obscurantists'.

Some would have Žižek's critique of ideology as a grotesque masquerade that seeks to pull back the drapes of a devilish democracy to reinstall some form of old-style Bolshevism. As one commentator put it, 'He is not offering warm, fuzzy Lennonism; this is cold, bloody Leninism' (*New Statesman*, 30 April 2007).

Yet others would regard Žižek as an enlightened prophet from behind the old 'iron curtain', possessing a firsthand experience of socialism and state violence that seemed like a breath of fresh air to many critics living in the Western democracies only experienced by proxy. Yet despite his role as the biggest box-office draw academic postmodernists have ever had, their best punch at the bestseller lists, and the press's fawning representation of him as an 'intellectual rock star', just how much of Žižek's ideas stand up to rigorous scrutiny? His acolytes argue that Žižek is trying to elasticise philosophy to cover the quotidian debris that philosophers have hitherto ignored. Yet what does Slavoj Žižek believe? For what does he argue? Under the veneer of critique, in what ways do Žižek's ideas offer us a subtle, new and nuanced perspective on postmodernism?

Many of his apparent critical allies on the Left appear yet to be persuaded that Žižek's project is more than philosophical pyrotechnics. Reviewing Žižek's *The Parallax View* (Cambridge MA, MIT Press, 2006), despite a sneaking sympathy for the scathing critique of 'the usual gang of democracy-to-come-deconstructionist-postsecular-Levinasian-respect-for-Otherness suspects', Terry Eagleton notes with jaundice that Žižek's intellectual brilliance is undermined by a pervasive stylistic similarity in all his books: 'He is never in the least obscurantist, though he lacks a certain gravitas and much of the time sounds more knowledgeable than wise. ... His mind is so robustly idiosyncratic that its presence in his books makes all of them sound somehow the same' (*Artforum International*, 22 June 2006). Reviewing the same book, Fredric Jameson declares himself to remain suspicious of Žižek's abyssmal project and suggests that 'Žižek may turn out to have produced a new concept and a new theory after all, simply by naming what it is probably better not to call the unnameable' (*London Review of Books*, 7 September 2006).

Nevertheless, Žižek, arguably what might have become known as a post-postmodernist cultural critic (if there is such a thing), is famous for his use of Lacanian analysis to foreground the ways that cultures can exhibit symptoms of the Real (the always-missing part of experience, that which lies outside language and resists symbolisation, that which is impossible to integrate into the symbolic order) in ways that surprise and confound their own symbolic networks. Žižek sees that ideology attempts to disguise impossibility and to reinterpret it as if it were a potentially removable obstacle. Žižek identifies insidious links between corporate globalisation and cultural subjectivity, a complicity between postmodern culture and that endorsed by the logic of capital. This is evident in two examples:

1. the pluralisation of identities provides an increasing opportunities for commodification and consumption, as ethnic identities are sold and packaged;
2. postmodernism's insistence on difference enforces a level playing field, in which one is required to respect all identities without prioritising any type of identity over another, thus rendering major global problems, such as world poverty or continental hunger, abstract and invisible.

As far as Žižek is concerned, we need to resist the conviction in postmodernism that forms of differential absorption are a bad thing, and he thereby implies a direct rejection of the postmodern prohibition on political prioritisation. Instead, he promotes a theory of a radical break with the postmodern rules of stressing difference and pluralisation within the existing social horizon. He recognises that an action from within the old symbolic order cannot be entirely named or judged within this order. As Žižek explains:

> An act does not occur *within* the given horizon of what appears to be 'possible' – it redefines the very contours of what is possible (an act accomplishes what, within the given symbolic universe, appears to be 'impossible', yet it changes its conditions so that it creates retroactively the conditions of its own possibility). (Judith Butler, Ernesto Laclau and Slavoj Žižek, *Contingency, Hegemony, Universality* (London, Verso, 2000), p. 121)

Therefore, a radical action has to redefine, or change, the criteria by which it will be understood. A radical act must transform the symbolic context, so that, after it has occurred, it seems the only course of events. Žižek's philosophy is therefore about steering a course through the shoals of ideological phantasms, using psychoanalysis to pass through the matrix of deceptive images and enabling a so-called *authentic act* to subvert ideology's shams and cons.

STOP and THINK

- At the risk of empiricism seeming dreary compared to the imaginative excesses of psychoanalysis, when using Žižek's theoretical method, is it possible to identify appearances of the real as opposed to the mere appearance of reality?

- To what extent might Žižek's freewheeling style, its spectacular montage of ideas, be regarded as an example of Lyotard's description of postmodernism as a smorgasbord of different cultures and geographical spaces?

- Žižek argues that what is often considered the most liberating aspect of postmodern technologies (like virtual reality) – their seemingly bi-lateral, interactive relation with the subject – must also be seen as the complete opposite: the liberating interactivity that subjects experience with postmodern technologies is simultaneously a disturbing 'inter-passivity'. To what extent do you agree?

Postmodernism and feminism

While the link proposed by the conjunction in 'postmodernism and feminism' suggests a necessary connection and reciprocity, this is far from straightforward. Feminism has always been a pluralist enterprise, yet one current issue for many feminists is the extent to which feminism can or will transform postmodernism, or the extent to which postmodernism can or will transform feminism; and fierce debates have occurred within feminist politics itself in addressing this matter (see, for example, Marianne Hirsch and Evelyn Fox Keller (eds), *Conflicts in Feminism* (New York and London, Routledge, 1990)). In some respects, the deconstructive recognition of interpretative multiplicity, of the indeterminacy and heterogeneity of cultural meaning, seems bound to attract feminism to postmodernism. Many feminist theorists, like Elizabeth Grosz, Judith Butler, Donna Haraway, Jane Flax, Seyla Benhabib, Rosi Braidotti and Moira Gatens, have engaged with postmodernist thought because of its ability to challenge essentialist gender identities. The thrust of this challenge is the main impetus for one of the most notable arguments that sex is constructed through language, namely Judith

Butler's *Gender Trouble* (New York, Routledge, 1990), which draws on, and critiques the work of, Simone de Beauvoir, Michel Foucault and Jacques Lacan. Butler criticises the distinction drawn by previous feminisms between (biological) sex and (socially constructed) gender. The tenor of Butler's argument in *Gender Trouble* is that the coherence of the categories of sex, gender and sexuality – the natural-seeming coherence, for example, of masculine gender and heterosexual desire in male bodies – is culturally constructed through the repetition of stylised acts in time. The repetition of these stylised bodily acts establish the appearance of an essential, ontological 'core' gender. This is the sense in which Butler famously theorises gender, along with sex and sexuality, as performative. While this gender performance is not a voluntary choice, the concept of performativity extends beyond the doing of gender and should be understood as a thoroughgoing theory of subjectivity. Although Judith Butler herself rejects the term 'postmodernism' as too vague to be meaningful, Linda Nicholson argues that feminist theory 'belongs to the terrain of postmodern philosophy' (Nicholson (ed.), *Feminism/Postmodernism* (New York and London, Routledge, 1990), p. 6), while Jane Flax puts it even more strongly: 'Feminist theorists enter into and echo postmodernist discourse' (Flax, *Thinking Fragments: Psychoanalysis, Feminism, and Postmodernism in the Contemporary West* (Berkeley CA, University of California Press, 1990), p. 2). The postmodern narrative of 'heteroglossia' appears to afford a ready theoretical ally to the feminist goals of opening up a new fluidity of boundaries and presenting the alternative perspectives of others. Three further aspects of where such a theoretical alliance seems appropriate are:

1. the celebration of the confusion of gender boundaries;
2. the erosion of the self in the face of the rigid demarcations of the masculine Cartesian universe;
3. the reconfiguration of the patriarchal fetishisation of the female body.

Donna Haraway's concept of the 'cyborg' as a metaphor for the 'disassembled and reassembled, postmodern collective and personal self [which] feminists must code' (Haraway, 'A Manifesto for Cyborgs', in Nicholson (ed.), *Feminism/Postmodernism*, p. 205) is just one powerful and influential model for a new, postmodern body which floats free of time, place and gender restrictions (see Chapter 7 for further discussion).

Susan Hekman has attempted to postmodernise feminism, since she perceives that postmodernism and feminism share an assault on anthropocentric definitions of knowledge. Feminism and postmodernism also share a critique of Enlightenment epistemology based upon rationalism and dualism. However, she recognises too that some tension exists between feminism and postmodernism. For example, feminism is critical of Enlightenment rationalism because of its gender bias in placing women in an inferior position with regard to the masculinisation of reason. In this respect, she argues that 'the feminist critique extends the postmodern critique of rationalism by revealing its gendered character' (Hekman, *Gender and Knowledge: Elements of a Postmodern Feminism* (Boston MA, Northeastern University Press, 1990), p. 5). However, feminism finds itself in a Catch-22: although it is critical of the Enlightenment for its patriarchal epistemology, it also seeks to avail itself of the modernist legacy of a unified emancipation through the exercise of the faculty of reason.

Other feminist arguments have criticised as another example of 'phallogocentricism' the socialist feminist effort to find a single, unified feminist perspective. Emanating from the perspective of French feminists such as Irigaray, Cixous, Julia Kristeva and Annie Leclerc, this means that any attempt to organise plural perspectives into a singular narrative is a further example of the exercise of male power. Such a unified narrative is also regarded as completely unfeasible because of women's different experiences across class, race and culture. Postmodernist feminists argue that by refusing to congeal and cement their differences into a unified, inflexible truth, they thereby resist patriarchal dogma. Picking up another vein of postmodernism, feminists such as Cixous and Irigaray have sought to show how 'sexuality' and 'textuality' merge. Cixous's 'Sorties' is a central essay for the objection to masculine logic and writing because they cast gender in binary terms upon which is built a patriarchal hierarchy. Cixous urges women to write themselves out of the world that men have constructed for them by putting into words the unthinkable/unthought. Irigaray suggests that women ought to mime the mimes that men have imposed upon them, taking the masculine images of women and reflecting them at men at twice the original size. This 'mimicry' preys on masculine logic and seeks to subvert the homogeneity of such representations.

For all these positive endorsements of feminism's *rapprochement* with postmodernism, just as many feminists have been extremely sceptical of the arguments of many of the postmodern theorists. Foremost in recent critiques has been Somer Brodribb's book, entitled *Nothing Mat(t)ers: A Feminist Critique of Postmodernism* (North Melbourne, Spinifex Press, 1993). Brodribb has produced an excoriating critique of attempts to ally feminism with postmodernism, which she perceives as an incorporation of feminism within a masculinist theory. Paraphrasing bell hooks, the influential, radical, African-American feminist theorist, Brodribb argues that the other sex is displaced and erased in the postmodern framing of difference, since ultimately postmodern theory effects a depoliticisation of feminism: 'Postmodernism exults [*sic*] female oblivion and disconnection; it has no model for the acquisition of knowledge, for making connections, for communication, or for becoming global, which feminism has done and will continue to do' (*Nothing Mat(t)ers*, p. xix). Highly critical of the likes of Hekman, Nicholson and Flax, Brodribb is ultimately concerned with the patriarchal politics of postmodernism. Postmodern arguments which stress the importance of micro-narratives and the collapse of the grand narratives of history have posed significant threats to an ideological critique of patriarchy based upon a 'grand narrative' of male domination. Such postmodern theories effectively subvert the potential for female agency and the radical political effectiveness of a feminist project based upon the analysis of a hegemonic male power. Understandably, feminists such as Brodribb are highly suspicious of an agenda for postmodern feminism derived from the ideas of male theorists such as Derrida, Lacan and Foucault.

STOP and THINK

- With Haraway's notion of the cyborg in mind, what sort of body is it that is free to change its shape and location at will, that can become anyone and travel anywhere? If the body is not a metaphor for the limitations of human perception and knowledge, then the body is no body at all. In what ways does Haraway's concept prove enabling or disabling for feminism?

- Consider the potential strengths and weaknesses of Iriga-ray's ideas of 'mimicry': for example, is there not a fine line between mimicking a position for subversive ends and fulfilling a definition?
- Is there a risk that in attempting to undo positions, women may fall back into them? Although Brodribb makes some pertinent arguments about the maculinist theoretical basis of postmodernism, does she risk falling into a trap of essen-tialising gender when she argues that feminism cannot use ideas from male theorists?

Postcolonialism and postmodernism

In so far as postmodernism is concerned with 'denaturalising' what has been taken for granted, postmodernist ideas have overlapped with those interested in deconstructing the common assumptions of racial hierarchies. It is not the case that there was no postcolonial discourse before postmodernism, for there has been oppositional discourse to colonialism from when the first settler's foot trod foreign soil. Rather, the dismantling of the structuring binary opposition of centre and margin evident in postcolonial discourse has in many ways found an intensification in postmodernism's commitment to deconstructing the authoritarian and logocentric master narratives of European culture. Postmodernism has there-fore prompted a renewed focus on non-Eurocentric cultural narra-tives, both in terms of the ways non-European cultures represent themselves, as well as in a focus on the politics of the representa-tions that the European has made of its 'other'. Although not always explicitly formulated as 'postmodern', this conceptual framework permeates a variety of critical perspectives, ranging from various ethnic theories, African-American studies and Commonwealth studies, to studies made by people seeking to 'rewrite' the histories of their respective nations and cultures.

Many of these writers and theories have derived a large impetus from the work of one of the most influential theorists on this subject, Edward Said, who in his book *Orientalism* (London, Routledge and Kegan Paul, 1978), strongly criticised the Enlightenment from a postcolonial position. He argued that the western intellectual tradition was completely bound up with the particular politics and interests of the West. In *Orientalism*, Said is deeply suspicious of any narrative that claims to be more than just a narrative, and he opposes western discourse on the so-called 'Orient' by constructing his own counter-narrative to provide an alternative story. By the time he had published *Culture and Imperialism* (London, Vintage, 1994) sixteen years later, Said had altered his position. In this book he suggests that Enlightenment views and colonialism are not that close, that Enlightenment is not tied so closely to a particular phase of European history, and that it is something less domineering. He points out that there are parts of the Third World which want to see the spread of Enlightenment values and that these are not the preserve of Europeans.

A major poststructuralist theorist of the way in which colonial power is represented is Gayatri Spivak. In recent years, Spivak has become associated with the Subaltern Studies group, and in particular with work on the cultural representations of India under British imperialism. The Subaltern Studies group is a collection of historians and cultural critics like Ranajit Guha, Partha Chatterjee and Dipesh Chakrabarty, among others, who have adopted the name 'subaltern'. Who, or what, is the subaltern? The term designates non-elite or subordinated social groups. It problematises humanist concepts of the sovereign, autonomous subject, since the subaltern has been overlooked in the accounts of and by the elite. The subaltern emerges not as a positive identity complete with a sovereign self-consciousness, but as the product of a network of differential, potentially contradictory identities. Through an engagement with the archives of the colonial administrators and with official historical sources, the Subaltern Studies group has been involved in a collective rewriting of the history of colonial India *from below*, or from the perspective of the peasant underclass. This takes the form of reading the presence of the 'other' or marginalised consciousness as a constitutive factor in the construction of the body of texts passed down by colonial administrators. It takes the form of trying to take account of the gaps and blanks in their historical records. Hence, subaltern studies offers a 'theory of change', at which it arrives by examining functional changes in sign systems, or what are called 'discursive displacements'. In these changes, Spivak detects a crisis of representation, and this crisis is exploited to rewrite the official history.

Yet despite Spivak's ideological allegiance to and sympathy with the project to formulate a counter-hegemonic history, she has criticised such views of subalternity as essentialist, albeit a strategic essentialism (see 'Subaltern Studies: Deconstructing Historiography', in D. Landry and G. McLean (eds), *The Spivak Reader* (London, Routledge, 1996), pp. 203–35). Spivak argues that the project is blemished by the fact that the Subaltern Studies group believes that there is a 'pure' subaltern voice which can be retrieved as the 'true' consciousness, untainted by the historical positions and determinations of the dominant social formation. In her view, the Subaltern Studies project must see itself as a reinscription as well as a rupture of the colonial narratives of power. As Robert Young puts it in his assessment of Spivak's work:

> Spivak shows how analyses of colonial discourse demonstrate that history is not simply the disinterested production of facts, but is rather a process of 'epistemic violence', an interested construction of a particular representation of an object, which may, as with Orientalism, be entirely constructed with no existence or reality outside its representation. Where such history does not take the form of a representation, Spivak argues that it generally consists of a historical narrative, usually one written from the perspective and assumptions of the West or the colonizing power. (Robert Young, *White Mythologies* (London, Routledge, 1990), pp. 158–9)

What emerges is Spivak's desire to construct a new ethical relationship between the so-called Third World and the First World, thus upsetting the First World's sense of pre-eminence. In place of a preoccupation with identity and the assertion of feminist individualism, Spivak offers the possibility of other perspectives and goals: 'I see no way to avoid insisting that there has to be a simultaneous other focus: not merely who am I? but who is the other woman? How am I naming her? How does she name me? Is this part of the problematic I discuss?' (Spivak, *In Other Worlds: Essays in Cultural Politics* (New York, Routledge, 1988), p. 150). By shifting the question from 'Who am I?' to 'Who is the other woman?', Spivak offers a heterogeneity and discontinuity which demonstrate the extent to which, although they share a common situation, each instance of being a woman is historically and culturally specific.

The postcolonial perspective forces people to rethink the limitations of the social sense of a 'collective community'. It insists that cultural and political identity are constructed through a process of *alterity* or *otherness*. In this respect, the postcolonial urges the end of metanarratives concerning the assimilation of minorities and marginalised groups into an organic notion of wholeness. Impelled by this recognition, Homi Bhabha has attempted to reconfigure the postmodern from the perspective of the postcolonial. Bhabha attempts to do so by deconstructing the old dichotomies of East/West, Self/Other and Centre/Margin, and explores the increasing *hybridity* and *liminality* of cultural experience. These are key terms for Bhabha, since his theories stress the mutual interdependence and construction of selfhood that exists between a coloniser and a colonised person. In biology, a *hybrid* refers to the offspring of two animals or plants of different breeds, varieties, species or genera; in Bhabha's definition, it refers to a 'third space' or 'in-between space' which emerges from a blend of two diverse cultures or traditions, like the colonial power and the colonised culture. Such a concept makes any claims for the hierarchical 'purity' of an original culture untenable. Bhabha's main discussion of hybridity is in 'Signs Taken for Wonders' in *The Location of Culture* (London, Routledge, 1994), where he states that in order 'to grasp the ambivalence of hybridity, it must be distinguished from an inversion that would suggest that the originary is, really, only an "effect". Hybridity has no such perspective of depth or truth to provide: it is not a third term that resolves the tension between two cultures' (*Location*, p. 113); that hybridity is an intervention 'in the exercise of authority not merely to indicate the impossibility of identity but to represent the unpredictability of its presence' (*Location*, p. 114); and that hybridity 'terrorizes authority with the *ruse* of recognition, its mimicry, its mockery' (*Location*, p. 115). *Liminality* derives from the Latin word 'limen' meaning 'threshold', and like 'hybridity' refers to an 'in-between space', or a space of symbolic interaction, which is distinguished from the more definite notion of a 'limit'. In all these descriptions, it is clear that Bhabha's concept of hybridity fits the poststructuralist attack on totalities and essentialisms, and dovetails with some of the postmodernist characteristics: surface instead of depth, the flattening of the sign, the simultaneous doubleness of perspective, and the critical effects of parody.

Bhabha's anti-essentialist model of postcolonial identity leads him to criticise both white colonial hierarchies and black nationalist positions, which he perceives as merely repeating the structures of social identification of western racism. Sceptical of the modernist prospect of resolving cultural differences teleologically, he construes postcolonial identity as differential and relational rather than fixed and essential, and he harbours no nostalgic desire for 'roots'. Instead, Bhabha's strategy is to seize the dominant narratives and lever them open for reutterance from postcolonial perspectives. Some have criticised Bhabha's position for privileging discursive modes over more materialist forms of resistance to colonial rule; others have been critical of the way his deconstructive theories appear to remove agency from the colonised subject. However, despite Bhabha's theoretical debt to the Lyotardian model of resisting new metanarratives for a matrix of practices embedded in the local and particular, he retains a cautious suspicion that such postmodern strategies may prove to be a new mode of the West's will to power over its other, if insufficient attention is paid to addressing the plight of the rest of the world. For Bhabha, it is important to recognise that the 'post' in 'postcolonial' does not merely mean 'after': rather the 'post' designates a space of cultural contest and change.

STOP and THINK

● What is the value of ideas which effectively remain Eurocentric and anti-grand narrative, when it is precisely the grand narratives of European history which have provided the impetus and models for the successful liberation movements in India, Africa and elsewhere?

- Or are postmodern ideas largely the concern of societies which are affluent and leisured, the luxury of a generation for whom scarcity seems remote, a generation concerned with liberty rather than necessity, with the individual rather than the collective? This may be one reason why so many countries still yearn for the attractions of modernity: does postmodernism only flourish when people become accustomed to modernity and take it for granted?
- One position argues that the 'post' in postmodernism is not the same as the 'post' in postcolonialism. Are attempts to correlate the two just one further example of Eurocentric imperialist processes?
- To what extent does the radical provisionality so fundamental to postmodernism counter the political dimension of identity so crucial to postcolonial literature?
- Might it be legitimately argued that those discourses which emphasise the inescapability of the coloniser–colonised from the discourse that constitutes them are merely reinscriptions of neo-colonial domination?

Postmodern theology: a contradiction in terms?

As this book will demonstrate, the philosophical and cultural debates concerning postmodern ideas have significant overlap with a number of other areas and disciplines. One such discipline that has strong interlinks with certain strands of postmodern philosophy is theology. Right from the outset in the 1960s, deconstruction and theology were clearly intertwined, and the subsequent development of Derrida and other allied philosophers like Blanchot and Levinas manifested similar theological concerns in their work, although not always Christian in orientation. For instance, one might consider Susan Handelman's *The Slayers of Moses* (1982) on links between the work of Harold Bloom, Jacques Derrida, and Geoffrey Hartman and Rabbinical exegetical practices. Recent years have seen a considerable flowering of debate in the area of 'postmodern theology', an intellectual consolidation in a discipline usually marked by the advent of subject 'Readers' such as Kevin J. Vanhoozer's

The Cambridge Companion to Postmodern Theology (Cambridge University Press, 2003) and Graham Ward's *The Blackwell Companion to Postmodern Theology* (Oxford, Blackwell, 2004). For another useful introductory overview, see the chapter 'Literature and Theology' by Kevin Mills, in Christopher Norris and Christa Knellwolf (eds), *The Cambridge History of Literary Criticism, IX* (Cambridge, Cambridge University Press, 2001), pp. 389–400.

On the face of it, this conjunction of postmodernist and theological concerns might appear to be surprising. Postmodernity eschews all absolutes and essences; yet theology's overwhelming concern lies in engaging the absolute, the essential. Therefore, in the face of the terminology of *anti-foundationalism and anti-essentialism* (see earlier in Chapter 1), combined with a critique of *metaphysics and metanarratives* (see earlier in Chapter 1), the notion of a postmodern theology would seem to be a complete contradiction in terms. So how does theology sit within postmodernity? Is theology even possible within a postmodern context?

Undaunted, Christian theologians have responded in numerous ways to the challenges of postmodernity. Surprisingly, in many respects, postmodern theology's engagement with postmodernism has been there right from the outset (for example, in the ethical terminology of Derrida's work and in the ethical philosophy of Lyotard in the late 1960s and subsequently, and in many critical assessments by theologians in the 1970s). Nevertheless, despite this early intellectual commitment, postmodern theology appears to have come of age largely in the 1990s and the early years of the new millennium. With the postmodern turn from metanarrative to narrative, from subjectivity to language, much of the religious philosophy addresses itself to the fundamental issue of postmodernity – the possibility of ethics: within a crisis of legitimation – in other words, by whose story, by whose authority, by whose criteria, should we live by, and why?

Various theologians have sought to map the territory of contemporary theology's engagement with postmodernism. Terrence W. Tilley argues that 'While some might say that theology after the death of God is like biology after the end of life – a discipline without a subject' (Tilley, *Postmodern Theologies: The Challenge of*

Religious Diversity (Maryknoll NY, Orbis, 1995), p. 124), he could nevertheless identify four general patterns of 'postmodernisms' in theology today: 'constructive' theologies (which attempt to formulate a coherent philosophy that is applicable to the component parts of a given faith's system of belief, with Helmut Peukert, David Ray Griffin, and David Tracy cited as examples); postmodernisms of 'dissolution' (which are a writing of the limits, affirming an otherness and difference without 'end', exposing the faults of totalising structures of 'truth' and exploring their 'remains' (exemplified in the work of Thomas J.J. Altizer, Mark C. Taylor and Edith Wyschogrod)); postliberal theologies (which advocate that since thought and experience are historically and socially mediated, a narrative approach to theology should be used (as proposed in the work of Hans Frei and George Lindbeck)); and 'communal praxis' (closely identified with Liberation Theology, which takes the view that Christian poverty is an act of loving solidarity with the poor as well as a political liberatory protest, as exemplified by Gustavo Gutierrez and other Latin American theologians, and James W. McClendon and Sharon Welch among North Americans). Although his examples and categories do not quite follow those of Tilley, Kevin J. Vanhoozer makes another attempt to lay out the territory across which postmodern theology follows its adventures in *The Cambridge Companion to Postmodern Theology* (Cambridge, Cambridge University Press, 2003), an excellent introductory reader on the subject. He identifies such questions as: 'Is postmodernity a "culture" into which the Gospel must be liberated? Are postmoderns on a mission to save theology or are theologians on a mission to save postmodernity . . . What shape will Christian wisdom take under the conditions of postmodernity'? (Vanhoozer, *The Cambridge Companion to Postmodern Theology*, pp. 22–5). Vanhoozer identifies two basic approaches to the issue of postmodernism: (1) there are those that approach theology via postmodernity, and (2) there are those that approach postmodernity from the perspective of theology, or from particular doctrinal perspectives. Others focus on the intellectual potential implicit in certain doctrines for offering correctives to particular postmodern tendencies (for example, investigating how the doctrine of the Trinity might allow one to conceive of difference in terms other than those of conflict).

Within the first of these twofold approaches, Vanhoozer offers a typology of postmodern theologies. These include six variants of postmodern theology, these being: (1) postliberal theology, (2) postmetaphysical theology, (3) deconstructive theology, (4) reconstructive theology, (5) feminist theology, and (6) radical orthodoxy. For some, like reconstructive theology, there is still room for metaphysics in postmodernity; for others, like postmetaphysical theology, all forms of ontotheology (which means the ontology of God and/or the theology of being, but the term has often been taken to refer to Western metaphysics in general) must be abandoned. In an effort to demonstrate the variety of positions on this spectrum, I will offer outlines of all these positions.

1.   Postliberal theology (also known as Narrative Theology) derives principally from the work of Karl Barth and Thomas Aquinas, but also from the linguistic philosophy of Ludwig Wittgenstein and the moral philosophy of Alasdair MacIntyre, and is rooted in the work of theologians at the Yale Divinity School in the 1980s, whose leading proponents are Hans Frei, George Lindbeck and Stanley Hauerwas. The term came into use largely as a result of the publication of Lindbeck's *The Nature of Doctrine: Religion and Theology in a Postliberal Age* (1984). This book proposed the idea that the Church's use of the Bible should focus on a narrative presentation of faith. In contrast to liberal individualism, which assumes an immediate religious experience common to all humanity, postliberalism leans toward more tradition-constituted and communitarian accounts of human rationality and personhood rather than an Enlightenment appeal to a 'universal rationality'. Employing a narrative approach to theology, postliberalism's postmodern characteristics can be found in its conviction that theological rationality is not to be rooted in the authority of the *individual* (*cogito ergo sum*) but in the language and culture of a living tradition of *communal* life.

2.   Postmetaphysical theology is particularly associated with the work of the French Catholic theologian, Jean-Luc Marion,

whose ideas are exemplified in his book *God Without Being* (1991). Marion is in turn indebted to Heidegger and Emmanuel Levinas, but also to the mystical theology of the late fifth and early sixth-century Dionysius the Aeropagite (also known as 'Pseudo-Dionysius'). Marion argues that God cannot be conceived in the language of 'Being' that has dominated Western metaphysics and its ontotheological conception of God as a 'supreme being'. 'God without being' is not meant to imply that God doesn't exist, 'but rather that any divine existence or nonexistence that human thought might ever imagine will fall short of the divine generosity that stands at the heart of revelation' (Thomas A. Carlson, 'Postmetaphysical Theology', in *The Cambridge Companion to Postmodern Theology*, p. 58).

3. Closely allied to this theological position is Deconstructive theology. The key theorists are a group of American theologians, heavily influenced by the death-of-God thinking from Hegel and Nietzsche and the linguistic turn taken by Wittgenstein and Heidegger, who saw in the work of Jacques Derrida the potential of deconstruction for developing their project of announcing the end of theology. *Deconstruction and Theology* (1982), edited by Thomas Altizer, featured essays by the most prominent of them: Thomas J. J. Altizer, Mark C. Taylor, Robert Scharlemann, and Carl Raschke. Mark C. Taylor published his full length study *Deconstructing Theology* in the same year, and followed this with his edited collection *Deconstruction in Context* in 1986. Developing Derrida's idea of dissemination in language, in which all language both posits and denies, defers and displaces meaning, these deconstructive theologians argue that all communication, any act of saying, betrays a similarity to negative theology (also known as the 'Via Negativa' (Latin for 'Negative Way') – a theology that attempts to describe God by negation, to speak of God only in terms of what cannot be said about God: both conceive of saying as an *avoidance* of saying something. Furthermore, they perceive in Derrida's explanations of justice in *Specters of Marx* (1994) and in his essay 'Force of Law' in *Acts of Religion* (2001) and the gift in *The Gift of Death* (1995) as 'yet-to-come', an invocation of the messianic 'beyond', anticipating two forms of religious discourse, the

prophetic and the mystical. Therefore, a theorist like John D. Caputo (*The Prayers and Tears of Jacques Derrida*, 1997) can argue that Derrida's affirmation of the impossibility of justice and the gift is not nihilistic despair, but one of faith: it is the desire for something *other* than what obtains in the present world order, a 'religion without religion'. With initial comparisons between Karl Barth and Jacques Derrida in the early 1990s, and others wanting to point to the similarities between Derrida's ideas and Buddhism (for example, Toby Forshay (ed.), *Derrida and Negative Theology*, 1992), many of these deconstructive theologians argue that deconstruction could only have been thought in the first place because theology pointed the way.

4.   A further development in postmodern theology has been Reconstructive theology, also sometimes referred to as 'Process theology', principally associated with David Ray Griffin's key early books *God and Religion in the Postmodern World* (1988), *Varieties of Postmodern Theology* (with William A. Beardslee and Joe Holland) (1989), and the edited collection *Sacred Interconnections: Postmodern Spirituality, Political Economy, and Art* (1990). Based heavily on Alfred North Whitehead's brand of metaphysical philosophy, reconstructive postmodern philosophy is oriented around the necessity for reconciling reason and religion. Seeking to undo the pernicious effects of the modern dualism between the ideas affirmed in theory and those presupposed in practice, Griffin emphasises the distinctively postmodern notions in Whiteheadian philosophy. He employs these notions for the deconstruction of classical and modern concepts and for ensuing reconstruction, and relates the resulting position to other forms of postmodern thought. Despite the fact that postmodernism believes that metaphysics is something we should go beyond, Whitehead's definition is not something beyond all experience, but he regards metaphysics as something in which every element of an experience can be interpreted, where a metaphysical 'system' is not a certainty but a tentative adventure. Consequently, Reconstructive theology denies that comprehensive thinking has hegemonic intentions.

5.   Feminist theology generally operates around positions of marginalised groups in Christianity and Judaism, to reconsider the

traditions, practices, scriptures and theologies of their religion from a feminist perspective. Some of the goals of feminist theology include increasing the role of women among the clergy and religious authorities, reinterpreting male-dominated imagery and language about God, determining women's place in relation to social roles such as motherhood, and studying images of women in the religion's sacred texts. Feminists have long attempted to counter stereotypical perceptions of women as morally or spiritually inferior to men, especially in the conventional Madonna–whore dichotomy; as a source of sexual temptation; as dedicated to childbearing, their homes, and husbands; and as having a lesser role in religious ritual or leadership because of such inferiority or dedication. Influential works include Pamela Sue Anderson's *A Feminist Philosophy of Religion: The Rationality and Myths of Religious Belief* (1998), C.W. Maggie Kim, Susan M. St. Ville and Susan M. Simonaitis's *Transfigurations: Theology and the French Feminists* (1993), and Susan Frank Parsons' *Feminism and Christian Ethics* (1996). 'Womanist Theology' also developed in the USA during the 1980s using the novelist Alice Walker's womanist–feminist dichotomy, which interpreted religious forms and practices in the light of the experience of African American women. Associated with and yet departing from Feminist Theology, womanist theology paid attention to the everyday realities of Black and other women of colour and what was perceived to be the lack of understanding of the special oppressions of Black women.

6. Finally, Radical Orthodoxy is a predominantly British, postmodern Christian theological movement that takes its name from the title of a collection of essays entitled *Radical Orthodoxy, A New Theology* (1999), edited by John Milbank, Catherine Pickstock and Graham Ward. Prior to this book, John Milbank described his own work as postmodern critical Augustinianism. Deriving influences from the work of the French Jesuit Henri de Lubac, French postmodern philosophy, and Greek Neo-Platonism, Radical Orthodoxy makes various attempts to recover the significance of patristic, medieval and Renaissance Christian doctrinal reasoning for contemporary philosophical theology. Highly critical of modernity for its exercise of instrumental rationality in the social domain and its

concomitant secularisation of society, theologians like Milbank
have argued that theology should not seek to make constructive
use of social theory, since only theology itself offers a comprehensive vision of all reality, extending to the social and political
without the need for social theory.

This proliferation of theological movements partly testifies to a
'return to the religious' in our apparently more secular world in
which materialism and worldly pleasures reign. Indeed, theoretical
contributions also occur from eminent philosophers like Gianni
Vattimo (*After Christianity* (New York, Columbia University Press,
2002)); with Richard Rorty, *The Future of Religion*, edited by Santiago
Zabala (New York, Columbia University Press, 2005); with John
D. Caputo, *After the Death of God*, edited by Jeffrey W. Robbins
(New York, Columbia University Press, 2006)), and Slavoj Žižek's
recent work includes extended treatments of key Christian thinkers
from Paul, Pascal, and Kierkegaard to G.K. Chesterton and C.S.
Lewis, while Christology and other theological themes have provided crucial points of reference in *The Puppet and the Dwarf: The
Perverse Core of Christianity* (Cambridge MA, MIT Press, 2003).
Yet while the political and social significance of religious belief
clearly plays a major role within our post-Rushdie, post-9/11 societies, admittedly not all religious persuasions contribute to these
theological debates in intellectually positive terms – many tendencies are the outcomes of a New Age commodification of spirituality;
fundamentalist middle America increasingly exerts considerable
conservative pressure on American democracy; religious booksell-
ers have numerous titles on the subject of excoriating the pernicious
influence of postmodern ideas on 'commonsense' Christian belief;
and this populist perspective is reinforced by numerous websites
and blogs challenging the value of postmodern theology. Nevertheless, it may be that the affinities that current theology has to postmodern philosophies indicate the underlying spirituality embedded
in a potent fashion in postmodern culture more generally.

Selected reading

Ashcroft, Bill, Gareth Griffiths and Helen Tiffin (eds), *The Post-Colonial
Studies Reader* (London, Routledge, 1995).

The section entitled 'Postmodernism and Post-colonialism' contains a good range of extracts which place the discussion in a clear context. Other sections in the book on 'Hybridity', 'Universality and Difference' and 'Issues and Debates' also offer interesting and useful discussions of pertinent concepts and arguments.

Best, Steven, and Douglas Kellner, *Postmodern Theory* (Basingstoke, Macmillan, 1991).

One of the better introductions to philosophical and cultural theory, with chapters on all the principal theorists of postmodernism – Michel Foucault, Jean Baudrillard, Jean-François Lyotard, Gilles Deleuze and Felix Guattari – and useful interrogations of their ideas. A thorough and sophisticated treatment, as well as investigating the critiques by various opponents.

Docherty, Thomas (ed.), *Postmodernism: A Reader* (Brighton, Harvester Wheatsheaf, 1993).

A monumental anthology of many of the key writings in postmodern debates, covering a wide range of cultural disciplines and their relation to postmodernist ideas. With an informative introduction, each section is preceded with a helpful explanatory contextualisation, and there is a comprehensive bibliography.

Foster, Hal (ed.), *The Anti-aesthetic: Essays on Postmodern Culture* (Port Townsend WA, Bay Press, 1983); reprinted in Britain as *Postmodern Culture* (London, Pluto Press, 1985).

An influential and accessible anthology containing a number of prominent and interesting essays on art, cultural theory, sculpture, feminism and architecture, by key people like Jürgen Habermas, Fredric Jameson, Baudrillard, Rosalind Krauss, Kenneth Frampton, Edward Said and Gregory Ulmer.

Grant, Judith, *Fundamental Feminism: Contesting the Core Concepts of Feminist Theory* (New York and London, Routledge, 1993).

Chapter 5 provides a useful survey of feminism and postmodernism.

Harvey, David, *The Condition of Postmodernity* (Oxford, Blackwell, 1989).

An important and influential book which covers a wide range of debate and material. Worthwhile reading for all students.

Hekman, Susan J., *Gender and Knowledge: Elements of a Postmodern Feminism* (Boston MA, Northeastern University Press, 1990).

A readable monograph which sets out many of the key arguments and debates about the viability of a *rapprochement* between feminism and postmodernism.

Nicholson, Linda (ed.), *Feminism/Postmodernism* (New York and London, Routledge, 1990).

An accessible collection of a variety of important and interesting essays on the subject of feminism and postmodernism.

Sim, Stuart, *Irony and Crisis: A Critical History of Postmodern Culture* (Cambridge, Icon Books, 2002).

Acts as an excellent sourcebook, tracing the emergence and subsequent developments of postmodernism across the full range of academic disciplines.

Tong, Rosemarie, *Feminist Thought: A Comprehensive Introduction* (London, Routledge, 1989).

Chapter 8 provides a useful survey of French feminist theory, which Tong describes as postmodern feminism.

Vanhoozer, Kevin J. (ed.), *The Cambridge Companion to Postmodern Theology* (Cambridge, Cambridge University Press, 2003).

An excellent introduction to the field of postmodernism and theology.

Ward, Graham, *The Blackwell Companion to Postmodern Theology* (Malden MA, Blackwell, 2004).

Another first class introduction to the field of postmodern theology.

3
Postmodernism and the literary arts

Postmodern fiction

It is in the field of literary studies that the term 'postmodernism' has received widest usage and most vexed debate. There have been many attempts to theorise the consequences and manifestations of postmodernism for literature, all usually running into problems of historical or formal definition. This chapter will explore the extent to which the term 'postmodernism' has been implicated in literary studies, particularly in relation to fiction, poetry and drama. Although the word is often used fairly indiscriminately about contemporary cultural production, it is possible to distinguish two particular uses: first, as a term which designates the contemporary cultural context as a whole; and second, as a description of a set of characteristics which are evident in selected texts. Often used as a periodising concept to mark the literature which emerged in the 1960s Cold War environment, it is also used as a description of literary formal characteristics such as linguistic play, new modes of narrational self-reflexivity, and referential frames within frames (the 'Russian doll' effect). Much postmodern fiction is suffused too with aesthetic representations of commodities and mass media entertainment; hence postmodern fiction's fascination with artifice, schlock and kitsch, animated as it frequently is by a desire to subvert the elitism of modernist high culture. Elizabeth Ermarth considers postmodernism to supplant 'the discourse of representation of the long and productive era that produced historical thinking' (Ermarth, *Sequel to History: Postmodernism and the Crises of Representational*

Time (Princeton NJ, Princeton University Press, 1992), p. 5). She goes on to characterise it as moving 'beyond the identity-and-similitude negotiations that characterise the construction of historical time and its rationalised consciousness' (*Sequel to History*, p. 6). Such periodising descriptions are difficult to maintain, though. They beg all sorts of complex questions about the validity of particular eras and chronological models, the politics of categorisation, and relationships with the styles of fictional precedents, such as naturalism and realism.

So-called postmodern writers were not homogeneous in their modes of writing. Yet amongst the multiplicity was a common purpose, which was to challenge the psychological realism in modernist fiction. In the 1960s, the use of the term 'postmodern' emerged to describe a frequent use of random techniques, mixed and merged styles, and increasingly provisional methods in certain types of fiction, although the concept only gained its dominance as a generic term in the 1980s. Over that time, the term has had a vexed and tangled history. This chapter does not view postmodernist fiction as a single style which begins with James Joyce's *Finnegans Wake* in 1939 and extends to Don DeLillo's fiction today; postmodern fiction is rather an ongoing process of problematisation or subversion of realist (mainstream) aesthetic ideology. One needs to be cautious about constructing a homogeneous narrative about the development of postmodern fiction as a movement. Periodisation is often a culturally imposed activity channelled by the dominant ideology. The 'post' in discussions of postmodernist fiction often relates to a succession or supersession of modernism. Nevertheless, there are several currents to modernism and postmodernism, and one's perception of the ideological significance of a postmodern text largely depends upon whichever construction of writing has been established as the normative model of modernism. As the following discussion makes clear, many people prefer speaking about 'anti-realist' rather than 'postmodernist' fiction, since that does not always have modernism as its touchstone. Indeed, as will become evident, there have been many suggested terms trying to account for the post-Second World War fictional developments: 'surfiction', 'post-contemporary fiction' (Jerome Klinkowitz), 'fabulation' (Raymond Federman), 'historiographic metafiction' (Linda Hutcheon), and

Susan Strehle's concept of 'actualism', which proposes that post-modern fiction is 'fiction in a quantum universe'. Nevertheless, among all the terminological wars of words, the following sections will attempt to isolate several repeated preoccupations in three areas of the literary arts – fiction, poetry and drama or performance.

Exhaustion and replenishment: postmodern fiction's attack on realism

> Everything there was to know about life was in *The Brothers Karama-zov*, by Feodor Dostoevsky. 'But that isn't enough any more.' (Kurt Vonnegut, *Slaughterhouse Five* (1970; London, Vintage, 1991), p. 87)

Kurt Vonnegut's entreaty to leave realism behind articulated a widely felt attitude that fiction had arrived at a cul-de-sac in its development. As Ronald Sukenick put it, 'What we think of as the novel has lost its credibility – it no longer tells what we feel to be the truth as we try to keep track of ourselves. There's no point in pushing ahead with fiction: we might as well write autobiography and documentary, or social criticism and other how-to books' (Sukenick, 'The New Tradition in Fiction', in Raymond Federman (ed.), *Surf-iction: Fiction Now and Tomorrow* (Chicago, Swallow Press, 1975), p. 36). One way out of this dead-end for fiction was demonstrated in William Burroughs' novel *The Naked Lunch* (1959): 'The world cannot be expressed, it can perhaps be indicated by mosaics of juxtaposition, like objects abandoned in a hotel room, defined by negatives and absences.' Burroughs' description alludes to the anti-foundationalism of postmodernism, which was discussed in Chapter 2 in relation to the ideas of Lyotard. Writers such as Thomas Pynchon, Kurt Vonnegut, John Hawkes, William Gass, Jerzy Kosin-ski, Richard Brautigan, Robert Coover, Donald Barthelme, Steve Katz and Gilbert Sorrentino all wrote a fiction defined by 'negatives and absences' in their challenge to modernism's literary formalism.

Postmodernism has been around in debates about fiction now for almost forty years and consequently has a substantial history. The category of 'postmodern fiction' covers a multitude of different writers, and one needs to be quite precise about the different types of writing with which one is engaging. It first appeared in the 1960s to describe fiction which sought to subvert its own structural and formal bases, and which implied that reality only existed in the language that described it, with meaning inseparably linked to writing and reading practices. So first, there was the fiction of writers like Federman and John Barth. Then the term 'postmodern' gradually moved during the 1970s and early 1980s to describe those works which also embodied within them explicit critiques of aspects of late capitalist society. This embraced fiction like that of the later Pynchon, DeLillo and Paul Auster. More recently, it has been applied to fiction which reflects the social ethos of late capitalism, like cyberpunk sci-fi and the so-called 'brat-pack' writers like Tama Janowitz, Bret Easton Ellis and Jay McInerney.

Yet if there is one note that dominates all these descriptions of postmodernist fiction, it is exhaustion. One of the founding definitions of the term 'postmodernism' in relation to literature occurs in the essays of Barth, a seminal writer in the 1960s development of new modes of fiction. Using the fiction of Vladimir Nabokov, Samuel Beckett and Jorge Luis Borges as archetypes, Barth's 'Literature of Exhaustion' (in Federman, *Surfiction* (1975), pp. 19–33) emphasised how literature had 'used up' the conventions of fictional realism. The dominant characteristic of these novels is the pretence that it is impossible to write an original work, and their paradoxical theme is writing about the 'end' of writing. Out of this yearning for silence emerges a fiction obsessively concerned with its own status as fiction. Consequently, art rather than nature became the object of imitation, and a self-conscious reflexivity emerged. Susan Sontag also argued that the fiction was concerned with silence (see *Against Interpretation, and Other Essays* (New York, Farrar, Straus and Giroux, 1966)), while Ihab Hassan reinforced this perspective with his books *The Literature of Silence* (New York, Knopf, 1968) and *The Dismemberment of Orpheus* (New York, Oxford University Press, 1971), defining silence as the disruption of all links between language and reality. Arguing that these novelists seek silence by abandoning the traditional elements of fiction such as character, plot, metaphor and meaning, Hassan proposes that there is an inexorable movement towards silence.

Also searching for a descriptive term adequate to the new fictive sensibility of the 1960s, Robert Scholes proposed 'fabulation', which meant fiction that insists on its unreality, that openly proclaims its artifice. In addition, Barth's second essay, 'The Literature of Replenishment' (1980), offered a 'restart' to literary practice, and emphasised the contributions of authors like Italo Calvino and Gabriel García Márquez, whose fiction merges the qualities of disjunction, simultaneity, irrationalism, anti-illusionism and self-reflexiveness with the more conventional narrative style of eighteenth-century realism. The increasing anxiety about the effects of rationalism and the subjection of citizens to the ideological dominance of the state led to a whole series of novels which sought to contest entrapment by celebrating unpatterned, resistant reactions to history, systems and codes. A novel like Joseph Heller's *Catch-22* (1961) exemplifies this particularly well, through charting a set of illogicalities and conspiracies fought out for no intelligible reason. The archetypal novelist of paranoia is Pynchon, whose *Gravity's Rainbow* (1973) may be taken as the epitome of postmodern fiction. Elsewhere, the treatment of contemporary history grew increasingly more surreal in works by Hawkes, Barth's *Giles Goat-Boy* (1966) and Brautigan's *The Confederate General of Big Sur* (1964), as the retrospective on the past produced mock-texts and fantasies of actuality.

STOP and THINK

- What have the self-reflexive explorations of the novel taught us? Have they made the fictional form more potent or more interesting, or were they nothing more than a form of decadent narcissism and regressive gimmick?
- To what extent have self-reflexive interrogations freed the novel from obsolete conventions?
- Is it useful or necessary to make a distinction between self-consciousness and self-reflection in fiction?
- Consider whether self-reflexive eighteenth-century novels such as Laurence Sterne's *Tristram Shandy* (1759–67) really perform the same task as twentieth-century fiction. For example, consider the historical differences between these self-reflections, the former in establishing itself as a respectable genre, the latter as reinvigorating an 'exhausted' genre.

Postmodern fiction and history

Just as the 'literature of exhaustion' flaunted its distinctiveness from the 'real' world by drawing attention to its artifice, so fabulists opposed realism with their critique of the myth of history as a set of 'innocent' facts and deeds. Scholes points to the attraction of novelists to the worn-out historical novel – Barth's *Sot-Weed Factor* (1960), Robert Coover's *The Public Burning* (1976), García Márquez's *One Hundred Years of Solitude* (English trans. 1970), John Fowles' *The French Lieutenant's Woman* (1969), Pynchon's *Gravity's Rainbow* and E.L. Doctorow's *Ragtime* (1975). In all these cases, Scholes argues that history is being demythologised. For it is postmodern fiction's ideological treatment of history that is one of the most controversial issues. Clearly, a new urgency to question the apparent distinctions between history and fiction emerged in the 1960s, partly in reaction to the obsessive privatisation of fiction in the 1950s and the political and social pressures of the 1960s. E.L. Doctorow said in a 1978 interview:

> Well, first of all, history as written by historians is clearly insufficient. And the historians are the first to express skepticism over the 'objectivity' of the discipline. A lot of people discovered after World War II and in the fifties that much of what was taken by the younger generations as history was highly interpreted history. ... And it turned out that there were not only individuals but whole peoples whom we had simply written out of our history – black people, Chinese people, Indians. At the same time, there is so little a country this size has in the way of cohesive, identifying marks that we can all refer to and recognise each other from. It turns out that history, as insufficient and poorly accommodated as it may be, is one of the few things we have in common here. I happen to think that there's enormous pressure on us all to become as faceless and peculiarly indistinct and compliant as possible. In that case, you see, the need to find color or definition becomes very, very strong. For all of us to read about what happened to us fifty or a hundred years ago suddenly becomes an act of community. (Richard Trenner (ed.), *E.L. Doctorow: Essays and Conversations* (Princeton NJ, Ontario Review Press, 1983), pp. 58–9)

Doctorow's description of a history in which social and cultural difference rather than universality was recognised marks a distinct reorientation of fiction in the 1960s. Historians and cultural critics such as Hayden White and Roland Barthes assaulted history's special status as an objective representation of reality by drawing attention to their shared use of linguistic and rhetorical structures. Malcolm Bradbury argues that:

> Though postmodernism is often seen as a break with representation and referentiality, it is clearly a fiction of the post-war world and its crises and anxieties. There is no doubt that the Second World War and the crises of representation and responsibility it posed had a crucial impact on Sixties fiction, and fed its preoccupation with the modern unreality. (Bradbury, *The Modern American Novel* (Oxford, Oxford University Press, 1984), p. 209)

However, many cultural theorists have argued that postmodernism anaesthetises the politics of literary works, and creates a *dehistoricising* fiction. Indeed, Doctorow's fiction is one of the literary examples used by Fredric Jameson to outline his theory of the disappearance of history in postmodern culture. Like Terry Eagleton, Jameson argues that postmodern fiction merely reproduces the past as nostalgia, which links it with the eclectic strategies of 'consumerist' popular culture and mass media. Postmodern fiction's implicit belief in a lack of linguistic referentiality, and the difficulty in believing in a history that has any ontological foundation other than that which is linguistically constructed, have led them to be wary of the ideological implications of texts which proclaim no obligation to the realm of reference. Such critics have argued that the linguistic self-referentiality of postmodernism severs the work from objective historical reality, thereby turning the art object into a formalist exercise unrelated to its social conditions of production.

Yet for Linda Hutcheon, postmodern fiction is interrogative and instructive rather than a reactionary cultural production. Acknowledging its ideological limitations, Hutcheon has described postmodern fiction as being Janus-faced with regard to the dominant culture. Describing it as 'historiographic metafiction', Hutcheon describes postmodern fiction as a mode which consciously problematises the making of fiction and history. Postmodern fiction reveals the past as always ideologically and discursively constructed. It is a fiction which is directed both inward and outward, concerned both with its status as fiction, narrative or language, and also grounded in some verifiable historical reality. Postmodernism tends to use and abuse, install but also subvert, conventions, through the use of either irony or parody. Hutcheon recognises a political ambivalence in her description of the way 'Postmodern texts paradoxically point to the opaque nature of their representational strategies and at the same time to their complicity with the notion of the transparency of representation' (Hutcheon, *The Politics of Postmodernism* (London, Routledge, 1989), p. 18). In place of a totalising vision of historical representation, Hutcheon finds postmodern fiction parodically subverts but also inscribes the conventions of realism. The literary text is both critical of and complicit with mimetic representation and the idea of the human at its centre. Hutcheon is quite clear that postmodern fiction is intricately tied to representations of history: the real issue for her is how and for whom those representations work. Metafiction is a central plank of any discussion of postmodern literature. Gass is generally credited with the coinage of the term, which refers to the fact that the novelist's business is no longer to render the world, but to *make* one from language: fiction is no longer mimetic, but constructive. Federman's manifesto 'Surfiction' suggests that reality only exists in the language that describes it and that meaning is only produced in writing and reading practices. Federman proposes 'Surfiction' as a descriptive term, as fiction which tries to explore the limits of fiction, which challenges the orthodoxies that govern it. 'Surfiction' exposes the fictionality of reality (*Surfiction,* p. 8). Pushing at and playing with the limits of fictionality, the stories and narratives of authors like Barth, Coover, Gass, Federman, Barthelme, Hawkes, Ronald Sukenick, Katz, Ishmael Reed, Pynchon, William Gaddis and Sorrentino increasingly became elaborate forms of complicity between author, text and reader. Their fiction displayed a plurality of forms, a scepticism towards generic types and categories, ironic inversions, a predilection for pastiche and parody, and a metafictional insistence on the arbitrariness of the text's power to signify. For example, Barth's *Lost in the Funhouse* begins with a 'Frame-tale' which works like a mobius strip:

> Once upon a time there was a story that began. (Barth, *Lost in the Funhouse* (New York, Bantam, 1969), pp. 1–2)

The tale establishes a parodic model for stories which turn in on themselves, endlessly repeating themselves in increasingly convoluted and inverted fashion. This play with fictional conventions recurs throughout the collection of stories:

> I see I see myself as a halt narrative: first person, tiresome. Pronoun sans ante or precedent, warrant or respite. Surrogate for the substantive: contentless form, interestless principle; blind eye blinking at nothing. Who am I. A little *crise d'identité* for you.
>
> I must compose myself.
>
> Look, I'm writing. No, listen, I'm nothing but talk; I won't last long. ('Autobiography: A Self-Recorded Fiction', *Funhouse,* p. 33)

In this story, Barth improvises with the notion of whether the existence of a self can or cannot be separated from writing, as well as with ideas of authorial control over the text, and the illusions of the *self*-writing or a *writing*-of-the-self embedded in the form of *auto*-biography.

Similarly for Patricia Waugh, metafiction represents a basic tension in all novels between the illusion of self-sufficiency and the unveiling of that illusion (see Waugh, *Practising Postmodernism Reading Modernism* (London, Edward Arnold, 1992)). Conventional notions of reality are challenged by such devices as exaggerated structural patterning, infinite textual regression, literary parodies, temporal and spatial dislocations and blurred boundaries of discourse.

Irony and transgression

Postmodern fiction can also be characterised by its transgression of the cultural boundaries erected between high and popular culture. Andreas Huyssen has made this the linchpin of his argument in *After the Great Divide* (Basingstoke, Macmillan, 1986), in which he sees postmodernism emerging in two distinct phases: (a) as a challenge to high art diluted by technological optimism in the 1960s, which (b) then transformed into an eclectic mode at once diverse and amorphous in the 1970s and 1980s. Postmodernism is not the great break with the past but is instead deeply indebted to that other trend in the culture of modernity – the historical avant-garde.

在定   保私

Postmodernism explores the contradictions and contingencies of high and pop cultures, motivated by a creative tension animated by the self-assertion of non-hegemonic cultures and the decentring of traditional notions of subjectivity.

A variety of theorists have offered economies of postmodern characteristics: David Lodge, Brian McHale, Ihab Hassan and John Mepham. Mepham has usefully described four categories in which postmodernist fiction can be understood:

1. historical narrative which usually pits postmodernism as a break with, or a transcendence of, many aspects of modernism;
2. philosophical argument which describes postmodernism as the cultural practice emerging from an allegiance to the poststructuralist philosophical assault on notions of stable linguistic meaning and the existence of an unmediated objective reality;
3. pedagogical or ideological impulse which seeks to raise our awareness of the structural armatures of our culture, through a disruption and 'problematisation' of conventional senses of reality and a laying bare of the conceptual structures of our world;
4. series of textual strategies employed by fiction and designed to foreground and highlight the textuality of the work ('metafictional strategies'), to draw attention to the fictional framing devices and the plurality of worlds. (John Mepham, 'Narratives of Postmodernism', in Edmund Smyth (ed.), *Postmodernism and Contemporary Fiction* (London, Batsford, 1991), pp. 138–55)

Mepham's discussion of postmodernism ranges broadly and usefully across the various debates and contradictions embedded in uses of the term to describe fiction.

In another formulation, McHale has argued that postmodernist fiction represents a conceptual shift in emphasis from the *'epistemological'* dominant of modernism to the *'ontological'* dominant of postmodernism. Producing a taxonomy of postmodern themes and techniques in *Postmodernist Fiction* (1987), McHale describes postmodernism as 'the shift of dominant from problems of *knowing* to problems of *modes of being* – from an epistemological dominant to an *ontological one*' (McHale, *Postmodernist Fiction* (New York and

London, Methuen, 1987), p. 10). McHale restates this as deploying 'strategies which engage and foreground questions like ... "Which world is this? What is to be done in it? Which of my selves is to do it?"' (*Postmodernist Fiction,* p. 10). Extending this argument in his second book, *Constructing Postmodernism* (London, Routledge, 1992), McHale states that '"Post-Modernism" foregrounds and lays bare the process of world-making (and -unmaking) and the ontological structure of the fictional world' (*Constructing Postmodernism,* p. 36). Problems emerge with McHale's model owing to his formalist approach, a catalogue of features and themes by which the postmodern can be recognised, and it is unclear whether postmodernism is linked to a specific economic formation, i.e. late capitalism. In addition, McHale's formulation seems oddly balanced between its definition of postmodernism as a plurality of voices on the one hand, and this stable tabulation of attributes on the other hand.

Hassan has produced one of the more influential discussions of postmodernism and literature in his book *The Postmodern Turn* (Columbus OH, Ohio State University Press, 1987), in which he isolates ten preoccupations and concerns of the idea, such as periodisation, definition and historical precedent. Hassan largely bases his idea of postmodernism on his neologistic concept of 'indeterminance' to designate two central tendencies in postmodernism, indeterminacy and immanence. In both cases, these are manifested in the workings of language. In attempting to distinguish the characteristics of postmodernism, he has drawn up a table of the features of modernism and postmodernism:

↓↑	⟷
Modernism	Postmodernism
Romanticism/Symbolism	'Pataphysics, Dadaism
Form (conjunctive, closed)	Antiform (disjunctive, open)
Purpose	Play
Design	Chance
Hierarchy	Anarchy
Mastery/Logos	Exhaustion/Silence
Art Object/Finished Work	Process/Performance/Happening
Distance	Participation
Creation/Totalisation	Decreation/Deconstruction

Synthesis	Antithesis
Presence	Absence
Centering	Dispersal
Genre/Boundary	Text/Intertext
Semantics	Rhetoric
Paradigm	Syntagm
Hypotaxis	Parataxis
Metaphor	Metonymy
Selection	Combination
Root/Depth	Rhizome/Surface
Interpretation/Reading	Against Interpretation/Misreading
Signified	Signifier
Lisible (Readerly)	*Scriptible* (Writerly)
Narrative/*Grande Histoire*	Anti-narrative/*Petite Histoire*
Master Code	Idiolect
Symptom	Desire
Type	Mutant
Genital/Phallic	Polymorphous/Androgynous
Paranoia	Schizophrenia
Origin/Cause	Difference-Differance/Trace
God the Father	The Holy Ghost
Metaphysics	Irony
Determinacy	Indeterminacy
Transcendence	Immanence

(quoted from Thomas Docherty (ed.), *Postmodernism: A Reader* (Brighton, Harvester Wheatsheaf, 1993), pp. 146–56)

Although Hassan acknowledges the necessary transience and equivocation that such a schematic inevitably requires, nevertheless certain problematic issues remain. For instance, there appears to be an unspoken approval of the characteristics in the right-hand column, suggesting that postmodernism is a 'good thing' and that it is just as well that modernism has been superseded. In addition, it is often unclear why some characteristics are positioned where they are (e.g. 'paranoia' in some accounts is a good postmodern feature). It might be argued that Hassan creates a straw-man modernism merely as an attempt to force some space between modernism and postmodernism as aesthetic movements.

STOP and THINK

- What sorts of contradictions do you find in Hassan's list of oppositions? For example, why do you think he places 'Dadaism' at the top of the 'Postmodernism' column, when it was an early twentieth-century art movement? Why characterise 'open' form as postmodernist when that classic modernist text, Ezra Pound's *Cantos,* is surely an open-form text? What are the strengths and weaknesses of Hassan's approach?

- Postmodernism is generally construed as having thrown off the hierarchical distinction between high and low cultures. Yet does the argument that postmodernism has effaced the 'great divide' between high and low culture depend for much of its power and effectiveness upon a particularly contentious construction of modernism, one designed to project the innovation and difference of postmodernism?

- Can you think of further examples where modernist writers have exploited popular-art models and genres without merely quoting them ironically or parodically?

Postmodern fiction by other means

Another group of writers who have produced a so-called 'fiction of insurgency' – Kathy Acker, Lynne Tillman and Constance de Jong, who in the mid-1970s lived in downtown Manhattan – have been described by Robert Siegle as engaging with postmodern fictional devices (Siegle, *Suburban Ambush: Downtown Writing and the Fiction of Insurgency* (Baltimore, Johns Hopkins University Press, 1989)). He characterises their writing as a guerrilla action that deliberately sets out to destabilise plot and character, to privilege marginal social groups, stressing issues of representation and language, the appropriation of images, and employing non-sequential structures to celebrate a fluidity that resists narrative totalisation, as in Acker's appropriation of pornographic clichés or science fiction (among many other forms of discourse) in her various 'punk' novels.

By contrast, the 1980s saw a different type of writing, to which the label 'postmodern' has still clung. The 'yuppie' fiction of Ellis,

McInerney, Janowitz and others is often suffused with nostalgia, in
their descriptions of the consumer culture of the 1980s. If postmodernism is generally taken to be a break with representation and
referentiality, then this fiction is postmodern in another sense, for
it works in a realist mould and does not make recognisably radical
narrative disruptions, but it does gesture to the postmodern world
in its content. Often described as the 'brat-pack' novelists, their
fiction is characterised by the insertion of new content into old
forms. In Ellis's *Less Than Zero* (1985) and McInerney's *Bright
Lights, Big City* (1984), novels set in the decadent environments of
Los Angeles and New York, topical references to cocaine, casual sex,
MTV, Ronald Reagan and Jordache jeans are sprinkled in with the
ennui and repetitiveness of life. The novels frequently deal with the
largely trivial and the narratives are fairly traditional. These are not
so much postmodern novels as novels about postmodern existence:
the postmodern consciousness emerges as the novels deliberately
portray the superficiality of contemporary existence.

Despite many of the observations that postmodernism is in terminal decline and that literary concerns have moved beyond the
well-worn metafictional 'games' of the 'high postmodern' era, the
1990s and early 2000s have seen key texts from many of the stalwart
American postmodernist novelists: William Gass' *The Tunnel* (1995),
William Gaddis' *Agape Agape* (2002) and *A Frolic of His Own* (1994),
Pynchon's *Vineland* (1990) and *Mason and Dixon* (1997), and more
recently *Against the Day* (2006), John Barth's *Coming Soon!* (2001),
Robert Coover's *The Adventures of Lucky Pierre* (2002) and *Step-
mother* (2004), and Don DeLillo's *Mao II* (1991), *Underworld* (1997)
and *Cosmopolis* (2003). Together with the works of other emerging
literary voices in the 1990s such as Richard Powers, David Foster
Wallace, Stephen Wright, Carole Maso, Rikki Ducornet, Percival
Everett, Jonathan Safran Foer and Dennis Cooper, the articulation
and exploration of language and representation in structuring
narrative appear to be real and urgent problems still addressed by
the experimental fiction situated within the literary avant-garde.
One further genre that has received much attention as an example of
postmodern fiction is the burgeoning new science-fiction genre
known as cyberpunk. Jameson has described 'cyberpunk' as 'the
supreme literary expression if not of postmodernism, then of late

capitalism itself' (Jameson, *Postmodernism, or the Cultural Logic of Late Capitalism* (London, Verso, 1991), n. 1, p. 491). For Jameson, cyberpunk is 'as much an expression of transnational corporate realities as it is of global paranoia itself' (*Postmodernism*, p. 38). Exploring the fiction of novelists like William Gibson, Bruce Sterling, John Shirley, Rudy Rucker, Pat Cadigan and Lewis Shiner, McHale also suggests the ways in which cyberpunk is postmodernist in its focus and character. In answering the question 'What is cyberpunk?' he seeks to chart a poetics of cyberpunk, with its dominant preoccupations and literary forebears in the work of Burroughs, Pynchon, Acker, Samuel Delany and Philip K. Dick. McHale regards science fiction as 'governed by the ontological dominant. Indeed, it is perhaps *the* ontological genre *par excellence*' (McHale, *Postmodernist Fiction*, p. 59). To the above list one might add the fiction of Neal Stephenson, Jack Womack and Stanislaw Lem. For many, Gibson's *Neuromancer* (1984) is the definitive cyberpunk novel, with its melange of genres, its compelling account of late commodity capitalism, and its decentring of the human consciousness in its innovative exploration of cyberspace. In *Reading By Starlight: Postmodern Science Fiction* (London, Routledge, 1994), Damien Broderick has also provided a good analysis of science fiction as a popular genre, showing how its intricately coded language and sophisticated self-reflexive vernacular are closely bound up with postmodern concerns. Both Broderick and Douglas Kellner (*Media Culture: Cultural Studies, Identity, and Politics Between the Modern and the Postmodern* (London, Routledge, 1995)) dedicate considerable space to Gibson's pathbreaking novel as a singular example of postmodern cyberpunk. Further discussion of the emergence of cyberculture and its social ramifications can be found in Chapter 7.

Although one might be tempted to suggest that postmodern fiction is largely an American and European affair, it was not exclusively so. The debate about the extent to which postmodernism has engaged with postcolonial texts is deeply involved and complicated (see Chapter 2's discussion of postmodernism and postcolonialism). Although British and American writers have been significant players in metafictional explorations, many South American novelists and writers from other cultures have emerged with a new voice.

The postcolonial writing which has emerged since the 1950s appears to have had other preoccupations. Writing from the margins emerges as a new and important source of fiction: from the Native Americans N. Scott Momaday, Leslie Marmon Silko, Sherman Alexie, Louise Erdrich, Gerald Vizenor and James Welch, the Asian Americans Maxine Hong Kingston, Amy Tan, Jessica Hagedorn and Cynthia Kadohata, the Chicana writers Sandra Cisneros, Ana Castillio and Gloria Anzaldua, and a whole host of African Americans like Toni Morrison, Toni Cade Bambara, Audre Lorde, Ishmael Reed, Nathaniel Mackey, Clarence Major and Octavia Butler, to writers like Salman Rushdie, Timothy Mo and Fred D'Aguiar in Britain. While not always exhibiting reflexive textual techniques, the 'local' and culture-specific narratives of such writers have been responsible for significant interventions in the dominant representations of national cultures and ethnic traditions.

Elsewhere, new writings from across the world have interrupted the canonical focus on the American-European literary context. South American magic realism in the fiction of Carlos Fuentes and García Márquez, as well as the more openly acknowledged postmodern authors J.L. Borges and Julio Cortazar, has had a significant impact on European writers. Latin American postmodernism has a well-established literary history, and a vibrant critical culture is evident in such texts as Raymond Leslie Williams' *The Postmodern Novel in Latin America* (New York, St. Martin's Press, 1995), Richard A. Young's *Latin American Postmodernisms* (Amsterdam, Rodopi, 1997), Bernard McGuirk's *Latin American Literature: Symptoms, Risks, and Strategies of Post-structuralist Criticism* (London, Routledge, 1997) and Cynthia Margarita Tompkins' *Latin American Postmodernisms: Women Writers and Experimentation* (Gainesville, University Press of Florida, 2006). Furthermore, there have been postcolonial writings in English from ex-British colonies in Africa, India and the antipodes. A writer such as André Brink in South Africa has demonstrated his interest in innovative forms of narrative and aesthetic experiment, and has increasingly utilised what some have considered 'postmodern' narrative techniques in his fiction, with which to investigate the politics of racism and apartheid. Brink has asserted that 'the study of history' is an abiding interest in his fiction, and some novels display what has been termed 'historiographic metafiction', wherein, rewritten from a 'knowing' retrospective perspective, history is consequently shown to be always dependent on its narrative *form* rather than 'objective' facts. A good example is *On The Contrary* (London, Secker and Warburg, 1993), set in the early colonial exploration of the Cape Colony in the 1730s, which shows explicit concerns with authorship, control of 'truth' and power, and employs intertextuality to engage with the lies of history and the search for 'truth'. At one point, the narrator remarks: 'This fascinates me: how each story displaces others, yet without denying or ever entirely effacing them' (*Contrary*, p. 134). Elsewhere, Brink's fiction self-consciously foregrounds the act of writing and narrating, as if to draw attention to the instabilities of stories as 'truth'. *States of Emergency* (1988) is a love story which is persistently self-referential, discontinuous and intertextual. With constant use of borders, demarcations, boundaries and divisions, the novel gradually places itself at the border of fiction and criticism through the inclusion of allusions and footnotes to Jacques Derrida's deconstructive work, semiotics and structuralism. All this has the effect of compelling the reader to reassess his or her practices of interpretation and evaluation, as the novel simultaneously inscribes and subverts the oppositions through which the love story has traditionally been narrated – self/other, love/politics, inside text/outside world. Through such narrative strategies, Brink urges the reader to consider the extent to which the love story is a naively humanist attempt to wish apartheid away; whether it displaces or domesticates the implications of political struggle by the familiarity of the genre; and whether a love story can effectively oppose apartheid and act as an effective transformative narrative structure for a future South Africa.

Writing from Canada, Australia and New Zealand has also all made an impact upon the contemporary consciousness, particularly the work of Margaret Atwood, Peter Carey, Timothy Findley, Robert Kroetsch and Michael Ondaatje. Although it must be acknowledged that much of this writing occurs within conventional realist narrative paradigms, it is nevertheless due to the ideological and cultural pressure exerted by postmodern ideas that the writings of non-Eurocentric cultures have been recognised as valuable cultural contributions. The impact of postmodernism on world literatures is valuably aided by the essays in Hans Bertens and Douwe W. Fokkema (eds), *International Postmodernism: Theory and*

Literary Practice (Amsterdam, John Benjamins, 1998). Japan has demonstrated significant intervention in the area of postmodern architecture (see Chapter 4), yet some of its writers are also well-known postmodern authors, such as Haruki Murakami and Banana Yoshimoto. *Postmodernism and Japan*, edited by Masao Miyoshi and Harry D. Harootunian (Durham NC, Duke University Press, 1989) and Fuminobu Murakami's *Postmodern, Feminist and Postcolonial Currents in Contemporary Japanese Culture* (London, Routledge, 2005) explore the fictional and critical work of contemporary Japanese writers.

In recent decades, with the downfall of Russian Communism, key comparative studies such as Mikhail Epstein's *After the Future: The Paradoxes of Postmodernism and Contemporary Russian Culture* (Amherst MA, University of Massachusetts Press, 1995), Mikhail Epstein, Alexander Genis and Slobodanka Vladiv-Glover's *Russian Postmodernism: New Perspectives on Post-Soviet Culture* (New York and Oxford: Berghahn Books, 1999) and Mark Lipovestsky's *Russian Postmodern Fiction: Dialogue with Chaos*, edited by Eliot Borenstein (New York and London, M.E. Sharpe, 1999) examine the two separate phases of Russian postmodernism, socialist realism and conceptualism, in contradistinction to the more seamless development of its Western counterpart. Acknowledging that the life-world of Las Vegas is not the same as the postmodernism in Petersburg, the ways in which postmodernism has had an impact upon post-Soviet writing is a particularly topical debate. 'Russian debutante' authors like Gary Shteyngart with his novels *The Russian Debutante's Handbook* (2002) and *Absurdistan* (2006), Lara Vapnyar with *There are Jews in My House* (2002) and *Memoirs of a Muse* (2006), David Bezmozgis with *Natasha* (2004), and Olga Grushin with *The Dream Life of Sukhanov* (2006), are emerging as part of a growing phenomenon of Russian émigrés who have become bestselling writers in the language of their adopted homelands.

Yet whether Russian postmodernism is an oxymoron or not, it would appear similar questions are also emerging in modern China, where simulations and skyscrapers abound in globalised cities like Shanghai. Few countries have been so transformed in recent decades as China and, with a dynamically growing economy and a rapidly changing social structure, China challenges the West to understand the nature of its modernisation. Using postmodernism as both a global frame of periodisation and a way to break free from the rigid ideology of westernisation as modernity, the diverse group of contributors in Arlif Dirlik (ed.), *Postmodernism and China* (Durham NC, Duke University Press, 2000), argue that the Chinese experience is crucial for understanding postmodernism. Based upon a special issue of *Boundary 2* (24:3, Autumn 1997), these essays juxtapose postmodernism with postsocialism and analyse China as a producer and not merely a consumer of the culture of the postmodern. Within the literary sphere, the contemporary experimental fiction of the Chinese avant-garde writers, such as Ge Fei, Yu Hua, and Ma Yuan, represents a new genre of storytelling defined by the writers' devotion to theatrics and their wilful apathy toward everything held sacred by the generation that witnessed the Cultural Revolution. The anthology *China's Avant-garde Fiction* (Durham NC, Duke University Press, 1998), edited by Jing Wang, selects provocative examples of this new school of writing, which gained prominence in the late 1980s. Contradicting many long-cherished beliefs about Chinese writers – including the alleged tradition of writing as a political act against authoritarianism – these stories make a dramatic break from conventions of modern Chinese literature by demonstrating an irreverence toward history and culture and by celebrating the artificiality of storytelling. Recent studies of China's cultural negotiations with postmodernism (including literature) occur in Jing Wang's *High Culture Fever: Politics, Aesthetics, and Ideology in Deng's China* (Berkeley, University of California Press, 1996), Xiaobin Yang's *The Chinese Postmodern: Trauma and Irony in Chinese Avant-Garde Fiction* (Ann Arbor MI, University of Michigan Press, 2002), and Sheldon Hsaio-Peng Lu's *Chinese Modernity and Global Biopolitics* (Honolulu HI, University of Hawai'i Press, 2007).

Key characteristics of postmodern fiction

One might summarise some of the key characteristics of postmodern fiction as follows. Postmodern fiction often shows:

1. a preoccupation with the viability of systems of representation;
2. the decentring of the subject by discursive systems, and the inscription of multiple fictive selves;

3. narrative fragmentation and narrative reflexivity; narratives which double back on their own presuppositions;
4. an open-ended play with formal devices and narrative artifice, in which narrative self-consciously alludes to its own artifice, thus challenging some of the presuppositions of literary realism;
5. an interrogation of the ontological bases of and connections between narrative and subjectivity;
6. an abolition of the cultural divide between high and popular forms of culture, embracing all in a mélange;
7. an exploration of ways in which narrative mediates and constructs history: e.g. Graham Swift's preoccupation with the relationship between story and history in *Waterland* (1983);
8. the displacement of the real by simulacra, such that the original is always already linguistically constructed: novels incorporate 'historical' fictions as fact, like Barth's *The Sot-Weed Factor*. See also the following discussion of DeLillo's *White Noise* (1985).

Postmodern fiction: an example

Arguably one of the most significant contemporary novelists, DeLillo has gradually come to be regarded as embodying the quintessential features of a postmodernist fiction. His most popular and widely acclaimed novel *White Noise* is a fine example of such preoccupations. It focuses on the Gladney family; Jack Gladney, a middle-class academic in Hitler Studies at the College-on-the-Hill, becomes sucked into the violent subculture of his home town. The novel is principally concerned with the problem of communication in an information age and the difficulty of selecting the important message from the 'white noise'. Related to this, the novel persistently argues that facts, sights and real events are mediated or constructed by the media, or are used as rehearsals for simulations of real events. In good postmodern fashion, *White Noise* demonstrates a society completely suffused with simulacra. One humorous example occurs in the aftermath of a toxic spill when the local population is being evacuated. Jack Gladney asks one civil defence organiser how the evacuation has gone:

> 'That's quite an armband you've got there. What does SIMUVAC mean? Sounds important.'

'Short for simulated evacuation. A new state program they're still
battling over funds for.'
'But this evacuation isn't simulated. It's real.'
'We know that. But we thought we could use it as a model.'
'A form of practice? Are you saying you saw a chance to use the real
event in order to rehearse the simulation?'
'We took it right into the streets.'
'How is it going?'
'The insertion curve isn't as smooth as we would like. There's a prob-
ability excess. Plus which we don't have our victims laid out where
we'd want them if this was an actual simulation. In other words we're
forced to take our victims as we find them. We didn't get a jump on
computer traffic. Suddenly it just spilled out, three-dimensionally,
all over the landscape. You have to make allowances for the fact that
everything you see tonight is real. There's a lot of polishing we still
have to do. But that's what this exercise is all about.' (DeLillo, *White
Noise* (1984; London, Picador, 1985), p. 139)

In a pure Baudrillardian moment, the real is preceded by the
simulacrum, the real measured and found wanting by the artificial
model. In another event, driving out past several advertisements
to see 'the most photographed barn in the world', Jack's colleague
Murray Siskind remarks, 'No one sees the barn ... Once you've
seen the signs about the barn, it becomes impossible to see the
barn ... We're not here to capture an image, we're here to maintain
one. Every photograph reinforces the aura' (*White Noise*, p. 12).
Siskind is pointing to the manner in which the advertisements
have caused people not to see the qualitative barn itself, but to see it
as an object of quantitative interest. In other words, the real barn
disappears behind the *image* of the barn.

Noel King, whose article 'Reading *White Noise:* Floating Remarks'
(*Critical Quarterly*, 33:3 (Autumn 1991): 66–83) has formed one
source for this reading, regards the novel as 'a series of shrewd
indications of this more general cultural condition of distorted
communication and information, specifically concerning the circulation of mass-mediated language and the relating of secondhand
information' ('Reading', p. 73). King's argument is that the novel
is postmodern because it demonstrates how 'we now inhabit a
historical moment where the "ficto–critical" replaces the binary
opposition of the "fictional" and the "critical"' ('Reading', p. 73).

The novel is a sustained study of some of the implications for a society saturated with signs and messages, and 'dramatises the problematic relationship between utterances and their origins, exposing the arbitrariness of any notion of there being a final point of discursive rest' ('Reading', p. 78). Lists pervade the novel, as if there is an obsessive-compulsive need in society to possess information. As example after example in the novel demonstrates, information exists as a perpetual parlour game of Chinese whispers, continually getting skewed and distorted in its transmission from person to person.

Elsewhere, the novel demonstrates a variety of postmodern preoccupations: the sense of character/subjectivity/individuality as a series of shifting and decentring constructs, or, as Gladney acknowledges, 'I am the false character that follows the name around' (*White Noise*, p. 17); the way in which the changing descriptions of the toxic airborne event show how discourse constructs and mediates the object; the superficiality and depthlessness of the supermarket culture and the concomitant packaging of people's lives; the reciprocal interplay of high and low culture; and the obsession with death, which may be perceived as a signification of a general lack of security and stability in people's belief-systems. Yet DeLillo's novel stops short of being a heavy-handed moralistic critique of contemporary society; in poking fun at many of the social characteristics of late twentieth-century western culture, the novel teases the reader into deciding whether DeLillo is critical of or complicit with the society he is describing. In this gaming element, or fictional 'play', DeLillo maintains the indecision of representation in the very form of the novel.

Postmodern poetry

The issue of what constitutes postmodern poetry is as vexed and controversial as the issue of postmodern fiction. Postmodern poetry has largely emerged from the verbal experiments of the European avant-garde, yet in another sense all poetry or use of language is in some sense 'experimental'. However, discussions of postmodern poetry often begin with the ideas of Charles Olson, a poet and a writer who was the rector of Black Mountain College,

North Carolina, an innovative and experimental liberal arts college founded in 1933 and at the height of its influence in the early 1950s. This functioned as an interdisciplinary centre for a wide variety of influential figures, including John Cage, Josef Albers, Merce Cunningham, Pierre Boulez and Robert Rauschenberg. Black Mountain poetics was born in this intellectual environment and derived largely from Olson's teachings, especially the essay 'Projective Verse' (printed in Robert Creeley (ed.), *Charles Olson: Selected Writings* (New York, New Directions, 1950)). Olson called for an 'open' poetry, where 'FIELD COMPOSITION' resisted the 'closed form' of mainstream poetry. Field composition was a poetics of improvisation and spontaneity, rather than using worn-out, inherited forms. He argued that 'ONE PERCEPTION MUST IMMEDIATELY AND DIRECTLY LEAD TO A FURTHER PERCEPTION' and that close attention must be paid to the breath of the line as a measure of utterance, which was to be reflected in the typography of the line. His principal poem *The Maximus Poems* (written 1950–70), a long, complex meditation on his metaphysical, cultural, geographical, historical and political environment, is often taken to be the beginning of the postmodern explorations in poetry. Other poets in residence at Black Mountain over the years included Ed Dorn, Robert Creeley, Hilda Morley, John Wieners and Robert Duncan, who are often regarded as important practitioners of 'open field' poetics. What distinguishes their poetry from that of their predecessors is a significant attention to speech patterns, a resistance to 'the lyrical interference of the ego' (Olson), and an increasing suspicion of language as a source of self-expression.

At a small arts gallery in San Francisco one evening in 1955, another significant gathering took place. Jack Kerouac described the event in *Dharma Bums:*

> Anyway I followed the whole gang of howling poets to the reading that night, which was, among other important things, the night of the birth of the San Francisco Renaissance. Everyone was there. It was a mad night. And I was the one who got things jumping by going around collecting dimes and quarters from the rather stiff audience standing around the gallery and coming back with three huge gallon jugs of California burgundy and getting them all piffed so that by eleven o'clock when Alvah Goldbrook [alias Allen Ginsberg] was

reading his wailing his poem 'Wail' [Howl] drunk with arms
outspread everybody was yelling 'Go! Go! Go!' (like a jam session).
(Kerouac, *Dharma Bums* (London, Deutsch, 1959), p. 13)

The association of poetry with jazz rhythms was a quintessential
part of the Beat poetics, although there was precedent for this in the
work of Robert Duncan, Jack Spicer and Kenneth Rexroth. Yet this
Six Gallery reading raised the profile of poetry as a public oral
performance and excited attention to alternative poetic developments within little magazines and small-press poetry publications.
The Beat poets like Allen Ginsberg, Gary Snyder, Gregory Corso
and Lawrence Ferlinghetti developed theories of spontaneous composition, verbal improvisation, and a direct, ecstatic and incantatory
writing. Ginsberg's *Howl* (1956) became the paradigmatic Beat
poem with its jazz measure, its agonised critique of contemporary
commodity culture, and its unabashed use of sexual imagery. However, its postmodern characteristics are somewhat diluted by distinct
Romantic yearnings, by marked foundationalist desires, and buried
narratives of a golden age. For example, Ginsberg's poetry pays
enormous homage to the American nineteenth-century Romantic
poet Walt Whitman, as well as suggesting, in his critiques of contemporary America and western culture, that there *are* mystical
truths to which one can gain some access, through poetry, Zen wor-
ship and Eastern forms of culture. This alternative to 'mad America'
was shared by a number of other poets such as Snyder, Philip
Whalen, Corso, and Duncan, who were also drawn to the cultural
'cures' and social potential of eastern forms of belief and social
organisation.

On the East coast, another group of poets were also producing
a poetry which displayed a fresh willingness to experiment with
the potential instability of language, the concern with poetry as
linguistic resource for knowledge, and an investigation into the way
language constructed rather than represented human consciousness. Kenneth Koch, James Schuyler, John Ashbery and Frank
O'Hara, central figures in the New York School, were strongly influenced by the European avant-garde, and developed a poetics which
espoused immediacy and directness, although their daring wit
and an unstudied refinement distinguished their work from the
brasher and more audacious Beats. O'Hara's mock proclamation,

'Personism: A Manifesto', established a new romanticism by arguing that poetry had to be born out of one's sense of interior address
to and dialogue with another, without being distracted by that relationship. Other significant developments within this period include
the 'ethnopoetics' of Jerome Rothenberg, which concentrated upon
poetries from non-European cultures; the 'deep image' poetics of
Robert Kelly; the 'aleatorical' or chance poetry of Jackson Mac Low
and John Cage, greatly influenced by Zen and the *I Ching;* as well as
the poetries of those gathered at readings at St Mark's Church in
New York, such as Ted Berrigan, Ron Padgett, Anne Waldman and
Bernadette Mayer.

Reading language writing

During the early 1970s, a new generation of writers, loosely focused
on a series of little magazines such as *L=A=N=G=U=A=G=E,*
Talks, Tottel's, Hills and *Poetics Journal*, and a handful of small
presses like Tuumba Books, The Figures, Roof and This, began to
stretch and push further at the legacy of these earlier poets. The
so-called 'Language' poets, such as Lyn Hejinian, Ron Silliman,
Robert Grenier, Clark Coolidge, Bob Perelman, Barrett Watten,
Charles Bernstein, Leslie Scalapino, Michael Davidson, Bruce
Andrews, Susan Howe, Carla Harryman and Steve McCaffery,
among the better-known names, began *consciously* to theorise their
work in the terminology of the cultural and philosophical ideas
which have informed postmodern theory. While many of these poets
would probably refuse the label 'postmodernist', nevertheless their
work frequently displays some of the preoccupations, interests and
excitements which have motivated postmodern theorists. Many
derive influences from the work of Gertrude Stein, Louis Zukofsky
and the Objectivist poets, the Russian Constructivists, and some
aspects of Black Mountain poetry, although they distance themselves from Olson's overbearing masculinism, as well as the claims
of presence and participation that underlie his practices and those
of the Beats and New York School.

Although 'Language' poetry has been castigated in some quarters as being the last gasp of modernism's experimental and oppositional fantasies (see, for example, Jameson's hostile and contradictory
reading of Bob Perelman's poem 'China' in 'Postmodernism and

Consumer Society', in Hal Foster (ed.), *Postmodernist Culture* (London, Pluto Press, 1985), where Jameson curiously suggests that the poem both is and is not indebted to modernism), the 'Language' poets themselves have nevertheless remained firmly committed to their sense of the necessity of a critique of social practices through language. 'Language' poets argue that the most important task of their poetry is to make us hear the ways in which the media pervade the most private recesses of our psychic lives. Consequently, there is an attempt to expose the alienating imposition of cultural codes and to exemplify the freedoms offered by art. Critical of the bardic, mystical impulses of the 1960s, the poetry explicitly focuses on the material of language itself. The 'Language' poets have themselves been prominent in entering the critical debate about poetry and have been instrumental in writing many theoretical essays attempting to explain their aesthetic practices. Some of the key figures of the 'Language' group set out their aims in a seminal essay entitled 'Aesthetic Tendency and the Politics of Poetry: A Manifesto' (*Social Text*, 19–20 (Fall 1988): 261–75). These are:

1. a denial of the centrality of the individual artist as expressive 'genius';
2. a deconstruction of the 'poetics of presence' invested in poetry's traditional reliance on the spoken word, and a concomitant devaluation of the oral in favour of the written word;
3. an interrogation of language's convention of communicative transparency;
4. the complementary development of poetic practice and theory;
5. the reciprocity of practice by a community of writers rather than a group of individuals.

In their vast output, many of the poets explore the power structures embedded in language and social reality, as well as the institutionalisation of poetic practice and aesthetic judgement in the United States.

Similar interests have developed in British poetry, albeit again eschewing the term 'postmodernist'. In this case, 'postmodernist' is often used to distinguish them from the poets who publish with mainstream presses (who have inherited the poetic mantle of the modernists like T.S. Eliot, W.H. Auden and Ezra Pound), and who have made a conscious effort to *theorise* their work as a resistance to the Romantic notion that poetry is the work of spontaneous emotion and artistic inspiration. With active writing centres in London, Cambridge and the north-east, this poetry has had close links with American developments over the past thirty years. During the huge popularisation of poetry by a variety of public media in its clamouring for accessible poems during the 1980s and 1990s, a strong corpus of writers who have not had access to the support of the mainstream presses or the bulk of the public funding for literature has nevertheless continued to exist by controlling their means of production. Poets included within this loose assemblage of writers are numerous and the list below is only a partial assortment, although a few of the more prominent names would include: Robert Sheppard, Barry MacSweeney, D.S. Mariott, Denise Riley, Gavin Selerie, Tom Clark, Bill Griffiths, Peter Middleton, Maggie O'Sullivan, Alan Halsey, Fred D'Aguiar, Allen Fisher, Tom Leonard, cris cheek, Adrian Clarke, Clive Bush, Wendy Mulford, Bob Cobbing and Ulli Freer. Generally speaking, the ideological and cultural history of these poets' work has largely been a development in conjunction with ideas and practices emerging from the Black Mountain writers, the San Francisco poets, and the 'Language' poets in the USA, as well as a variety of largely ignored British traditions, like the poetry of Basil Bunting and regional and dialect poetry.

Some of these poets have seen a few cautious incursions by large publishers into publishing their work in Britain, and the 1980s saw a contemporary poetry series in Paladin (the *re/active* anthologies); volumes like *The New British Poetry Anthology* (1994), *A Various Art* (1990), and the collections of poets such as Fisher, Griffiths, MacSweeney and Douglas Oliver; and more recently, Iain Sinclair's anthology *Conductors of Chaos* (1996) published by Picador. Nonetheless, these poets have mainly produced their writing on a basis of self-determination and a committed belief in the ideological rectitude of their interrogative cultural activity. Rather than being mesmerised by the 1980s economics of privatisation, they have continued writing steadily despite the cultural and ideological hostilities they have faced, and the spread of journals, magazines, presses and publications continues apace, albeit at the cost of individuals' pockets and their private time. Various influential magazines have grown up and some passed away since 1975, such as *Reality Studios, Pages, Parataxis, Angel Exhaust, First Offense, Object Permanence, The Many Review* and *fragmente* (to name only a few of the proliferation of magazine publications). The ongoing support of Reality Street Editions, *Spanner* Publications, Equofinality Editions, North and South and Salt Press (to name only a handful of the presses) has been crucial in the development of established poets' work, and has played an important role in attracting and encouraging a generation of new, younger voices, like Miles Champion, Marriot, Drew Milne and Caroline Bergvall. The disseminating importance of readings like Gilbert Adair's *Subvoicive* in London, the readings at Cambridge, the *Verbals* readings in Wales, the annual Six Towns poetry festival, and numerous other readings around the country, has established a major network for small-press poetic activity. In many cases, these reading venues have provided continued associations with US and Canadian writers, among whom Creeley, Ginsberg, Dorn and David Bromige have been invited to read, as well as 'Language' poets like Perelman, Hejinian, McCaffery, Bernstein, Watten, Howe and Harryman.

Although many university departments of English around Britain would not have heard of many of the writers I have mentioned here, nevertheless, some academic institutions have attempted to keep contemporary poetry production as an important part of cultural debate: the major series of Cambridge Contemporary Conferences on Poetry since 1990, largely organised by Rod Mengham; Peter Middleton's series of conferences at Southampton University; and Robert Hampson's day conferences at Senate House at London University; although there are other pockets of activity elsewhere around the country. Supplementing this academic interest, a small number of critical books have appeared which have sought to map out the writing strategies of many of these groups: Anthony Easthope and John Thompson's *Contemporary Poetry Meets Modern Theory* (Brighton, Harvester Wheatsheaf, 1991); Robert Hampson and Peter Barry's *New British Poetries: The Scope of the Possible* (Manchester, Manchester University Press, 1994); Denise Riley's *Poets on Writing* (Basingstoke, Macmillan, 1995); and Clive Bush's *Out of Dissent: A Study of Four Contemporary British Poets* (London, Talus Editions, 1997). Furthermore, the advent of new computer technology has opened up new possibilities with CD-Rom technology – see for example the CD work of cris cheek (*Skin Deep* (London, Sound and Language, 1996) and Hazel Smith and Roger Dean, *Nuraghic Echoes* and *The Riting of the Runda* (Rufus Records, Sydney, 1996) – as well as the World Wide Web opening more immediate avenues to activities within North America, like the Electronic Poetry Center at the University of New York at Buffalo, maintained by Loss Glazier (http://wings.buffalo.edu/epc/) and the journal in Britain, *Angel Exhaust* (http://angel-exhaust.off world.org/).

A whole host of issues form the material for the poetry of this period, but one might argue that as for the 'Language' poets, it is the 'politics of the sign' which preoccupies these writers. Their poetry involves a struggle over the means of representation, as well as a politics of identity (regional, class, racial and sexual). Allen Fisher's 'Place' project of the 1970s, his 'Gravity as a Consequence of Shape' project of the 1980s, the edition of *Floating Capital: New Poets from London* (1991), as well as a number of other publications by cris cheek, Ken Edwards and Roy Fisher, and more recently Aidan Dun's *Vale Royal* (1995), have sought to describe histories of London, Birmingham and urban space; Tom Pickard, Leonard, MacSweeney, Peter Finch, Edwin Morgan and others have a more (albeit not exclusive) regional focus to some of their work; John Agard, Grace Nichols, D'Aguiar and Levi Tafari use language to raise consciousness specifically about racial perspectives. Still others have questioned the construction of sexuality and femininity (Riley, Caroline Halliday, and some of the work collected in the anthology *Out of Everywhere* (1995)) and masculinity (interrogated for example by Peter Middleton in *A Portrait of an Unknown Man* (1986)). Most poets possess a sense of subjectivity constructed through language, usually (but not always) as a result of a conscious, unapologetic and unashamed engagement with recent developments in literary and cultural theory.

So far, this section has focused on what might be regarded as the British poetic subculture. However, the term 'postmodernism' has been associated at one time or another with other (more mainstream) poets, like James Fenton, Robert Crawford, Ian McMillan, W.N. Herbert and, in an Irish context, Paul Muldoon. The critical work of Alan Robinson (*Instabilities in Contemporary British Poetry* (Basingstoke, Macmillan, 1988)), Ian Gregson (*Contemporary Poetry and Postmodernism: Dialogue and Estrangement* (Basingstoke, Macmillan, 1996)), David Kennedy (*New Relations: The Refashioning of British Poetry 1980–1994* (Bridgend, Seren, 1996)), Peter Barry (*Contemporary British Poetry and the City* (Manchester, Manchester University Press, 2000) and *Poetry Wars: British Poetry of the 1970s and the Battle of Earls Court* (Cambridge, Salt, 2006)), or Dennis Brown (*The Poetry of Postmodernity: Anglo-American Encodings* (Basingstoke, Macmillan, 1994)), pose an alternative if somewhat controversial balance to the more 'subcultural' interests of Hampson, Barry, Easthope and others.

STOP and THINK

- As part of their writing strategies, postmodern poets concede the intertextuality of the world and their writing in it. Consequently, they tend to acknowledge openly their debt to writers present and past. You may want to consider the historical genealogy of postmodern poetics and what it owes to modernist and Romanticist ideas: for example, consider 'personism' and its Romantic underpinnings; the techniques of defamiliarisation in Russian Constructivism and those in 'Language' poetry; Objectivist poetry's legacy to 'Language' poetry; and the Romanticism in the New York School and Beat spontaneity.
- In the light of this, is it the case that postmodern poetics has made an absolute break with previous poetic traditions? If not, what are the relationships between various postmodern poetic practices and their precursors? Are these relationships all the same?
- To what extent do you agree with Jameson's argument that 'Language' poetry is complicit with the logic of late capitalism (see Jameson, 'Postmodernism and Consumer Society', in Foster (ed.), *Postmodern Culture,* pp. 111–25)?
- What is the practical relevance of little magazines and small poetry presses in an age of global capitalism, where everything is incorporated into capitalist structures? Can

poetry retain a socially critical function if it is mediated through the production processes of large corporate publishing houses?

Key characteristics of postmodern poetry

Although poetic practices and aims vary immensely, and many poets would resist the notion of being pigeonholed as 'postmodern', one may chart key common characteristics across poetry as follows:

1. a resistance to preconceived forms dictating the arrangement of language and ideas;
2. a resistance to closure, espousing open forms like 'open field' composition, the 'new sentence', and forms other than those handed down by orthodox poetry;
3. a challenge to the 'lyric subject' – the unified voice which orders the consciousness in the poem – and the adoption of a more dispersed, multiple voice;
4. a suspicion of the 'poetics of presence' embedded in the priority accorded to oral forms, and a rigorous exploration of the written or textual dimension of language;
5. an insistence on the materiality of the signifier, and a delight in opening up the possibilities of that recognition;
6. commitment to a 'politics of the referent': in other words, their 'play' with language and its 'rules' is a deliberate challenge to the ideological power invested in dominant linguistic formulations or patterns;
7. an insistent emphasis on the shared practices of a poetic community, as opposed to the ideology of individualism.

Postmodern poetry: an example

In order to make this discussion as accessible as possible, I have selected an extract to discuss from the widely available Norton anthology *Postmodern American Poetry*, edited by Paul Hoover (New York, Norton, 1994). Lyn Hejinian's *My Life* (1980/1987) was written in 37 sections to reflect her age when it was written. Each section is positioned alongside a phrase from another section.

The work is a good example of the discontinuous prose style adopted by many of the 'Language' poets. In a very succinct and pertinent essay entitled 'The Rejection of Closure', Hejinian has written that 'closure is a fiction', since she finds 'the world vast and overwhelming; each moment stands under an enormous vertical and horizontal pressure of information, potent with ambiguity, meaning-full, unfixed, and certainly incomplete. ... The open text is one which both acknowledges the vastness of the world and is formally differentiating' (Hoover, *Postmodern*, p. 653). Here is part of a section from *My Life:*

> *Like plump birds* Summers were spent in a fog that rains.
> *along the shore* They were mirages, no different from those
> that camel-back riders approach in the fac-
> tual accounts of voyages in which I persis-
> tently imagined myself, and those mirages on
> the highway were for me both impalpable
> souvenirs and unstable evidence of my own
> adventures, now slightly less vicarious than before. The person too
> has flared ears, like an infant's reddened with batting. I had claimed
> the radio nights for my own. There were more story-tellers than
> there were stories, so that everyone in the family had a version of
> history and it was impossible to get close to the original, or to know
> 'what really happened.' The pair of ancient, stunted apricot trees
> yielded ancient, stunted apricots. What was the meaning hung from
> that depend. The sweet aftertaste of artichokes. The lobes of auto-
> biography. Even a minor misadventure, a bumped fender or a
> newsstand without newspapers, can 'ruin the entire day,' but a child
> cries and laughs without rift. The sky droops straight down. I lapse,
> hypnotized by the flux and reflux of the waves. (Hejinian, in Hoover,
> *Postmodern*, pp. 385–6)

The relationship with the reader opened up by this piece is based less on the reception of generically or stylishly encoded work, than on the reader's participation with a relatively 'open' text. If, as is suggested, there is autobiography here, then it is not the expressivism of a Romantic outpouring of an 'inner self'. On the contrary, there appears to be a specific flattening of the register, a shifting site of enunciation, and an extensive use of non sequitur and discontinuity, which diminishes the role of the lyric subject in favour of neutral or multiple voices. Does the 'I' remain the same throughout the piece? The observations appear to be those of an 'I' whose consciousness changes. There is no attempt to unify perceptions and organise them into a single, ordered perspective: instead, the local and particular jostle with the general and abstract, forcing the reader to find or make connections between the linguistic units. Self-reflexive about the blurry distinction between objective facts and imaginative stories, originals and copies, language and its absent referents, and where the 'I' fits into the articulation of narrative, the poem is concerned with the gap that opens up between what is said and what happened; in other words, the piece relishes and takes pleasure in the condition that words are the world that we inhabit. This is language as inquiry, as inquisitiveness, as a revealed process of getting to know the world.

Two further characteristics may be noted: the condensation and displacement of linguistic elements into brief fragmentary phrases, which has the effect of displacing any unified narrative, creating a constantly changing semantic environment; and the syntactical work in what has been called the 'new sentence', which refers to the deformations of normal sentences so as to alternate ways in combining them within larger structures. Consequently, the poem does not offer up pre-existent meanings, but the passage demands that one attend to the material basis of the meaning production within its own context. As Hejinian states in her essay: 'We delight in our sensuous involvement with the materials of language, we long to join words to the world – to close the gap between ourselves and things, and we suffer from doubt and anxiety as to our capacity to do so because of the limits of language itself ... While failing in the attempt to match the world, we discover structure, distinction, the integrity and separateness of things' (Hoover, *Postmodern*, p. 658).

Postmodern theatre and performance

Theatre has shifted from a dominant place in our culture to a relatively minor one. In a world where everything appears to be theatricalised, theatre is more easily presented through television, film, computers and other technologies. More so than fiction or poetry, drama tends to have difficulty in making a straightforward distinction between modern and postmodern theatre, perhaps because what is modernist about theatre has a more vaguely outlined history. It is not my intention to present a clear-cut guide to 'postmodern theatre' here. Nevertheless, there are some practitioners and companies who have been identified with the ideas which have fed into postmodern theories, especially with theatre as a basis for an exploration of physical gestures as semiotic systems. Owing to its residual position within our culture, theatre is considered by some to be a radical form, as it goes against the grain of our dominant technological and cultural practices. Challenging the boundaries of what constitutes classical drama, as well as the space in which that drama occurs, much of postmodern drama might be called performances, or happenings, and overlaps with the performance in body art (see Chapter 5). The realm of performance reaches into dance, art-happenings, theatre and even pop concerts (think of the 'performance' that might be given at a Michael Jackson or a Madonna concert). Within the realm of theatre, postmodernist influences can be seen in the work of established playwrights, in the work of directors' interpretations, and in critical attempts to theorise what a postmodern theatre ought to be. This short discussion will attend to the basis for this new growth in performance, as well as survey the contributions of some of the significant protagonists within the area.

There are many contemporary playwrights whose work has been produced within the context of the postmodern debate about the representation of history and the politics of that practice. In Britain, the work of playwrights such as Howard Barker, Caryl Churchill, Howard Brenton and Brian Friel is often discussed within these terms, dealing as they do with the relation of history to the political sphere, the equivocal nature of 'reality' and the inequalities of social power based on gender differences. Yet although their drama frequently questions the prevailing ideological practices of contemporary society, it remains within largely recognisable theatrical conventions.

It is with the work of the contemporary avant-garde – that of groups and directors like the Welsh site-specific drama group Brith Gof, the American experimental Wooster Group and its founder Elizabeth LeCompte, the Welfare State International, the American experimental directors Robert Wilson, Richard Foreman and Richard

Schechner, the German playwright Heiner Muller, the Polish director Jerzy Grotowski and his Laboratory Theatre, and the Canadian
director-writer Robert Lepage – that the real influence of poststructuralist and postmodernist ideas has been manifested. Much of this
change is measured from the upsurge in performance and experimental theatre in the 1960s. Authors such as Peter Handke, Samuel
Beckett and Heiner Muller began presenting texts which, although
delivered by actors as a form of dialogue, could no longer be interpreted as representations of 'real life', e.g. Beckett's *Happy Days*
(1961), in which a middle-aged woman chatters away, seemingly
oblivious to the fact that she is buried first waist-high, then neck-
high in sand. The theatre was treated as a discursive space which
refused any clear-cut consciousness of character, and, as Parvis
has put it, 'the text is maintained as an object of questioning, the
workings of codes, rather than a series of situations and allusions
to a subtext which the spectator ought to feel' (Parvis, 'The Classical
Heritage of Modern Drama: The Case of Postmodern Theatre',
Modern Drama, 29:1 (March 1986): 10). Texts are treated as possessing an infinite openness to significance and a space for the
perpetual deferment of conclusive meaning.

A significant early influence in these changes in the conception
of theatre lies in the work of Allan Kaprow. Explaining his interest
in chance procedures (drama with only outlines of actions on which
actors then improvise), anti-totalisation (dramas which refuse a
'fitting' closure or ending), and non-teleological dramatic happenings (staged events which appear to have no goal or motive other
than the spectacle itself), he remarks on the importance of the
juxtapositional dynamics of collage: 'In this way a whole body of
non-intellectualized, non-culturized experience is opened to the
artist and he's free to use his mind anew in connecting things he did
not consider before' (Kaprow, 'Events', in *Assemblages, Environments, and Happenings* (New York, Abrams, 1966), p. 46). Tadeusz
Kantor has made similar observations in his 'Impossible Theatre'
(1972) about his attempts to effect a break with realist theatre: 'The
great good sense of the collage method is that it re-opens to question the exclusive right of the creator to shape the work; no longer
is the creator the only one to form, to imprint, and to express'
(*Twentieth-Century Theatre: A Sourcebook*, ed. Richard Drain (London,

Routledge, 1995), p. 65). Such deconstructive practices in theatre
have also been theorised by Herbert Blau, whose ideas are a careful
working through of complicity and illusion in theatre and theory,
or, as he put it in his article 'Ideology and Performance', 'the unre-
mitting meticulousness of the thinking through of illusion' (Blau,
'Ideology and Performance', *Theatre Journal*, 35:4 (December
1983): 460). According to Blau, a radical politics of theatre emerges
from under-cutting these frames of realist reference.

Richard Foreman's involvement with theatre has been a constant
subversion of the frames through which we have been structured to
perceive the world. In 'Unbalancing Acts' (1992), Foreman writes:

> Society teaches us to represent our lives to ourselves within the frame-
> work of a coherent narrative, but beneath that conditioning we *feel*
> our lives as a series of multidirectional impulses and collisions. We're
> trained to see our lives as a series of projects, one following the next
> along the road of experience, and our 'success' depends upon how
> well we progress from project to project. But traveling this narrow
> road shuts out a multitude of suggestive impulses and impressions –
> the ephemeral things that feed our creative insight and energy. ...
> I like to think of my plays as an hour and a half in which you see the
> world through a special pair of eyeglasses. These glasses may not block
> out all narrative coherence, but they magnify so many other aspects
> of experience that you simply lose interest in trying to hold on to
> narrative richness and instead, allow yourself to become absorbed
> in the moment-by-moment representation of psychic freedom.
> ('Unbalancing Acts', in Drain (ed.), *Twentieth-Century Theatre*, p. 68)

Foreman is interested in theatrical forms which refuse totalising
experiences and resist ironing out contradictions. His 'ontological-
hysterical theatre' exemplifies the multiplicity with which contemporary theatre can operate, bombarding the audience with a
sophisticated plurality of visual and auditory events. For Nick Kaye,
whose sense of postmodern performance is a disruption of the move
towards self-containment and self-sufficiency, Foreman's theatre
exemplifies a disruption of closure through systematic distortions
and constantly frustrating continuities and coherences. In a discussion of Foreman's piece *Pandering to the Masses: A Misrepresentation*
(1977), Kaye describes how:

> the performance undercuts itself as it traces out, at each successive
> moment, expectations that are systematically let down. This leads,

> Foreman suggests, to a critique that 'is the body and flesh of the
> play', and that, because it is the very substance of the performance,
> becomes, paradoxically, 'the critique of a play that isn't there'. It is
> a 'play' whose elements seem continually to come into view but
> which never finally appears, a play whose realisation and so closure
> is perpetually staved off. (Kaye, *Postmodernism and Performance*
> (Basingstoke, Macmillan, 1993), p. 54)

Kaye discusses two other important figures in the development
of a theatre which disrupts the structural and formal boundaries
of theatrical representation since the 1960s – Michael Kirby and
Robert Wilson. Both Kirby and Wilson continually activate the contingency of meaning and the ambiguity of structure, which Kaye
regards as practices which 'resist the effort to penetrate the surface
of the work, frustrating the reading of structure, sequence, pattern
and image' (Kaye, *Postmodernism*, p. 69). Adopting culturally reso-
nant images from mass circulation, like cowboys and Indians, Stalin,
and Einstein, Wilson then indicates that the meaning ascribed to
them is arbitrary. His focus rests with the surface of representation,
and he does not rupture representation so much as relativise it.
Quite clear about the impact that commodification has on images,
he nevertheless celebrates their value as spectacle. Ultimately, Foreman, Kirby and Wilson are artists whose work 'amounts to an attack
not only on the autonomy of the work of art but the specularity of
the sign, as the attempt to read, to discover depth, is persistently
deflected, de-centred, thrown back upon itself, in an exposure of the
contingency of the "work" and that which the viewer discovers in
the moment of its presentation' (Kaye, *Postmodernism*, p. 70).

Another dimension of contemporary theatre is dance. The term
'postmodern' has long been associated with dance, especially since
Merce Cunningham's association with Black Mountain College in
the 1960s. An oxymoronic image of the classical muse of dance
in leisure shoes acts as the title for Sally Banes's book, *Terpsichore in
Sneakers: Postmodern Dance* (Middletown CT, Wesleyan University
Press, 1987), and this figure gestures to the way in which postmodern dance seeks to break with the conventions of western conceptions
of classical grace and harmony. This has interesting resonances with
conceptions of the postmodern as a shattering of the harmonies of
Euclidean geometry (e.g. postmodern fiction as part of the quantum
universe). Dancers and performance artists, like Laurie Anderson,

Botho Strauss, Carolee Schneemann, Yvonne Rainer, Lucinda
Childs, Meredith Monk, Steve Paxton, Pina Bausch and Trisha
Brown, have been instrumental in challenging the strict canons of
physical aesthetics on the ballet floor. Banes dates this new style in
dance from Michael Kirby's definition in the 1975 issue of the
Drama Review devoted to postmodern dance, in which he wrote:

> In the theory of post-modern dance, the choreographer does not
> apply visual standards to the work. The view is an interior one:
> movement is not pre-selected for its characteristics but results from
> certain decisions, goals, plans, schemes, rules, concepts, or problems.
> Whatever actual movement occurs during the performance is accept-
> able as long as the limiting and controlling principles are adhered to.
> (Kirby, 'Introduction', *Drama Review*, 19 (March 1975): 3)

Rejecting musicality, meaning, characterisation, mood and atmo-
sphere, Banes argues that since this date postmodern dance has
gone through a variety of stages, from analytic postmodern dance,
which sought to redefine movement in the late 1960s and 1970s, to
the rebirth of content in the 1980s. Often producing a variety of
cooperative ventures among artists, like Lucinda Childs', Philip
Glass' and Sol LeWitt's collaboration *Dance*, or Trisha Brown's and
Robert Rauschenberg's collaboration on *Glacial Decoy*, choreogra-
phy has gradually turned to new sources for exploring movement,
like the meditative Zen influences and the mesmerising movement
of Tai Chi. In this respect, if postmodernism has caused a reassessment of representation and discourse, then it has also opened theatre
to other cultures. Augusto Boal's *The Theatre of the Oppressed* (1974;
London, Pluto Press, 1979) produces exercises for a revolutionary
theatre, theatrical strategies which act as resistances to passive complicity with an oppressive situation.

STOP and THINK

●   Is theatre the same as performance? If not, where does the-
     atre end and performance begin? Consider the different
     meanings of the word 'performance': do the alternatives
     offer interesting ways into definitions of what constitutes
     a postmodern theatre? For example, what is the distinction

between 'performing' and 'performance'? In what ways does 'performance' traverse and disrupt different discourses? How are the traditional notions of 'role', 'writer' and 'director' altered?

- Many performance artists base their work on their own bodies or their own autobiographies instead of characters previously created by other artists. What particular interpretative difficulties does dance or body performance produce for theories which concentrate on the *textual* or *written* word? In what ways can one theorise physical movement as an aesthetic practice, and in particular, how does one account for a specifically 'postmodern' theory of physical movement?

- How might one conceptualise postmodern performance in terms of Lyotard's distinction between grand narratives and local narratives? Consider the parody, pastiche and ironic citations of the Wooster Group's reworkings of Thornton Wilder, Arthur Miller, Eugene O'Neill and others. You may also want to consider the way in which performance appears to become more and more about itself and its processes, and less and less about an objective reality and life in the world.

Selected reading

Postmodern fiction

Baker, Stephen, *The Fiction of Postmodernity* (Edinburgh, Edinburgh University Press, 2000).
A study of postmodern fiction in the work of DeLillo, Morrison, Rushdie, Pynchon, and Amis, viewed in relation to critiques of the culture industry, analyses of the postmodern condition, and theories of simulacra.

Greaney, Michael, *Contemporary Fiction and the Uses of Theory: The Novel from Structuralism to Postmodernism* (Basingstoke, Palgrave Macmillan, 2006).
Focuses on the interrelationship of literary theory and fiction from the 1970s to the present, analysing the 'fictionalisation' of radical literary theories.

Green, Jeremy, *Late Postmodernism: American Fiction at the Millennium* (Palgrave Macmillan, 2005).
Addressing the issue of whether postmodernism can be written off as a *fin-de-siècle* trend, this investigates new directions in US experimental fiction since the 1990s.
Gregson, Ian, *Postmodern Literature* (London, Arnold, 2004).
An accessible approach to postmodernism that compares and contrasts it with modernism, and places it in its historical context.
Heuser, Sabine, *Virtual Geographies: Cyberpunk at the Intersection of the Postmodern and Science Fiction* (Amsterdam, Rodopi, 2003).
A detailed study that offers a working definition of cyberpunk within the postmodern culture, considering its offspring in domains like literature, film, music, and feminism.
Hoffman, Gerhard, *From Modernism to Postmodernism: Concepts and Strategies of Postmodern American Fiction* (Amsterdam, Rodopi, 2005).
Discusses the US postmodern novel in its historical, cultural and aesthetic context between 1960 and 1980, covering Pynchon, Barth, Vonnegut and Sorrentino.
Hutcheon, Linda, *A Poetics of Postmodernism: History, Theory, Fiction* (London, Routledge, 1988).
A sophisticated account of postmodernism, but still easily accessible and wide-ranging. Considers issues like the role of parody, 'ex-centricity', intertextuality, metafictionality, and discourse and history.
Hutcheon, Linda, *The Politics of Postmodernism* (London, Routledge, 1989).
A very useful and approachable introductory discussion of debates concerning postmodern fiction. Also contains discussions of fiction and history, photography and performance.
McHale, Brian, *Postmodernist Fiction* (New York and London, Methuen, 1987).
A good place to start on the formal characteristics of postmodern fiction.
McHale, Brian, *Constructing Postmodernism* (London, Routledge, 1992).
Extends the argument first expounded in *Postmodernist Fiction*. Has good chapters on Thomas Pynchon, Don DeLillo, and cyberpunk fiction. Wide-ranging and readable.
Nicol, Bran (ed.), *Postmodernism and the Contemporary Novel: A Reader* (Edinburgh, Edinburgh University Press, 2002).
An excellent source of key texts and statements, covering many areas of the postmodern debate.
Slocombe, Will, *Nihilism and the Sublime Postmodern* (London, Routledge, 2006).
This book examines the relationship between nihilism and postmodernism in relation to the sublime.

Smyth, Edmund (ed.), *Postmodernism and Contemporary Fiction* (London, Batsford, 1991).

Contains a number of useful essays on contemporary fiction in Britain, America, France, Italy and Spain, and others on ideology, politics and feminism, with especially helpful pieces by John Mepham, David Seed, Linda Hutcheon and Thomas Docherty.

Postmodern poetry

Andrews, Bruce, and Charles Bernstein (eds), *The L=A=N=G=U=A=G=E Book* (Carbondale and Edwardsville, Southern Illinois University Press, 1984).

A collection of the seminal essays and short pieces by the key poets and practitioners involved with the *L=A=N=G=U=A=G=E* magazine. A major resource.

Barry, Peter, and Robert Hampson (eds), *New British Poetries: The Scope of the Possible* (Manchester, Manchester University Press, 1993).

Contains some seminal essays and some very interesting discussions of contemporary poetry in Britain. Also offers some useful 'case-studies' of poets' work.

Davidson, Ian, *Ideas of Space in Contemporary Poetry* (Basingstoke, Palgrave Macmillan, 2007).

A study of the relationship between the 'spatial turn' in cultural and social theory and its representation in contemporary poetry and poetics.

Easthope, Anthony, and John Thompson (eds), *Contemporary Poetry Meets Modern Theory* (Brighton, Harvester Wheatsheaf, 1991).

A wide-ranging collection of essays from some of the key critics on American and British contemporary poets and their practices.

Eclipse: http://english.utah.edu/eclipse/

Edited by Craig Dworkin, Department of English at the University of Utah, Eclipse is a remarkable free on-line archive focusing on digital facsimiles of the most radical small-press writing from the last quarter century, as well as also publishing carefully selected new works of book-length conceptual unity.

Funkhouser, C.T., *Prehistoric Digital Poetry: An Archaeology of Forms, 1959–1995* (Tuscaloosa AL, University of Alabama Press, 2007).

This book documents and analyses the history of digital poetry and its major practitioners as they have used technology to foster a new aesthetic.

Hartley, George, *Textual Politics and the Language Poets* (Bloomington IN, Indiana University Press, 1989).

An advanced yet interesting discussion of the politics of contemporary poetry from a Marxist perspective.

Hoover, Paul (ed.), *Postmodern American Poetry: A Norton Anthology* (New York, Norton, 1994).
A useful anthology of material, although not always offering the best examples of the range of innovation and experiment by the respective writers. It does include some very useful statements on poetics as an appendix.

Huk, Romana (ed.), *Assembling Alternatives: Reading Postmodern Poetries Transnationally* (Middletown CT, Wesleyan University Press, 2003).
In 24 essays, this book focuses on how national differences have inflected poetic experimentation and analyses the provocative differences in strategies of resistance, constructions of self, use of voice and use of technology.

Perloff, Marjorie, 'The Word as Such: L=A=N=G=U=A=G=E Poetry in the Eighties', in *The Dance of the Intellect* (Cambridge, Cambridge University Press, 1985), pp. 215–38.
A good, approachable introductory essay by a major champion of the 'Language' poets' activities and practices.

Perloff, Marjorie, *Radical Artifice: Writing Poetry in the Age of Media* (Chicago, Chicago University Press, 1991).
An excellent advanced discussion of contemporary American poetics in relation to its forebears and contextual cultural practices.

Rheinfeld, Linda, *Language Poetry: Writing as Rescue* (Baton Rouge, Louisiana University Press, 1987).
A good introductory discussion of a variety of the main issues which are pertinent to the poetic practices of the 'Language' poets.

Sheppard, Robert, *The Poetry of Saying: British Poetry and Its Discontents, 1950–2000* (Liverpool, Liverpool University Press, 2005).
Investigates the 'secret history' of fifty years of experimental British verse, revealing the work of British poets as well as the role of poetry magazines.

Silliman, Ron, *The New Sentence* (New York, Roof, 1989).
Key essays from one of the major theorists and practitioners of the 'Language' poets. Contains the essay on the 'new sentence'.

Tuma, Keith, *Fishing by Obstinate Isles: Modern and Postmodern British Poetry and American Readers* (Evanston IL, Northwestern University Press, 1998).
Explores the complex relations of recent British and American poetries, challenging reductive American views of a British poetry dominated by anti-modernism.

Watten, Barrett, *Total Syntax* (Carbondale and Edwardsville, Southern Illinois University Press, 1984).

A significant discussion of the practices and poetic precedents of the 'Language' poets, which is accessible and wide-ranging.

Postmodern theatre and performance

Auslander, Philip, *Presence and Resistance: Postmodernism and Cultural Politics in Contemporary American Performance* (Ann Arbor MI, University of Michigan Press, 1992).

A study of the political nature of postmodern performance and the strategies employed by such performers as Laurie Anderson, Spalding Gray, Andy Kaufman and Sandra Bernhardt as they combat the mediatised contemporary culture.

Auslander, Philip, *From Acting to Performance: Essays in Modernism and Postmodernism* (London, Routledge, 1997).

Chapters on the politics in postmodern theatre, gender and the body, alteration and identity. From the Ecstatic theatre of the 1960s to the performance theatre of the 1990s, Auslander argues that performance is the postmodernism which ousts the theatricality of modernism.

Banes, Sally, *Terpsichore in Sneakers: Postmodern Dance* (Middletown CT, Wesleyan University Press, 1987).

An excellent account of the changes in dance from modernist to postmodernist practices.

Birringer, Johannes, *Theatre, Theory, Postmodernism* (Bloomington and Indianapolis IN, Indiana University Press, 1991).

Analysing the dehumanising and dematerialising effects of postmodernism, Birringer calls for theatre to have a 'critical connection to postmodern culture', and to develop a resistance to postmodern impoverishment.

Briginshaw, Valerie A., *Dance, Space, and Subjectivity* (Basingstoke and New York, Palgrave, 2001).

By focusing on site-specific dance, the mutual construction of bodies and spaces, body–space interfaces and 'in-between spaces', this book contains readings of American, British and European postmodern dances informed by feminist, postcolonialist, queer, and poststructuralist theories.

Campbell, Patrick (ed.), *Analyzing Performance: A Critical Reader* (Manchester, Manchester University Press, 1996).

A selection of useful and informative essays on the subject of feminism and performance art.

Carlson, Marvin, *Performance: A Critical Introduction* (London, Routledge, 1996).

An overview of performance and how it has developed in various fields. Especially good on the relationship of performance, postmodernism and the politics of identity.

Huxley, Michael, and Noel Witts (eds), *The Twentieth-Century Performance Reader* (London, Routledge, 1996).

An introduction to all types of performance (dance, drama, music, theatre, live art), through the writings of practitioners, theorists and critics.

Kaye, Nick, *Postmodernism and Performance* (Basingstoke, Macmillan, 1993).

A good critical survey of the territory, focusing on performance and dance, attempting to delineate the development of the plurality of practices which have emerged in contradistinction to those of modernism.

Schmidt, Kerstin (ed.), *The Theater of Transformation: Postmodernism in American Drama* (Amsterdam, Rodopi, 2005).

This book offers an innovative reading of the contemporary experimental American theatre scene and navigates through the contested and contentious relationship between postmodernism and contemporary drama.

4

Postmodern architecture and concepts of space

Architecture was one of the first areas in which the subject of postmodernism was debated and defined, partly because buildings have a highly visible public profile, affecting most people's lives. Beginning in the late 1960s, the argument concerning what replaced modernist architecture has received close attention from all quarters: from Charles Jencks, the most famous and prolific theorist of postmodernist architecture, to Charles Windsor, the Prince of Wales. In addition to architects and princes, the debate concerning lived space has also involved engagements by geographers, collaborations with philosophers, critiques from urban sociologists and town planners, and arguments from cultural theorists. The impact of this wide-ranging debate has been registered in the tabloid newspapers as well as university treatises; and public consciousness about the construction of urban space has been raised to a high level in North America, Western Europe and Southeast Asia. In analysing these debates and definitions, this chapter will focus on the key theorists and their arguments, as well as the principal influential books and buildings.

Modernist architecture

Postmodernism in architecture emerged as a series of architects' reactions against what was increasingly perceived to be the stultifying effects of the modernist interest in functionalism. The most influential modernist architects were Walter Gropius (1883–1969),

Le Corbusier (born Charles-Edouard Jeanneret, 1887–1965) and
Ludwig Mies van der Rohe (1886–1969), who together formed the
main theoretical exponents of the Bauhaus School. Le Corbusier, an
architect, town planner and designer, developed the central tenets
of modernist architecture in a series of trenchant manifestoes, of
which the most influential was *Vers une Architecture Nouveau
(Towards a New Architecture* (Paris, Editions Cres, 1923; London,
Butterworth Architecture, 1927, rpt 1987)). This manifesto proclaimed that utility and functionalism ought to be the presiding
features of modern architecture, with such emphatic assertions
as 'The great problems of modern construction must have a geometrical solution' and 'Without plan we have the sensation, so
insupportable to man, of shapelessness, of poverty, of disorder, of
wilfulness' (*Towards a New Architecture,* pp. 2, 48). Le Corbusier's
principal architectural characteristics were an insistence on low
cost, rationalised and standardised architecture for mass production, a defence of functionalism, a rejection of the nineteenth
century's preoccupation with 'style', and a firm stand against elaborate, non-structural decoration. The basic cell-like house in his
Maison Citrohan (1922) displays his preoccupation with function
rather than form in his deliberate pun on the French car Citroën,
implying something mass produced with mechanical efficiency. His
famous aphorisms, 'A house is a machine for living in' and 'A curved
street is a donkey track, a straight street, a road for man', reflect Le
Corbusier's intention to promote an architecture of democracy,
with an emphasis on simplicity, regularity and purity. Partly generated by the necessity of postwar urban housing regeneration, in a
grand utopian gesture, architecture was to become not just a reflection of, but a decisive agency in the creation of, a new society. This
can be seen in his building Unité d'Habitation (1947) in Marseilles,
a large apartment block built of prefabricated, reinforced concrete
which housed 1,600 people as a small organic community. The
building sought to integrate private dwelling spaces with collective
activities, like a gymnasium and a shopping centre, providing a
shared life with no sacrifice of individuality. Although subject to a
huge public protest, the building was envisaged as a radical alternative to suburban sprawl, governed by collective participation in
the unity of a single habitation. This utopian aspect is best captured

in one of Gropius' Bauhaus maifestoes, in which he resoundingly states:

> The ultimate aim of all visual arts is the complete building! . . .
> Together let us desire, conceive, and create the new structure of the
> future, which will embrace architecture and sculpture and painting
> in one unity and which will one day rise toward heaven from the
> hands of a million workers like the crystal symbol of a new faith.
> (Walter Gropius, 'Programme of the Staatliches Bauhaus in Weimar'
> (1919), in Ulrich Conrads (ed.), *Programmes and Manifestoes on
> Twentieth-Century Architecture* (London, Lund Humphries, 1970),
> pp. 49–53; p. 49)

What came to be known as the International Style emerged from Le Corbusier's architectural polemics, from the Bauhaus School under the guidance of Gropius, and from the CIAM (Congrès internationaux d'architecture moderne), established in 1928 to advance the cause of modern architecture. Interacting with Cubist constructions of smooth planes set at right angles, the International Style expressed a simple, geometrical intensity. Mies van der Rohe exemplified the uncompromising simplicity of the International Style in the 1950s with his designs for the apartments on Lake Shore Drive in Chicago, two rectangular blocks placed at right angles, which are so disciplined as to be coldly impersonal; and it is seen perhaps most completely in the clean purity of the Seagram Building (1954–58) at 375 Park Avenue in New York (Figure 1), a great prismatic shaft of austere brown and bronze rectilinear slab with a curtain wall of sheer glass hung on a hidden steel frame. The wealth and power of the corporation are reflected in an all-powerful image conveyed by an unbending rectangular uniformity and a monumentality in its consistent devotion to logic and clarity of structure.

To sum up, three main features are embodied in the totalising impulse of modernist architecture – reductivism, determinism and mechanism. The principal characteristics of the International Style might be formulated as follows:

1. Style was removed from the vocabulary of form in favour of a new ascetic geometry. The tyranny of historicism in architecture was rejected, as 'ornament was crime'.

Figure 1 Mies van der Rohe, Seagram Building, 375 Park Avenue, New York City (1954–58)

2. A radically functional approach to architecture was taken, in which the imperative was Mies' notion that 'form follows function'.
3. Regularity, rationalisation and standardisation, and a clarity of outline and geometry, became the principal organisational features, as the architects sought a universalist and abstract style.

The International Style was at its best nearly international, its purist impersonal image dominating the architectural scene the world over, and at its most influential in Western Europe, North America and occasionally Japan and South America after the Second World War. It was devoid of local or regional characteristics, and promoted a simple, uncluttered, repetitive and modular design, eliminating the ornament that expressed local style or personal eccentricity. Yet although it was guided by a desire to design democratic housing and business quarters for a mass population, ironically it became a technocratic monument to the impersonalism of big business and international capitalism.

Postmodernist reactions

'Modern Architecture died in St. Louis, Missouri on July 15, 1972 at 3.32 pm.' So Charles Jencks ironically stated upon the blowing-up of the infamous Pruitt-Igoe housing development, which had sucked in thousands of dollars in renovation plans and repair bills for severe vandalism. Dynamited along with the block of flats was the vision of social equality which underscored Gropius' belief that clean lines, purity and simplicity of form would play a social and morally improving role in society, for there was by now clear evidence that such housing projects were unable to solve modern social problems.

For Jencks, this event solidified a set of multiple resistances to the hegemony of modernist architectural preoccupations during the first half of the twentieth century. People emerged with a series of devastating attacks, from the withering scorn of Jane Jacobs in *The Death and Life of Great American Cities* (London, Jonathan Cape, 1962), to the sardonic cynicism of Tom Wolfe's caustic social critique of modernist architecture and the evolution of postmodernist

alternatives in *From Bauhaus to Our House* (1982), in which he sar-
castically described the Avenue of the Americas in Manhattan as
'Row after Mies van der row of glass boxes' (Wolfe, *From Bauhaus to
Our House* (1982; London, Abacus, 1983), p. 4). The causes of the
failure of the modern movement in architecture were manifold; but
in addition to the unacceptably prescriptive nature of its architectural theories, one of the principal reasons was that it was unable
to deliver an architecture which was free from the influence of
corporate capital. As David Harvey has argued:

> Some of the ideological claims [of modernism] were grandiose. But
> the radical transformations in the social and physical landscapes of
> capitalist cities often had little to do with such claims. ... Even when
> contained by planning regulations or oriented around public invest-
> ments, corporate capital still had a great deal of power. And where
> corporate capital was in command (especially in the US), it could
> happily appropriate every modernist trick in the architect's book to
> continue that practice of building monuments that soared ever higher
> as symbols of corporate power. (Harvey, *The Condition of Postmoder-
> nity* (Oxford, Blackwell, 1989), p. 71)

The development of postmodern architecture during the second
half of the twentieth century has inevitably meant that many theorists have considered its position as a manifestation of late consumer
capitalism. Perhaps the most sustained critique in this respect has
been that of Fredric Jameson, who perceives postmodern architecture to be an unapologetic celebration of aestheticism. The focus for
his critique is John Portman's megalithic Bonaventure Hotel
(1974–76) in Los Angeles, which Jameson describes as inaugurating
and symbolising the development of a radically new kind of 'postmodern hyperspace' that 'has finally succeeded in transcending the
capacities of the individual human body to locate itself, to organise
its immediate surroundings perceptually, and cognitively to map its
position in a mappable external world' (Jameson, *Postmodernism, or
the Cultural Logic of Late Capitalism* (London, Verso, 1991), p. 44).
He points out that the hotel, with its huge, reflective glass skin,
appears to dissociate itself from the city, and that 'this disjunction
from the surrounding city is different from that of monuments of
the International Style, in which the act of disjunction was violent,

visible, and had real symbolic significance – as in Le Corbusier's great *pilotis,* whose gesture radically separates the new Utopian space of the modern from the degraded and fallen city which it thereby explicitly repudiates' (*Postmodernism,* p. 41). Unlike the consciously interventionist and polemical confrontation posed by Le Corbusier, the Bonaventure Hotel displays an indifference to the city beyond, seeming content to repel it through aesthetic dissociation and aloofness. Jameson argues that postmodern architecture functions aesthetically to undermine democratic urban space, since it merely imitates the cultural logic of late capitalism, which is a consumer-led triumphalism.

The very universal nature of the International Style's application led to designs which failed to recognise the different functions of various buildings. Housing, offices and cultural institutions all looked similar, and this stylistic uniformity was criticised for its inability to add anything to their environment. The evisceration of historical reference demanded by the International Style was recognised as stylistically restrictive, rootless and meaningless; and consequently, in the rejection of modernist architecture, along with an explicit adoption of 'pop' styles, historical traditions have become the source of contemporary quotation and imitation.

What there is to learn from Las Vegas

The year that saw the demolition of Pruitt-Igoe saw another demolition job on modernist architecture from Robert Venturi, who was to become the prophet of postmodernist architecture in North America, with his aggressive use of decorative moulding, traditional symbol and popular culture. The terms for much of the discussion of postmodernist styles of architecture emerged partly from the seminal work of Venturi, Steven Izenour and Denise Scott Brown, in an important book entitled *Learning from Las Vegas* (1972). In its revaluation of commercial shlock, this book established a celebration of popular styles at the expense of the ascetic minimalism of the International Style. It developed some of the points Venturi had made in his earlier book, *Complexity and Contradiction in Architecture* (1966; rpt London, Butterworth Architecture, 1988), in which he lambasted the modernists for their restrictive and stultifying allegiance to architectural simplicity and purity. Venturi sets out his own architectural manifesto:

> Architects can no longer afford to be intimidated by the puritanically moral language of orthodox Modern architecture. I like elements which are hybrid rather than 'pure', compromising rather than 'clean', distorted rather than 'straightforward', ambiguous rather than 'articulated', perverse as well as impersonal, boring as well as 'interesting', conventional rather than 'designed', accommodating rather than excluding, redundant rather than simple, vestigial as well as innovating, inconsistent and equivocal rather than direct and clear. I am for messy vitality over obvious unity. I include the non sequitur and proclaim the duality. I am for richness of meaning rather than clarity of meaning; for the implicit function as well as the explicit function. I prefer 'both-and' to 'either-or', black and white, and sometimes gray, to black or white. (*Complexity and Contradiction*, p. 16)

Parodying Mies's famous dictum 'less is more', Venturi states that a complex and contradictory architecture embraces 'the difficult unity of inclusion rather than the easy unity of exclusion. More is not less' and follows this with the damning 'Less is a bore' (*Complexity and Contradiction*, pp. 16–17).

Elaborating upon this excoriating condemnation, *Learning from Las Vegas* sought to redefine the territory of architecture by stressing issues such as history, language, form, symbolism and the dialectics of high and popular culture. Asking 'is not Main Street almost all right?' (*Complexity and Contradiction*, p. 104), Venturi studies the banality of the American strip in its most exuberant form and seeks to establish how the so-called avant-garde has lost its dynamism and how Las Vegas has become the cutting edge of architectural style. Opening himself to the popular culture embedded in Las Vegas, Venturi promotes an imitation of kitsch, of the vast flashing neon signs and pop culture. Venturi states that:

> the order of the Strip *includes;* it includes at all levels, from the mixture of seemingly incongruous land uses to the mixture of seemingly incongruous advertising media plus a system of neo-Organic or neo-Wrightian restaurant motifs in Walnut Formica. It is not an order dominated by the expert and made easy for the eye ... The Strip shows the value of symbolism and allusion in architecture ...

> Allusion and comment, on the past or present or on our great commonplaces or old clichés, and inclusion of the everyday environment, sacred and profane – these are what are lacking in present-day Modern architecture. (Venturi, Scott Brown and Izenour, *Learning from Las Vegas* (Cambridge MA, MIT Press, 1977), pp. 52–3)

Venturi rejects the universalising thrust of modern architecture and argues for an architecture which is rooted in the regional and the historical. Furthermore, he insists on the importance of the communicative function of architecture. What architecture can learn from Las Vegas is inclusion, allusion, articulation; and it can also learn the communicative and symbolic power of iconographic ornament and decoration. Both *Learning from Las Vegas* and *Complexity and Contradiction in Architecture* demonstrate that architecture must incorporate a multiplicity of architectural languages, as opposed to the single, prescriptive language of purity and self-sustaining simplicity which underpinned modern architecture. In other words, Venturi sought to introduce notions of irony, playfulness, multivalenced lexicons and a celebration of the ordinary into architecture, resisting the austere, monumental and heroic quality of modern architecture; and in so doing, he sought to make architecture bend to the demands of place, more responsive to the immediate historical and cultural environment of its location of buildings.

Venturi's celebration of hybridity over purity, and complexity over straightforward simplicity, can be seen in his designs like Venturi and Rauch's famous Franklin Court, Philadelphia (1972–76), which sets up an open frame of stainless steel as an approximation of Franklin's old mansion in the centre of surrounding restored buildings, with the archaeological remains encasing the 'ghost' building, knitting together the old and the new. Venturi's 'difficult unity' and Pop detail became the basis for designs like Venturi and Rauch's Guild House (1960–63), the house for his mother Vanna Venturi in Pennsylvania (1963–65), and their Gordon Wu Hall (1982–84) at Princeton University. Other American architects, like Robert Stern, developed many of Venturi's symbolic and ornamental ideas, exemplified in Stern's Bozzie Residence (1982–83) on Long Island, and his hybrid office building Point West Place (1983–84) near Boston. Others again, like Charles Moore in his Piazza d'Italia (1976–79) in New Orleans, and Michael Graves in his Portland Public Services Building (1980–82) in Oregon and his Humana Medical Corporation HQ (1982–85) in Louisville, Kentucky, demonstrate this same historical and cultural pluralism, as well as reusing the Venturi team's experiments with idiosyncratic corners, odd walls and 'postmodern' space.

Charles Jencks and 'dual-coding'

If Venturi argued that architecture ought to pay renewed attention to the semiotic dimension of architecture, to architecture as a *language* which signifies and communicates, then this was explicitly formulated by Charles Jencks. The terms of Jencks' discussion of postmodernist architecture partly emerged from Venturi's landmark work, although Jencks was concerned to distinguish postmodern architecture from what he perceived to be 'Late Modern' architecture. Emerging simultaneously with postmodernism, according to Jencks, the latter was merely an exaggeration of what modernist architects were already doing, flaunting its high-tech character with occasional ironic asides, as in the new Lloyd's Building in London, with its inversion of the modernist desire to hide the guts of a building beneath a smooth and pure exterior. Arguably, the emergence of historicism in the United States came with the major works of Johnson in the early 1960s. Yet it was with Johnson and John Burgee's audacious AT&T Corporate Headquarters building (1979–84) in New York, with its celebrated split pediment being tagged as a 'Pop icon of a "Chippendale Highboy"', that Johnson set about creating an architecture of 'bricolage' (a French term for improvisation or makeshift work, often applied to collage or assembled artworks), which plays with historical implication and latent and manifest symbolism. This mimicry is continued in their Republic Bank Center (1981–84) in Houston, with its imitation of a Middle European *Rathaus* or town hall, or their office building at 580 California (1984), San Francisco, with Muriel Castanis's iconographic statues of death placed on its roof.

Yet arguably, postmodernism in architecture can be seen to date from the late 1950s with the developments of the Italian Neo-Liberty architects like Luigi Moretti, Franco Albini and Paolo Portoghesi. All their buildings demonstrated traits of vague or repressed historical allusions to Roman, medieval or Baroque styles, although not without influence from the modernism of Mies van der Rohe, Gropius or Le Corbusier. This historical ambivalence is one of the principal features of postmodernist architecture, which generally refers to a building which works on two semiotic levels: it addresses other architects and a concerned minority who care specifically about architectural meanings; and it addresses the public at large, or the local inhabitants, who care about issues of comfort and a way of life. This is what Jencks has termed postmodernism's 'dual-coding' or 'double-coding', or a conscious schizophrenia, which amounts to nothing less than architectural irony, or pastiche.

The term 'post-modern' was first used in an architectural context in 1949 by Joseph Hudnut, in the article 'The Post-Modern House'; and then by Nikolaus Pevsner in his attack on the 'anti-Pioneers' (1966), when he was berating buildings with sculptural decoration or unusual 'kinks' in them. Subsequently, largely due to the influential histories and explorations of Jencks' several books, among which are *The Language of Post-Modern Architecture* (1st edition, London, Academy Editions, 1977), *Free-style Classicism* (London, Architectural Design, 1982) and *What is Post-Modernism?* (1986; London, Academy Editions and New York, St. Martin's Press, 1989), the architectural term has come to refer to buildings which treat architecture as a language or a discourse. That is, buildings which self-reflexively 'quote' historical characteristics and make ironic use of local context; which utilise a certain metaphorical quality in their design; which encapsulate a pluralism or hybridity of style; and which construct a new ambiguous space. As such, Jencks has argued that Post-Modernism (as Jencks writes it) is basically a plural concept which incorporates a variety of architectural styles and influences. This creates an architecture of 'narrative content', which suggests that the bare demands of utility are supplemented by ornamental or symbolic features, which lift the building out of its primary relationship to *function* and place it within a new relationship with *fiction*. A good example of this might be Foster's design for the new airport at Chep Lap Kok in Hong Kong (1998), which not only functions as an airline passenger and freight terminal, but is built in the shape of a vast airliner.

Jencks' definitions of postmodern architecture become progressively more sophisticated as he attempts to distinguish between different trends within postmodern practices. He has produced a series of increasingly more refined genealogies for movements within contemporary architecture, as well as a series of categorisations of their characteristics. One of the more widely quoted examples occurs in his essay 'The Emergent Rules', where Jencks outlines a series of eleven characteristics concerning the definition of postmodern architecture: dissonant beauty, pluralism, urbane urbanism, anthropomorphism, anamnesis, radical eclecticism, double-coding, multi-valence, tradition reinterpreted, new rhetorical figures, and a return to the absent centre. Jencks regards these 'rules' as a set of evolving practices rather than a set of inflexible categories. Yet his notions of postmodern architecture may be supplemented with other definitions by practising architects. Stern, often cited as a prime mover in establishing the postmodern reaction to the International Style, states that:

> post-modernism recognizes that buildings are designed to mean something, that they are not hermetically sealed objects. Post-modernism accepts diversity; it prefers hybrids to pure forms; it encourages multiple and simultaneous readings in its effort to heighten expressive content. Borrowing from forms and strategies of both modernism and the architecture that preceded it, post-modernism declares the pastness of both. The layering of space characteristic of much post-modernist architecture finds its complement in the overlay of cultural and art-historical references in the elevations. For the postmodernist, 'more is more'. (Stern, *New Directions in American Architecture* (New York, George Braziller, 1969), pp. 134–5)

Like Jencks, Stern emphasises the new ornamentalism and cites three dominating principles in postmodernist architecture: (a) contextualism, (b) allusionism, (c) ornamentalism. Paulo Portoghesi also regards postmodern architecture as the ironic reintroduction of the past and history into spatial constructions: 'The Postmodern in architecture can therefore be read overall as a re-emergence of archetypes, or as a reintegration of architectonic conventions, and thus as a premise to the creation of an *architecture of communication*, an architecture of the image for a civilization of the image' (Paulo Portoghesi, *Postmodern: The Architecture of the Postindustrial Society* (New York, Rizzoli, 1982), p. 11). Eschewing the dogmatic assertions of the functionalist statutes 'form follows function', 'architecture must coincide with construction' and 'ornament is crime', Portoghesi sees a Lyotardian description of the demise of grand narratives in postmodernist architecture: 'In place of faith in the great centred designs, and the anxious pursuits of salvation, the postmodern condition is gradually substituting the concreteness of small circumstantial struggles with its precise objectives capable of having a great effect because they change systems of relations' (*Postmodern*, p. 12). He also stresses the important notion of 'the presence of the past' in contemporary architecture: 'The return of architecture to the womb of history and its recycling in new syntactic contexts of traditional forms is one of the systems that has produced a profound "difference" in a series of works and projects in the past few years understood by some critics in the ambiguous but efficacious category of Postmodern' (*Postmodern*, p. 14).

STOP and THINK

- Jencks has described 'dual-coding' as 'the most prevalent aspect of postmodernism', inscribing and challenging different tastes and opposite forms of discourse in its 'use of irony, ambiguity and contradiction' (Jencks, *Post-Modernism: The New Classicism in Art and Architecture* (New York, Rizzoli and London, Academy Editions, 1987), p. 340). What might an 'ironic' or 'ambiguous' building look like?

- Can you think of examples in your local environments where buildings demonstrate an openness to 'fiction' as well as 'function'? Does the fictional element of the building merely serve an ornamental purpose, or does the 'fiction' serve a symbolic *function?*

- Compare Jencks' concept of 'dual-coding' with other similar ideas: for example, Venturi's insistence on the 'double-functioning element' in architecture, its 'both–and' signification, and the 'multifunctioning building' (terms from *Complexity and Contradiction*); Derrida's concept of writing as a mime, parasitism, equivocation, montage, super-imposition, a layered signification, or super-imprinting one text on another (one important discussion occurs in his book *Dissemination* (1972; English trans. Chicago, University of Chicago Press, 1981)); or Linda Hutcheon's concept of postmodernism as parody, in which literature simultaneously inscribes and subverts conventions. In what other discourses can you find similar concepts of 'doubleness'? Are there ways in which these accounts of 'doubleness' differ?

Architectural languages

British architects have also been leading lights in the development of postmodern architecture. James Stirling has synthesised many of the postmodern characteristics, evolving a hybrid aesthetic that combines the old and new within the local urban context. His *pièce de résistance* is the Neue Staatsgalerie (Stuttgart Art Gallery, 1977–84), which is a series of quoted styles built over a parking garage. The building echoes Venturi's ghosted buildings (like the Franklin Court design mentioned above), embraces high-tech materials and symbolic ornamentation, and gestures to popular culture with its pink and sky-blue dayglo handrails. Stirling's high-profile buildings include the Clore Gallery Extension to the Tate Gallery (1982–87) in London, and the Tate Gallery and Albert Dock Development in Liverpool in the late 1980s. Along with the designs of Norman Foster and Richard Rogers, these architects have set new standards and styles for postmodern architecture from which Europeans, North Americans and Japanese have learned. The urban classicism of Stirling is developed in the work of Ricardo Bofill and his Taller de Arquitectura, especially evident in such giant palatial complexes as Les Espaces d'Abraxas (1978–82) at Marne-la-Vallée, near Paris, Les Arcades du Lac (1972–83), near Paris, and La Place du Nombre d'Or (1978–84), in Montpellier. Bofill's designs demonstrate an amplification and displacement of architectural elements, owing as much to the Renaissance as to the modernist tradition.

Another important European architect in his development of an urbanist typology and a style of contradiction, or *'coincidentum oppositorum'* as he calls it, is O.M. Ungers. His Frankfurt Fair Hall (1972–82) combines a glass gallery set against a red masonry shed, as the building focuses on Ungers' principal preoccupations of space, geometrical organisation and the transformation of types. His German Architectural Museum (1982–85) and Skyscraper (1983–85), both in Frankfurt, have become archetypes of the style of 'oppositional' architecture. Finally, Robert Krier with the IBA in his Ritterstrasse Block (1984) in Berlin, and his brother Leon Krier, have been hugely influential in the development of the new classical urbanism, with their utopian and arcadian designs incorporating the social and political dimensions of decentralisation in their use of public space and small-block planning. The Krier brothers, along with Aldo Rossi and other Rationalists, have had to fend off criticism that their work is fascist in its use of the monumental in perpetuating and maintaining a collective historical memory; although architectural semantics are not free of historical or ideological overtones any more than any other discourse, and echoes of Albert Speer's or Stalinist projects might well taint such styles for many more decades yet.

A further development in postmodern architecture has been the use of metaphor and similes in buildings. Conceiving of architecture as a literal 'language', it encodes parts of the body, the outlines of animal forms and other physical features into the building. Certain anthropomorphic metaphors occur in buildings like Stanley Tigerman's Hot Dog House (1975–76) and his phallus-shaped Daisy House (1976–77), or Kazumasa Yamashita's Face House in Kyoto, Japan. Other metaphors include gestures to types of writing, like Minoru Takeyama's Beverly Tom Hotel (1974), which mimics the shape of the phallic Shinto 'tenri' symbol, a detail which is repeated throughout the design of the hotel. Architects like Graves and Jencks also practise metaphoricism in architecture, which creates a postmodern semiotic irony in explicit or implicit codings. Many Japanese architects adopt a similar architecture of symbolism or the manifestation of language games and signs in buildings. Most prominent is Arata Isozaki's Tsukuba Civic Center (1980–83), in which the motif of 'absent presence' in the building is self-confessedly influenced by the work of other postmodernists, like the designer Ettore Sottsass, the cultural critic and philosopher Roland Barthes, and the architect Philip Johnson. Isozaki's Museum of Contemporary Art (MOCA) (1982–86) in Los Angeles, as well as the work of other prominent Japanese architects like Minoru

Takeyama, Takefumi Aida, Monta Mozuna, Kazuhiro Ishii and Hiroshi Hara, bind together various symbolic systems, including Jungianism, Platonism, Christianity, Buddhism and Shintoism.

Deconstructive architecture

More recently, postmodern architecture's concern with unclear boundaries, exaggerated perspective, ambiguous spacing, the idiosyncratic collision of walls, and various transformations of the part's relation to the whole has been felt in a direct association with Derrida's philosophy of deconstruction. Postmodern architecture includes a great variety of buildings, from the 'high-tech' of Norman Foster's Hong Kong and Shanghai Bank, or Renzo Piano's and Richard Roger's Pompidou Centre in Paris, to the less ostentatious style of I.M. Pei's Pyramid in the Louvre (1993) or Cesar Pelli's Pacific Design Center (1975) in Los Angeles. Yet arguably one of the most radical and innovative architectural developments in postmodern architecture is that of the 'deconstructivist' buildings, from architects like Peter Eisenman, Bernard Tschumi, Zaha Hadid, Hiromi Fujii, Rem Koolhaas, Frank O. Gehry, Daniel Libeskind and Coop Himmelblau. Deconstructivist architecture has openly challenged the humanist construction of space, or the way in which conceptions of space have relied upon unities and harmonies established in reason, representation and truth. As the style's name indicates, it is motivated by a close theoretical engagement with poststructuralist theories of language, and has led to some dubbing its practice 'archetexture'. Its two principal exponents, Tschumi and Eisenman, have collaborated with Derrida on several occasions and clearly conceive their work in relation to his philosophical ideas. It is an architecture which adopts an 'aesthetics of fragmentation', as it decentralises the conventional syntax and iconography of buildings. Aiming to strip the architectural model of the aura and familiarity which normally reconcile us to it, deconstructive architecture makes us see the emperor unclothed; and by dismantling space constructed upon humanist notions of space, it has produced some controversial and interesting buildings.

Specifically concerned to break away from the automatic link between architecture and habitation, architectural deconstruction seeks to prevent any conventional or 'naturalising' conception of architecture dominating the discipline. Tschumi conceives of his architecture as disruptive and 'unsettling', aiming to pose the question as to whether it can both house and settle at the same time as disturb and unsettle. It is this sense of dislocation that also informs Eisenman's deconstructionist subversion of expectations, projections and desires: 'Even as architecture shelters, functions and conveys aesthetic meaning, a dislocating architecture must struggle against celebrating, or symbolising these activities; it must dislocate its own meaning. Dislocation involves shifting but not obliterating the boundaries of meaning, and since meaning necessarily implies absence through the absent referent, then a dislocating architecture must be at once presence and absence' (Eisenman, 'Misreading', in *Peter Eisenman: House of Cards* (Oxford and New York, Oxford University Press, 1987), p. 185). Architecture thus leads to a continual sense of placement and displacement. Eisenman recognises the paradox that one cannot escape what is handed down from the past, and yet attempts to prevent architecture from being policed and controlled by that history. While incorporating previous traditions cannot help but perpetuate architectural concatenations, Eisenman seeks the 'unthought' in an architecture of implication, as he demonstrates in his House No. VI with its Escher-like optical illusions. Dubbed 'radical eclecticism' by Jencks, the characteristics of this style are buildings constructed as 'adventures' in possible spaces, emphasising the mysterious, ambiguous, sensual, with features such as skew-angled walls which disorient scale and distort perspective. The challenge posed by their work is the attempt to understand the relationship between interpretation and deconstruction in buildings.

Tschumi has explicitly stated his interest in how the spaces of buildings organise and shape unconscious desire and the sensual or erotic aspects of humans (Tschumi, in *The Manhattan Transcripts* (1981; London, Academy Editions, 1994) and *Questions of Space* (London, Architectural Association, 1990)). Architecture is repeatedly analysed and associated with the erotic and violent implications that it has for the spatial organisation of bodies:

> The pleasure of space: . . . Approximately: it is a form of experience –
> the 'presence of absence'; exhilarating differences between the plane

and the cavern, between the street and your living room; symmetries
and dissymmetries emphasizing the spatial properties of my body;
right and left, up and down. Taken to its extreme, the pleasure of
space leans toward the poetics of the unconscious, to the edge of
madness. (Tschumi, *Architecture and Disjunction* (Cambridge MA,
MIT Press, 1994), p. 84)

Architecture simultaneously establishes spaces which are personally
appropriated and rearranged, as well as imposing and violating
personal spaces already in existence: 'First, there is the violence that
all individuals inflict on spaces by their very presence, by their
intrusion into the controlled order of architecture. … Bodies carve
all sorts of new and unexpected spaces, through fluid or erratic
motions . . . Each architectural space implies (and desires) the
intruding presence that will inhabit it' (*Architecture and Disjunction*,
p. 123). Then there is the violence performed by architectural spaces
on bodies – for example, with narrow corridors on large crowds –
a violence which has generally been ignored by architecture's
aesthetic imperative that it 'should be pleasing to the eye, as well as
comfortable to the body' (*Architecture and Disjunction*, p. 125).
Describing the history of architecture as complicit with hegemonic
power, with the 'adaptation of space to the existing socioeconomic
structure . . . [reflecting] the prevalent views of the existing political
framework' (*Architecture and Disjunction*, p. 5), Tschumi looks to the
manner in which city spaces can generate unexpected social and
cultural manifestations. He seeks to use this characteristic of urban
space as a form of political resistance and subversion:

> It might be worthwhile therefore to abandon any notion of a Post-
> Modern architecture in favour of a post-humanist architecture, one
> that would stress not only the dispersion of the subject and the force
> of the social regulation, but also the effect of such decentring on the
> entire notion of unified, coherent, architectural form. (Tschumi,
> 'Parc de la Villette, Paris', in A.C. Papadakis (ed.), *Deconstruction in
> Architecture* (London, Architectural Design, 1988), p. 33)

Wanting to think in terms of 'questioning structures' rather than
'formal composition', Tschumi aims to challenge our established
icons and notions of urban space, and to show the city as a fractured
space of accidents.

One of the most stunning examples of deconstructive architecture is Tschumi's Parc de la Villette in northern Paris (Figure 2). It is laid out on a grid structure that connects fire-engine red architectural elements with a 'cinematic promenade' comprising a series of provocative, frameworked vistas that unroll as you walk through the campus. Tschumi has deliberately flouted the modernist hierarchy of structure over ornamentation. The insides of structures are, in places, exposed as exteriors and used as decoration; and the result is profoundly disorientating, as the Parc emerges as a complex organisation of ambiguous spaces and shapes, and 'thus can be seen to encourage conflict over synthesis, fragmentation over unity, madness and play over careful management. It subverts a number of ideals that were sacrosanct to the Modern period and, in this manner, it can be allied to a specific vision of Post-Modernity' (Tschumi, 'Pare', p. 38). The Parc always stresses the self-reflexive spatial organisation of consciousness, in the belief that being aware of one's position and location are contemporary imperatives: 'Excentric, dis-integrated, dis-located, dis-juncted, deconstructed, dismantled, disassociated, discontinuous, deregulated ... de-, dis-, ex-. These are the prefixes of today. Not post-, neo-, or pre-' (*Architecture and Disjunction*, p. 225). The Parc's fire-engine red constructions of enamelled steel, called 'folies', are meant to signify both British eighteenth-century garden 'follies' and the French notion of 'madness'. Placed every 120 metres on a grid pattern, this conjunction of irrationalities can be interpreted as a pleasurable kind of instability. Derrida has described this deconstructionist architecture as a 'socius of dissociation':

These folies destabilize meaning, the meaning of meaning, the signifying ensemble of this powerful architectonics. ... By pushing 'architecture towards its limits', a place will be made for 'pleasure'; ... the structure of the grid and of each cube – for these points are cubes – leaves opportunities for chance, formal invention, combinatory transformation, wandering. ... Architect-weaver. He plots grids, twining the threads of a chain, his writing holds out a net. A weave always weaves in several directions, several meanings, and beyond meaning. ... An architecture of heterogeneity, interruption, non-coincidence ... aimed at a spacing and a socius of dissociation. (Derrida, 'Point de Folie – Maintenant Architecture', *AA Files*, 12 (Summer 1986): 65–75)

Figure 2 Bernard Tschumi, 'Folies', Parc de la Villette, Paris (1982–)

Here is architecture revelling in absences and presences, in which space becomes the pleasurable invention for the walking, perusing subject. The Villette project is meant to stimulate rather than repress the multiplicity of spaces. Tschumi uses spatial metaphors which disrupt and deform passive, lived experience, self-consciously exciting our sense of the erotic and sensual potential of our quotidian existence, rather than working with the temporal or periodic arrangement of styles and forms.

Eisenman is another architect concerned with the obscurantist effect that attention to temporality (history) has on the social consciousness of space: 'The tradition of history in fact covers up potential types which evolve today ... not in what we see in history but what we have not seen in history' (Eisenman and Leon Krier, 'My Ideology is Better than Yours', in A.C. Papadakis (ed.), *Reconstruction, Deconstruction* (London, Academy Editions, 1989 rev. edn 1994), p. 13). Eisenman's practical answer has been to develop an architecture which self-consciously 'lays bare' the organisation of space and the shaping of social movement. His 'textual architecture', with its punning names and emphasis on the importance of syntax and text, has created an architecture as an infinite text of superpositions. Structured (or better, 'destructured') by transfiguration, displacement, trace, through the material deconstruction of space, Eisenman's buildings, like his House No. VI or his 'El even Odd' building, flagrantly open the door to interrogations of the conventional assumptions about what constitutes shelter, foundations, boundaries, constructions – indeed, the whole relationship between self-identity and the specificity of the space(s) one inhabits. Eisenman and Tschumi are concerned with challenging the boundaries between inside and outside, as well as those oppositions which have traditionally structured architecture – figure and ground, ornament and structure, aestheticism and functionalism. There is no completely rational space – space is 'now-here' and 'no-where', like the city of Bellona in Samuel R. Delaney's science fiction epic *Dhalgren* (1975) or Berlin in Thomas Pynchon's vast metafiction *Gravity's Rainbow* (1973) – with the result that their disruptive spatial logics refigure and reconceive entrenched relations between bodies and spatial experiences.

'Monstrous carbuncles' or rural retreats?

Postmodern architectural ideology has always embraced a strong community element and concern with locale. A prominent example of this is Ralph Erskine's development of Byker (1972–74), a working-class area in Newcastle. In this case, the community was involved in the design through a consultative process with the architect, and the result incorporated old buildings into the pattern to protect the communal environment. In Britain, it is an architectural practice with which Prince Charles has prominently and controversially associated himself. He burst into the architectural debate with his speech to the Royal Institute of British Architects in 1984, when he attacked the planned extension to the National Gallery in Trafalgar Square as a 'monstrous carbuncle' on the face 'of a much loved friend'. Devastating attacks on bureaucratic planning and insensitive modern architecture in general have followed, although his support for community architecture, conservation and the young Classical Revivalists has been raised from the level of practice into a nostalgic and sentimental ideology for a simplified organic community without any social differences and without a history, such as that represented in Quinlan Terry's Richmond Riverside Development (1984). The practice of the architect consulting the people for whom he or she is designing was taken a stage further in Lucien Kroll's design for the Medical Faculty Buildings (1970–77) at the University of Louvain in Belgium, where the students were divided into flexible and changing teams to solve design and technical problems. The result was a varied and piecemeal building which arose from decisions which had been taken gradually over time.

Postmodern architecture is thus a multifaceted category, embracing a wide variety of concerns, styles and techniques. Nevertheless, one might argue that they all demonstrate a coherent set of resistances to and transformations of modernist architecture: abstraction and geometricism give way to an interest in referential and gestural styles; the self-regarding concentration on the building as an autonomous entity defers to an awareness of the context in which a building occurs; ahistoricism and purity give way to a critical engagement with the past; preoccupations with plurality and hybridity replace the desire for simplicity and non-contradiction; popular and mass culture get precedence over the rules of the elite.

The politics of these differing positions within the discourse of architecture is similarly complex. It is crucially and influentially discussed in Kenneth Frampton's article 'Towards a Critical Regionalism' (in Hal Foster (ed.), *Postmodern Culture* (London, Pluto Press, 1985)) which argues that architecture must develop a critical 'consciousness', which will cause the human subject to be constantly alert to the historical specifics of a place. The result is a 'regional-ism' which shuns pastoral myth, but remains open to the possibi-lities of different traditions. However, he is not sympathetic to Jencks' architectural ideology, since Frampton perceives in that the encouragement of the commodity aesthetics and standardisation of consciousness of a late capitalist society. Indeed, postmodern architecture finds itself bound up in various ideological contradic-tions and ironies within its general principles. A central paradox is that its principal goal was the reversal of the theoretical scaffolding of modernity and its discourse of mass produced, standardised and dehumanised planning, instituting instead a new language of difference and plurality. Yet as postmodernist architecture develops on a world-wide scale, it ironically seems to depend upon the very means of mass production so scathingly attacked as the linchpin of modernism. The 'hybrid', 'complex' and 'schizophrenic' language of postmodernist architecture claims to inscribe an innovative sense of rootedness, locality and regionality, and yet as this 'plurality' is now so universally pervasive in most of the world's capital cities, it merely becomes another style transmitted across the globe as speedily as a fax of the latest design alteration. Despite its anti-universalist rhetoric, postmodernist architecture is thus to be found everywhere. As with postmodernist theory in other spheres, the postmodernist architect needs to find ways of protecting the value of difference and plurality, without circumscribing and effectively debilitating that difference.

Architecture into the new millennium: new complexity, 'blobmeisters' and ecological enterprises

'Complexity' has been a buzzword inextricably tied up with post-modern architecture from the very outset, with the publication of Robert Venturi's *Complexity and Contradiction in Architecture* (1966). However, in the seventh edition of *The Language of Postmodern Architecture* (now entitled *The New Paradigm in Architecture* (New Haven CT, Yale University Press, 2002)), Charles Jencks has speci-fically added a chapter entitled 'The New Complexity'. Developed partly from ideas first outlined in his *The Architecture of the Jumping Universe: A Polemic* (Ann Arbor MI, University of Michigan Press, 1995), Jencks argues that the calls by Venturi and others in the

1960s for a complex architecture are finally being realised in the 1990s–2000s in a new and complex architecture aided by computer design. Often curved, warped and fractal in shape, this architecture is more welcoming, affective and articulate than the Modern architecture it challenges. Carried forward by architects such as Frank Gehry, Daniel Libeskind, Zaha Hadid, and Peter Eisenman, there is also a vast amount of other work on the edge of the new paradigm by the Dutch architects Rem Koolhaas, Ben van Berkel and MVRDV, or other Europeans like Santiago Calatrava and Coop Himmelb(l)au, or those who have moved on from High-Tech in England, such as Norman Foster. These architects, as well as those that flirted with Deconstruction – Hadid and Morphosis – look set to take on the philosophy. The computer is now at its heart but its history, which Charles Jencks traces, is built on that postmodern desire for an architecture that communicates with its users, and one based on the heterogeneity of our cities and global culture.

Jencks argues that a linear science of simplicity underpinned the modern world-view and that this was replaced by a non-linear science of complexity in the 1980s, which underpins the postmodern world-view. This 'new complexity' derives from a number of sources, such as Ilya Prigogine's study of dissipative structures, and the science of chaos that investigated self-organising systems, such as Benoit Mandelbrot's *The Fractal Geometry of Nature* (1977), which demonstrated the peculiar beauty of repetition with minor variations. Developing alongside the advent of major computing power in the late 1970s, these ideas enabled the simulation and modelling of non-linear systems of growth. In parallel, an interest in a continually changing set of differences in theories of folds and curves reinforced the new interest in a syntax of ever-varying patterns in which a pluralism of styles is the defining feature. From graceless blobs to elegant wave-forms, from jagged fractals to impersonal datascapes, this shift in architectural grammar sees nature and culture as growing out of the narrative of the universe, a story that Jencks argues has only recently been sketched by the new cosmology in the last thirty years (Jencks, *Critical Modernism: Where is Post-Modernism Going?* (5th edition, Chichester, John Wiley, 2007)). Attempts to design buildings that meet contemporary organic and ecological demands have resulted in what Jencks terms

'Organi-Tech' designers, architects who produce surprising structural metaphors that celebrate the organic nature of structure, the bones, muscles and rippling skin of the human body. Such architects include Nicholas Grimshaw, Norman Foster and Santiago Calatrava, the latter having designed an expressive skeleton meant to dazzle the eye, especially when the sun is out. Calatrava's fantastic Turning Torso, in Malmö, Sweden (2005), a 190m tall concrete and steel residential tower that twists 90 degrees from top to bottom, is modelled upon a twisting human spine or a DNA strand, a potent reminder of the relationship between architecture and the body.

Another identifiable group, producing rounded fractals, was christened the 'Blobmeisters' in New York. The term 'blobmeister' was first used by Los Angeles architect Wes Jones to describe the digital architects who utilise computer program as a facilitator for form. The label 'blobmeister' implies several truths, not all of them flattering. First that these 'meisters' were determined to capture the field, and do so with 'blob grammars' and abstruse theories based on computer analogies – cyberspace, hybrid space, digital hypersurface were some of the other terms. Often the 'Blobmeisters' were young university professors and their students engaged in the usual turf wars. One member of this group, Greg Lynn, has argued in a series of books that the blob is really a developed form of the cube. Handling more information than the dumb box, it is more complex and therefore potentially more sensitive. However, the grammar needs to be treated with scale and skill to ensure a correlate with function. So many blobs are simply the result of stacked geodesics, like Grimshaw's Eden project, a series of globular bubble-forms. By contrast, Norman Foster's Swiss Re headquarters building at 30 St. Mary Axe (the London 'gherkin') (2004), evoking both natural images and a rocket spiralling upwards, is a perfected, stretched blob conceived as a city landmark, once again aided by the computer to produce self-similar forms.

Foster's partial shift from a Cartesian to blob grammar marks a turn of mainstream practice towards the new paradigm. It follows many sculptural experiments, for instance those of Will Alsop in Marseilles and in his design for the Peckham Library, London, and Frank Gehry in Europe, Japan and America. Ever since Gehry's Guggenheim Museum opened in Bilbao (1997), architects realised a new kind of building type had emerged, and that there was a standard to surpass. With a single undulating skin, his landmark building pulls this former industrial city and its environs together – the river, the trains, cars, bridges and mountains – and with its titanium panels endlessly repeating as they fold into new forms, the building echoes the shifting moods of nature, the slightest change in sunlight or rain. Most importantly its forms are suggestive and enigmatic in ways that relate both to the natural context and the central role of the museum in a global culture. Indeed, because of what is called the 'Bilbao Effect', what Jencks terms the 'enigmatic signifier', or implicit allusion veering away from explicit symbol, has become the reigning method of designing large, monumental civic buildings, especially museums. This emergent strategy, whose precursor might be seen in a small way during the 1950s with Ronchamp and the Sydney Opera House, has now become a dominant convention of the new paradigm. Peter Eisenman, Rem Koolhaas, Daniel Libeskind, Coop Himmelb(l)au, Zaha Hadid and Morphosis produce suggestive and unusual shapes as a matter of course, as if architecture had become a branch of surrealist sculpture. Furthermore, this architecture produces unusual and disorienting spaces, such as the exhibition hall in Hadid's Phaeno Science Center, at Wolfsburg, Germany (2005), and Rem Koolhaas/OMA's Casa da Musica, at Porto, Portugal (2005), a building which was caustically described by one Dutch critic as a 'hasty meteorite attack on Porto'. The language of fluidity is further demonstrated in Zaha Hadid's four stations for the Nordpark Cable Railway, at Innsbruck (2007), as do her designs for the Guangzhou Opera House in China (currently under construction) and the Cagliari Contemporary Arts Centre (also currently under construction). Always interested in such fluid shapes, Peter Eisenman's current City of Culture of Galicia in Santiago de Compostella in Spain has wave-like buildings on an artificial hill, in a ghost-like echo of the old medieval town; while other examples include Coop Himmelb(l)au's Akron Art Museum, in Ohio (2007), with its three-part structure of the Crystal, the Gallery Box, and the Roof Cloud, Tschumi's New Acropolis Museum in Athens (currently under construction), and Gehry's Science Library at Princeton University, New Jersey, which is nearing completion.

The postmodern architectural impulses to playfulness and elaboration are now often tempered by the increasing environmental imperatives, an alliance principally developed in the burgeoning new 'ecological architecture'. Ecological architecture merges the interests of sustainability, environmental consciousness, green, natural, and organic approaches to evolve a design solution from these requirements and from the characteristics of the site, its neighbourhood context, and the local micro–climate and topography. A good introduction to this subject occurs in James Steele, *Ecological Architecture: A Critical History* (London, Thames and Hudson, 2005). Steele discusses a variety of 'green' and environmental architectural initiatives, the terminology and the repeated themes of ecological architecture, and focuses on some case studies, such as the work of the Jordanian architect Rasem Badran, whose designs are human-scaled, responsive to their environment and aim to meet the social and cultural requirements of the people who use them. In a series of highly innovative site-sensitive projects, including designs for the Lucille Halsell Conservatory in San Antonio, Texas (1988), the Master Plan for the Universal Exposition at Seville (1992), and the Fukuoka Prefectural International Hall (1995), Emilio Ambasz has become arguably the leading exponent of an ecological grammar in architecture that recognises how locations of buildings have a direct impact on their performance. Philip Jodidio's *Architecture: Nature* (Munich, Prestel, 2006) offers further extraordinary examples of architecture's engagement with the natural world, such as Renzo Piano's Paul Klee Center, Bern (2005), where the flow of the land is used as a source of architectural inspiration for its three 'hills'; Edouard François' Flower Tower, Paris (2004), which, owing to a façade covered with 380 large flowerpots, seems to sprout bamboo from every level and corner of the building; and Diller and Scofidio's Blur Building (2002), an exhibit at the Expo '02 at Yverdan-les-Bains, Switzerland, which seems to hover uncannily in a cloud above Lake Neuchâtel.

A great deal of architectural energy is currently going into major public projects around the world. A major building with a high international profile can have a massive publicity and tourist effect, successfully resituating a whole city within international consciousness (witness Bilbao). Yet whether all these architectural developments in recent years in themselves mark a new emergent paradigm in architecture remains an open question. Nevertheless, that architectural trend–spotter Charles Jencks is clear in his mind that a new wind is stirring architecture, and that at least it is the beginning of a shift in theory and practice, even if it takes time for people to adjust their sympathetic tack.

STOP and THINK

General

- What is lost (if anything) in postmodern architecture's abandonment of Le Corbusier's architectural vision?
- Is the recent trend towards historical allusion in buildings a retrogressive, nostalgic step, or is it an indication of a radical intervention in present architectural practices?
- Do architectural forms such as the dome, the tower, the column, the pediment and so on, have fixed symbolic contents associated with them permanently?
- Considering its reliance on massive financial patronage, does postmodern architecture inevitably usher in a triumphant corporate monumentalism; or can it resist such capitalist structures in its reworkings of space, as deconstructive architects like Tschumi and Eisenman suggest? Are all buildings which utilise modern materials (glass, steel, plastics) modern?

Specific

- A good deal of the debate surrounding recent developments in architecture has to do with the impact of the developments on local communities. Is such contextualism merely another form of aestheticism, or is it rather a real attempt to open up architecture to the community? What 'community' is being addressed? Are the communities envisaged by Prince Charles, Byker's Wall and the University of Louvain the same?
- What has happened to the 'community' in London's East End as a result of the Docklands Development in the 1980s?

Key characteristics of postmodernist architecture

1. *A celebration of spectacle.* The aesthetic features of architecture are celebrated for their own sake, as opposed to the way in which modernist architecture sought to subordinate form to function. As Harvey writes, 'the theatricality of effect, the striving for jouissance and schizophrenic effect are all consciously present. Above all, postmodern architecture and urban design of this sort convey a sense of some search for a fantasy world, the illusory "high" that takes us beyond current realities into pure imagination. The matter of postmodernism ... is "not just function but fiction"' (Harvey, *Condition*, p. 97). Consequently, postmodernist architecture tends to be more aesthetically complex, playful and 'fantastic', exhibiting a new classicism and monumentalism in such buildings as Bofill's Les Espaces d'Abraxas, Eisenman's Wexner Center for the Visual Arts, and Kohn Pedersen Fox Associates' Procter and Gamble headquarters (1982–85) in Cincinnati, Ohio.

2. *Radical eclecticism.* Unlike modernism, which sought a purity of styles and codes, postmodernist architecture utilises a wide variety of styles, traditions and codes. It is this multiplicity that produces the 'schizophrenic' aspect that many theorists of postmodern architecture have identified. Furthermore, as Venturi's books make clear, whereas modernist architecture tended to adopt its sources from 'high culture', postmodernists erase the high modernist distinction between high and low culture, often exploiting the latter for its aesthetic effects. Examples of this eclecticism are Stirling's Stuttgart Art Gallery, Moore's Piazza d'Italia, Graves' Humana Medical Corporation HQ, and Isozaki's Tsukuba Civic Center.

3. *Random historicism.* Part of the radical eclecticism is the tendency for postmodern architecture to put together a collage of historical styles. Jameson has defined this as 'the random cannibalisation of all the styles of the past, the play of random stylistic allusion, and in general ... the increasing primacy of the "neo"' (Jameson, *Postmodernism*, p. 18). The important issue is the randomness of history here: history as a meaningless collection of aesthetically interesting images. An example of this is Stirling's Clore Gallery Extension.

4. *Irrational space.* Modernist architecture sought to rationalise and standardise space, organising it according to predictable and regular geometric shapes. Postmodernism abandons this emphasis, and 'suspends normal categories of time and space, social and rational categories which are built up in everyday architecture and behavior, to become "irrational" or quite literally impossible to figure out' (Jencks, *The Language of Post-Modern Architecture* (London, Academy Editions, 1984), p. 124). Examples include Eisenman's abstract houses and Tschumi's designs for La Parc de la Villette.

5. *Parodic metaphor.* Along with the stress on spectacle, postmodern architecture frequently parodies architecture's anthropomorphic tendency to communicate meaning. Buried vestiges of faces and bodies in pre-postmodern architecture are now made exaggeratedly explicit. Examples of this include Takeyama's Beverly Tom Hotel (shaped like a huge penis) and Yamashita's Face House. Other parodies gesture towards toys (e.g. Aida Takefumi's Toy Block House III (Tokyo, 1980–81)), feudal battlements (e.g. John Burgee's Trump Castle) and Norman Fosters' new Hong Kong airport at Chep Lap Kok (shaped like a giant airliner).

Postmodern architecture: some examples

There are a huge number of different types of postmodern buildings, but a good example of a building which exhibits a 'double-coding' is Stirling's Stuttgart State Gallery (Figure 3). This example shows many of the principal features of postmodern architecture listed above, some of which can also be exemplified in Stirling's buildings in Britain, to which I will refer. The building is structured as a collage of quotations from a variety of architectural historical styles, like the 'traces' of the past so much desired by Venturi. There is the reference to the Egyptian pylon at the entrance with its red and blue steel temple, Romanesque arches and windows, Egyptian cornices, and a rotunda with a 'domeless dome', as well as other features like a sunken Doric portico facing a modern staircase. (Similar historical echoes can be seen in Stirling's Clore Gallery Extension, where in addition to the stylistic quotations, he also uses what one might call a 'chameleon' technique of blending the end of the Gallery's façade

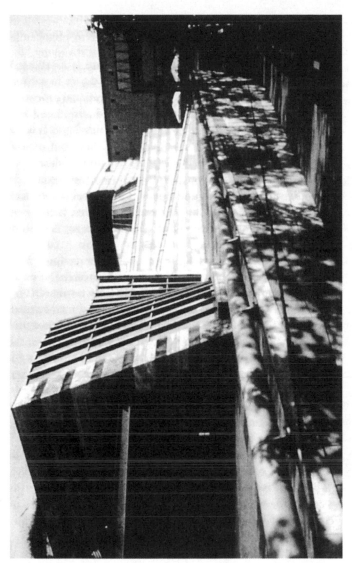

Figure 3 James Stirling, Neue Staatsgalerie, Stuttgart (1984)

with the brickwork in the adjacent Lodge building.) In addition to
this defamiliarisation through eclectic stylistic citations, the Stuttgart Gallery has a colour scheme of two-tone brown stone and
concrete, contrasting starkly with the dayglo pink and sky-blue
handrails which hold the lighting fixtures, suggesting something
of a 'punk' allusion. These colour elements attempt to popularise
the building, playing a joke in colour on the expectations of the
building's users as to what constitutes a colour scheme for a monument of 'high' culture in a state art gallery. In addition, there are
other 'jokes' played with the building: the car park beneath the
gallery has a few stone blocks 'pushed out' on to the grass, leaving
a hole resembling an eighteenth-century 'ruin'; yet on closer inspec-
tion, the fallen blocks prove to be a sham and are in fact functional,
providing ventilation for the enclosed car park. Jencks has described
the building as 'the most impressive building of Post-Modernism
up to 1984 ... For the Neue Staatsgalerie is both a very popular and
a profound building. It appeals to many different tastes, the prime if
not the only goal of Post-Modern architecture, and illustrates many
of its strategies, including ironic representation and contextual
response' (Jencks, *Post-Modernism: The New Classicism in Art and
Architecture* (New York, Rizzoli, 1987), p. 274).

A further example of postmodernist architecture is Eisenman's
Fin D'Ou T Hou S. In keeping with Eisenman's desire to subvert
the traditional understanding of architecture as a rational process of
composition based upon hierarchised, centralised and closed systems of ordering, this house is built according to a new logic. It is
not the logic of known orders and human-centred values, but instead
plays with presence and absence in shape and volume. A decompo-
sitional 'folie', it presumes that its own origins are unknowable, as
the building dissimulates with ambivalent spaces and teases with
indeterminate closure. As its punning name indicates, there are a
number of deconstructive possibilities occurring here: 'Find out
house', 'fine doubt house', 'find either or' (French 'ou ... ou'), 'end
of where' (French 'fin d'ou'), as well as various other readings.
Like a Rubik cube of lived experience, the house is conceived of as
an object in process, going nowhere and emerging from nowhere.
This is a building which clearly rejects representation and manifests
an openly flaunted artificiality. Another of Eisenman's architectural

projects which is less abstract in its conception, but which nonetheless demonstrates similar features to the Fin D'Ou T Hou S, is his design for the Ohio State University Wexner Center for the Visual Arts in Columbus, Ohio (1985–89) (Figure 4). In a subtle interlinking of the past and the present, the building is located between the existing buildings and resurrects the old Armory once located near by. Furthermore, in seeking to respond sensitively to the history and context of the campus, the building integrates the geometries of the street grid of Columbus and the oval of the campus. However, the building itself is fractured and incomplete-looking, thus resisting any holistic or straightforward unification with the campus or wider community. Used to house contemporary art, the building attempts to offer a continuous transformation of memory through the inventions of art and architecture.

Figure 4 Peter Eisenman, Ohio State University Wexner Center for the Visual Arts, Columbus, Ohio (1985–89)

Spatial experience and geography

Discussions of postmodern architecture inevitably overlap with experiences and conceptions of space in the late twentieth century, especially urban geography. The debate concerning postmodern lived spaces has affected geography as much as any other discipline. In fact, some theorists like Harvey, Edward Soja and Jameson have argued that whereas the modern era was preoccupied with temporality, the postmodern era is dominated by spatiality. Space is the new cultural dominant. In this section, I want to consider the ideas of some of these geographers and position their arguments within the overall debate about postmodern experiences of space.

Jameson asserts that 'space is for us an existential and cultural dominant', having described postmodernism's dependence on a 'supplement of spatiality' that results from postmodernism's depletion of history and its consequent exaggeration of the present (Jameson, *Postmodernism*, p. 365). Although Jameson's project is the recuperation of history and the analysis of 'real' temporality rather than its synthetic pastiche, he nevertheless alerts us to a new lexicon gaining ascendancy within cultural analysis in recent years – geography, place, space, locale, location. The politics of space, the cultural function of geography, and the importance of place are increasingly being contested and asserted. The territory of these arguments is marked out in the diverse work of people like Michel Foucault, Gaston Bachelard, Harvey, Soja, Doreen Massey, Derek Gregory, bell hooks, Gillian Rose, Pierre Bourdieu and Michel de Certeau. Foucault has argued that the twentieth century has brought about a correction to the nineteenth-century obsession with temporality, which occluded a critical sensibility to the spatiality of social life. In his article 'Of Other Spaces', Foucault describes his concept of a 'heterotopia' as 'something like counter-sites, a kind of effectively enacted utopia in which real sites, all the other real sites that can be found within the culture, are simultaneously represented, contested, and inverted' (Foucault, 'Of Other Spaces', *Diacritics* (Spring 1986): 22–7). Recent years have witnessed far-reaching calls for the spatialisation of critical consciousness, as in the work of Derek Gregory. The proliferation of theories of space within sociological work have opened up new perspectives on the organisation of consciousness and subjectivity within urban and geographical space. The discussions of the nature and utilisation of space in 'postmodern' architecture by such architects as the Krier brothers, Aldo Rossi, Eisenman and Tschumi (and the latter's joint architectural projects and writings on spatial frameworks with Derrida), as well as the 'semiotics of environment' in the work of Venturi and Jencks, have contributed to this debate on the social consciousness of space. Furthermore, there has been a wealth of socio-economic cultural studies on postmodern urban space, amongst which Mike Davis's analysis of Los Angeles in *City of Quartz* (London, Verso, 1990), Dayan Sudjic's analysis of the development of postmodern urban sprawls in *100 Mile City* (London, Flamingo, 1993), and Sharon Zukin's analyses of the commodifying function of capital upon cities and inner-city gentrification in *Landscapes of Power* (Berkeley, University of California Press, 1991) are exemplary. Regarded now as primarily representations or as imagined environments, cities need to be reconceived as new models and metaphors emerge in response to structural changes in the organisation of capital, which in their turn transform people's sense of self, consciousness and society.

In this 'spatial turn', many of these theorists acknowledge their debt to Henri Lefebvre's *The Production of Space* (Oxford, Blackwell, 1991), in which he rigorously argues that space is the key component in the analysis of economic production. Although many of these people criticise postmodern theories of space from an openly avowed Marxist stance, they have nonetheless been instrumental in shaping the parameters of the debate. As a consequence, historical analysis can no longer ignore the politics of spatialisation embedded within production. Where Jameson once exhorted 'Always historicise!', Henri Lefebvre has added 'Always spatialise!' Lefebvre explores the 'production of space', maintaining that space is produced and reproduced, thus representing the site and outcome of social, political and economic struggles. Arguing that new modes of production exist in concomitant relation to new conditions of space, Lefebvre deconstructs the illusions of the naturalness and transparency of space and erects a typology of spatialities. Taking his cue from Lefebvre, Soja's call to theoretical arms is similar: 'Demystifying and politicizing the spatiality of social life is the critical nexus of

142 Beginning postmodernism

contemporary retheorization' (Edward Soja, 'Regions in Context', *Environment and Planning D: Society and Space*, 3:2 (1985): 178). He argues that there is a new turn to spatiality in postmodernism, and that the consequence is a different and new sense of social subjectivity and ontology: 'the existential link between spatiality and human agency: Being, consciousness, and action are necessarily and contingently spatial, existing not simply "in" space but "of" space as well. To be alive intrinsically and inescapably involves participation in the social production of space, shaping and being shaped by a constantly evolving spatiality' (Soja, 'Regions', p. 177). Los Angeles serves as his case-study for the contemporary struggle for control over the social production of space, as Soja argues for a radical rethinking of the dialectics of space, time and social being. According to him, this new attention to spatiality is a theoretical demystification similar to that of 'Marx's treatment of the commodity form under capitalism. Behind and within what appears to be a thing-like collection of properties and attributes is hidden and obscured the fundamental structuration of social relations and human life' (Soja, 'Regions', pp. 177–8). Whereas history has been construed in the past as disguising our 'real' relations, Soja argues that space ought to be subject to the same scrutiny: 'We must be insistently aware of how space can be made to hide consequences from us, how relations of power and discipline are inscribed into the apparently innocent spatiality of social life, how human geographies become filled with politics and ideology' (Soja, *Postmodern Geography* (London, Verso, 1989), p. 6). Soja's postmodern geography builds upon Lefebvre's and Foucault's ideas of spatiality, and is a creative recombination and extension of a focus on 'real' material space and 'imagined' representations of space, developing what he calls a 'thirdspace', a multiplicity of real-and-imagined places. Indeed, as early as the 1970s, Foucault was conceding the need for attention to geography and space in critical theory, especially since he perceived spatial organisation as an important aspect of social, economic and political strategies in various contexts – such as the control and division of space, and the organisation of the carceral space of the body, which are so vital to surveillance techniques.

Arguably, postmodernism has been a challenge to these spaces of a modernism which sought to establish a complete rationalism in all

sites of everyday life. The instrumental rationalisation, standardisation and uniformity of space that occurred in the architecture
and town planning of concepts like Le Corbusier's cities had the
dialectical twist of a total annihilation of space – it turned it into a
completely uniform arena. Critiques levelled against a functional
landscape, which destroyed sensitive urban place-making and
ignored human perspectives, have sought to reintroduce human
sensibilities and human proportions into urban design. As David
Ley has put it, 'In urban design the transition from the cubist grid
to what geographers have called a sense of place reveals a more
complex attention to theories of space in the plural styles of what
has become known as postmodern architecture' (Ley, 'Modernism,
Post-modernism, and the Struggle for Place', in J.A. Agnew and
J.S. Duncan (eds), *The Power of Place: Bringing Together Geographical and Sociological Imaginations* (Boston MA, Unwin Hyman,
1989), pp. 44–65; p. 53). Ley goes on to quote Charles Jencks's
new stress on architecture as symbolic communication in postmodernism, seeing in '"the return of the missing body", an attempt
to restore meaning, rootedness and human proportions to place in
an era dominated by depersonalizing bulk and standardization'
(Ley, 'Modernism', p. 53).

Significant voices have taken these spatial constructions to task
for their male-centredness, arguing that the absence of a feminine
urban space or architecture is scarcely reflected upon. Gillian Rose's
Feminism and Geography (Cambridge, Polity Press, 1993) seeks to
explore women's entrapment within the city and to lay the groundwork for a 'feminist geography'; and there is a movement which
concerns itself with the place of women within the profession
of architecture. Massey has been prominent in her critiques of
Harvey's and Soja's arguments, particularly in her book *Space,
Place and Gender* (Cambridge, Polity Press, 1994). Her principal
point is that individudal perspectives are taken to be universal, specifically that of the white, male heterosexual. Both Soja and Harvey
are blind to the way in which gender constructs their conditions of
postmodernity. Massey and Rose seek a geography which does not
hide difference behind the screen of universal masculinity. Another
theorist within the 'thirdspace' perspective is bell hooks, who defines
an alternative spatiality of continual disruption in which the politics

of location and identity are constantly being reformed and questioned: 'this space of radical openness is a margin – a profound
edge. Locating oneself there is difficult yet necessary. It is not a
"safe" place. One is always at risk. One needs a community of resistance' (hooks, *Yearning: Race, Gender, and Cultural Politics* (London,
Turnaround, 1991), p. 149). Arguing that marginality is a space of
resistance, hooks urges a new arrangement of place, politics and
identity, which coincides with a number of other arguments concerning dislocating space. Since men and women experience space
differently, hooks' work is concerned with analysing the differences
of gendered spaces.

Allied to these new interests in 'postmodern geographies' and
the spatial consequences is the newly emerging interdisciplinary
field of 'mobilities'. Affected not just by geographical considerations, but also by the increasing concerns over globalisation, the
concept of 'mobilities' encompasses both the large-scale movements
of people, objects, capital, and information across the world, as well
as the more local processes of daily transportation, movement
through public space, and the travel of material things within everyday life. One key thinker to have made a significant impact in relation
to theories of migration, globalisation and transnationalism is Arjun
Appadurai, in works like *Modernity at Large: Cultural Dimensions of
Globalization* (Minneapolis MN, University of Minnesota Press,
1996) and *Globalization* (Durham NC, Duke University Press,
2001). Straddling the interests of several disciplines, within the
work of people like Arjun Appadurai, John Urry, Fredric Jameson
and Slavoj Žižek, globalisation has really been a major concern for
several decades. However, this is not to confuse nomadism with
migration or travel. Humans have always migrated and travelled,
without necessarily living nomadic lives, and this has long been a
focus of economic and geographical studies. A recent article defined
this new breed of nomads: 'Even if an urban nomad confines himself to a small perimeter, he nonetheless has a new and surprisingly
different relationship to time, to place and to other people through
the use of mobile technology' ('Mobility: Nomads at last', *The
Economist*, 10 April 2008). The 'production of mobilities' and
the ways in which the convergence of mobile technologies transform many aspects of economic and social life with new fluidities

of communication are discussed in Tim Cresswell's *On the Move: Mobility in the Modern Western World* (London, Routledge, 2006) and John Urry's *Mobilities* (Cambridge, Polity, 2007). Geographers and sociologists in particular are trying to figure out how mobile communications are changing interactions between people, while anthropologists and psychologists are investigating how mobile and virtual interaction spices up or challenges physical and offline chemistry, and whether it changes young people's autonomy. Architects, property developers and urban planners are changing their thinking about buildings and cities to accommodate the new habits of the 'nomads' that dwell in them. Yet until recently, one of the most dominant forms of mobility, 'automobility', has remained largely ignored. As a sub-division of this new interest in mobility studies, 'automobility' examines the social, cultural and spatial dimensions of driving. The car and its promise of autonomy and mobility are examined in *Automobilities* edited by Mike Featherstone, Nigel Thrift, and John Urry (London, Sage, 2005). Mobility – flows, movement and migration in social life – have therefore emerged as a central area of exploration in the past decade, as geographers and sociologists attempt to come to grips with the changing social and spatial practices caused by shifting technological developments within globalised cultures.

Selected reading

Benjamin, Andrew, 'Derrida, Architecture and Philosophy', in Andreas Papadakis (ed.), *Deconstruction in Architecture* (London, Academy Editions, 1988), pp. 8–11.
A complex yet provocative analysis of the debts philosophy owes to architectural metaphors, and of how Jacques Derrida and Bernard Tschumi seek to deconstruct these foundations in their respective work in deconstructive philosophy and the deconstructive folies of the Pare de la Villette.
Gregory, Derek, *Geographical Imaginations* (Oxford, Blackwell, 1994).
An exciting survey of the discipline and discourse of geography. Mapping human geography on to contemporary social theory, Gregory addresses, reinterprets and questions key theoretical issues within the debates concerning postmodernism.
Jencks, Charles, *The New Paradigm in Architecture: The Language of Postmodernism* (New Haven CT, Yale University Press, 2002).

Completely rewritten with the addition of two new chapters, this seventh edition of *The Language of Postmodernism* brings the history of postmodern architecture up to date with the latest twists in the narrative and the turn to a 'new complexity' in architecture.

Jencks, Charles, *Post-Modernism: The New Classicism in Art and Architecture* (New York, Rizzoli, and London, Academy Editions, 1987).

A sumptuously illustrated book, which attempts to categorise postmodern art within five streams of 'classicism' and architecture within four streams of 'classicism', arguing that postmodernism is a blend of the modern with an ironic return to the classical past.

Jencks, Charles, *What is Post-Modernism?* (1986; 3rd rev. enlarged edn, London, Academy Editions and New York, St. Martin's Press, 1989).

A very readable consideration of the concept of postmodernism as it relates to the arts and literature. It offers a spirited defence against modernist reaction. Distinguishing between Late Modernism and Postmodernism, this is a useful, if polemical, introductory tract.

King, Ross, *Emancipating Space: Geography, Architecture, and Urban Design* (New York and London, Guilford Press, 1996).

A first-class account of postmodernism and its intersection with the debates concerning architecture, geography and other spatial discourses. Incorporates useful discussions of the ideas of Tschumi, Peter Eisenman and Derrida, as well as others such as Michel Foucault, Henri Lefebvre, Edward W. Soja, David Harvey and Fredric Jameson.

Massey, Doreen, *Space, Place and Gender* (Cambridge, Polity Press, 1994).

An excellent collection of her essays which interrogate spatial theory and postmodern ideas from a feminist perspective in a stimulating and provocative manner.

Massey, Doreen, *For Space* (London, Sage, 2005).

Arguing for a reinvigoration of the spatiality of our implicit cosmologies, Massey examines how best to characterise these so-called spatial times, how it is that implicit spatial assumptions inflect our politics, and how we might develop a responsibility for place beyond space.

Massey, Doreen, *World City* (Cambridge, Polity, 2007).

Concerning identity, place, and political responsibility in the changing geographies of our times, this book focuses on the City of London as an example of the rise of a new class, of deepening inequality, and of the geographical imaginations that are mobilised to legitimate the increasing dominance of cities around the world as they strive to be global.

Norris, Christopher, and Andrew Benjamin, *What is Deconstruction?* (London, Academy Editions, 1988).

A sophisticated pair of essays which seek to explain Derrida's method of reading, in which conflicting textual 'meanings' are shown to undermine any fixed interpretation. The discussions are illustrated with references to the work of visual artists like Cy Twombly and Anselm Kiefer, and architects like Eisenman, Zaha Hadid, Tschumi and Daniel Libeskind.

Papadakis, A.C., *Deconstruction in Architecture* (London, Architectural Design, 1988).

Important essays by Jencks and Andrew Benjamin on Derrida, architecture and deconstruction, as well as illustrations and essays on Tschumi's Parc de la Villette and Eisenman's Wexner Center, essays by Frank O. Gehry, Hadid, Emilio Ambasz and Coop Himmelb(l)au, and an interview with Eisenman.

Papadakis, A.C., *Reconstruction, Deconstruction* (London, Academy Editions, 1989, rev. edn 1994).

Focuses on the work of Eisenman, Tschumi, Rem Koolhaas and Arquitectonica, with a significant interview between Leon Krier and Eisenman presenting the conflicting ideologies of reconstruction and deconstruction. Lavishly illustrated, it touches on the importance to architecture of ideas like history, universal values, presentness, tradition, modernity and change.

Portoghesi, Paulo, *Postmodern: The Architecture of the Postindustrial Society* (New York, Rizzoli, 1982).

Based on the Venice Biennale of 1981, an influential account of postmodernism as it is understood by a variety of architects as a way to confront the principal themes of postindustrial society. Offering a critical profile, it focuses on architects like Aldo Rossi, Eisenman, Ambasz, Ricardo Bofill, Michael Graves and Stanley Tigerman, and seeks to explain why postmodernism constitutes a decisive turning point in the history of architecture.

Soja, Edward W., *Postmodern Geography: The Reassertion of Space in Critical Social Theory* (London, Verso, 1989).

A major discussion of the relationship of new theories of space to postmodernism. Offers a critique of a number of contemporary theorists like Foucault and Lefebvre, and contains a good analysis of Los Angeles from this perspective.

Steele, James, *Architecture and Computers: Action and Reaction in the Digital Design Revolution* (London, Laurence King Publishing, 2001).

An introduction that explores the theory of cyberspace and traces the effects that technology has had on society, followed by five chapters exploring different aspects of the computer in architecture.

Urry, John, *Global Complexity* (Cambridge, Polity 2003).

Examines how the ideas of chaos and complexity can aid us in our examination of global processes, drawing out how complexity forces us to reorganise our main categories of sociology.

Urry, John, *Mobilities* (Cambridge, Polity, 2007).
Developing what he calls the 'new mobilities paradigm' for the social sciences, Urry shows how this paradigm makes comprehensible social phenomena which were previously opaque. He analyses the intersecting implications of 'mobility systems' for social inequality, for social networks and meetings, for the nature of places and for alternative mobility futures.

5

Postmodernism in visual art, sculpture and the design arts

There are significant overlaps between the debate concerning postmodernism in architecture and that in the visual and plastic arts. For example, the architect Frank Gehry began work as an artist; Michael Graves' architectural drawings are highly sought after; various architects like Stanley Tigerman, Aldo Rossi and Zaha Hadid are also well-known designers of domestic furniture, silverware, jewellery and sculpture; some critics like Charles Jencks engage with both art and architecture; and the aspect of play in recent architecture has often led architects to produce sculptural artefacts, just as artists have produced 'site-specific' works which involve spatial and architectural considerations. The boundaries are thus notoriously slippery. Such artists and sculptors as Andy Warhol, Robert Rauschenberg, Francis Bacon, David Hockney, Mary Kelly, Anselm Kiefer, Jasper Johns, Ron B. Kitaj, Sol LeWitt, Roy Lichtenstein, Nam June Paik, Christo, Rasheed Araeen, Carl André and David Salle have all in their various ways been associated with postmodern aesthetics. Even visual art itself has become something of a mongrel breed, comprising the traditional medium of painting and yet blurring into 'sculpture' with the advent of various new media, like photography, computers, video and television installations, and unorthodox materials, like (in the case of Joseph Beuys) lard and fur. Furthermore, visual design as 'fashion' has entered into virtually every walk of our lives, as the 'designer labels' in the current 'Style Dictator' column in the *Guardian Weekend* supplement testify. This dimension of visual art, which has attracted postmodern aesthetic discussion – of fashion and domestic designers, in the work of people like Vivienne Westwood, Jean-Paul Gaultier, Ettore Sottsass and Rossi – will also be considered as part of the general discussion. Design in the plastic arts is multifaceted. The boundaries between visual art, sculpture and design are flexible; and this chapter will attempt to chart the influence of theories of the postmodern in a variety of these areas.

Visual art

Postmodernism in the visual arts has an extremely vexed and complex history. It is not so much a recognisable 'school' as a tendency which invades and infringes upon a wide range of art 'isms' and groups. Many theorists shy away from the use of the term 'postmodern' in art theory, since they feel that it flattens out the wide variety of techniques and practices evident in the sphere of visual art during the last thirty years. The philosopher of art, Arthur Danto, prefers to speak about 'post-historical' art, referring to its practice of erasing history (Danto, *After the End of Art* (Princeton NJ, Princeton University Press, 1997), p. 12); while Marco Livingstone prefers the term 'pluralism' because of the variety of 'isms' during the 1960s (Livingstone, 'Pluralism Since 1960', in David Britt (ed.), *Modern Art: Impressionism to Post-Modernism* (London, Thames and Hudson, 1989)). Nevertheless, despite the lack of an agreement on a satisfactory terminology, in broad terms postmodern art refers to the art produced after the 'death' of modern art in the late 1960s. These movements include, for example:

- *Pattern Painting:* a mid-1970s vogue in American art for celebrating patterns, whether geometric or non-geometric. Reacting against the puritanism of minimal and conceptual art, among its principal practitioners were Brad Davis, Robert Kushner and Cynthia Carlson.
- *Neo-Expressionism:* a late 1970s and early 1980s 'return' to the more traditional art forms of painting and sculpture, in a practice which owed a debt to German expressionists of the early twentieth century. The work of artists such as Georg Baselitz, Kiefer, Sandro Chia, Susan Rothenberg, Salle and Julian

Schnabel was typically large, figurative and crudely executed, emphasising the personal, imaginative and subjective experience.

- *Neo-Geo:* a mid-1980s penchant for neo-geometric art, usually abstract and using dayglo colours, often parodying earlier movements. A complete contrast to the Neo-Expressionists, the art of people such as Ashley Bickerton, Jeff Koons and Ross Bleckner was 'cool', calculated and impersonal.

- *New British Sculpture:* the sculpture of artists such as Tony Cragg, Anish Kapoor, Julian Opie and Bill Woodrow, the characteristics of which tended to be (a) a synthesis of pop and kitsch, (b) a bricolage (assemblage) of the decaying UK urban environment and the waste of consumer society, (c) an exploration of the way in which objects are assigned meanings, and (d) a play of colour, wit and humour.

- *Super-Realism:* also called Photo-realism, this was developed in the 1960s and 1970s by artists such as Richard Estes, Malcolm Morley, Michael Gorman and Robert Cottingham. They attempted to challenge the accuracy of photography in painting. However, their interest lay more in the technical problems of rendering tones and light across a surface rather than mere verisimilitude.

One might point to a host of other movements and tendencies which gained a foothold in the anti-modernist stance. Sandy Nairne points out in *The State of the Art* (London, Chatto and Windus, 1978), that many 'postmodern' artists and theorists appear to be motivated by a reaction to the position of Clement Greenberg, the influential, American modernist art critic, on modernist art in the 1960s and 1970s. Greenberg's position derives from the early twentieth-century British theorists of modernism, Clive Bell and Roger Fry, who applauded modernism's 'lines and colours combined in a certain way, certain forms and relations of forms, [which] stir our aesthetic emotions. ... These aesthetically moving forms I call "Significant Form"; and "Significant Form" is the one common quality to all works of visual art' (Clive Bell, *Art* (1928; London, Chatto and Windus, 1958), p. 7). This universalism and formalism of modernism found their way across the Atlantic after the Second World War, and Clement Greenberg championed and established the ideology of 'Late Modern' American painting, applauding its desire for purity, clarity and order. Greenberg's argument was that painting can only rely on its characteristic features to determine what is unique and irreducible in painting: 'Content is to be dissolved so completely into form that the work of art or literature cannot be reduced in whole or part to anything not itself' (Greenberg, 'Kitsch and Avant-Garde', in Charles Harrison and Paul Wood (eds), *Art in Theory: 1900–1990* (Oxford, Blackwell, 1992), pp. 531–2). The classic definition of modern art occurs in Greenberg's essay 'Modernist Painting' (1960), a position which led straight to the colour-field abstractions of artists like Mark Rothko and Ad Reinhardt:

> the unique and proper arena of competence of each art coincided with all that was unique to the nature of its medium. The task of self-criticism became to eliminate from the effects of each art any and every effect that might conceivably be borrowed from or by the medium of any other art. Thus would each art be rendered 'pure' and in its 'purity' find the guarantee of its standards of quality as well as of its independence. 'Purity' meant self-definition, and the enterprise of self-criticism in the arts became one of self-definition with a vengeance. (Greenberg, 'Modernist Painting', in Harrison and Wood (eds), *Art*, p. 755)

Broadly speaking then, postmodern art thus emerged as a reaction to modern art's obsession with a clinical purity of form and autonomous abstraction. Bored with the incessant drive for ever-increasing minimalism and abstraction, postmodernism was part of a reintroduction of ornament, morals, allegories and decoration into art. However, in narrower terms, the description 'postmodernist' applies to art that exemplifies in form and content the postmodern condition of post-history and stylistic pluralism. Whereas in 1967 art magazines were full of sleek cubic forms, by 1969 these had been replaced by natural substances, ongoing processes, photographic images, language and art 'happenings' in real time. This disillusionment with the art object, with consumer culture and with the scientific pretence of objectivity, together with a distrust of the artificial world, produced art which retrospectively made modernism look austere and reductive, its purity look puritanical and its preoccupation with perfect structure seem formalistic. In a broad-ranging description, Kim Levin, reviewing the end of the modern art era, attempted to summarise the advent of the new:

> Post-modernism is impure. It knows about shortages. It knows about inflation and devaluation. It is aware of the increased cost of objects. And so it quotes, scavenges, ransacks, recycles the past. Its method is synthesis rather than analysis. It is style-free and free-style. Playful and full of doubt, it denies nothing. Tolerant of ambiguity, contradiction, complexity, incoherence, it is eccentrically inclusive. It mimics life, accepts awkwardness and crudity, takes an amateur stance. Structured by time rather than form, concerned with context instead of style, it uses memory, research, confession, fiction – with irony, whimsy, and disbelief. Subjective and intimate, it blurs the boundaries between the world and self. It is about identity and behaviour. (Levin, *Beyond Modernism: Essays on Art From the '70s and '80s* (New York, Harper and Row, 1988), p. 7)

Levin's wide-ranging description captures something of the feel of an all-encompassing change that occurred within art circles at the end of the 1960s, as new styles emerged virtually every month.

Many of these new styles owed their existence to the critique of modernist art launched by the Conceptual artists in the second half of the 1960s. No single descriptive phrase secured widespread acceptance in describing the Conceptual artists' practices. One of the more influential statements of Conceptual art's ideas can be found in Sol LeWitt's 'Sentences on Conceptual Art' (1968) (reprinted in Ursula Meyer (ed.), *Conceptual Art* (New York, Dutton, 1972), pp. 174–5). The salient characteristics tended to be an emphasis on the work of art as idea, attention to the critical function itself, and drawing attention to the languages which surround art objects and which mediate their meaning. The work questioned the material status of the artwork, interrogated the conventional association of art with the 'traditions' of painting and sculpture, and queried the art system as a social institution. These challenges paved the way for various kinds of political art in the 1970s, like feminist art and community art. Groups like Fluxus, and Art and Language (Mel Ramsden, Joseph Kosuth, Michael Baldwin), perceived language as an all-important medium of expression, and their critiques of the individualism of earlier art led to a gradual 'dematerialisation' of the art object. Livingstone suggests that 'Given the existential emphasis within Abstract Expressionism, by which every brush-mark was judged an authentic sign of the artist's personality and a gesture indicative of his or her free will, it was almost inevitable that subsequent generations would seek a demystification of both process and content as a release from this romantic inwardness' (Livingstone, 'Pluralism' p. 359). From this perspective, postmodernist art can be conceived of as launching an attack on the humanist and modernist conception of art as 'expression', through strategies of pastiche and a critique of 'originality'. Brandon Taylor argues that 'What post-modernism claims is that the humanist paradigm of the artist as a "subject" who can "act" on his environment is ideologically unsound, bourgeois, a mystification, a capitalist deviation, and so forth' (Taylor, *Modernism, Post-modernism, Realism* (Winchester, Winchester School of Art Press, 1987), p. 46). Artists who questioned this modernist stress on originality, such as Salle, Sigmar Polke and Schnabel, became the leading figures of this new assault on the conventions of art.

Paul Crowther has also been active in articulating a theory of postmodernism in visual art, relating it especially to the category of the sublime (an affirmative or elevating feeling through aesthetic experience). Drawing on Edmund Burke's, Immanuel Kant's and Jean-François Lyotard's theories of the sublime, Crowther argues in *Critical Aesthetics and Postmodernism* (Oxford, Clarendon Press, 1993) that critical postmodern art offers the sublime as an 'affective jolt' which has the effect of reawakening and rejuvenating our sense of being alive. The means may be banal or ludicrous, but it offers the notion of a life-enhancing force in the midst of social monotony and accelerating standardisation and reification. Burke's theory of the sublime, formulated in the eighteenth century, was organised upon notions of positive shock and horror, whereas Kant's theory, outlined in his *Critique of Judgement* (1790), involved a rational containment of excess which leads to a kind of transcending of the mundane self. Deconstruction has opened up the instability of the correspondence between concept and object. Crowther relates this to the sublime in the following way: if meaning is only producible within an unstable field, then the relation of self to work, and to its own understanding, is at best provisional. It is constantly being renegotiated and remade, as the overall field of meaning itself undergoes reconfiguration.

The matrix of postmodernism began to emerge as a cluster of oft-cited words, amongst which perhaps the most repeated was 'appropriation', by which is meant, roughly, leasing or borrowing. Artists such as Jean-Michel Basquiat, Keith Haring, Jeff Koons and Sherrie Levine practised this 'appropriation' in a variety of ways. As Levine wrote in 1981, representation could not be 'original' any more: 'The world is filled to suffocating. Man has placed his token on every stone. Every word, every image, is leased and mortgaged. . . . Succeeding the painter, the plagiarist no longer bears within him passions, humours, feelings, impressions, but rather this immense encyclopaedia from which he draws' (Levine, 'Statement', in Harrison and Wood (eds), *Art,* p. 1067). Like the poststructuralist notion that all anyone can do is borrow from an already-existing database of images, words, terms, these artists practised a systematic borrowing, an *appropriation* of images which looks back self-consciously to earlier art, both imitating previous styles and taking over specific motifs or even entire images. 'Appropriation', like myth, is a distortion rather than a negation of prior semiotic images. It maintains but shifts the former connotations to create a new sign, and accomplishes this covertly, making it all seem ordinary and 'natural'. The principal theorists of this strategy are Craig Owens, Hal Foster, Douglas Crimp and Benjamin Buchloh. Their argument is that appropriation displaces the implicit suggestion of a 'guiding father' in the older term 'influence', shifting the inquiry into predecessors towards the still active agents of signification in society, and thus illuminating historical context. 'Appropriation' cuts away the privileged autonomy of the art object, or at least allows that stated autonomy to be negotiated.

Contrary to this position is Donald Kuspit's argument that 'Appropriation art is informed by the decadence syndrome; the sense of the decline and impending death of art . . . appropriation art is a crisis in the sense of the purpose of art' (Kuspit, *The Cult of the Avant-Garde Artist* (Cambridge, Cambridge University Press, 1993), pp. 106–7). Kuspit is extremely wary of the disguised vestiges of conservatism in postmodern art, especially with regard to its characteristic mélange of styles: 'Each new appropriation of a style, making it into a personal mannerism, testifies to the individuality of the neo-avant-garde artist – not to the historical staying power of the style. From a neo-avant-garde perspective, this is an imperial extension of personality, a kind of self-deification' (*Cult*, pp. 24–5). Sneaking the cult of the hero back into art, postmodern art betrays a self-satisfied complacency with its own smart image: 'Postmodernist art does not embody and epitomise the experience of the object for the sake of the subject – does not mediate sense presentations and feeling presentations that suggest the subjective character of experience . . . Rather it overobjectifies art, reifying it until its subjective implications seem beside its visible point, its spectacular appearance. This is a kind of narcissistic self-assurance, as it were' (*Cult*, p. 13).

Hal Foster has tried to take account of both these radical and reactionary axes of postmodern practices. He has argued that there are two kinds of postmodernism: a postmodernism of *reaction* and a postmodernism of *resistance*. The first is exemplified by artists (e.g. Carlo Maria Mariani) and theorists (e.g. Jencks) who celebrate the cynical recycling of worn-out styles like neo-classicism. The second tends to be an amalgamation of artists from the left wing and feminism who explicitly deal with political issues and critiques of various suffocating hegemonies like the art world, patriarchy, heterosexuality and racism. It is a matter for debate, however, as to what exactly these two persuasions of postmodernism react against or resist.

Craig Owens: postmodernism as the return of allegory

The return of the allegorical also features in the work of Craig Owens, a theorist who has made an influential analysis of postmodernism in the visual arts. His theories were outlined in a two-part essay in the journal *October*, entitled 'The Allegorical Impulse: Towards a Theory of Postmodernism' (1980). In an 'allegory', a story or visual image carries with it a second distinct meaning partially hidden in its literal or visible meaning; in other words, it is a metaphor extended into a narrative structure. A famous example in literary terms is John Bunyan's *Pilgrim's Progress* (1678), where each character embodies an idea within a Christian concept of salvation. Well-known examples of allegorical visual art are the engravings by Hogarth entitled *The Rake's Progress* (1735), or Picasso's *Guernica* (1937), an embodiment of the cruelties of war. Borrowing his ideas from the German Marxist theorist Walter Benjamin, Owens argued that the return of allegory in recent art marks the advent of the

postmodern; it creates an art which 'no longer proclaims transcendence, but rather narrates its own contingency, insufficiency,
lack of transcendence' (Owens, 'The Allegorical Impulse: Towards
a Theory of Postmodernism', in Harrison and Wood (eds), *Art*,
p. 1052). In other words, the principal characteristic feature of
postmodernism in visual art is its interrogation of the modernist
emphasis on the artwork as self-sufficient and universal in its
essence; and it contests the vestiges of Romantic expressivism in
modernism, which privileges the formal and expressive over the
discursive. That is to say that postmodernism challenges the notion
that the artwork is the coherent fusion of accurate empirical observation and the incisive expression of the perceptions and emotions
of the artist who has a particularly heightened and penetrating
intelligence. Instead, postmodernism understands the artwork as
produced by the network of inconsistent social structures and
contradictory ideologies.

The advent of allegory in postmodern art sustains a mood of
mystery and catastrophe in the work of artists such as Eric Fischl,
Salle, Schnabel and Ron Kitaj. Like Craig Owens, Kitaj is a provo-
cateur of allegory, and his paintings *If Not, Not* (1975–76) or *The
Autumn of Central Paris (After Walter Benjamin)* (1972–74) are also
clearly indebted to Benjamin's sense of allegory, an enigma and
suggestion which nevertheless appear as an allegory without a plot.
Owens argued that 'The allegorical work is synthetic; it crosses
aesthetic boundaries' producing a 'confusion of boundaries' (Owens,
'Allegorical', p. 1055). In outlining these ideas, he suggested that
'Appropriation, site-specificity, impermanence, accumulation, dis
cursivity, hybridisation – these diverse strategies characterise much
of the art of the present and distinguish it from its modernist
predecessors' (Owens, 'Allegorical', p. 1056):

1. *The appropriation of images:* the use of photo-mechanical
   reproduction of imagery in single or multiple form in order to
   challenge the uniqueness of the art image and its specific 'aura',
   often by emptying the images of their resonance or significance
   by, 'artists who generate images through the reproduction of
   other images'. Examples are the appropriated images of Marilyn Monroe, Mao or Campbell's soup tins in Warhol's images,

the parodic photographic reproductions by Levine, and the multiple television installations by Nam June Paik.

2. *Site-specificity:* the construction of sophisticated environments, installations and sites which embed works firmly within a defined context, subverting the apparently timeless and universal persistence of a great painting within a prestigious gallery. Deliberately impermanent, they affirm the arbitrariness and transience of their status by resisting recuperation by the institution of a gallery. Examples are Robert Smithson's *Spiral Jetty* (1970), built in the mud and rock of the Great Salt Lake, Utah; or Christo's *Surrounded Islands* (1980–83), in which eleven islands in Biscayne Bay, Miami, Florida, were encircled by pink polypropylene fabric floating on the water.

3. *Transience or impermanence:* the construction of works from perishable materials – perishable either in their physical substance or in their content, drawn from mass/popular images – in order to snub the privileged status upon which gallery art is founded. Examples are the earth art of Richard Long, or the kitsch sculptures by Koons.

4. *Agglomeration or accumulation:* the hoarding or 'piling up' of fragments in the construction of a work, using a repetitive logic; 'The projection of structure as sequence', through the production of works in series – Warhol's *Marilyn Monroe* – which can have the effect of transforming the mundane and the banal into the symbolic. Examples are Trisha Brown's *Primary Accumulation,* or the work of the sculptor Carl André, like his infamous 'pile' of bricks.

5. *Discursivity:* allowing an interaction between the sensuous appeal of imagery and the discursive reflection of a written commentary in the same piece, making the silent artwork articulate and argumentative. This produces a 'reciprocity . . . between the visual and the verbal: words are often treated as purely visual phenomena, while visual images are offered as script to be deciphered'. Examples are Mary Kelly's *Post-Partum Document,* a psychoanalytical and cultural documentation of her relationship with her baby son, and the conceptual art of Robert Barry and Lawrence Weiner.

6. *Hybridisation:* the amalgamation of materials, genres and historical referents to produce singularly eclectic constructions,

in both content and form, again contravening the purity of the art object. An example is Schnabel's practice of sticking bits of broken crockery and other found objects onto his painted canvases.

Owens presents allegory with a critical function, as it replaces the redemptive, purified and organic concept of form with textuality and the arbitrariness of meaning as it exists in fragments.

Feminist art

Feminists perceived modernism as heavily patriarchal, and post-modernism to that extent was a political victory against the weight of a previously male-dominated aesthetic culture. However, there are many female artists who perceive this masculine culture at work within postmodernism as well, and have sought to use the strategies of postmodernism to encourage a redirection of artistic efforts into an aesthetics more specifically informed by identity and gender politics. Often principal activists in the use of 'appropriation' (see Owens' description above), Barbara Kruger, Cindy Sherman, Levine, Judy Chicago and others have sought to inject a significant dose of gender critique into the aesthetic practices of postmodernist art.

Feminist art organisations like WAR (Women Artists in Revolution) were established in the 1960s to combat the male-dominated art world, and these were accompanied by journals such as *Women and Art* (1971) and *Feminist Art Journal* (1972). Feminist artists distinguish themselves by deliberately addressing feminist issues in the content and form of their work, and arguing that the goals of feminism ought not to be incorporated as a new 'ism' into the wealth of pluralist postmodernism. In 1980, the influential feminist art critic Lucy Lippard proclaimed feminism as opposed to modernism:

> Feminist methods and theories have instead offered a socially concerned alternative to the increasingly mechanical evolution of art about art. The 1970s might not have been pluralist at all if women had not emerged during the decade to introduce the multi-coloured threads of female experience into the fabric of modern art. (Lippard, 'Sweeping Exchanges', in *The Pink Glass Swan* (New York, New Press, 1995), p. 171)

Feminism was just as vociferous in rejecting Greenberg's modernism, but as Griselda Pollock has argued, feminist art is more complex

than merely a substitution of pluralism for purity, of critical engagement for abstraction and (apparent) objectivity. It entails 'a political
reassessment of the relations between a range of potential practices
and the sites of their effective deployment within a field contested
by official and emergent cultural strategies' (Rozsika Parker and
Griselda Pollock (eds), *Framing Feminism: Art and the Women's
Movement 1970–1985* (London, Pandora, 1987), p. 104).

Many feminist artists have therefore been committed to interrogating and reworking the mass media stereotypes of femininity,
exploring eroticism and sexuality as represented and perpetuated by
masculine hegemonies, and contesting the dominant iconographies
of women in art as sex objects of objectified spectacle. Feminist artists argue that sexuality is non-essentialist and that sexuality is a set
of effects and positions which artistic practices confront, are implicated in, or may dislocate. The sociality of sexuality is well explored
in the work of artists such as Louise Bourgeois, Eva Hesse, Bridget
Riley, Laurie Anderson, and Judy Chicago's massive collaborative
project *The Dinner Party* (1973), which was a kind of feminist last
supper and was designed as homage to the hidden achievements of
39 women whom the artist considered to be major female figures in
western history, plus 999 others.

A particularly prominent example of feminist art in the late 1970s
occurred in Kelly's *Post-Partum Document,* in which she carefully
documents her work into the construction of cultural identity from
a feminist and psychoanalytical perspective. On the birth of her son,
Kelly performed an examination of the mother–child relationship
based on the idea that the mother's and child's personalities are formed
at the crucial moment of childbirth. Avoiding the literal figuration of
the mother or child, the work instead focuses upon diverse memo-
rabilia from various stages of the child's development: used diapers
with traces of the infant's faeces; plaster handprints; examples of
the child's first writing; extracts from the mother's diary commentary on the child's development. With a heavily psychoanalytic
impetus to the work, Kelly relies upon the work of Sigmund Freud,
Jacques Lacan and Julia Kristeva to examine conscious and unconscious struggles over femininity, ideas of motherhood and how a
child enters language, or the symbolic realm (documented in Kelly,
Post-Partum Document (London, Routledge and Kegan Paul, 1983)).

The use of text in a combination with many other elements was typical of postmodernist feminist practice. Griselda Pollock has remarked upon the fact that whereas words and texts were taboo in modernist works, they mark a characteristic presence in postmodernist works: rather than being simply an extrinsic theoretical commentary, the text becomes an intrinsic part of the aesthetic practice. Kelly created her work out of varied representational processes, combining text, artefacts and natural fragments, presented as if an exhibit in a museum, in order to allow viewers to construct their own images. Her use of text demonstrates that no single narrative could account for the multiplicity of human experience, and that there is no single theoretical discourse to explain all forms of social relations and political praxis.

Initially, many feminist artists who emerged in the 1980s and 1990s were at pains to distance themselves from the 'essentialist heresy' (the notion that gender reflects a natural rather than socially constructed difference between men and women) with which contemporary theory has increasingly characterised feminism of the 1970s. Yet postmodernist theory has left a bitter aftertaste in the mouths of many feminist artists; although postmodernism has attacked the theoretical foundation of 1970s essentialist feminism on seemingly logical grounds, it has generally ignored the diverse artistic organisation that emerged from it. This perpetually deconstructive, negative and hostile stance has proved unproductive for many feminist artists, since in opening up the ontological question of what is real, it has deprived women of their history by dismissing as beneath consideration virtually all that women have accomplished in their history. Hence, despite all the clamour concerning the cataclysmic change brought about by postmodernist theory, feminists like Lippard and Pollock, and performance artists like the Guerilla Girls (a group of women artists and activists formed in 1985 with the express purpose of combating sexism and racism within the art world), have criticised postmodern artists for maintaining their links with the modernist heroicisation of the artist, and remaining universalist and blind to their complicity with the gender structures of masculine authority. As Christopher Reed has written, 'Where, at the opening of the eighties, the art world espoused a postmodernism defined in opposition to the identity-based practices associated with feminism, by the end of the decade, the development and articulation of identity was central to this kind of postmodern artistic practice' (Reed, 'Postmodernism and the Art of Identity', in Nikos Stangos (ed.), *Concepts of Modern Art* (London, Thames and Hudson, 1981) pp. 271–93, p. 286). Indeed, many critics and theorists have had to reassess their attitude to postmodernism during the 1980s, and people like Owens, Douglas Crimp and Hal Foster have acknowledged that there is a necessity for an increased awareness of identity politics within postmodern theory. The imperative to examine identity and to expose the structures of oppression which circumscribe it has become one of the principal features of postmodern art at the end of the 1990s.

Yet contentious issues nevertheless remain within feminist art. Women are still concerned about whether there is a specifically feminist or matriarchal aesthetic; whether feminist art can escape the fate of being merely an additional category within a pluralist perspective; and whether it can achieve its goal of radically transforming both art and society. Furthermore, women still have to resist their marginalisation within the art establishment and institutions.

Photography

It has been argued by Arthur Danto in his book *The State of the Art* (London, Prentice Hall, 1987), and by other theorists, that photography proved to be such a significant rupture to traditional modes of representation that it marks the advent of the postmodern itself. Indeed, many theorists, like Crimp, have argued that it is in the realm of photography that postmodernism in the visual arts has really blossomed. The main reason for this is that it is a medium which most effectively exposes the notion of artistic 'originality' as a myth perpetuated by modern culture. The critique of the traditional art object with the desire for a renewed social content led many to an engagement with photography, video and performance. 'Art' photography has attempted to subvert expressionism and to displace any attempts to recuperate 'aura'. This means that photography has used its technical processes to undercut and bring into question the mystique or sacred 'halo' which has surrounded art for hundreds of years. Instead, people such as Sherman, Kruger, Hans Haacke, Levine, Victor Burgin, Martha Rosier, Laurie Simmons and others have made extensive use of techniques offered by photography to interrogate the issue of 'authenticity' and 'origins' in art. In particular, they have sought to query the expressivity of the unique artefact. Others like Robert Rauschenberg have sought to graft photography into their works, offering a form of technical collage. This is an argument put forward strongly by Linda Hutcheon in *The Politics of Postmodernism* (London, Routledge, 1989), who suggests that owing to the paradoxes inherent in its medium, photography is in many ways the perfect postmodern vehicle. In particular, photography is able to challenge the apparent neutrality of objective recording through its subjective framing perspective. In addition, it alerts viewers to 'culturally determined codes' by its ability to 'revision' objects and scenes. For Hutcheon, always aware of this potential for double vision, art photography is uniquely able to manifest the postmodernist consciousness of the tensions of the interplay between text and image, discourse and representation.

The work of Sherman has become something of a by-word for postmodernist art photography. Since the 1970s, she has presented photographs which, despite their appearance as film stills, are actually staged self-portraits. Sherman has stated that 'My "stills" were about the fakeness of the role-playing as well as contempt for the domineering "male" audience who would mistakenly read the images as sexy' (interview in 1988). Early feminist criticism tended to emphasise the manner in which the photos drew attention to the cultural construction of 'femininity' as a result of media manipulation. Sherman offers 'types' of women, posed within a series of roles defined by specific but unknown narratives at which the viewer can only guess. Playing with mimesis, she began with images of the *femme fatale* from *film noir*, setting them in ambiguous poses, often highlighting female self-surveillance as a form of subservience to patriarchy. Later work is more concerned with the association between films, fashion advertisements or features, and illustrations for romantic fiction. Poses as a 'little girl' or 'tomboy' are plentiful – as victim, frightened or worried. Relying on a complicity with the viewer, one has to know the generality of the looks rather than the actual poses or styles. Sherman interrogates the fantasy of roles we play and of the selves we adopt: as Laura Mulvey has written, 'the wordlessness and despair in her work represents the wordlessness and despair that ensues when a fetishistic structure, the means of erasing history and memory, collapses, leaving a void in its wake' (Mulvey, 'A Phantasmagoria of the Female Body: The Work of Cindy Sherman', *New Left Review*, 188 (July/August, 1991): 136–50). In more recent work, Sherman has foregone the whole for body fragments and pieces, which echoes the disturbing way in which contemporary consumer society fetishises displays of the female body. Such disruptions of gender stereotypes equally occur in the photographic explorations of eroticism by Robert Mapplethorpe, as his pictures of S&M erotica and sexual violence testify.

STOP and THINK

- Is the return to 'nature' – something found, not used – as opposed to 'culture', a depoliticisation of art, resulting from the pressures of institutional, social, economic and market forces?
- Do you agree with Owens' argument that since all quotation represents authority, postmodernist artistic citations are really a return of authoritarianism disguised as anti-authoritarianism? If so, is postmodern art really an acquiescence with authority proclaimed as a radical act?
- Many theorists (like Kuspit and Danto) have been critical about postmodern art's erasure or neutralisation of history. Does the return of the past as scraps of quotation or stylistic mimicry in postmodern art demonstrate that the past is never simply over; that it is the locus of meanings by which one still lives, struggles over, and competes in the present? Or does it mark a sense of the timelessness and immutability of the values of the present status quo (i.e. that nothing has really changed)?
- Do references to the vernacular in contemporary art open the art institution to the wider world and establish an interrogation of the values of 'art' and 'mass media'? Or are they an uncritical citation of the vernacular, with a mixture of condescension and awe, to add some 'street cred'

to 'high art'? Perhaps one needs to decide the extent to which postmodern art is being appropriated by a neo-conservatism which smuggles in a reaffirmation of conservative values within a rhetoric of renewal.

Key characteristics of postmodern visual art

1. Postmodern artists, especially painters, exhibit a nonchalance in dealing with seemingly incompatible styles, practise an aesthetic pluralism, and combine a number of different styles of art in one work, rather than keeping to the purity of form desired by modernists. Postmodernism also implies a period where several styles coexist, rather than the single strand of development implied by modernism.
2. Postmodern art involves a return of the vernacular (the daily and local language of the people), which goes against the modernists' attempts to deprecate and disparage 'mass culture'. 'High' and 'low' art mingle freely.
3. It has a joy in the unconstrained use of colours and shapes, along with a wealth of imagination and a feeling for decorative effects.
4. It demonstrates a carelessness towards orthodox aesthetic conformity and a lack of any systematic approach; it celebrates contradiction, and has a superfluous playfulness and a general lack of respect towards any aesthetic conventions whatsoever.
5. In postmodern art, the ego is displayed unrestrainedly and demonstratively, sometimes in a narcissistic or exhibitionistic way, sometimes radiating a polymorphous eroticism not confined by convention.

Postmodern visual art: some examples

As examples of postmodern visual art, I intend to focus on the work of two very different artists: Jean-Michel Basquiat and Barbara Kruger. Born in Brooklyn, New York, but also part-Puerto-Rican and part-Haitian, Basquiat's perspective manifested itself in an eclectic and hybrid play of signifiers in bright, multicoloured images, which cumulatively produce a harsh and grating critique of contemporary America and the position of black people within it. Basquiat's debut in the 1970s in New York made him instantly famous and wealthy, and, together with artists such as Salle and Schnabel, he became one of the artists to be most widely associated with a postmodern 'pluralism' during the 1970s and early 1980s. His art is extremely exhibitionist, combining heterogeneous and vastly different influences, and pluralism is evident in every aspect of his work, from technique to materials. His paintings are constructed not merely out of canvas and paper, but from cut-off doors, loose boards, boxes, window frames and other poor-grade detritus from everyday life. He draws frequently from the European influences of Jean Dubuffet's *Art Brut*, Pablo Picasso's primitivism and Paul Klee's mysticism, but also upon American Abstract Expressionist styles. He amalgamates these impulses from art history with images from popular culture and the mass media, juxtaposing figurative and abstract elements with figures derived from cartoons, street graffiti, and African-American jazz culture. Many of his paintings incorporate words and phrases that have been altered, erased or replaced with better versions. The pervasive editing of this surfeit of information and excess of signification suggests a perpetual struggle to articulate and clarify signs. The emphases and crossings-out indicate a continual mutation of signs and meanings, as they refuse to remain still and be easily defined.

Basquiat's principal interest appears to lie in appropriating different images and then sending them off in new and unusual directions. With a thoroughly postmodern carelessness for history, he quotes European myths as well as contemporary American popular images, which demonstrates a levelling of high and low culture by intermixing popular images and traditional archetypes. One such example is *Melting Point of Ice* (1984) (acrylic, oil paintstick, and silkscreen on canvas, 86 × 68 inches) (Figure 5), which combines and enlists fragments of different signifying codes, like the popular children's story image of Barbar the Elephant with the classical Egyptian reference to the Eye of Horus, and the graffiti image of the skull-like head in the top right; as well as other combinations, like the sacred and the banal, the high and low culture, and the everyday (the graffiti and the © symbol) and the specialist (the mention of

Figure 5 Jean-Michel Basquiat, *Melting Point of Ice* (1984)

the hygrometer, an instrument to measure the relative humidity of the air).

In Basquiat's flagrant disregard for art historical decorum in this disjunctive syntax, there appears to be a consciousness that one can only deal with the existing fragment rather than any original whole. The painting suggests an artist who thinks that all he can do is draw from a bank of already-existing images and techniques, and that any pretence to originality and uniqueness in representation is an

aesthetic fallacy. This postmodern consciousness of a society saturated in images which somehow 'in-form' the individual's articulations suggests Basquiat's work knowingly appropriates parts of a
prefabricated culture. For instance, a figurative drawing in the
bottom left corner of a Biblical image of peasant and donkey is juxtaposed with the image of what appears to be a cartoon-like super-
character punching the air in the centre-right, with a star and 'Bip!'
etched next to it. Abstract scrawls in the centre are themselves
set off by the inclusion of words and letters. This juxtaposition
suggests something about the fallacious division and separation
of culture. The simultaneous reliance on and evacuation of representation by the use of simulacra and incongruous materials also
has the effect of highlighting theatrical constructedness and an
anti-illusionism.

Basquiat's paintings emerged within a new, sophisticated critical
discourse of 'coding', 'ironic distance' and 'eclecticism', as a painting like *Melting Point of Ice* self-consciously explores the limits of
cultural and artistic conventions. It problematises meaning through
unresolved conflicts, discontinuities and reversals, as well as producing a dehierarchisation of aesthetic elements and substances.
The collection of 'used things' in Basquiat's art (like street images
here, but his more famous use of African-American imagery and
discarded items) undermines the dominant romantic posture of the
heroic isolation of the artist and the sense of art as self-expression.
One question mark which constantly hovers over Basquiat's work,
though, as with that of his friends Salle and Schnabel, is the extent
to which these cultural borrowings preserve difference, as some
would argue, or, on the contrary, flatten out difference in the attempt
to forge a new cultural unity.

On the face of it, Kruger's work is a complete contrast. Unlike
Basquiat's formalist experimentations with cultural genres, Kruger's
photographs are overtly radical in their politics, explicitly feminist
in their ideological interrogations, and assertively aggressive in
their argument. Characteristically, Kruger's images are a montage,
combining appropriated black-and-white photos with some brief
didactic or clichéd phrase in white lettering in a red slash across the
picture. They are strongly suggestive of advertisements. Kruger is
concerned with the manner in which images and messages position,

manipulate and subject the social body. Her technique might be described as one of 'semiotic interference': the images intercept codes that signify power, commodity status and gender identity, and then redirect them, interrogating the sites of the enunciation of the message and the politics of that discourse. A typical example might be *Your Gaze Hits the Side of My Face* (1981) (photograph, 140 × 104 cm) (Figure 6). The message down the side of the bust suggests the immobilising and literally petrifying power of the male gaze, or what Owens has called 'the Medusa effect'. Indeed, women are often captured in static or supine poses, and Kruger seems to be examining the manner in which women are represented as passive objects by a patriarchal gender machinery. The frequent structure of the 'You/We', 'I/You', in the messages demonstrates the interpolation of gendered identities by language, an assignment that is caustically subverted by Kruger's inversion of the phrase. Appropriated photographic images are overlaid with gender-laden slogans which call attention to the imbalance in western patriarchal power.

Kruger has said that she desires to welcome a female spectator into a man's world. Her visual/textual strategies collaborate to disrupt the power imbalance associated with the gaze in western culture. Kruger's exploration of the way in which the eye objectifies the woman and can act as a tool of masculine aggression is part of her larger project in examining the interconnection of gender, the commodity and the market place:

> I am concerned with who speaks and who is silent. I think about works which address the material conditions of our lives and the oppression of social relations on a global level: in work which recognises the law of the father as the calculator of capital. I want to speak and hear outlandish questions and comments. I want to be on the side of surprise and against the certainties of pictures and property. (Statement in Bonn, 1984, quoted in Sandy Nairne, *State of the Art*, p. 162)

Blending psychoanalytical and poststructuralist ideas derived from Freud, Lacan, Kristeva, Michel Foucault and Jean Baudrillard, Kruger's appropriative strategies refuse the mystique of the unique art object, assert a vigorous materialist critique of commodity capitalism, and constantly blur the boundaries of high art and their

Figure 6   Barbara Kruger, *Your Gaze Hits the Side of My Face* (photograph, 140 × 104cm) (1981)

continuous traffic with the low cultural forms of the market place. Her work emphasises the postmodern contention that there is no unmediated access to the real, and that it is only through represen- tations that we know the world. She gives this a sharp political tweak by demonstrating that although reality is a matter of representation, it is the power invested in the discourses surrounding these images which gives the representation its social impact. As an artist, Kruger is a manipulator of existing signs rather than a producer of new objects; and in this respect, her work appears to partake of the same postmodern impulse as Basquiat's abduction of cultural discourses and kidnapping of social codes.

Sculpture, plastic and performance art

In many respects, the traditional mediums of painting and drawing have played a secondary role in the development of a postmodernist art. Part of the reason is that painting and drawing are closely identified with the modernist tradition; by extension, they were tainted tools. 'Natural' forms, like land art, installations, performance art, and video and electronic media have come to the forefront and become highly politicised as a result. Robert Morris set the tone for this in his 'Notes on Sculpture, Part 3' (*Artforum,* 5:10 (Summer 1967): 29), where he argued for the priority of sculptural practice over the traditions of painting. Attacking the notion of an improvised art for private contemplation, Morris stated that the forms utilised in contemporary three-dimensional work have 'the feel and look of openness, extendibility, accessibility, publicness, repeatability, equanimity, directness, immediacy . . . Such work would undoubtedly be boring to those who long for access to an exclusive specialness, the experience of which reassures their superior perception.' The new assumptions which emerged in this sculpture might be categorised as follows:

1. Sculpture rightly claimed for itself viewing conditions that emphasised its hermetic integrity, its radical unlikeness to other things. The typical gallery space was the bare, whitewashed room, free from all possible distractions.
2. The spectator's interest in processes, procedures and techniques of fabrication was properly subordinate to the total effect of the finished work. The construction of the piece was secondary to being in the aura of the work's presence.
3. Sculpture ought properly to be made out of rigid materials and had one stable and authentic physical form. Hence, welding, bolting, moulding and turning became established as practices of sculpture.

4.   The integrity of sculpture was a matter of the syntactical coher-
     ence of its disparate parts.

The very term 'sculpture' changed not simply to designate three-
dimensional artistic objects, but to claim aesthetic privilege for
certain sorts of activities as against others. In 1969, Gilbert and
George dubbed themselves 'Living Sculptures', creating what they
called 'Interview Sculpture' and 'Nerve Sculpture'. Richard Long
used the term for his practice of walking to mark out depressions
and marks upon the earth's surface. Sculptors such as Tony Cragg,
David Nash, Bill Woodrow and Barry Flanagan increasingly formed
their work from found natural objects and the 'detritus' of contemporary society. Counterposed to the concept of sculpture as a wilful
and expressive exploitation of malleable material was the notion of a
more passive view, predicated on a sense of achieved reconciliation
with the world. This means that normal processes of weather,
growth, ageing and so on be admitted into the work, as necessary
forming agencies in human culture.

Rosalind Krauss: postmodernism and land art

As part of the group centred on the journal *October*, Rosalind Krauss
has been another influential critic and theorist of postmodernity in
art. In a much anthologised and significant essay entitled 'Sculpture
in the Expanded Field' (first published *October* 8 (Spring 1979)),
Krauss has argued that postmodernity lies with the development
of land art, or following Owens' term, 'site-specific' art. This is also
known as earth art or environmental art, and was a radical sculpture
movement which sought to subvert the commodifying and feti-
shising influences of the institutional museum and gallery on the
practice of art. Occasionally called 'site construction', it was concerned with the work of art as a total environment, and the works by
these practitioners, especially in the United States, took up vast
spaces in inaccessible regions and involved the direct interaction of
humans with nature. The earth became a raw sculptural material
and, given the enormous size of North America, the works of the
principal figures, such as Michael Heizer, Dennis Oppenheim,
Robert Smithson, Mary Miss, Alice Aycock, Richard Serra, Richard
Long, Robert Irwin, Robert Morris and Walter de Maria, were

usually associated with large-scale enterprises. Others, such as the British artists Richard Longo, Hamish Fulton and David Tremlett, and the Bulgarian artist Christo, travelled to regions as various as Australia, Paris, Greenland and Tibet in search of suitable locations.

The actions performed on the land often involved digging and removing soil and stones, and the restructuring of a site into a symbolic form. De Maria's *50m³* (1968) was a construction of 1,600 cubic feet of earth; Miss' *Perimeters/Pavilions/Decoys* (1978) was a delicate structure of wooden beams set in a pit in the middle of a field; Smithson's *Spiral Jetty* (Great Salt Lake, Utah, 1970), was a 1,500 ft-long curl of mud, rock and salt crystals into the Great Salt Lake; while his *Spiral Hill* (Emmen, 1971) was a hill made of black topsoil and white sand and had a 75 ft circumference at its base. Other works involved the subtle relocation of natural elements demonstrating the mark of human beings in a hitherto untouched area. Long's *England* (1968) consisted of a large X shape made on a grassy field by the removal of the heads of daisies; while his *Walking in a Line in Peru* (1972) was the result of walking backwards and forwards along a plotted line until a path had been worn into the earth. By nature transient and temporary, these works were documented by photograph and left to the observer to reconstruct the physical experience for himself or herself. Other works were more sculptural in a traditional sense, as in the works by Christo such as his *Wrapped Coast* (Sydney, 1969), and *Valley Curtain* (Colorado, 1971), in which the shape of large areas of land was articulated by massive quantities of cloth.

Land art would seem to indicate a nostalgic desire to escape from civilisation as well as from the corruption of art by its commercial exploitations. Yet its very irrationality, with thought, labour and materials expended to make a temporary mark of no apparent significance, is a form of protest against the exploitation of people and materials, against the increasing demolition by which we recognise the modern city, and against the wanton destruction of nature by humans in search of their accumulative pleasures. In her influential essay, Krauss describes these artists as postmodern because of their 'structural transformation of the cultural field' of sculpture, and states that their work consequently resists assimilation by the dominant modernist concepts of sculpture. These *site constructions* explored the interface between what is sculpture and not-sculpture, and ruptured the *siteless* spatial aspirations of modernism – sculpture as the loss of site, the monument as an abstraction – in a deconstructive behaviour. Once again, one can see the rationale of space and mapping at the heart of the logic of postmodernism.

Installations and performance art

The use of space also dominates installations and performance art, which have become the focus of much postmodern artistic experiment. They provide an ideal manifestation of the deconstructionist idea of the world as a 'text' whose intent can never be fully known even by its author, so that 'readers' are free to interpret it in the light of their own understanding. In effect, it offers viewers the opportunity to co-write the 'text'. The principal precursor of installation and contemporary performance art must be Joseph Beuys (see below). Installations are also often a bridging of conventional art boundaries: public and private, individual and communal, high style and vernacular. Although a broad category encompassing a variety of activities, styles and intentions ranging from the formalist to the political, installations and performance art revive art as entertainment. In the age of being entertained by the television, electronic media have also offered a considerable resource for installation artists, perhaps none more so than Nam June Paik with his sophisticated video displays. Delay mechanisms, electronic recording facilities, slow motion and split screens all offer unique technical means for exploring multiple identities, representation and mimesis, as well as the interrelations of text and image. William Wegman is a video artist who also plays on the failure of images to live up to words, while Krzysztof Wodiczko projected slide images on to the sides of buildings in an attempt to create spectacular visual commentaries on architectural forms and their socio-political meanings. Other performance artists of note include Vito Acconci, Richard Foreman, Yvonne Rainer, Gilbert and George, and Chris Burden (who arranges happenings in which his life is put at risk, like being kicked down a flight of stairs).

With postmodernism's dominant interest in pluralism and popular culture, performance art offered further examples of how a 'radical' art could be embodied in new media. Deriving from Dada, 'happenings' and the alternative theatre of the 1960s, performance art appeared able to resist the commodification of art (it could not be easily bought or sold), and frequently replaced the usual materials of art with the human body. Under the influence of post-structuralism, the focus of contemporary performance art has shifted from the text to the body, from authority to effect, to the spectator's freedom to construct and alter meanings. Body art encompasses a wide range of activities too vast to be encapsulated here; but some of its principal preoccupations include narcissism, masochism and sexuality. Body art and performances often marked a reaction to the spare minimalism of Conceptual art and the aseptic quality of computer art in the 1960s. Among body art's principal protagonists were Gina Pane, Stuart Brisley, Barry La Va, Bruce Nauman and Rebecca Horn, although there are clear precedents in the work of Yves Klein. Frequently crossing over with the work of feminist theatre (see Chapter 3), performance art heightens those sensibilities usually attributed to sculpture – such as the texture of material or objects in space – which it is felt become even more tangible in live presentation. Tending to be one-off occasions, per-formances are responses to what are construed as society's anaes-thetisation and alienation processes. More than anything else, it is the sense of 'being there' which governs the presiding experience of the installation or performance.

The 1990s saw installation art move from a peripheral to a central practice within the art world, as well as moving from site-specific to more portable pieces. In parallel, the 1990s also witnessed a technological development of unprecedented speed for the digital medium, the so-called 'digital revolution'. What has become known as 'Digital Art' or 'New Media Art' embraces a wide variety of multiple practices. Indeed, as computers have become less cumber-some, the advent of computer art (which first developed in the late 1960s and early 1970s) and its recent digital applications have become central to developments in installation, performance and video art. The implications of the computer for postmodernism are considerable. Many examples of computer art (for example, those by practitioners like Manfred Mohr, Michael Noll, Torsten Ridell, Vera Molnar) are effectively, as one critic has put it, 'the result of systematic or random distortions introduced into the development of a system of calculation' (Florence de Mèredieu, *Digital and Video Art* (Edinburgh, Edinburgh University Press, 2005), p. 98). Marking the end of an aesthetic dominated by natural light, digital art also breaks away from the traditional conception of considering the natural world as a reservoir of images to be preserved, captured and recorded. Echoing so many of Baudrillard's words, computer and digital art advance a world of 'enhanced reality', a relief that ordinary vision does not allow, an excessive representation of a reality more real than nature itself, and where 'virtual reality' enables a space of possibility or impossibility formed by illusionary addresses to the senses. 'Digital Art' opens up practices based upon mathematical distortions, simulations, hybrid images and multimedia art, fluid and dynamic shapes (like those of William Latham, Karl Sims and Louis Bec), digital sculpture, interactive and virtual environments, the development of fractal images and 3D images using virtual reality goggles by visitors to installations, as well as addressing itself to a range of issues that overlap with other popular culture concerns (see the discussion of cyberculture in Chapter 8), such as telepresence and telerobotics, gaming and narrative hypermedia environments, artificial life, and net art. Excellent introductions and explorations of the multiplicity of these art developments occur in Christiane Paul's *Digital Art* (London, Thames and Hudson, 2003), Julian Stallabrass's *Internet Art* (London, Tate Publishing, 2003), Rachel Greene's *Internet Art* (London, Thames and Hudson, 2004), Oliver Grau's *Virtual Art: from Illusion to Immersion* (Cambridge MA, MIT Press, 2004) and Bruce Wand's *Art of the Digital Age* (London, Thames and Hudson, 2006). Many of these books address themselves not only to the practices and the key figures like Char Davies, Erwin Redl and John Klima, but also to the politics of this art, interactivity, surveillance, data forms, the relationships of space and time to each other, the commercial reactions and appropriations of network art, as well as the challenges posed by internet art to art institutions.

STOP and THINK

- Where do the boundaries between visual and plastic art, performance art, and other forms of cultural activity begin and end? Performances frequently open up questions of subjectivity (who is speaking/acting?), location (in what sites/spaces?), audience (who is observing?), commodification (who is in control?), conventionality (how are meanings produced?) and politics (what ideological positions are being interrogated or reinforced?).

- Try these questions out on a performance piece of your choice, and consider how your answers are the result of the performance itself, or the critical theories you bring to it. Can a performance stand alone, or is it inalienably bound up with your interpretative categories?

Key characteristics of sculpture, plastic and performance art

1. An increase in the use of technological media, such as videos, televisions, computers, and other domestic and electronic machinery.
2. A specific attention to the body as a site of artistic investigation.
3. A challenge to conventional gallery spaces as the exclusive site for artistic display, which has produced site-specific constructions and an interest in everyday public spaces.
4. An increasing interest in process and procedure as opposed to the finished artefact.
5. A redefinition of what constitutes sculpture: an opening of the sculptural object to the natural processes of weathering, ageing and deterioration.

Postmodern sculpture and performance art: some examples

I have selected three examples of postmodern sculpture and performance art to examine here. The first is the work of Robert Smithson, in particular his *Spiral Jetty* (1970) (Figure 7). This became a hugely influential example of the new minimalism in sculpture, which fed into postmodern notions of sculpture, especially as it was formulated by Krauss. Smithson chose to locate his design on the shores of the Great Salt Lake in Utah, producing an artwork which would derive from reading the local topography and be designed in conformity with its surrounding environmental site. The site for the spiral combined several symbolic concerns: (a) there was a local

Figure 7 Robert Smithson, *Spiral Jetty*, Great Salt Lake, Utah (1970)

legend about the Great Salt Lake being connected to the ocean
through some vast underground tunnel, which revealed itself in the
middle of the lake as an enormous whirlpool; (b) like the famous
infinitely recursive shape of the Mandelbrot set in fractal geometry,
the overall spiral is reproduced in the molecular lattice of the salt
crystals that coated the rocks on the water's edge. Hence, the spiral
was a symbolic key to both the macroscopic, mythological, as well
as the microscopic worlds. The language with which Smithson
described the spiral is clearly concerned with entropy as a measure
of disorder: he described the spiral as 'coming from nowhere, going
nowhere', 'shattered', 'fractured', open and irreversible, a lexicon
which clearly dovetails with the postmodern emphasis on multiplicity, open-endedness, fragmentation, and the absence of origins.
Spiral Jetty has sometimes been regarded as the quintessential
heroic human gesture in the landscape, in which man conquers the
wilderness by imposing his magnificent marks upon its surface,
with its monumentality rivalling prehistoric works like Stonehenge
and the Pyramids. However, Smithson was acutely self-conscious
about the 'primitiveness' of the artwork, and insists that it is a site
of the multiple results of the universal force of entropy. Indeed,

those forces of entropy have continued to work inexorably. As it has been submerged since 1972, owing to the unexpected rise of the water-level of the Great Salt Lake, it has also become a work which only exists in 'textualised' form, in documents, drawings, photographs and Smithson's film of its production. Albeit inadvertently, this ironically adds to its postmodern status, since it is now an artwork which relies entirely on discursive systems for its 'existence'.

Joseph Beuys has attained the status of European guru of postmodern art. Shaman, seer, sculptor, maker of happenings, performance artist, he has achieved almost mythic proportions with his conviction that everyone is an artist; that art is a kind of being or doing rather than making:

> Every human being is an artist. In my work man appears as an artist, a creator. By artists I don't mean people who produce paintings or sculpture or play the piano, or are composers or writers. For me a nurse is also an artist, or, of course, a doctor or a teacher. A student, too, a young person responsible for his own development. The essence of man is captured in the description 'artist'. All other definitions of this term 'art' end up by saying that there are artists and there are non-artists – people who can do something, and people who can't do anything. (Joseph Beuys, quoted in Sandy Nairne, *State of the Art*, p. 93)

This challenge flies in the face of the artist as an embodiment of the creative ideal, or as hero. The 'great artist', genius, innately born rather than trained, is bunk! Beuys widens the definition of artist to the 'process of living' in a radically democratic gesture. His work tends to focus repeatedly on survival, and his significant materials of felt and fat embody a special symbolic potency. Shot down during the war in the Russian Caucasus, he was rescued by Tartars, who kept him alive by wrapping him in felt and lard. Over the years, he has transformed his suffering into art – partly as an exorcism of the German national trauma. He firmly believed that art was a way to heal the wounds of society, as a form of social therapy. His shamanistic and ritualistic invocation of animal totems – stags, hares, bees, coyotes – addresses those unconsciously disenchanted with modernity and its elevation of the rational order that is scientifically and technologically realised. His shamanistic art also stands squarely in opposition to the abstraction of modernist art, as he invokes

allegories and symbolic narratives at every turn in an attempt to
overcome the bifurcation of modern sensibility into thinking
and feeling. Beuys' 'Theory of Sculpture' summarises his artistic
healing effect, calling it 'the passage from chaotic material to ordered
form through sculptural movement'. One of his famous performance happenings occurred in 1965, entitled *How to Explain Pictures
to a Dead Hare*. Beuys appeared smeared with honey and covered in
gold leaf, an iron plate tied to his right foot, muttering inaudibly
to the animal's corpse cradled in his arms for three hours. This
mock-shamanistic ritual appears to suggest a state of pre-civilised
consciousness and a tragic sense of history with the impending
disintegration of Europe. A further detailed discussion of this
performance can be found in Gregory Ulmer's book, *Applied Grammatology: Post(e)-Pedagogy from Jacques Derrida to Joseph Beuys*
(Baltimore, Johns Hopkins University Press, 1985).

My third example is the work of an influential feminist performance artist, Carolee Schneemann. Schneemann's installation work
has consistently been characterised by explorations of forgotten
visual traditions, pleasure wrenched from suppressive taboos, and
the body of the artist in dynamic relationship with the social body.
Schneemann interrogates the restrictions of traditional western
categories by creating a space of complementarity and mutuality,
and she has transformed the very definition of art especially with
regard to those discourses concerning the body, sexuality and gender. Often explicitly centred upon the female body as a source for
narrating the erasures of women from history, as in *Interior Scroll*
(1975), her performances have promoted a heightened awareness of
cultural differences, and the ways in which discursive and gender
meanings are delimited, generated, occluded, transgressed and
multiply interpreted.

In her large installation entitled *Cycladic Imprints* (1992),
Schneemann uses a multi-image procedure, which incorporates
well-known art historical representations of the female body from
painting, sculpture and photography onto a wall-bound assemblage
of mechanised violins and painted hourglass-shaped silhouettes.
This morphological exploration challenges what Schneemann
perceives to be the dominant narrative of artistic creation, in which
the man of genius finds his inspiration in the female nude as muse.

The ghostly juxtaposition of the violins, the traces of hourglass shapes on the wall, and the shadow of the woman's body in Figure 8 throw into ironic relief masculine stereotypes of female physical beauty, perpetuated by the presentation of the 'vital statistics' of female models in beauty parades, and immortalised in Holden Caulfield's adolescent erotic reveries about 'a woman's body [being] like a violin and all, and that it takes a terrific musician to play it right' (J.D. Salinger, *The Catcher in the Rye* (1951; London, Penguin, 1982), p. 98). Schneemann's arrangement of body, instruments, shadow-shapes and machines effectively transforms the female image from passive form into active subject, and assaults the Romantic model of expression and its association with masculine strategies of possessive power. As with most performance art, the explicit use of the body is also a direct challenge to the suppression of sexuality and somatic activity in the history of western culture, a seductive liberation of physical form from the hierarchial priority accorded to the mental process.

Figure 8 Carolee Schneemann, *Cycladic Imprints* (1992), installation, four synchronized projectors, dissolve units, 17 motorised violins mounted on walls approximately 20 × 36 ft, walls stained with double-curve strokes, 240 overlapping dissolving images of Cycladic sculptures, violin forms and human torsos. Sound loop, duration: approximately 15 minutes, dimensions variable

Creative design

Design is everywhere: it infuses all our objects, surfaces and depths in the material world, as well as providing form to immaterial processes like services and factory production. Design is a central representation of cultural values, a fact not often acknowledged by the principal philosophers of modernism and postmodernism. Postmodernist design is dominated by the three As – Archigram, Alchymia, Archizoom – which have all in various ways been responsible for the development of a style of jewellery, silverware, textile, pottery and domestic design which turned its back on the dominant master narrative of modernist design, functionalism.

Archigram was an organisation of architects and designers led by Peter Cook, based in London and the United States in the 1960s and early 1970s. Archigram delighted in experimental projects – plug-in cities, clip-on architecture, capsule dwellings, instant and walk-in cities – partly inspired by the advanced technology emerging from NASA's space programme. In Italy, 'radical design' emerged with Archizoom, which was formed in Florence in 1964 by Andrea Branzi, who later worked with Alchymia and Memphis. Along with other sixties groups like Gruppo Sturm and Superstudio, they absorbed aspects of pop design into what was designated 'anti-design' or 'banal design', as for example in the 'Dream Beds'. As Branzi has described it in his major survey of 'Italian New Wave' design, *The Hot House* (Cambridge MA, MIT Press, 1984), the design impulse was anti-functional and super-sensual. In a shift from function to expression, for Branzi design was a way of constructing the self and forging one's identity. His 'Domestic Animals' (1985) was a series of furniture which investigated the way in which natural materials like bamboo and untreated wood have been used in furniture manufacture, and manifest a neo-primitivism which he perceived as introducing a new magic and ritual into social contexts. In explaining the shift away from modernism, Branzi states:

> New Design is thus interested in putting together a different domestic culture, in recovering a system of ties and functions that cannot be explained in purely ergonomic or functional terms, that involve man in his relationship to his domestic habitat from a wider cultural and expressive point of view. (*Hot House*, p. 148)

Ettore Sottsass, another significant figure in this development of Italian 'anti-design', has provided a variety of furniture, domestic appliances, textiles and jewellery which also depart from modernist clarity of form and static functionalism. In the late 1970s, Sottsass became a member of the Alchymia studios at Milan, which pursued a vigorous, irreverent, usurping style, before he went on to establish Memphis in 1981, with such other designers as Barbara Radice, Michele de Lucchi, Shiro Kuramata, Marco Zanini and Nathalie du Pasquier. The title of the co-operative studio intentionally alludes to magic and mystery, combining the classicism of Ancient Egypt and the populism of American rock and roll. Pluralistic in gesture, with the strong belief that objects should have a powerful intrusive presence in the domestic environment, the studio's ironic use of historical styles, their inappropriate decorative fabrics, pastel colours, irrational shapes, their cultivation of 'bad taste' and references to pop culture and the 'banal', all mark their reaction against the uniformity and dullness of international design. Sottsass has distinguished the Memphis designs from postmodern design on the basis that postmodern designs are inclined towards restoration and historicism, whereas the 'neo-modern' Memphis is concerned with the present. However, Italian 'New Wave' and postmodern design clearly share roots and interests in their determination to find a new language for design. This can be seen in Sottsass's Beidermeier Sofa (1982) and his Lemon Sherbert bookshelf (1987), which utilise unorthodox colour schemes and ironic allusions to other furniture history. Sottsass' work on patterned surfaces, printed on to plastic laminate, were largely inspired by banal sources like the mosaic floors of suburban bars and the wire netting of suburban fences; they were, he said, 'extracts from a figurative iconography found in spaces uncorrupted by the sophistication of the standard culture of private design' (quoted from the Introduction to *A Catalogue for Decorative Furniture in Modern Style, 1973–1980* (Milan, 1980), p. 2).

Memphis' objects explicitly related to the world of consumption and use, competing for attention with the plethora of mass-mediated images that infiltrate everyday life. Many architects have infiltrated the world of design as well, so that people like Michael Graves, Hans Hollein, Aldo Rossi, Zaha Hadid, Arata Isozaki, Robert Venturi, Charles Moore, Stanley Tigerman and Charles Jencks have

all produced designs for various studios. Some of the most innovative of these in recent years have come from the deconstructive
designs of Hadid. Her furniture utilises colour in ways which
echo De Stijl juxtapositions, and her sofas imply a movement and
weightlessness quite evident in her architectural designs.

Postmodernism in design can refer to almost anything which is
not a celebration of the inter-war 'heroic period' of modern architecture and design. It remains principally a post-pop art style in
its reactions against pure ideas of 'good form'; but in so far as it
continues to use modern materials like laminates and plastic, it
extends rather than denies modernism's technical achievements.
Designer chic can even be seen in mundane household objects, like
the Dyson vacuum cleaner, whose striking colours mark it out as
more than a merely functional object. Indeed, modernist functionalism has itself become a *style* in its own right, as can be seen in
recent designs for Braun shavers. A Jamesonian dehistoricisation is
also evident in a recent advertisement for the Olympus LT Zoom
camera, which boasts a 'coloured leather style body and brash
chrome front . . . that captures all of the energy of the past and
brings it bubbling into the 1990s'. Redolent of the decadent late
1920s, evoking the flapper dresses, Bugattis, strings of pearls and
wind-up gramophones of the Jazz Age, the advertisement suggests
that 'the retro feel' of the camera will lose you 'in an era of elegance
and style, of fun and laughter, of romance and travel'. The entire
advertisement plays on the notion that purchasing the camera will
allow you to substitute for your present the lost age of *The Great
Gatsby* (1925).

The restrictive vocabulary of modernism was not only felt by
domestic designers: its semantic limitations were also felt by the
fashion business. Yet what constitutes postmodernism in clothes
design is often perplexing and not altogether straightforward. On
first showing, aggressive and 'outré' fashion statements seem to be
the name of the game when it comes to dress design, and these
do not appear to be the province of any single designer. However,
even a business in which to shock is virtually *de rigueur* has its
postmodern rebels, from the funk and punk of Vivienne Westwood
to the imitative parodies and 'pop' styles of Jean-Paul Gaultier.

Westwood's designs draw upon a rich visual syntax, generating a greater sense of freedom to express affinities with different 'life-styles'. Her association with Malcolm McLaren led her to the influence of the Sex Pistols and punk rock in the 1970s, when she launched her Punk Collection at her shop Seditionaries; her Pirates Collection in 1981, 'plundering' styles and images from the bucca-neering age, emerged in conjunction with McLaren's work with the pop group Adam and the Ants and their combination of Geronimo face-paint and pirate costumes; her Savage Collection had ethnic references; her Buffalo Collection drew its inspiration from the American folk heritage; and her Nostalgia of Mud Shop drew upon African styles. Playing games with cultures and history, Westwood challenges expectations and traditions at virtually every turn. Simi-lar anti-status clothes which break down the accepted western views of fashion and sexuality can be seen in Rei Kawakaburo's designs, the presiding spirit at Comme des Garçons. Although Japanese in style, it is the Japan of stylised, ritual violence to which she appeals, with creased, torn and slashed clothes evoking a vulnerable, aban-doned, shorn-of-sophistication look. With visibility being everything to contemporary fashion, haut couture even makes its appearance as the lead in contemporary film. Gaultier's designs for Luc Besson's film *The Fifth Element* (1997) are typical, as the PR material for the film promotes the new genre of 'style-led' action thrillers with a 'definite fashion statement'.

In its preoccupation with surfaces, *style* has itself become the presiding rationale for postmodernism. The social or radical cul-tural politics of a subculture is rapidly undermined by the relentless commercialisation of style, as it becomes an 'off-the-peg' option available at a variety of High Street retail shops. For example, punk was once regarded as the affirmation of the working-class urban reality of unemployment. However, it quickly became absorbed into mainstream culture and its outcry against the establishment was neutralised by the way in which ready-torn and slashed clothes appeared pervasively. Postmodern style is inalienably linked to big business, as a company like Esprit demonstrates, with shops designed by Norman Foster and Shiro Kuramata, and interiors by Sottsass and Antonio Citterio.

Key characteristics of creative design

1. A use of 'pop' themes and allusions, or an ironic and parodic rearticulation of previous styles; a 'sampling' of elements of different styles or eras.
2. An inclusion of anti-functional design features, like a complex use of garish colour, explicit decoration and ornament, or texture.
3. A return to the individual, private consumption of goods rather than the mass use of public space.
4. A use of 'styling' and image control in the design process, like 1950s 'retro' designs in refrigerators.
5. A play with visual language, creating new readings of familiar objects.
6. A break with the homogenisation of the mass market, and a search to express the paradoxes and contradictions of post-industrial society.

Postmodern design: some examples

Hans Hollein, a successful Austrian architect and designer, has produced some remarkable examples of postmodern design. Perhaps his most celebrated piece is a sofa entitled 'Marilyn', designed for Poltronova, Italy (1981) (Figure 9). It combines in one fell swoop classicism, screen deco, sexuality, pop and kitsch: its hybrid style mingles a Hollywood casting couch, a deco screen goddess couch, and a neo-classical couch. Like many postmodern artefacts, its name also plays with a number of other historical referents: it alludes to the pop kitsch seats designed by Studio 65 in the 1960s, which were shaped like a pair of lips and coloured red; as a tribute to Marilyn Monroe, this sofa was itself a modernised version of the original 'Mae West Lips' sofa made in 1937 to Salvador Dali's design; which in turn refers to Dali's painting *The Face of Mae West* (1935). Hollein's play with signifiers in his designs is also evident in his silver coffee and tea set designed for Alessi in 1983 (Figure 10), in which the tray is shaped like an aircraft carrier, ready to 'take off' in the user's hands. Hollein's designs are marked by an iconography and syntax that are often historicist, but also highly idiosyncratic in their referential allusions.

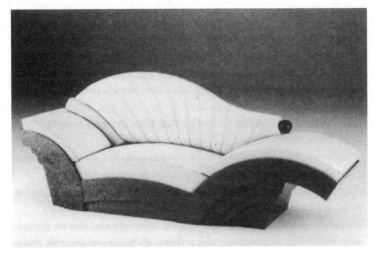

Figure 9 Hans Hollein, 'Marilyn' sofa in wood and fabric for Poltronova, Italy (1981)

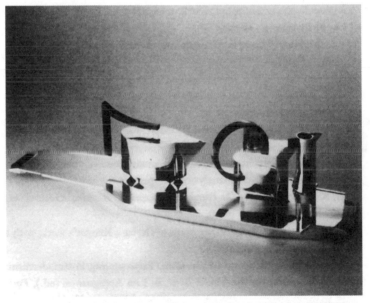

Figure 10 Hans Hollein, silver coffee and tea set, for Alessi, Italy (1983)

Selected reading

Archer, Michael, *Art Since 1960* (London, Thames and Hudson, 1997).
A wide-ranging book on the changes in art during the last 40 years. Includes a useful timeline of movements, key figures and world events. Chapters focus on ideology, postmodernism, assimilation, referentiality, identity and difference.

Baker, Steve, *The Postmodern Animal* (London, Reaktion, 2000).
A fascinating study of how animal imagery has been used in recent and contemporary art and performance, and in postmodern philosophy and literature, to shape ideas about identity and creativity.

Bate, David, *Photography After Postmodernism: Barthes, Stieglitz and the Art of Memory* (London, I.B. Tauris, 2008).
In life 'after postmodernism', photography, cinema, television and the internet have all already changed the way we think about pictures. Bate demonstrates the complex ways in which photographic images resonate across public and private spaces, carrying a slippage of meaning that is never quite fixed, always social and contingent.

Branzi, Andrea, *The Hot House: Italian New Wave Design* (Cambridge MA, MIT Press, 1984).
A wide-ranging and comprehensive account of Italian 'new wave' design, generally considered to be the leading edge in postmodern design.

Burton, Johanna (ed.), *Cindy Sherman* (Cambridge MA, MIT Press, 2007).
Contains critical essays on Cindy Sherman's metamorphosing self-portraits and appropriation of genres, which can be seen as a continuous investigation of representation and its complicated relationship to photography.

Collins, Michael, with Andreas Papadakis, *Post-Modern Design* (London, Academy Editions, 1989).
Probably one of the most definitive books currently available on the subject, with lavish illustrations, and a thorough history of creative design since the late 1960s.

Harrison, Sylvia, *Pop Art and the Origins of Post-modernism* (Cambridge, Cambridge University Press, 2001).
Examines the critical reception of Pop Art in America during the 1960s and compares the ideas of critics such as Leo Steinberg, Susan Sontag, and Max Kozloff, demonstrating the striking similarity of their ideas to deconstructive post-modernism.

Heartney, Eleanor, *Postmodernism* (Cambridge, Cambridge University Press, 2001).
An introduction to the intellectual movement known as Postmodernism and its impact on the visual arts.

Isaak, Jo Anna, *Feminism and Contemporary Art* (London, Routledge, 1996).
A series of essays which focus upon the comic critique proposed by
feminist art of the traditional approaches to the theory and history of art.
It has good discussions of people like Barbara Kruger, Cindy Sherman
and Mary Kelly amongst others.

Iversen, Margaret, Douglas Crimp and Homi Bhabha, *Mary Kelly* (London,
Phaidon, 1997).
A series of informative interviews, critical essays and reflections on the
nature of Kelly's work on subjectivity and power, discursivity, and the
reception and distribution of art.

Kaye, Nick, *Site-specific Art: Performance, Place and Documentation* (London,
Routledge, 2000).
Charts the development of the fascinating historical antecedents of
today's installation and performance art, focusing on spaces and
mappable space, place events, bodies in space frames.

Kelly, Mary, *Post-Partum Document* (London, Routledge and Kegan Paul,
1983).
Carefully documents her work into the construction of cultural identity
from a feminist and psychoanalytical perspective.

Kocur, Zoya, and Simon Leung, *Theory in Contemporary Art Since 1985*
(Oxford, Blackwell, 2004).
Brings together a selection of important contributions to the fields of
contemporary art, theory, and culture, that focus upon key theoretical
and aesthetic issues such as cultural/multicultural theory, identity
politics, AIDS, post-colonialism, globalization, and spectatorship.

Linker, K., *Love for Sale: The Words and Pictures of Barbara Kruger* (New
York, Harry N. Abrams, 1990).
A good collection of large illustrations of Barbara Kruger's work, with a
good, accessible commentary.

Newman, Michael, 'Revising Modernism, Representing Postmodernism:
Critical Discourses of the Visual Arts', in Lisa Appignanesi (ed.), *Postmodernism: ICA Documents 4* (London, ICA, 1986), pp. 32–51.
An excellent introductory piece, which covers the development of
modernist and avant-garde art, through conceptual art, to postmodernism. The extensive discussion of postmodernism works through a critical
lexicon, i.e. terms like allegory, bricolage, simulation and parody.

Oliveira, Nicolas, Nicola Oxley, and Michael Petry, *Installation Art in the
New Millennium* (London, Thames and Hudson, 2003).
Analyses the shifts in practice in the late 1990s in the field of installation art.

Poynor, Rick, *No More Rules: Graphic Design and Postmodernism* (New
Haven CT, Yale University Press, 2003).

Offering a complete overview of the graphic revolution during the post-modern period, this book investigates the key themes of the multifaceted field of graphic design: the origins of postmodern design; deconstructionist design and theory; issues of appropriation; the revolution in digital type; questions of authorship; and critiques of postmodern graphic design.

Sandler, Irving, *Art of the Postmodern Era: From the Late 1960s to the Early 1990s* (New York, HarperCollins, 1996).

An exceptionally informative book, which ranges widely across the various ideas and diverse concepts which inform postmodern art practices. Well acquainted with the artworks and the theories, the book offers an outstanding bibliography, organised by artist as well as by books, articles and exhibition catalogues, making this a major resource.

Schneemann, Carolee, *Imaging Her Erotics: Essays, Interviews, Projects* (Cambridge MA, MIT Press, 2003).

A collection of material depicting and analysing many of Schneemann's key projects with an excellent array of illustrations.

Taylor, Brandon, *Modernism, Post-modernism, Realism: A Critical Perspective for Art* (Winchester, Winchester School of Art Press, 1987).

A very good introductory text exploring the interrelationship of the various aesthetic styles in visual art. Offers a wide range of illustrative examples.

Taylor, Brandon, *Art Today* (London, Laurence King Publishing, 2004).

Charts the ideas and practices of contemporary art across a wide international spectrum, from Minimalism and Conceptualism to video and film, from painting and sculpture to performance and installation. Reviewing the major controversies of the later twentieth century and the early years of the twenty-first, it also includes a discussion of the impact of the internet and digital art.

Welchman, John C. (ed.), *Art After Appropriation: Essays on Art in the 1990s* (Amsterdam, OPA, 2001).

Considers how art has moved beyond and thought through issues of appropriation, a key postmodern characteristic in art.

Woodman, Jonathan M., *Twentieth-Century Ornament* (New York, Rizzoli, 1990).

Charts the development of twentieth-century design clearly, with the last two chapters dedicated to design in postmodernism and 'after', the marketing of 'individualism' in the 1990s.

6

Postmodernism, popular culture and music

Andreas Huyssen has commented that 'Pop in the broadest sense was the context in which a notion of the postmodern first took shape . . . and the most significant trends within postmodernism have challenged modernism's relentless hostility to mass culture' (Huyssen, *After the Great Divide*, p. 16). In the visual arts, it was the work of pop artists like Claes Oldenburg, Roy Lichtenstein, Andy Warhol and others that began the first assault on the tenets of modern art; similarly popular culture has always been established in opposition to the puritan ideology of aesthetic purity and highbrow intellect in modernist culture. Postmodernism as a term has entered all walks of popular culture, from youth culture magazines and record sleeves to the fashion pages of *Cosmopolitan* and *The Face*. Following the incorporation of modernist 'high' culture into the canon, a re-evaluation of what constitutes popular culture occurred in Britain and the United States in the 1950s and 1960s. Popular culture became the expression of, as well as the construction of, youth culture and ultimately enabled the formation of sites of enunciation for a variety of 'marginal' groups. Indeed, Dick Hebdige, an influential theorist of contemporary popular culture, has sought to define non-hegemonic cultures as 'subcultures':

> Subculture forms up in the space between surveillance and the evasion of surveillance, it translates the fact of being under scrutiny into the pleasure of being watched. It is hiding in the light.
>
> The 'subcultural response' is neither simply affirmation nor refusal, neither 'commercial exploitation' nor 'genuine revolt'. It is

neither simply resistance against some external order nor straightforward conformity with the parent culture. It is both a declaration of
independence, of otherness, of alien intent, a refusal of anonymity, of
subordinate status. It is an *in*subordination. And at the same time it is
also a confirmation of the fact of powerlessness, a celebration of
impotence. Subcultures are both a play for attention and a refusal,
once attention has been granted, to be read according to the Book.
(Hebdige, *Hiding in the Light* (London, Routledge, 1988), p. 35)

In their deliberately ambiguous and heterogeneous situations – one
might almost say in their deconstructive sites – subcultures appear
to be characteristically postmodern phenomena. Yet popular culture
(that is culture which lies outside the domains of hegemonic cultural practices) has always existed and is not a new phenomenon. In
recent years, popular culture has seen a fantastic explosion. Tied to
the postwar economic boom, to the advent of the teenager in the
1950s and then youth culture in the 1960s, as well as the expression
of minority cultural identities, it is a sphere which has excited much
critical and cultural debate since the 1970s, and has seen a huge
growth in cultural analysis.

Debates in popular culture

As a field of study, the genealogy of cultural studies emerged from
the work of structuralists such as Roland Barthes and Marxists like
Raymond Williams, Richard Hoggart and Stuart Hall's work with
the Centre for Contemporary Culture at the University of Birmingham. In many ways, these theorists had to struggle against the
German musicologist and philosopher Theodor Adorno's monolithic view of popular culture, which was then prevalent: in response
to his notion that popular music constructed a rationalised, standardised product, and produced a pseudo-individualised response
and a 'false consciousness' in the audience, they condemned his
blinkered, high-cultural dismissal of the aesthetics of popular music
and his pervasive pessimism about the political value of popular culture. It is perhaps their introduction of the theoretical work of the
Italian Marxist Antonio Gramsci which prepared the way for a postmodern conception of popular culture. For his ideas allowed people
to recognise that ideology is not directly imposed upon people; but

is continually composed through a mobile strategy of shifting alliances and compromises which he termed 'hegemony'. Williams defines hegemony as:

> ways of seeing the world and ourselves and others [which] are not just intellectual but political facts, expressed over a range from institutions to relationships and consciousness ... it is seen to depend for its hold not only on its expression of the interest of a ruling class but also on its acceptance as 'normal reality' or 'commonsense' by those in practice subordinated to it. (Williams, *Keywords* (London, Fontana, 1983), p. 145)

In other words, introducing the concept of hegemony seeks to explain how people are complicit with their own ideological construction: ideology works in and through us, forming our very identity and sense of self. Consequently, a cultural semiotics was fashioned (well illustrated in the work of Hebdige and Hall), where people 'read' popular cultural forms as the sites of political contests over language.

Hence, the importance of reading popular culture as forms of coded desire grew. Signs now took on increasing importance in the contemporary world, which caused people to pay new attention to the heterogeneous surface activities of everyday life. A sensitivity to what is local, partial and temporary has demanded that theorists pay closer attention to the complexities of mobile meanings, shifting connections, temporary encounters and the world of intertextual connections. The very existence of departments of cultural studies in academic institutions in recent years, which analyse anything from pop music, soap operas, everyday artefacts such as washing-up boxes and menus, to the latest haircuts and the design of magazines like *Wired* and *The Face* (which featured an interview with postmodern guru Jean Baudrillard in vol. 2, no. 4 (January 1989)), testifies to the significant power and pervasive influence of these popular artefacts and processes in our consumer culture. I say 'consumer' deliberately, because popular culture is inextricably linked to the commodification of our lives, the commercial exploitation of our leisure time, and the reliance upon a surplus income to indulge these fabricated cultural desires. Everything is commodified and this process is constantly reinforced by a barrage of television advertising.

The postmodern is understandably widely associated with societies in which consumer lifestyles and mass consumption dominate
the lives of their citizens. Fashions and tastes are eclectic and consumer culture aims for globalisation – Big Macs, Tommy Hilfiger,
Coke, *Dallas*, Levi 501s, Sony, Nike are on most High Streets
and in many shops throughout the world. Consequently, it ought to
come as no surprise that most of the debates in popular culture centre upon the ways in which culture forms identity, the central claim
being that there are major factors outside 'high' culture which constitute people's identities. Indeed, one of the principal arguments
of postmodern theorists of popular culture is that the opposition
low/high is subverted and blurred by contemporary postmodern
culture. Postmodern theories have forced cultural critics away from
the search for 'immanent' meaning in a text, towards the sociological interrelationship between images and different cultural forms
and institutions. In her focus upon new formations of cultural identity in *Postmodernism and Popular Culture* (London, Routledge,
1994), Angela McRobbie argues that postmodern theory opens up a
more pluralistic vision of social practices than other theories hitherto. McRobbie lambasts structuralist analyses of popular culture
for their inability to deal with multimedia performances, as well as
for their neglect of the context and the audience of popular cultural
consumption.

She is severely critical of what she perceives to be Fredric Jameson's implicit deprecation of 'low' culture for its celebration of
glamour, glitz and glitter, things which the left has generally taken
to be signs of capitulation to commodification and complicity with
capitalism. McRobbie regards this 'low' culture as a new form of
'camp', using similar cultural techniques to those Susan Sontag
identified in her analysis of 'camp sensibility', in which she perceived a 'love of the unnatural: of artifice and exaggeration'.
McRobbie sees postmodern popular culture as the site of 'new
agency': as a way in which new pluralist forms of possible identity
are being constructed, which often lie outside the traditional perspective on the formation of identity. For this reason, postmodernism
is useful as:

> an analytical/descriptive category whose momentum derives from
> its cutting free from the long legacy of meanings associated with

modernity. The term, postmodernity, indicates something of the scope and the scale of the new global and local social relations and identities set up between individuals, groups and populations as they interact with and are formed by the multiplicity of texts, images and representations which are a constitutive part of contemporary reality and experience. (McRobbie, *Postmodernism*, p. 26)

Contrary to Jameson's pessimistic critique of postmodernism's production of schizophrenic subjectivity and its celebration of depthlessness and surface, McRobbie optimistically sees popular culture as the site where possibilities for new identities are emerging:

To lament the decline of full wholesome subjectivity is literally to cast aspersions on unwholesome, un(in)formed, partial and hybridic identities [and to ignore] how second-hand, do-it-yourself plundering of culture, particularly on the part of both black and white young people who are as yet unformed as adults, ... can give them space to impregnate a scornful, often condemning adult social order with the politics of their adolescent identities. (McRobbie, *Postmodernism*, pp. 3–4)

Thus, McRobbie carefully outlines what she takes to be the landscape of postmodern culture: an embrace of pastiche, a defiant pleasure in being dressed up or 'casual', an exploration of fragmented subjectivity, the incursion of imagery and communication into areas and spaces hitherto considered private (Baudrillard's 'ecstasy of communication'), and the way one set of media practices become the reference points for another (how soap-opera characters form the basis for Saturday morning teenage television phone-ins, etc.). In her wide-ranging analyses of various popular cultural phenomena, she continually explores how these characteristics are in fact constitutive of much of our contemporary consciousnesses.

Lawrence Grossberg, the pre-eminent American theorist of postmodern popular culture, has also sought to demonstrate how popular culture allows for an 'empowerment' of and 'investment' in new cultural identities. Yet he is wary of the complicated baggage that the term 'postmodern' carries, and seeks to define post-modernity as:

a crisis in our ability to locate any meaning as a possible and appropriate source for an impassioned commitment. It is a crisis not of faith, but of the relationship between faith and common sense,

a dissolution of what we might call the 'anchoring effect' that articulates meaning and affect. ... Postmodernity demands that one live
schizophrenically, trying on the one hand to live the inherited meanings and, on the other hand, recognising that such meanings cannot
enable one to respond to one's affective situation. (Grossberg,
Dancing in Spite of Myself (Durham NC, Duke University Press,
1997), pp. 223–4)

Consequently, Grossberg's analyses of music, film, television and
other forms of popular culture investigate the *popularity* of these
forms. He concludes that popular culture offers sites where individuals can empower themselves, although not necessarily in the
form of resistance. Grossberg ultimately understands postmodern
popular culture as a new 'sensibility' which structures our everyday
environment: 'one of the dominant sensibilities put into place
by popular culture is what I have called a "postmodern logic" of
"authentic inauthenticity." It legitimates and even privileges an
ironic cynicism: You know you are faking it and you don't care.
Everything is an image and so you put on an image' (*Dancing*,
p. 281). This new postmodern sensibility is not 'an experience of
subjects or a representation of an external reality, but a form of
practice that produces particular sorts of affective alliances' (*Dancing*, p. 19). As far as Grossberg is concerned, it is important to
recognise that popular culture offers positions from which a politics
of cultural resistance *may* be formulated, since the postmodern
sensibility is an 'affective economy' which 'sacrifices the negativity
of resistance for the positivity of its own celebration and survival'
(*Dancing*, p. 188). Hence, it is incumbent upon theorists to formulate a politics of everyday life by 'winning back [popular culture's]
empowering positivity for progressive political investments, to rees-
tablish a connection between ideological difference and affective
identity' (*Dancing*, p. 188).

One significant focus for this political attention in cultural studies has been the construction of female identities, and the matrix of
feminism, postmodernism and popular culture creates a redefinition and re-evaluation of popular culture as an area of political and
representational struggle. McRobbie's concern for the new identities forged by postmodern popular culture includes a specific focus
on feminist interests; and these are shared by feminist theorists of

popular culture like Ros Coward, Meaghan Morris, Judith Williamson, Tania Modleski, Elspeth Probyn and Ann Brooks. Taking issue with what she perceives to be the characteristic feminisation of mass culture (for example, in Huyssen's work), Morris questions 'the myth of a postmodernism still waiting for its women' and argues that in many ways it is feminism which has paved the way for a discourse *about* postmodernism. As Grossberg acknowledges, 'it is fair to say that there is no cultural studies which is not "post-feminist", not in the sense of having moved beyond it but rather in the sense of having opened itself to the radical critique and implications of feminist theory and politics' (Grossberg, *Bringing It All Back Home* (Durham NC, Duke University Press, 1997), p. 199). Arguably, it has been the feminist theorisation of the notion of 'resistance' in popular culture that has grounded some of the more abstract debates; and it has been work on the specific consumption of popular cultural modes or images (like romance or Madonna) that has led to new insights about the construction of female identity in popular culture. As Brooks demonstrates in *Postfeminisms: Feminism, Cultural Theory and Cultural Forms* (London, Routledge, 1997), in the debate concerning the effectiveness of postmodernism for feminism, some feminists have noted that it may not be so debilitating after all. Drawing on the concepts of simulation, artifice and 'make-overs', it has been pointed out how such Baudrillardian concepts may challenge the stability of gender as sexual difference and the normative edifice of heterosexuality.

As the essays in C. Swichtenberg's *The Madonna Connection* (New South Wales, Allen and Unwin, 1993) make clear, a key figure in this analysis has been Madonna, who has been the central focus for a number of studies about the ways in which a popular cultural icon can deconstruct sex as the basis of identity and open up the issue of how all bodies are constructed. One can feel that something of a Madonna industry has grown up to the exclusion of other areas of popular music in these debates; but as feminists argue, Madonna's images make a particularly clear strategic use of simulation, masquerade and fantasy to prise open a crack in stable sexual identity and offer a sexual pluralism which does not reflect a political reactionism. Indeed, Madonna's bodily reconstructions and the implicit 'plastic body' become a postmodern paradigm, a discussion which will recur in Chapter 7 in relation to cyborgs and the new technology.

Pop music and eclectic styles

Simon Frith has argued that pop/rock music is the most important popular cultural medium, crucial to the analysis of the function of popular culture because it works so intensely with emotions, affects and peer pressure. It is not easy to categorise the development of a postmodern pop music after a modernist style. In many respects, by its very definition, popular music has always been postmodern in its trafficking in popular cultural images and its resistance to 'high' art forms. Most frequently the ambit of youth or minority cultural groups, pop music has traditionally operated on the fringes of the cultural establishment, marking itself out as the postmodern form of music itself. However, with pop music now a multimillion-dollar business, with commercialism and international finance deeply involved in its success, it is increasingly difficult to isolate pop music as a marginalised culture.

Nevertheless, recent years have seen several concerted efforts to provide a historical analysis of popular music, thereby attempting to chart the development of postmodern characteristics. Perhaps the pathbreaking attempt to understand rock music in postmodern terms was Fredric Jameson's essay 'Postmodernism and Consumer Society', in which he crudely described the Beatles and the Rolling Stones as examples of 'high modernism', and the Clash, Talking Heads and the Gang of Four as 'postmodern'. As Andrew Goodwin has sought to demonstrate, this fails to take account of musical differences within the two historical moments, like rock 'realism' (the Clash) and rock 'modernism' (Talking Heads), and of rock 'authenticity' (the Stones) and pop artifice (the Beatles) (Goodwin, 'Popular Music and Postmodern Theory', *Cultural Studies*, 5:2 (1991): 184). However, other theorists have sought to argue that there are distinctively postmodern characteristics to music in recent years. Specific trends towards direct and explicit mixing of styles, the 'infiltration' of other genres of music in a self-conscious way, as well as the stitching together, remixing, quoting of different musics, sounds or instruments to create sub- or pan-cultural identities, have all been cited as examples of postmodern pop music.

Dominic Strinati has argued that reggae, rap, house and hip-hop all demonstrate the postmodern concerns:

> with collage, pastiche and quotation, with the mixing of styles which remain musically distinctive, with the random and selective pasting together of different musics and styles, with the rejection of divisions between serious and fun music, and with the attack on the notion of rock as serious artistic music which merits the high cultural accolade of the respectful concert – a trend started by punk. (Strinati, 'Postmodernism and Popular Culture', in John Storey (ed.), *Cultural Theory and Popular Culture: A Reader* (Brighton, Harvester Wheatsheaf, 1994), p. 435)

His principal example is Jive Bunny and the Master Mixers, whom he regards as typical of 'an eclectic ransacking of the history of pop with no attempt to go beyond the simulations and dissimulations this involves' (Strinati, 'Postmodernism', p. 435).

Jon Stratton has continued this debate, offering a different trajectory to popular musical history in order to account for the recent emergence of a postmodern music. He perceives popular music to have three moments: the first is the period around 1954 and the formulation of rock and roll; the second is the years 1964–68, when pop music shifted from a working-class discourse to one which included the middle classes; the third is the emergence of postmodern pop music between 1975 and 1978, when punk, and postpunk plurality, 'was integrated in its material practices within the coterminous concerns of so-called high cultural avant-garde' (Stratton, 'Beyond Art: Postmodernism and the Case of Popular Music', *Theory, Culture and Society*, 6:1 (February 1989): 32). Stratton perceives postmodern popular music to be defined by the alliance of style with pleasure, producing an aesthetic which, 'operating within a concern with emotion and involvement, is based on excess' ('Beyond Art', p. 54). Following this history of pop's development, Stratton concludes that postmodernist pop 'operates within the present concern with "nostalgia" which, itself, is an attempt to come to terms with the loss of time as a linear, fixed entity. The preoccupation with nostalgia, however, is not simply with a "return" to a "past" but, simultaneously, reworks that past as self-conscious representation' ('Beyond Art', p. 54).

Iain Chambers also describes the musical self-consciousness that punk induced as forcing:

> a stark reappraisal of pop's own sounds. The simple distinction between 'mainstream' and margin, between avant-garde and popular, between music and 'noise' were confused. The singular history of pop, seen as a set of successive waves – rock'n'roll, beat, progressive rock – were set aside and replaced by multiple histories. Crossover and synthesise becomes the choice: black rhythms and heavy metal, funk and punk, jazz and beat. (Chambers, *Popular Culture* (London, Methuen, 1986), pp. 172–3)

Punk attacked rock and roll in its 'progressive rock' phase, as a gesture against groups such as Genesis, Yes, Pink Floyd, and Emerson, Lake and Palmer, and their pretensions to high intellect and serious art. Punk ransacked postwar subcultures for the purposes of recycling and reusing them in a celebration of surfaces, styles and artifice. Subsequently, we now have a music based upon a cosmopolitan culture which, derived from America to Africa, from New York to Nairobi, not only coexists but quotes and alludes internally. Paul Simon's *Graceland,* an album made with Ladysmith Black Mambazo, mixes homage to Elvis with the a cappella oral sounds of South African shanty towns; Scritti Politti can release a record which alludes to the European philosopher of deconstruction, entitled *Jacques Derrida*; while British Asian artists produce a new sound combining bhangra music with western rock.

Terry Bloomfield has suggested a chronology of pop music since the 1960s, in which he associates a '*pre*modernist realism' with rock music in that decade, with 'its adherence to the depth model of the cultural object (what songs are "about")' and its 'rock singer who expresses the real feelings of a generation of alienated youth, or positively articulates counter-forms to those of the dominant culture'; while the punk explosion, with bands like the Clash, the Sex Pistols, the Slits, X-ray Spex, the Damned and their followers, was the real locus of modernist music, with its repudiation of 'the sixties hermeneutic of integrity of message and authenticity of feeling' (Bloomfield, 'It's Sooner Than You Think, or Where Are We in the History of Rock Music?', *New Left Review,* 190 (November/ December, 1991): 70).

As to what constitutes postmodernist music, Bloomfield is a bit more chary. In answering the question 'what is the postpunk world of popular music like?' he points out two often-cited defining characteristics: that rock music in the 1980s:

1. 'endlessly plagiarizes and recycles 1960s styles in a (doomed) attempt to rekindle their original legitimacy – in Jameson's terms the transmutation of modernist styles into postmodern codes', or a 'pastiche' of the grand individual styles of modernity;
2. 'has lost its youth-cultural (rebellious) meanings to take its place as one of a circle of signifiers no longer anchored in an "independent reality"' where pop music becomes embroiled in an endless chain of 'autoreferentiality'. ('Sooner', p. 71)

However, Bloomfield clearly demonstrates that these so-called postmodern definitions of post-punk music ignore the fact that bands who utilise pastiche (like Blondie or the Primitives) do not intend a satiric criticism of past styles. Furthermore, he points out that auto-referentiality (referring back to the lyrics or styles of earlier bands in a parodic or ironic way) need not inherently blunt the critical edge of a band's politics. Consequently, Bloomfield is less interested in isolating whether a band is 'postmodern' or not, and more concerned with whether certain musical cultural practices resist commodification, and therefore occupy a culturally progressive site in late capitalism. He goes on to analyse 'indie' record labels, rave culture, acid house, sampling, rap, hip-hop and house styles, citing the new modes of contemporary resistance to commodification in dance music which takes place in clubs.

Cornel West has suggested that it is precisely in music styles like rap that a black postmodernism is evident. Interviewed on the subject of what constitutes a postmodern black popular culture, he responds that in rap 'a tremendous *articulateness* is syncopated with the African drumbeat, the African funk, into an American postmodernist product: there is no subject expressing originary anguish here but a fragmented subject, pulling from past and present, innovatively producing a heterogeneous product' (West, 'Interview', in Andrew Ross (ed.), *Universal Abandon? The Politics of Postmodernism* (Minneapolis, University of Minnesota Press, 1988), pp. 280–1). Arguing that 'postmodernism ought never to be viewed as a homogeneous phenomenon, but rather as one in which political contestation is central' ('Interview', p. 276), West regards rap as 'a mode of resistance' to the dominance of white racial stereotypes, a fight for representation and recognition in the multivalent and complex postmodern world. It is worth noting though, that rap is a mode of repression as well, with some very sexist and antisemitic tendencies on occasions.

On the face of it, then, pop music in recent years has demonstrated all the characteristics one might associate with postmodernism: a triumph of style over substance, a breakdown of the distinction between high and low culture, a series of eclectic mixings and ironic 'thefts' of past music, and an interrogation of the notions of authenticity and creativity. One even has 'the death of the author' in Prince's high levels of irony in his new name, AFKAP – 'The Artist Formerly Known As Prince'. This 'decentring' of the artist is evident in the increasing trend towards singles being made off the back of advertisements, films, soaps, videos, i.e. singles are no longer being driven by the music alone. However, the influential theorist of popular music Andrew Goodwin has remained highly sceptical about the value of claims that recent music has become postmodern. He has acknowledged that technological developments (such as drum machines and digital music computers) have brought about 'sampling' and sequencing, which have eroded the divisions between originals and copies, and between human and machine performed music. Authenticity and creativity appear to have been placed in crisis by this music, not just because of 'theft', but because of the automated nature of their mechanisms (Goodwin, 'Sample and Hold: Pop Music in the Digital Age of Reproduction', *Critical Quarterly*, 30:3 (Autumn 1988): 37–8). As Goodwin points out, a group like M/A/R/R/S can produce a massive success with 'Pump Up The Volume' at the end of the 1980s, a record which is compiled from about 30 other records. Yet he wants to demonstrate that despite these apparently postmodern characteristics, recent pop music is still linked to earlier preoccupations. For example, the success of Britpop's sound is its 'modernist' yearning (consider the nostalgic and evocative string introduction to Verve's 'Urban Symphony' and Oasis' Beatles sound).

The postmodern critique of creativity and authenticity is undercut by the musicians' and producers' own explanations of their techniques of 'sampling' or plundering other records, since they still seem to work with fairly traditional notions of authenticity and creativity; while the selectivity and plundering, rather than being a pastiche which denies pop history, instead *recuperates* it. Goodwin suggests that 'the self-conscious hype [of this music] is doomed precisely because its postmodern premises (audiences aren't interested in truth or creativity any longer) defy pop's romantic aesthetic' (Goodwin, 'Sample', pp. 34–49). Goodwin cites the Pet Shop Boys as an instance of a group who defy the discourse of authenticity, but only by invoking it through claiming authorship of their own image and acting as the source of their own 'truth' (although this 'truth' is itself a representation of either a pop group, or two camp aesthetes, or their show sets). Furthermore, Goodwin argues that modern technology does not replace the 'live' concert but allows for a simulation of 'real', 'live' performances, thus perpetuating the celebration of pop 'aura'. Although groups like Frankie Goes To Hollywood, New Order and Depêche Mode engage in an explicit celebration of playfulness as a self-conscious exposure of their own craft, this is not inherently indicative of an abandonment of the metanarrative of originality and cult hero-worship.

STOP and THINK

General

• Since pop music emerges alongside the emergence of postmodernism in the 1950s, does this make all pop music postmodern? Rather than a simple linear historical model of the development of pop music, what other structural models might help to escape an either/or description of pop music (either modernist *or* postmodernist)? For example, consider Williams' dominant/residual/emergent model of culture in his widely anthologised essay 'Base and Superstructure in Marxist Cultural Theory' (in *Problems in Materialism and Culture* (London, Verso, 1980), pp. 31–49). This model tries to account for the fact that cultural practices emerge in parallel with one another, often challenging each other's cultural dominance.

- Popular culture is a product: yet in its turn, this pop commodity also produces the pop viewer and its public. How does one introduce resistance into this culture industry? Can mere interruption or disturbance act as a resistant feature, in the hope that it will engender critical self-reflection?

- Given the centrality of 'authenticity' to debates in popular culture, how useful are Baudrillardian concepts of simulation, artifice and the simulacrum for establishing an understanding of alternative practices and politics of popular culture?

- Do you agree with the sanguine attitude of critics like McRobbie and Grossberg that there are new possibilities for agency and the formation of identity in popular culture; or do you take the more pessimistic Baudrillardian view that popular culture merely offers arbitrary signs and manipulates identity?

- To what extent is the element of nostalgia in postmodern pop music due to the ageing of the market for popular music?

Specific

- Contrary to the image of corporate power and industrial organisation in the record business, it would appear that companies are often unable to predict the consequences of their musical releases into the charts or the dance clubs. This might suggest that any straightforward categorisation of popular music into 'marginal' (or 'alternative') and 'mainstream' is not always as easy or as profitable as it may seem. Consider the different ways in which the distribution and reception of music might cut across such simple distinctions between incorporated and resistant popular music. Think of the history of Abba: from being winners of the Eurovision Song Contest in 1976, they had huge success during the 1970s and 1980s as a popular band with many number one chart hits, to be returned to success in the 1990s on the back of the Australian film *Muriel's Wedding* (1994), as part of a wave of nostalgia for the disco music of the 1970s. Indeed, a hit like 'Dancing Queen' had already become ironised in gay clubs, where the song was a regular number. How does one explain the factors involved in this trajectory? Is Abba now a 'postmodern' group, where they were once examples of pop modernism? What does this suggest about the nature of production and consumption in relation to postmodern popular culture? What does make for a radical politics in popular music? Consider the explicitly political lyrics and self-consciously cultivated anti-authority stance of rap groups like Niggers With Attitude and Ice-T: are these in themselves enough to give a popular music group a radical politics? When it comes to other forms, like acid house, what do the characteristic, repetitive, erotic 'talk-overs' suggest about the representation of gender?

Key characteristics of postmodern pop music

1. The techniques of 'sampling', 'theft' and appropriation of other records constitute some form of satirical or self-reflexive pastiche of past styles.
2. Techniques of 'sampling', 'rap' and 'sequencing' introduce the critique of authenticity and creativity.
3. These postmodern features are themselves part of a technology which simulates 'real', 'live' music.
4. A popular culture is characterised by a 'new materialism', an aesthetics of transitory and tactile reception. In its sensitivity to what is local, partial and temporary, it is also an aesthetics of immediate participation and expendable criteria.

Postmodern pop music: some examples

This discussion of examples of postmodern music is heavily indebted to Hebdige's brilliant analysis of the video by Talking Heads entitled *The Road to Nowhere* (1984) in his book *Hiding in the Light*. David Byrne, the lead singer and prime mover of the band, has developed a reputation for highly self-conscious, technically virtuoso innovation in the field of popular music. Drawing upon an eclectic range of material – visual and aural – to create a pastiche or 'house style', Talking Heads sought to push at the boundaries of what constituted definitions of rock/pop/art/performance/video in the mid-1970s. *The Road to Nowhere* mocks and satirises categories of 'popular' and 'serious' cultural forms, and is thus a song from a self-consciously postmodern group. As Hebdige points out, Byrne continually exploits a postmodern sensibility, as is evident in his fascination with the play of signification, representational and generic codes. The group's songs constantly invoke issues of simulation, substitution, impostors, mimicry and copies, raising to a high degree the blurring of levels, categories, signs and identities which characterises postmodern discourse. In particular, Hebdige describes *The Road to Nowhere* as a video which proffers a diffusion of modernist art styles, allusions to films like *Citizen Kane* (1941), and motifs from American iconography like the 'open road' and road movies. Describing the video as a 'writhing chain of signifiers', Hebdige argues that the deconstructions and alienations created in it are jokes rather than didactic points, and it is this ironic humour which makes the song postmodernist rather than modernist.

'Experimental' music: well-tempered music and bad-tempered debate

Given that one of the principal assaults of postmodernism is on the false dichotomy of high and low culture, it is something of an anomaly to refer to 'experimental' or 'serious art' music in contradistinction to 'pop' music. Nevertheless, this distinction has been propagated by many theorists who seek to distinguish between the avant-garde modernists and the 'experimentalist' postmodernists. There is a considerable body of music which is regarded as 'postmodern' within the 'serious art' music category, although the term itself is not often used. Postmodernism within contemporary music is not a particularly live issue. In fact, if anything, it is positively reviled by most contemporary composers: mention the 'P' word in their company and you will not see them for dust! However, given the characteristics that certain composers and music demonstrate, it is possible to chart the topography of 'postmodern' music. The formal and aesthetic features are evident, even if an explicit ideological affiliation is not. Of the composers whose work has been occasionally described as postmodern, the most prominent are the Minimalists (see below), while others are John Cage, Robert Ashley, Luciano Berio, Pauline Oliveros, William Bolcom, Richard Pinhas, Louis Andriessen and Henri Pousseur, as well as some of those whose work has been produced at IRCAM (Institut de Récherche et Coordination Acoustique/Musique) in Paris, although these composers are not always related to postmodernism in the same ways.

In much the same way that postmodernism in the visual art world grew out of the aesthetic and ideological challenge to a Greenbergian modernism (see the discussion in Chapter 5 about modernist visual art), so the challenge to modernism in music was a confrontation with serialism in the late 1960s. Serialism in music grew out of the collapse of tonal music with the atonality of 1900–10, and was the product of the Second Viennese School of the 1920s – Arnold Schoenberg, Alban Berg and Anton Webern. Serialism focused tightly on the organisation of pitch, and might well be compared with Abstract Expressionism in visual art – where a highly rationalist and structuralist aesthetic which aspired to a pure, universal language of sound was developed. Serialism prescribed an aesthetic completely antithetical to tonality, which also amounted to an assertion of total disdain for popular music, based as the latter is on a tonal system geared to harmony and melody. The popular remained 'other' to serial musical modernism. Serialism gradually became the dominant aesthetic of musical modernism, and was championed with great power by Adorno.

However, although dominant, serialism was not the only 'high' musical tendency in the early 1920s and 1930s. The musical avant-garde remained far from unitary, and serialism was shadowed by two competing musical dispositions:

1. the neo-classicism of composers like Igor Stravinsky and Paul Hindemith, who sought to reinvigorate the present with the principles of eighteenth- and nineteenth-century music;
2. the more populist or folk-oriented composers like Aaron Copland, Claude Debussy, Francis Poulenc, Darius Milhaud,

George Gershwin, Bela Bartok and Ralph Vaughan Williams,
who appropriated styles from jazz, folk and popular idioms.

Nevertheless, serial modernism gained great impetus after the
Second World War, and with increased intensification, it became the
ideological gathering point of the postwar European avant-garde,
with its leading exponents Pierre Boulez and Karlheinz Stockhausen, and in the United States, Milton Babbitt. This led to what
is called 'total' or 'integrated' serialism, in which the discourse of
rationalism, determinism and control stretched not only to pitch,
but to all aspects of composition: rhythm, dynamics, timbre, etc.
Furthermore, it increasingly became involved with science, acous-
tics and the physics of music, which scienticised the conceptual
basis of composition with a new mathematical rigour.

Typical of this clarion call for a scientific groundwork to music
was the leading serial theorist Babbitt's article 'Who Cares If You
Listen?' (1958). Owing to the perceived public indifference to and
intellectual misunderstanding of serial music, Babbitt argued for a
more protected academic environment for the composers and their
music. His discourse stresses the rationalistic and scientific basis of
the music, in which there is an increased 'efficiency' of communication and 'increased accuracy' of the transmission of music from
performer to listener, and where a higher degree of 'determinacy'
and autonomy in the music has resulted in 'greater efficiency, economy and understanding'. Furthermore, with advances in technology,
music was increasingly becoming 'research' into the parameters of
physical sounds, carried out with sophisticated technological apparatus and often only feasible in highly equipped scientific institutions.
This scientific, rationalistic, determinist, formalist and theoretical
discourse greatly aided the legitimisation of serialism within academic institutions and universities, as it gradually became established
as the dominant modernist musical aesthetic ideology. The peak of
this technological 'total serialism', which amalgamated serialism
with science and electronics, was perhaps most clearly reached in
Stockhausen's desire to produce a systematic repertoire of artifi-
cially generated timbres, analytically ordered and suited to serial
manipulation.

Whilst 'total serialism' was busy absolutising and purifying itself
and deriding its opponents with some vitriolic condemnation,

a strong opposition to its aesthetic tenets gradually developed. Henri Pousseur, a Belgian composer, sums up much of this in his radical critique of serialism in 1966:

> Serial music is often thought of as the fruit of excessive speculation and the result of an exclusive mustering of the powers of reason. Everything that occurs within is constructed according to pre-established quantities and is justified by the rules of a strictly combinatorial logic. Except for the rules and quantities themselves, nothing seems to have been left within the realms of free invention, to gratuitous inspiration or to a more subjective intuition. In short, a pitiless regimentation would seem to rule over this music, controlling the course of events even in their most intimate details ... Precisely where the most abstract constructions have been applied, it is not seldom that one has the impression of finding oneself in the presence of the consequences of an aleatory free play. (Henri Pousseur and David Behrman, 'The Question of Order in New Music', *Perspectives of New Music*, 5:1 (1966): 93–111)

One of serialism's main postwar alternatives sprang from the experimentalism of the American John Cage. With other American composers like Morton Feldman, Christian Wolff, Earle Brown and Cornelius Cardew, Cage sought to liberate the parameters of sound from the hypercontrol of serialism by introducing chance and indeterminate procedures. In an article describing this movement as a 'New Simplicity', the British composer Michael Nyman has argued that in Cage's music, 'the radical concept is, of course, that of *unfixing relationships*, since all Post-Renaissance music has been concerned with fixing with increasing exactitude the relationships between sounds' (Nyman, 'Against Intellectual Complexity in Music', in Thomas Docherty (ed.), *Postmodernism: A Reader* (Brighton, Harvester Wheatsheaf, 1993), p. 210). These composers also turned to anti-rationalist cosmologies (Cage and his penchant for Zen and eastern mysticism), while others turned to other alternative belief systems such as Maoism. Most of their music broke away from the highly annotated and complex scores of the serialists, often presenting only the briefest of notes to give the maximum interpretative room for manoeuvre during the performance.

Against the pitch of serialism, Cage proposed time as central to music and sound; and against the linearity of duration and the mathematically quantifiable, these composers argued for non-cumulative, non-directional, static music, in which rhythm was cyclical, repetitive and, importantly, *processual*. In rebellion against the teleological drive of classical serialist forms, Cage wanted a 'purposeless music'. This is perhaps best illustrated in his now infamous piece, *4′ 33″* (1952). The published score shows sections I, II, III all *'tacet'* – the player plays nothing in all three timed sections. The piece reinvents the performer as listener and observer, and reinvests the listener with an active/creative (rather than passive) role. Rather than being simply a huge practical joke at the expense of the audience, *4′ 33″* demonstrates that silence is non-existent, since there is a whole series of non-intentional sounds which permanently surround us; that they are worth attention, and that these 'environmental' sounds are just as aesthetically useful as the sounds produced by the world's musical structures. Hence, rather than a negation of music, *4′ 33″* turns out to be an avowal of its universality.

In addition to these challenges, the music of these composers frequently made reference to non-western forms and popular music, and in a throwback to some of the early forefathers of modernist music like the American Charles Ives, and the Frenchmen Eric Satie and Debussy, they treated other styles of music with pastiche, parody and musical montage, all anathema to serial modernists. Furthermore, many of these 'experimental' composers were influenced by ritual and the participatory nature of non-western music, and they were much concerned with social and live performance. As Nyman's book *Experimental Music: Cage and Beyond* (London, Studio Vista, 1974; reprint Cambridge, Cambridge University Press, 1999) seeks to explain, this opened the way for their insistent critique of the composer's traditionally authoritative role in western music, as well as their desire to erase the hierarchical musical segregation of labour between the composer as creative authority, the performer as constrained interpreter, and the listener as passive receiver. Nyman suggests too that these 'experimental' musicians, although also committed to research into sound, combated the high-tech of the serialists with low-tech research, experimenting with small, flexible and portable technologies like valve radios, microphones, home-made circuitry, and water pipettes. Even the act of composing has been ideologically overthrown; since as Nyman points out, 'sitting down to compose' is a metaphor drawn from traditional composition, which has little to do with experimental music, where the traditional idea of the 'craft of musical composition' is bypassed (Nyman, 'Against', p. 213 n. 4).

One further aspect of this 'postmodern' reaction to serialism is a certain demasculinisation of music from the male hegemony of serial modernism. In a sphere where notoriously few women composers have achieved international reputations, there has been a loosening of 'experimental' music as the preserve of 'male rigour', with a marked increase in women composers like Judith Weir, Pauline Oliveros, Kajia Saariaho and Elaine Barkin achieving serious attention. Although not necessarily composing in a 'postmodern' fashion, these women have benefited from the postmodern crisis of representation when it comes to sexuality and music. However, this is not to say that the bastion of male conservatism in music has been breached and that the walls are falling all around us. The domain of 'experimental' music composition still remains predominantly masculine, as opposed to the realms of popular and folk music, where there is a great deal more gender equality.

Minimalism developed out of the Cagean reaction to total serialism in the early 1970s. Minimalism (also known as 'process music') marked a restoration of tonality, but in distinction to the harmony of the past four centuries, this was a cyclical rather than hierarchical tonality. Whereas western tonality had organised relationships of tones with reference to a definite centre, the 'tonic' and a set of closely related keys, now tone was organised according to structures of repetition and gradual change effected within 'ostinato textures', or a set of repeated patterns. Consequently, there is no sense of completion and closure in much of the Minimalists' music: it just stops. Often incorporating crossovers with rock and pop forms, including musical influences from other countries like Ghana, Indonesia and Bali, the 'impurity' and pluralism of this music has incited one critic to castigate it as 'pop music for intellectuals'. Despite these features, the leading exponents, such as the Americans John Adams, Philip Glass, Terry Riley, Steve Reich and La Monte Young, and in Britain, Gavin Bryars and Nyman, explicitly disavow any connection with postmodernism. Nevertheless, Nyman's description of the so-called 'New Simplicity' (an ideological rejection of

the 'complexity' of total serial modernism), describes many of the
characteristics which one might consider postmodernist:

> Perhaps the reaction of experimental composers to the so-called
> intellectual complexity of *avant-garde* music is a reaction not against
> intellectual complexity itself, but against what brings about the need
> for such complexity, as well as its audible result. We should perhaps
> speak of the qualities that serial music denied and which have resur-
> faced in experimental music; symmetrical rhythms (i.e. regular beat);
> euphony; consonant, diatonic, or modal materials; absence of theat-
> ricality and grandiloquence, of drama, of sound used as symbol.
> (Nyman, 'Against', pp. 211–12)

This explicitly acknowledges the reintroduction of ornamentation
and spectacle to music, after a period where music was 'rationalised'
by the modernist interest in atonal and serial composition: a renewed
interest in style, rather than simply an efficient, scientific and
abstract exercise. Like the architectural postmodernist reaction to
the rationalised and objective approach to building in modernism,
so the 'postmodern', 'experimental' music described by Nyman is
concerned with reintroducing elaboration, ornament and decoration. Commenting specifically on the musical strategies of Reich's
Minimalism, Nyman argues that the music 'still retains the basic
non-traditional characteristics shared by all experimental music;
that of stasis and a non-directional, non-dramatic, non-dynamic
approach to musical structure; there are no hierarchies, no transitions, no tension, no relaxation, and change is quantitative rather
than qualitative' (Nyman, 'Against', p. 212). In his own manifesto
for 'process music', entitled 'Music as a Gradual Process', Steve
Reich argues that music must remove the composing self, either as
'expressive player' (process music removes the need for improvisation) or as controlling composer:

> While performing and listening to gradual musical processes one can
> participate in a particular liberating and impersonal kind of ritual.
> Focusing in on the musical process makes possible that shift of atten-
> tion away from *he* and *she* and *you* and *me* outwards to *it*. (Reich,
> 'Music as a Gradual Process' (1968), in *Writings About Music* (New
> York, New York University Press, 1974), p. 11)

However, despite their popular appeal and their relative success
as composers of contemporary music, not all postmodern music

emerges from the Minimalist composers. Even some one-time seri-alists have turned their music to more eclectic and parodic forms. The Italian composer Luciano Berio, often considered one of the leading postwar composers, has produced a number of pieces of music which have been regarded as postmodern in their use of musi-cal pastiche. One frequently cited example is his *Sinfonia*, scored for orchestra, singers and speakers. Combining musical allusions to Gustav Mahler's Second Symphony (*The Resurrection*) (1894), as well as to Bach, Debussy, Strauss, Schoenberg, Boulez and others, with readings from passages of James Joyce, Samuel Beckett, Claude Levi-Strauss and others, the first performance was given by the popular a cappella group, the Swingle Singers. Michael Chanan has considered this piece an archetypal instance of postmodern music:

> Whatever Berio is trying to do here, there is no attempt at congruity: the movement hangs together only by its statement about the non-synchronicity, the contrast 'between the time when the symphonic form was strained by the breakup of the familiar narratives, and the contemporary moment when formal coherence is abandoned'. The music of Mahler here tells us that there is *no* resurrection of the past, which recedes as the noise of the everyday gains ground. Berio reminds us 'of discontinuous time and space, where the old distinc-tions between speech and poetry disappear, where narratives lose their endings as well as their origins' . . . In short, where the past is present but impossible, while the present is ungraspable except as an anarchy of conflicting utterances. (Chanan, *Musica Practica: The Social Practice of Western Music from Gregorian Chant to Postmodern-ism* (London, Verso, 1994), p. 277)

Elsewhere in the United States, composers like William Bolcom, John Corigliano and Michael Daugherty have asserted a cross-fertilisation between traditional and vernacular repertoires. Bolcom's music in particular makes extensive use of parodic allusion. This elimination of traditional musical boundaries through musical crossovers, now extends into a whole gamut of different musical spheres: Philip Glass' *Low Symphony* is based on themes from David Bowie's 'Low'; Paul McCartney, composer of 'I Want to Hold your Hand', made news headlines for his *Liverpool Oratorio*; while Henryk Górecki's Third Symphony, or 'Symphony of Sorrowful Songs', achieved an astonishing climb up the British pop charts in 1993.

In recent decades in Britain, the debate about 'postmodernism' in music appears to have shifted to the context of the debate over 'complexity' and 'simplicity' in music. An uncompromising musical complexity marks the work of Brian Ferneyhough, as well as others like Michael Finnissy, Chris Dench and Roger Redgate, the last having composed several pieces in the 1980s inspired by the post-structuralist philosophy of Jacques Derrida, like *Eidos* for piano, *mais en étoile* for ensemble, and *Eperons* for oboe and percussion. In reaction to this complexity, the postmodernists have established a wide-ranging eclecticism: composers like Robin Holloway, Dominic Muldowney, James MacMillan, Steve Martland (who worked with the Loose Tubes jazz orchestra), Mark-Anthony Turnage and Martin Butler all demonstrate an interest in crossovers with jazz, pop and Minimalism, as well as extensive allusions to other earlier composers' work, and in the case of Holloway, even recomposing them.

Whereas minimalism was once considered to be the model for postmodernism in music, the picture is beginning to change in the new millennium, with new musical tendencies developing some of the recognisable postmodern concerns. As Judy Lochhead and Joseph Auner put it, postmodernism trickled into music with little debate about how the term might apply (see Judy Lochhead and Joseph Auner (eds), *Postmodern Music/Postmodern Thought* (New York, Routledge, 2002)). One key development is 'postminimalism', which surfaced in the late 1970s, reaching maturity in the 1980s and 1990s. According to the influential composer-critic Kyle Gann, postminimalist music 'tends to be tonal, mostly consonant (or at least never tensely dissonant), and based on a steady pulse. The music rarely strays from conventional musical sounds, although many of the composers use synthesizers. Postminimalist composers tend to work in shorter forms than the minimalists, 15 minutes rather than 75 or 120, and with more frequent textural variety' (Kyle Gann, 'Minimal Music, Maximal Impact', *New Music Box: The Web Magazine from the American Music Center* (http://www.newmusicbox.org/index.nmbx, 2001). Gann's excellent web-articles detail the history of minimalism and postminimal developments, and he regards the first piece of postminimalist music to be William Duckworth's *The Time Curve Preludes* (1977–78), twenty-four short pieces for piano. This piece established a number of precedents and

typical characteristics for the style called postminimalism: a continued utilisation of minimalism's regular beat and diatonic tonality,
but demonstrating an inclusiveness bringing together ideas from a
daunting array of musical sources. In addition to Duckworth's
Southern Harmony (1980–81), a choral cycle based on shaped-note
hymns and his *Imaginary Dances* (1985/88) for piano, other key
influential figures and works include Jonathan Kramer's *Moments
In and Out of Time* (1981–83); Elodie Lauten, who greatly freed up
the rhythmic limitations of minimalism in her Concerto for Piano
and Orchestral Memory (1984), and her postminimalist opera, *The
Death of Don Juan* (1987); and Paul Epstein, who has used many
algorithmic systems in a postminimalist context, such as in *Chamber
Music: Three Songs from Home* (1991). By the 1990s, the postmini-
malists had achieved a repertoire of enthralling music markedly
dissimilar to the minimalists' *oeuvre*. In addition to his own music,
Gann cites a range of young American composers whose works
might be regarded as postminimalist, including such notable pieces
as Janice Giteck's *Om Shanti* (1986), a Sanskrit-language prayer
for AIDS patients buried in Balinese textures; Daniel Lentz's
Apologetica (1992–95), his hour-long homage to native peoples;
Elodie Lauten's *Tronik Involutions* for overdubbed synthesiser
(1993); pieces by Beth Anderson, like her Piano Concerto and *Rose-
mary Swale*, although she is principally known for her text-sound
works, in which voices speak words, phrases and phonemes to create
a sort of rhythmic, percussive music, where the literal meanings of
words are incidental; Paul Dresher's *Double Ikat* for trio (1988–90);
Mary Jane Leach's *Mountain Echoes* (1987) and other sensitive
works for women's chorus; Stephen Scott's *Minerva's Web* (1985),
known for a technique he developed where he 'bowed' the strings of
the piano, creating long sustained tones rather than the generally
percussive tones associated with that instrument; Mary Ellen
Childs's *Carte Blanche* for ensemble (1991); David Borden's mam-
moth cycle *The Continuing Story of Counterpoint* (1976–87); Guy
Klucevsek's gentle *Viavy Rose Variations* (1989) based on melodies
from Madagascar.

For all its divergences from minimalism, this postminimalist tendency still demonstrates many of the list of 'traits' of postmodern
music usefully compiled by the late Jonathan Kramer, outlined in

his stimulating essay 'The Nature and Origins of Musical Postmodernism'. For Kramer, postmodern music

1. is not simply a repudiation of modernism or its continuation, but has aspects of both a break and an extension;
2. is, on some level and in some way, ironic;
3. does not respect boundaries between sonorities and procedures of the past and of the present;
4. challenges barriers between 'high' and 'low' styles;
5. shows disdain for the often unquestioned value of structural unity;
6. questions the mutual exclusivity of elitist and populist values;
7. avoids totalising forms (e.g., does not want entire pieces to be tonal or serial or cast in a prescribed formal mould);
8. considers music not as autonomous but as relevant to cultural, social, and political contexts;
9. includes quotations of or references to music of many traditions and cultures;
10. considers technology not only as a way to preserve and transmit music but also as deeply implicated in the production and essence of music;
11. embraces contradiction;
12. distrusts binary oppositions;
13. includes fragmentations and discontinuities;
14. encompasses pluralism and eclecticism;
15. presents multiple meanings and multiple temporalities;
16. locates meaning and even structure in listeners, more than in scores, performances, or composers. (Kramer, in Judy Lochhead and Joseph Auner (eds), *Postmodern Music/Postmodern Thought* (New York, Routledge, 2002), pp. 16–17)

Since postmodern music is not a neat category with rigid boundaries, Kramer adds the caveat that these traits should not be used as a checklist to help identify a given composition as postmodern or not. We are further urged to consider the continuing vibrancy of surrealist aesthetics in contemporary music by Anne LeBaron (*Postmodern Music/Postmodern Thought*, pp. 27–73), who argues that on this basis, studies of postmodern music should not exclude musicians experimenting on the borders between 'jazz', 'rock' and 'serious music'. Such musicians include the likes of John Zorn, with his smorgasbord of selections in *Cobra* (1984–85), or the 'plunderphonics' (self-referential audio collage) of John Oswald in works like

Plexure (1993), or Beck and Björk, who have utilised postmodern concepts and techniques like layering, parodying, and heterogeneity in their music. Others have argued that postmodernism in music manifests itself as much in the marketing as the content of the music itself. The brief flash-in-the-pan of 'totalism' in the late 1990s (the term never caught on, but was associated with the blend of high and low music cultures in the music of Arthur Jarvinen, Mikel Rouse and Ben Neill), drawing on musical traditions from classical music, pop, rock and world music, was indicative of this feature in postmodern music for its self-conscious publicity and marketing strategies.

STOP and THINK

- Despite the use of non-western forms and instruments in the music of 'experimentalist' composers, does a distance still remain between eastern and western musical practices? There is little use of commercial forms, and these composers' use of 'popular' music is often limited to folk, ethnic or non-western music. Does this suggest that there is still some residue of an idealised and untainted, non-commercial, authentic people's music, and a disdain for the aesthetics and sites of commercial popular music?
- Even when 'experimental' composers like Glass, Reich, Adams, Laurie Anderson and Nyman do make use of pop and rock music in an attempt to reach a wider audience, does their music still remain a form which is distinct aesthetically, ideologically and institutionally from commercial popular music?
- Glass's operas are performed at the New York Metropolitan Opera and at the English National Opera, and Nyman's music at the Institute for Contemporary Art and the Festival Hall in London: does this suggest that their pluralism of musical reference is based upon an antagonism to, rather than an exclusion from, the centres of high cultural legitimation?

Key characteristics of postmodern 'experimental' music

1. It combats the self as expressive agent in music, so that chance processes, non-determinism or indeterminism become main compositional principles.
2. There is a rejection of rational and scientist systems in favour of irrational, mystical or non-rational belief systems. Confronting the ordered hierarchy of a system of priorities and dualisms, a new equality is introduced where nothing is given priority over anything else.
3. In contradistinction to the complex and cerebral music of serialism, a physical, performative 'new simplicity' is espoused.
4. Instead of being highly notational and text-centred, it is practice-centred; for example, in the new reliance on 'environmental' sounds.
5. Against the linear, cumulative and teleological (see the discussion of this term in Chapter 1) direction of the serialists, the music was conceived of as cyclical, repetitive and static; for example, John Cage's tape collage, *Fontana Mix* (1958).

Postmodern music: an example

Since it is difficult to present a meaningful analysis of a piece of postmodern music here, I will instead focus upon a composer and what might be construed as the postmodern characteristics of his work. Philip Glass is an American composer, prominently associated with Minimalism, which commenced in the early 1970s. Glass's music might be construed as postmodern owing to several factors: its subversion of the dominant Eurocentric classical and modernist logics of musical tonality and rhythm; its attempt to conceive of the musical work as process rather than as object; Glass's resistance to inscribing a recognisable narrative and teleological progression in the music; and the concomitant disruption and disorientation in a music which lulls the listener into the false comfort of repetition, as Glass constantly reconfigures the composer–listener relationship.

Born in Baltimore in 1937, Glass was educated variously at the Peabody Conservatory, Baltimore (1949–52), the University of Chicago (1952–56), and the Juilliard School of Music, New York (1959–61), before going to Paris to study with Nadia Boulanger

(1963–65). While in Paris, he worked with the Indian sitar player Ravi Shankar and the tabla player Allah Rakha, from whom he learned several important lessons about musical rhythm and measure. Out of this, Glass developed a small-scale '*ostinato*' technique. An '*ostinato*' refers to a persistent musical figure which is repeated throughout a composition. Yet as Glass's work has moved into bigger spheres, he has expanded the method in order to cover larger musical structures. His solution has been to return to Baroque large-scale forms, like the *chaconne* or *passacaglia*, forms of continuous variation, with distinct melodies over a repeating eight- or sixteen-bar bass. Influenced by the minimalist experimentation of Cage, Glass's music typically first constructs a melodic unit which is then altered and extended very gradually over a period of time. Simple patterns emerge which change minutely and constantly, combining the two principal features of his composition technique, which he has defined as 'additive process' and 'cyclic process'. Additive process takes a simple measure of notes and then expands or contracts it, allowing it to manifest a different rhythmical shape while maintaining the same melodic configuration. Cyclic process refers to a 'wheels within wheels' concept of composition, where different musical phrases join each other after separate but similar trajectories.

Many of Glass's early works demonstrate an interest in conceptual performance, such as *Strung Out* (1967) for solo violin, the violinist following the music laid out in a long line around the room; or *Pieces in the Shape of a Square* (1967) for two flutes, where the music is placed in the shape of a square and flautists perform it going in alternate directions. He formed the Philip Glass Ensemble in 1968, and this group became the medium for his avant-garde performances in galleries and performance spaces in the late 1960s and early 1970s. A large number of chamber and instrumental pieces were written, including *How Now* (1968), *Music in Contrary Motions* (1969), *Music in Fifths* (1969), *Music in Twelve Parts* (1971–74), *Façades* (1981) and *Glassworks* (1981). His other works include numerous orchestral pieces like *Company* (1983) and *The Light* (1987); a large number of choral and vocal pieces like *Itaipu* (1988) and *Hydrogen Jukebox* (1990); soundtracks for films like Reggio's *Koyaanisqatsi* (1981) and *Mishima* (1985); various other incidental music for plays like Beckett's *Mercier and Camier* (1979) and *End-game* (1984); and the opening and closing music to the Summer Olympics in Los Angeles in 1984. Glass has often collaborated with other artists such as Sol LeWitt, Robert Wilson and Richard Serra to produce innovative multimedia projects, and his association with Paul Simon, Suzanne Vega, David Byrne and Laurie Anderson resulted in the pop lyrics *Songs From Liquid Days* (1986).

Yet it is with his operas that this collaboration has been massively successful and popular. The subjects of Glass's operas have been imposingly large – science is presented in *Einstein on the Beach* (1975, with Robert Wilson), politics in *Satyagraha* (1980) (the early political struggles of Ghandi), and religion in *Akhnaten* (1983) (Egyptian theism) – while shorter works include *The Photographer* (1982) about the photographer Eadweard Muybridge; *The Juniper Tree* (1986); his collaboration with Doris Lessing on her science fiction text entitled *The Making of the Representative for Planet 8* (1987); an adaptation of Poe's *The Fall of the House of Usher* (1988); and his more recent works *1000 Airplanes on the Roof* (1988) and *The Voyage* (1992), a tricentennial celebration of Columbus's voyage to the United States, the opera triptych based on Jean Cocteau's works (1993–96), and the large grand scale opera *Waiting for the Barbarians* (2005), based upon the novel by J.M. Coetzee. Other developments within the past decade include the score for the fourth in the 'Qatsi' films by Godfrey Reggio, entitled *Naqoyqatsi* (2002), a Hopi phrase meaning 'Life at war'; a chamber opera entitled *The Sound of a Voice* (2003), the large cantata *The Passion of Ramakrishna* (2006), and *Appomattox* (2007) based on events in the American Civil War. He has also continued his work on highly acclaimed film scores, such as *Kundun* (1997), *The Truman Show* (1998), *The Hours* (2002), *The Illusionist* (2006) and *Notes on a Scandal* (2006). Argu-ably he has developed a more lyrical and romantic style in recent years, evident in several of his recent symphonies, but particularly in the widely praised *Études for Piano* (1994–95) written for his long-standing friend, the conductor Dennis Russell Davies, where a clear classical, post-minimalist development can be found. Glass's music attains length not through the classical musical patterns of evolution and development of material, but through repetition. The operas are all set pieces (arias, choruses, interludes, etc.) but without recognisable melodic or harmonic change. Called 'mesmeric' and 'mystic', Glass's music is perceived by some to be too static and rudimentary, although these qualities appear necessary to the Minimalist who wishes to direct his music towards a public which seeks withdrawal from the world.

Glass has insisted that the best music is conceived of in 'world terms', and he has always embraced a wide variety of musical styles, from popular music through to non-western influences; and if postmodernism is measured by some as a breaking down of the barriers between popular and art cultures, then he has written for a wide variety of purposes, ranging from advertisements for Cutty Sark Whiskey, performances in rock clubs, and an appearance at the Kool Jazz Festival (1984). Indeed, his huge popular appeal owes much to the fact that his music keeps open the bridges between pop and classical audiences. His music is closer to rock, his operas exhibit open tunefulness, and the transformations of his original motifs are easily perceived. It also uses the developments of music in other cultural spheres, like eastern tonal principles, the use of the sitar and tabla with Shankar and Rakha, and Balinese gamelan music. With this musical intertextuality, Glass and Reich have put western listeners in touch with large parts of music from other cultures which the West would otherwise have made little attempt to explore or understand. However, unlike La Monte Young and Terry Riley, Glass's introduction of eastern influence in his music is not connected to mysticism. Despite the potential his music offers for escape, its power lies in its affirmation of clear structures and a rigorously planned consideration that his music 'is not characterised by argument and development. It has disposed of traditional concepts that were closely linked to real time, to clock-time. Music is not a literal interpretation of real life and the experience of time is different. It does not deal with events in a clear directional structure. In fact there is no structure at all' (Philip Glass (ed.) and supp. Robert T. Jones, *Music by Philip Glass* (New York and London, Harper and Row, 1987), p. 22). Furthermore, he adds that 'Music no longer has a meditative function, referring to something outside itself, but rather embodies itself without any mediation. The listener will therefore need a different approach to listening, without the traditional concepts of recollection and anticipation. Music must be listened to as pure sound-event, an act without any dramatic structure' (*Music by Philip Glass*, p. 23). In postmodern style, Glass conceives of his music as having abandoned teleological elements, being left with mere duration and stasis, in a concentration of perception and physical being on the immediate moment and thus on particularity of place. Conventional ideas of music as a totality therefore become invalid, as the music becomes a perpetually self-reflexive process which constantly generates its own shifting structure.

Selected reading

Attali, Jacques, *Noise: The Political Economy of Music* (Manchester, Manchester University Press, 1985).
  Considers the shifting boundaries of 'noise' and 'music' and offers a reading of contemporary music which utilises many of the concepts of contemporary theory.
Bernard, Jonathan W., 'Minimalism, Postminimalism, and the Resurgence of Tonality in Recent American Music', *American Music*, 21:1 (Spring 2003): 112–33.
Cox, Christoph and Daniel Warner (eds), *Audio Culture: Readings in Modern Music* (London, Continuum, 2004).
  Through writings by philosophers, cultural theorists, and composers, the book explores the interconnections among such forms as minimalism, indeterminacy, *musique concrète*, free improvisation, experimental music, avant-rock, dub reggae, Ambient music, HipHop and Techno.
Fink, Robert, *Repeating Ourselves: American Minimal Music as Cultural Practice* (Berkeley, University of California Press, 2005).
Gann, Kyle, 'Minimal Music, Maximal Impact', *New Music Box: The Web Magazine from the American Music Center* (Internet. http://www.newmusicbox.org/index.nmbx, 2001).
Grossberg, Lawrence, *Dancing in Spite of Myself: Essays on Popular Culture* (Durham NC, Duke University Press, 1997) and *Bringing It All Back Home: Essays on Cultural Studies* (Durham NC, Duke University Press, 1997).
  These two volumes offer a vast array of debate about the conjunction of popular culture and postmodernism from one of the leading American theorists of popular culture. More advanced in content and argument.

Guilbert, Georges-Claude, *Madonna as Postmodern Myth* (Jefferson NC, McFarland, 2002).
Analyses Madonna's mythical status and her role in debates about contemporary sexuality, identity, religion and cult standing in the world of popular culture.

Hebdige, Dick, *Hiding in the Light: On Images and Things* (London, Routledge, 1988).
Probably one the principal works on postmodern popular culture, which contains excellent material and in-depth analyses.

Huq, Rupa, *Beyond Subculture: Pop, Youth and Identity in a Postcolonial World* (London, Routledge, 2006).
Investigates a series of musically-centred global youth cultures, including hip-hop, electronic dance music and bhangra, and presents case-studies and interviews with consumers and producers.

Kramer, Jonathan, 'Beyond Unity: Toward an Understanding of Musical Postmodernism', in Elizabeth W. Marvin and Richard Hermann (eds), *Concert Music, Rock, and Jazz since 1945: Essays and Analytical Studies* (Rochester NY, University of Rochester Press, 1995), pp. 11–33.

Kramer, Jonathan, 'The Nature and Origins of Musical Postmodernism', *Current Musicology*, 66 (1999): 7–20; Reprinted in Judy Lochhead and Joseph Auner (eds), *Postmodern Music/Postmodern Thought* (New York, Routledge, 2002).

Lochhead, Judy and Joseph Auner (eds), *Postmodern Music/Postmodern Thought* (New York and London, Garland, 2000).
Addresses itself to the question of what is postmodern music and how it differs from earlier styles, including modernist music; the roles that electronic technologies and sound production have played in defining postmodern music; how postmodern music has blurred the lines between high and popular music; and the appropriation and reworking of Western music by non-Western bands.

McRobbie, Angela, *Postmodernism and Popular Culture* (London, Routledge, 1994).
From a leading figure in postmodern popular cultural studies, this book contains a number of important essays on feminism, popular culture and postmodernism.

Mertens, Wim, *American Minimal Music* (London, Kahn and Averill, 1983).
A useful introduction to the work of the principal figures and ideology of musical Minimalism, La Monte Young, Philip Glass, Steve Reich and Terry Riley.

Nehring, Neil, *Popular Music, Gender, and Postmodernism* (London, Sage, 1997).

Rebuts the cynicism of academic postmodernism and music journalism, and argues for the political significance of the emotional performance of defiance in hip–hop and rock.

Nyman, Michael, 'Against Intellectual Complexity in Music', *October*, 13 (1980): 81–9; reprinted in Thomas Docherty (ed.), *Postmodernism: A Reader* (Brighton, Harvester Wheatsheaf, 1993).

A significant attempt to outline the debates concerning experimental music in a postmodern or contemporary context. Strongly recommended.

Strinati, Dominic, 'Postmodernism and Popular Culture', in John Storey (ed.), *Cultural Theory and Popular Culture: A Reader* (Brighton, Harvester Wheatsheaf, 1994), pp. 428–38.

An excellent introduction to the characteristics of postmodernism and their relation to a variety of cultural practices.

Whiteley, Sheila, Andy Bennett and Stan Hawkins (eds), *Music, Space and Place: Popular Music and Cultural Identity* (Aldershot, Ashgate, 2004).

Examines the urban and rural spaces in which music is experienced, produced and consumed, exploring how identity is constructed through the exchanges that occur between displaced peoples of the world's many diasporas.

Listed below are some of the sites on the internet which will give further information about the contemporary popular music scene:

- BPI: <http://www.bpi.co.uk/>
- Music Week: <http://www.dotmusic.com/MWhome.htm>
- Internet Music Resource Guide: <http://www.teleport.com/~celinec/mus_gurl.htm> This site gives access to numerous other sites.

7

Postmodernism, film, video and televisual culture

When Jean Baudrillard announced somewhat dramatically that 'The cinema and TV are America's reality!' (Baudrillard, *America* (London, Verso, 1988), p. 104), he was describing the extent to which late capitalist American society is dependent on televisual constructions for its sense of social and cultural identity. In the 'age of the image', it has frequently been remarked that television is *the* postmodern medium, since it keys into debates about representation, images and information in so many vital ways. In many ways, media culture has become virtually synonymous with 'the postmodern condition'.

The televisual media are closely associated with popular culture, and it will be evident from the previous chapter that there are many overlaps between the establishment of subcultures and their allegiance to styles, images or technologies derived from the televisual media, perhaps most noticeably 'cyberculture'. But punk, new wave, rap and other forms all feed into video and television, which in turn feed back into everyday life and social practices. Consequently, many of the discussions of television, music video and cyberculture in this chapter ought to be considered in relation to the issues about popular culture raised in Chapter 6.

Television: zipping and zapping

If there is any one single medium which exemplifies Fredric Jameson's thesis of the 'depthlessness' of postmodern culture, then it must be televisual cultures, of which television is the most dominant. However, if television is taken to be the archetypal cultural medium of postmodernity, as many people have commented, it is difficult to periodise this, for where and when was TV's modernity? What was TV modernism against which there has been a reaction? Some have sought to argue that TV becomes 'postmodern' with the advent of the new, conservative economic, social and ethical hegemonies in the late 1970s, whilst others have argued that TV has always been a 'proto-postmodern' medium.

Nevertheless, TV has always offered theorists of postmodernity a perfect playground for their apocalyptic messages of a doomed and illiterate culture resulting from the commodified inanities and puerilities of contemporary television programmes. Pessimism of this sort emerges from Baudrillard, a particularly influential figure within television studies, largely for the theories of the 'simulacrum' and the 'hyperreal' which were discussed in Chapter 2. As we saw, his concept of the 'simulacrum' refers to the fact that 'the ecstasy of communication' in the postmodern era has caused 'reality' and 'fiction' to coalesce (see Baudrillard, 'The Ecstasy of Communication', in Hal Foster (ed.), *Postmodern Culture* (London, Pluto Press, 1985), pp. 126–34). His concept of 'the ecstasy of communication' suggests that society has entered an information overload, and that the only powerful mode of resistance left to us lies in a rejection of the commodified images which invade our consciousnesses. According to Baudrillard in his essay 'The Masses: The Implosion of the Social in the Media' (in Mark Poster (ed.), *Jean Baudrillard: Selected Writings* (Cambridge, Polity Press, 1988), pp. 207–19), the televisual media are postmodern in their emblematic status owing to their 'implosion' of meaning. Meaning has 'imploded' because of our intensive exposure to the mass media. Hence, Baudrillard's infamous remark that 'the Gulf War did not take place'. In an article of the same name republished in the *Guardian*, 11 January 1991, his argument was that the war was so mediated through the images constructed by the media that one was not able to see the 'real' war. Instead one received a 'simulation' of the war, a war made with media condoms and the 'televisual subterfuge' suggested that what was really at stake was the very status of war itself, its representation, its meaning and its future. Christopher Norris produced a speedy polemical rebuttal of what he perceived to be the dangerous conclusion in the excesses of this Baudrillardian position. He pointed out that the logic of Baudrillard's argument meant that reality as a product of signs and discourses leaves one with no power to change the discourse: there can be no appeal to a higher truth, nor can one get outside the discourse itself. Norris argued that the Gulf War *did* exist, but that some accounts were mendacious whilst others were closer to the truth. Just because we live in a society where there are. competing media narratives or claims does not make us foolish dupes, nor does it mean that soldiers and civilians did not die. These two positions exemplify quite starkly the opposing sides involved in the debate about postmodernity: Baudrillard's position offers a reality which is wholly constructed by signs and images with no outside referent, and Norris's position argues that a knowledge of the real world which lies outside the discourses used to describe it is possible.

The apotheosis of postmodern TV must be the advertisement. Television commercials pull apart cultural signifiers of every kind and allow them to float around in a loose space, which Baudrillard calls hyperreality, where they attach themselves to commodities. As Judith Williamson demonstrates very clearly in her important study of advertising, *Decoding Advertisements* (London, Boyers, 1978), the very structures of advertisements themselves – the play of signifiers, the manipulation of history and the erasure of temporal differences to evoke nostalgia, the use of linguistic and visual puns, the arrangement of fragments, absences, substitutions and synecdoches (where a part is used to signify the whole) – suggest a postmodern medium. There has been a change in the strategy of advertisers over the years, moving from promoting the product directly to adverts which say less about the product and more about the cultural representations of the advertisement itself as opposed to its referential product. Advertisements frequently quote and allude to other ads, and emphasise style and surface as opposed to utilitarianism. Often these changes can be traced to shifts in social and cultural 'taste': where once it was acceptable to associate cigarettes with certain lifestyles (for example, the Marlboro association with the rugged, outdoor cowboy life), it has now been legally necessary for tobacco companies to advertise a commodity obliquely (and hence the award-winning campaigns by Benson and Hedges and Silk Cut, where the visual puns brilliantly indicated the absent

products). In any event, advertising in a variety of forms, but especially on the television, has become more attentive to the *look* of the
advertisement than to the product it is selling.

This preoccupation with style in itself is not particularly critical.
However, the story of the debilitating effects of television often
emerges from the right wing which nostalgically laments a golden
age, or from the left who make a knee-jerk association between popular culture and right-wing ideology. One typical example of this
argument about the public succumbing to the culture of the visual
image is Neil Postman's suggestion that TV is specifically responsible for the decline of reason: 'the epistemology created by television
not only is inferior to a print-based epistemology but is dangerous
and absurd' (Postman, *Amusing Ourselves to Death* (London, Methuen, 1987), p. 27). Another example is Michel Foucault's assertion
that TV and cinema act as an 'effective means . . . of *reprogramming
popular memory'* in which 'people are shown not what they were but
what they must remember having been. . . . Since memory is a very
important factor in struggle . . . if one controls people's memory,
one controls their dynamism' (Foucault, *Foucault Live* (New York,
Semiotext(e), 1996), p. 92).

Other postmodern theorists, however, are not quite so pessimistic
and perceive television as a liberating medium, with vast educational
and innovative potential. Postmodern television indeed exhibits
many of the features which dominate all other forms of postmodern
culture: frequent borrowings and splicings, a relentless intertexua-
lity and the pillage of other genres (*Twin Peaks*), abrupt transitions
and a fragmented relativism (*NYPD Blue*), pastiche and a reworking of pop culture (*Miami Vice*), an effacement of history (*Miami
Vice*) and the dissolving of boundaries between high and low art
(*L.A. Law*). In all respects, postmodern television privileges the
medium over the message, style over substance and form over
content. Nicholas Abercrombie has produced what he considers to
be an economy of postmodernism in television in his book *Television
and Society* (Cambridge, Polity Press, 1996). These six features are
as follows:

1.   Postmodern theorists of television suggest that we no longer
      live in reality, but in *images* or *representations* of that reality.
      We are no longer able to perceive any difference between the

image and the reality. For example, when we travel to the West Indies, we do not see the real islands, but the way they are mediated through advertisements for Bacardi, glamorous locations in James Bond movies, and so on. Consequently, we now live in an image-saturated society, in which the collapse of image and reality results in a 'simulational culture' (Baudrillard).

2. 'Contemporary societies are about creating an image, refining a *look*, presenting a *style*' (Abercrombie, *Television and Society*, p. 38). This preoccupation with 'surface appearance' is closely linked with consumerism as people are encouraged to buy an image. Jameson's notion of 'depthlessness', a superficial culture which is reflected in and promoted by TV, is perhaps most evident in shows like *Miami Vice* or *Moonlighting*.

3. The break with traditional boundaries which postmodern culture promotes – high/low, or different historical periods or geographical areas – is evident in many TV shows, which show no respect for 'authenticity', are dominated by pastiche, and are amalgamations of different elements, genres, styles. Such characteristics are evident in *Twin Peaks*.

4. The self-referentiality of postmodern culture is evident in the way in which television feeds off itself, taking itself as material for its own programmes in chat shows and even news programmes. Many comedy shows depend upon TV for their jokes: for example, *Have I Got News For You?* or *Drop the Dead Donkey*.

5. Postmodern television does not follow the conventions of realism and narrative; rather it plays with these conventions, like *Twin Peaks* and *The Singing Detective*. In the early days of television, producers made every effort to hide the cameras and the production equipment; now a series like *Moonlighting* can finish with the crew coming on to the set and dismantling the apparatus around the actors.

6. Postmodern culture is fragmented; bits of it do not add up to a whole. E. Ann Kaplan demonstrates this most effectively with regard to MTV; yet the experience of much TV is one of disjunctive pieces.

Although some television shows demonstrate these characteristics, Abercrombie acknowledges that the bulk of television shows remain predominantly realist. Therefore, he perceives the need to move away from the merely formalist definitions of postmodern television suggested by this list, to interrogate the preconceptions that motivate producers and the concepts that inform audiences and their reception of television programmes.

Just such a shift in critical focus is undertaken by John Fiske in *Television Culture* (London, Routledge, 1989), which attempts to analyse the viewer's interpretation of programmes. Although acknowledging that television produces an ideologically dominated society, Fiske's analyses of television are concerned with elaborating a position from which the 'subordinate' decoders (that is, the viewers, who are supposedly just watching 'passively') can produce resistant readings and refuse ideological manipulation. He has sought to move away from analyses of how texts position the viewer, towards what the viewer does with the text: in other words, he has moved from sites of textual construction and production to sites of textual consumption. One of his principal examples of postmodern television is *Miami Vice*, with its foregrounding of leisure as pleasure and style as content. Readily distinguishable from the gritty realism of *Cagney and Lacy* or *Hill Street Blues, Miami Vice is* its look: the series concentrates upon the shots of Tubbs and Crockett cruising the street in their pastel clothes to the latest Top Twenty hits and voluptuous photography. The pure pleasure of *Miami Vice* lies in the way 'leisure displaces labor, consumption displaces production, and commodities become the instruments of leisure, identity, and social relations' (Fiske, *Television Culture*, p. 259). Spectacle is the source of pleasure in the show, as even the masculine self is shown to be produced and affirmed through a series of theatrical gestures and displays, as a *spectacle:*

> These images of style in *Miami Vice*, in music videos, title sequences, or commercials, open the viewer to a postmodernist pleasure. The fast editing, the dislocation of narrative sequence, the disruption of the diegesis may produce the sensation of fragmentariness, of images remaining signifiers, of the signifieds being not sold, but swamped, by the sensualities, of the physical uniqueness of experience rather than its meaning. Images are neither the bearers of ideology, nor the representations of the real, but what Baudrillard calls 'the hyperreal': the television image, the advertisement, the pop song become more

'real' than 'reality', their sensuous imperative is so strong that they *are* our experience, they are our pleasure. Denying the narrative domain of these objects dislocates them from the ideological one as well. The pleasure here is not in resisting ideology, nor in challenging it with a 'better' one, but in evading it, in liberating oneself from it. (*Television Culture*, p. 260)

By championing the 'subordinate' decoder of television images as a type of resisting reader, Fiske attempts to demonstrate how television may serve the interests of 'subordinated' or oppressed groups. For Fiske perceives television as a contradictory medium, a state which allows it to promote the hegemonic ideology while at the same time promoting an oppositional and different cultural value for the marginalised sections of society. Television is a site where conflicting power interests coalesce: 'Far from being the agent of the dominant classes, it is the prime site where the dominant have to recognise the insecurity of their power, and where they have to encourage cultural difference with all the threat to their own position that this implies' (*Television Culture*, p. 326). Fiske's project is to analyse how the viewer manages to negotiate the conflicting images and ideologies without becoming a mere puppet of the televisual medium.

Lawrence Grossberg also makes *Miami Vice* one of the linchpins of his cultural analysis of television. His principal interest lies in how one can make sense of postmodern texts as televisual practices within a broader, historical configuration of the popular: what 'postmodern' practices does television appropriate, and what does the popularity of such televisual practices suggest about certain struggles and relations of power in the cultural terrain? Like Fiske, Grossberg regards *Miami Vice* as cops putting on a fashion show to a Top 40 soundtrack with Miami as the catwalk. With a narrative that is less important than the images, Grossberg sees the protagonists 'not so much patrolling Miami as cruising it, only to rediscover the narrative as an afterthought in the last few minutes. Narrative closure becomes a mere convenience of the medium' (Grossberg, 'The In-Difference of Television', *Screen*, 28:2 (Spring 1987): 29). The outcome of this is a difficulty in distinguishing between the actor and the character. TV generates an 'in-difference' to the effects of its own blurring of the line between reality and fantasy: 'If semiotics teaches us that identity is constituted out of difference, and postmodernism teaches us that identity has disappeared with the erasure of difference, I want to argue that the effectivity of TV is precisely the complex effects it generates by operating, in specific ways, on the line of in-difference' (In-Difference', p. 32). This in-difference is announced by its use of irony, repetition and excess, and in order to negotiate these, Grossberg suggests that television effectively establishes a new subjectivity. Echoing Gilles Deleuze and Felix Guattari's concept (see Chapter 2), this 'nomadic subjectivity' is:

> a subjectivity which is always moving along different vectors and changing its shape, but not always having a shape.
>   Nomadic subjectivity describes a post-humanist theory of the subject. Rejecting the existential subject who has a simple unified identity that somehow exists in the same way in every practice, it proposes a subject that is constantly remade, reshaped as a mobilely situated set of vectors in a fluid context. ('In-Difference', pp. 38–9)

Ultimately, because affective relations have been lost in society, 'TV re-establishes a site of and source for affective living within its democratic economy. It does this by constituting an empowering form of identity – the masculine exotic. It celebrates the ordinariness of the exotic and the exoticism of the ordinary. It locates identity in the absence of any difference by effectively investing in the difference of the same' ('In-Difference, p. 45). It is arguable that ultimately Grossberg capitulates too much to the logic of postmodern television ('TV is . . . in-different to the difference between subordination and resistance' ('In-Difference', p. 45)), which merely serves to reinforce the ideological constructs of dislocated subjectivity, political impotence and social passivity.

Whilst acknowledging the importance of Fiske's analyses of television, Feuer regards them as lacking historical specificity. Questioning the notion of the 'resisting reader' as being too generalised and insufficiently historicised, Feuer argues in *Seeing Through the Eighties: Television and Reaganism* (Durham NC, Duke University Press, and London, BFI Publishing, 1995) that the formal features of postmodern television have to be placed within the historical, social and cultural circumstances within which they developed. And for Feuer, TV postmodernity 'correlates to the development of the Reaganite cultural formation' (*Seeing*, p. 7), as she asserts that 'television and Reaganism formed mutually reinforcing and inter-penetrating imaginary worlds' (*Seeing*, p. 12). In addition to *Dallas* and *Dynasty*, *L.A. Law* and *thirtysomething* are regarded as arche-typal 'yuppie' shows emblematic of a Reaganite ethos, where tele-vision and Reaganomics are construed as mutually causing and effecting each other. According to Feuer's analysis, postmodern television programmes, no longer simply formally mechanistic or unidirectional, are involved in a complex process of reflection and construction of the specific political and social environment which constituted Reaganism.

Much of the debate concerning television and postmodernism hinges upon the nature of the ideological relation between program-ming production and interpreting audience. If these cultural readings demonstrate a concern for the activity and relations of politics and power within the sphere of television, then Arthur Kroker and David Cook appear to have relinquished any hope that viewers may exercise any autonomous strategic political manoeuvre with regard to television. For them, television is synonymous with postmodernity: 'In postmodernist culture, it's not TV as a mirror of society, but just the reverse: *it's society as a mirror of television*' (Kroker and Cook, *The Postmodern Scene: Excremental Culture and Hyper-aesthetics* (Macmillan, Basingstoke, 1988), p. 269). In this society where people imitate popular and cultural images, 'social cohesion is provided by the pseudo-solidarities (pseudo-mediations) of electronic television images' (*Postmodern Scene*, p. 268). Televi-sion emerges as an ideologically suspicious surrogate for sociality as a result of the total collapse of social unity. For example, TV and radio soaps are not just serials about *characters:* they are all mainly about *communities – Coronation Street, Brookside, EastEnders, Emmerdale Farm, The Archers* and *Neighbours* all provide a substi-tute neighbourhood for their audiences. Where novels are mainly 'character'-centred, soaps are much more 'place'-centred by com-parison. Kroker and Cook's grand vision of a society utterly dependent upon the spectacle generated by the illusions of televi-sion owes more than a little to the formulations of Baudrillard's overpowering cultural pessimism:

> Our general theorisation is, therefore, that TV is the real world of postmodern culture which has *entertainment* as its ideology,

the *spectacle* as the emblematic sign of the commodity-form, *lifestyle advertising* as its popular psychology, pure, empty *seriality* as the bond which unites the simulacrum of the audience, *electronic images* as its most dynamic, and only, form of social cohesion, *elite media politics* as its ideological formula, the buying and selling of *abstracted attention* as the locus of its marketplace rationale, *cynicism* as its dominant cultural sign, and the diffusion of a *network of relational power* as its real product. (*Postmodern Scene*, p. 270)

Gone is any sense of the potential for ideological interrogation, say Kroker and Cook, as viewers become mere playthings or ventriloquists' dummies for the technological imposition of commodity culture in late capitalism.

STOP and THINK

- How have recent changes in TV and communications reconfigured the public and private spheres? In his book *Understanding Media: The Extensions of Man* (London, Routledge and Kegan Paul, 1964), Marshall McLuhan warned that although we create the technologies, they also create us: in what ways do you perceive the contemporary individual becoming a 'made' entity, a postmodern pastiche of different styles? Consider your answer in relation to the last section of this chapter, which deals with developments in cyberculture and televisual constructions.

- It has often been pointed out that most popular television like *Coronation Street* and *EastEnders* still uses realist aesthetics and strong, conventional narrative lines. To what extent, then, is postmodern television dependent on the existence of these forms as the dominant aesthetic ideology?

- With specific attention to Fiske's arguments about the 'subordinate' group, is one able to grant the group the homogeneity that Fiske seems to suggest? What, for example, happens when the stakes of one 'subordinate' group (say, black women) collide with the interests of another (say, white gay men)? How likely is it that all 'resistant' readings or appropriations of television will all prove 'radical' in the same ways? If, as Fiske implies, all people can subvert and thereby resist television, is there any need for reforming television?

● Do you agree with Feuer's argument that TV's postmodernity corresponds to the Reaganite cultural formation, and where does that leave histories of TV in Britain, Europe or the rest of the world? Or is it that global sales of American television programmes (like *Dallas, Dynasty, thirtysomething* or *L.A. Law*) force all nations into the American ideological mould?

● With regard to advertising, are you convinced by the argument that there are specific methods and techniques which are pertinent to *postmodern* advertising as opposed to advertising in general? What would you cite as examples of a specifically postmodern advertising? In what ways do these advertisements differ from other advertisements? Are the particular differences ones of kind or degree?

VJs displace DJs: music videos and MTV

Of all the televisual media in recent decades which have attracted the most concerted descriptive analyses of postmodernism, music videos or promos have been at the top of the list. Music videos exemplify pastiche, a knowing appropriation of other audiovisual media right across the range, self-reflexive and ironic approaches in their portrayal of stars, and montage strategies with intertextual cross-referencing at all times. In a gesture that now looks full of premonition, MTV launched in 1981 with The Buggles' 'Video Killed the Radio Star'. With the MTV video-jock replacing the *Top of the Pops* disc-jockey as the primal scene of music consumption, rock videos have been construed by several theorists as presenting a challenge to the dominant form of television, since they make no pretence at showing 'the Real'. For example, Peter Wollen has described music videos as the archetypal inscription of postmodernism. He considers them postmodern for four distinct reasons:

1. Music videos disrupt the conventional distinction between television and video art. With new post-production technologies, both these aspects converge in one form.

2. Music videos break down familiar genre distinctions with the
    development of new mixed-media forms. Rock videos combine
    elements of live musical performance, film and television to
    produce an 'electronic mini-operetta' or 'an animated record
    sleeve'.
3. Music videos bring about a tremendous amount of hybridisa-
    tion, blurring categories of programme and advertisement. For
    example, one has the Spice Girls selling salt and vinegar crisps
    with reference to Gary Lineker's earlier crisp advertisements,
    and to their song 'Wannabe'; or one has Michael Jackson's
    Pepsi advertisements. Alternatively, one has the *Max Headroom
    Show* treating music videos as programmes, which produces
    a new and complex interaction between programming and
    marketing.
4. Music videos also hybridise the fashion event. David Bowie and
    Malcolm McLaren paved the way for this straddling of music
    and fashion, but music has moved into fashion and perfor-
    mance, with clothes displayed on catwalks to the sounds of the
    latest pop hits.

Wollen describes postmodern art's 'typical forms as eclecticism
and historicism. It plunders the image-bank and the word-hoard
for the material of parody, pastiche, and, in extreme cases, plagia-
rism' (Wollen, 'Ways of Thinking about Music Video (and Postmodernism)', *Critical Quarterly*, 28:1–2 (Spring–Summer 1986):
167–70). Wollen continues by arguing that music videos need a
more pluralised mode of cultural understanding, since they defeat
any existing critical apparatus available to comprehend them:
'The polarized distinction between avant-garde and kitsch, high
and low art; the doctrine of the purity of genres; the cluster of
aesthetic concepts around the idea of artistic originality – all
these are useless for any serious engagement with a hybrid and
technologically sophisticated form such as music video' (Wollen,
'Ways', p. 169).

In her specific analysis of the rock videos shown on MTV,
Kaplan's book *Rocking Around the Clock: Music, Television, Postmodernism and Consumer Culture* (London, Methuen, 1987) argues that
the music television channel phenomenon is a singular expression

of postmodern culture. Drawing on Baudrillard's theories of the collapse of 'fiction' and 'reality' into a single realm of 'simulacra', Kaplan argues:

> The new postmodern universe, with its celebration of the look – the surfaces, textures, the self-as-commodity – threatens to reduce everything to the image/representation/simulacrum. Television, with its decentred address, its flattening out of things into a network or system, the parts of which all rely on each other, and which is endless, unbounded, unframed, seems to embody the new universe; and within television, MTV in particular manifests the phenomena outlined by Baudrillard. (*Rocking*, p. 44)

Kaplan describes MTV's postmodern characteristics as the effacement of distinctions between past, present and future, the collapse of separated traditions and genres, and the creation of unstable subject positions that fall outside the usual categories. She suggests that MTV operates through a process of deferred satisfaction, constantly inviting audiences to watch the next video to achieve plenitude. The analysis identifies five different types of music video: (a) romantic, (b) socially conscious, (c) nihilist, (d) classical and (e) postmodernist. The last type of video is merely an extreme version of the tendencies which Kaplan considers all rock videos to possess: each textual element is undercut by others; narrative is undercut by pastiche; signifying is undercut by images that do not form a coherent chain; the text is 'flattened out'; and the spectator is decentred, fixated on one particular image, and eager for the next video to give satisfaction.

Fundamentally disagreeing with Jameson's despairing and pessimistic analysis of popular culture's elision of forms, and Grossberg's sense of music videos as heralding some impending cultural death, Kaplan's perspective is far more optimistic. She suggests that the elision of boundaries is 'an exhilarating move toward a heteroglossia that calls into question moribund pieties of a now archaic humanism' (*Rocking*, p. 148). MTV and music videos emerge as a form of resistant, counter-hegemonic cultural form, in which 'The creativity and energy of rock videos could represent a refusal to be co-opted into the liberalism that has brought America to its present crisis' (*Rocking*, p. 148).

Andrew Goodwin, on the other hand, is very critical of the positions adopted by theorists like Wollen and Kaplan about the postmodernity of MTV and rock videos. He is principally concerned with the deficiencies in the arguments concerning pastiche, and the issues of depth and surface. He concludes that pastiche is not always the most appropriate term for the 'quotational modes' used by videos; and that postmodern analyses of 'pastiche' are not sufficiently flexible or subtle enough to account for 'slippage' between different uses and subtleties of citation in music videos. Goodwin discerns at least six modes of 'visual incorporation' or citation in his exploration of a variety of music videos (the examples are Goodwin's, from *Dancing in the Distraction Factory: Music, Television and Popular Culture* (London, Routledge, 1993)):

1. *Social criticism:* There is social criticism evident in some videos, for example in the news footage and excerpts found in videos by Bruce Springsteen ('War') or The Clash ('Radio Clash').
2. *Self-reflexiveness:* Some music video parodies take music video itself as the target, e.g. Dire Straits' invocation of MTV in 'Money For Nothing'.
3. *Parody:* There are rather few examples of this in music video.
4. *Pastiche:* A significant concept in relation to music video, e.g. the citation of Fritz Lang's *Metropolis* in Queen's 'Radio Ga Ga', or Michael Jackson's 'Thriller' and his use of horror films.
5. *Promotion:* music video offers promotion and homage, selling movies as well as records, often acting as a 'trailer' for the movie, e.g. David Bowie's 'Absolute Beginners' or Duran Duran's 'A View to a Kill'.
6. *Homage:* some music videos abandon parody altogether in favour of a tribute to a specific director, or cultural form. For example, Big Audio Dynamite's '$E = MC^2$' uses clips from Nick Roeg's films, in order to illustrate a song that is itself a tribute to Roeg.

Goodwin's criticisms are impelled by a conviction that postmodernist accounts of music television are devoid of adequate accounts of historical context: 'the literature of postmodernism, while it sometimes celebrates popular forms, rarely demonstrates concrete, historical links between the aesthetic and its mode of production' (*Dancing*, p. 167). Goodwin maintains a rigorously historical understanding of music television in relation to its production context, and consequently suggests that there are ways of comprehending pastiche which do not simply lapse into reductive arguments of how rock videos 'express' the dominant postmodern aesthetic/ social structure. As examples, he cites the way in which the textual incorporation of film, video or other elements leaves open the possibility for textual criticism; he argues that pastiche cannot be overlooked as a 'cover for cross-promotion', where quotation from other videos is a form of advertisement; and he suggests that although pastiche may be technically 'blank' (where the music videos provide a viewer with no position from which to critique or endorse the citations), it is nevertheless a socially and ideologically laden manoeuvre. From his historical perspective, Goodwin also argues that 'it is evident that production practices in music television are responsible for *particular* shifts in the representation of popular music' (*Dancing*, p. 176), and demonstrates its effects on three areas of rock videos: gender construction, racial prejudice in the allocation of video budgets, and the representation of stars.

So far from being a 'depthless' medium which lacks history, Goodwin argues that postmodern analyses of music video leave several lacunae in our understanding of this popular cultural phenomenon:

> Contrary to the postmodern literature on this topic, music television does not, generally speaking, indulge in a rupture with the Symbolic; nor does it defy our understanding or attempt to elude logic and rationality through its refusal to make sense. Far from constituting a radical break with the processes of meaning production, music television constantly reworks themes (work, school, authority, romance, poverty, and so on) that are deeply implicated in the question of how meaning serves (or resists) power. (*Dancing*, p. 180)

Whether or not MTV and music videos embody the archetypal postmodern form, Goodwin, Kaplan and Wollen all agree that the advent of MTV and the music video are an important feature of late capitalist popular culture. It remains for posterity to decide whether the displacement of DJs by VJs in the 1980s did herald the dawn of a new, postmodern era.

STOP and THINK

- MTV poses a variety of contradictions resulting from its use of pastiche in videos. How do the economic demands of the multinational record and TV companies conflict with the liberal spirit of great freedom projected by MTV?
- Similarly, consider the extent to which MTV's very youthful, alternative, inventive, hip appearance is the result of a global marketing business, and whether its postmodern style is the effect of a big-business financial ploy.
- Finally, given that music video and advertisement have now merged as one medium, what route of access is there for traditionally marginalised 'others' to the mainstream sources of musical promotion? How does one explain the huge success of black rap and women artists? Can one distinguish qualitative musical signs in their work, or are they merely another good marketing ploy?

Screening the image: postmodern film

Even before television emerged, cinema was exploring the construction of images within twentieth-century society. Yet upon its arrival in the early stages, although a modernist artefact, cinema was paradoxically more wedded to realism than modernism, as it held out the potential for reproducing reality with an incomparable exactitude. For popular mainstream narrative cinema, a whole technological apparatus was geared towards creating the illusion of reality through the production of a seamlessness in its production practices. The evolution of a modernist cinema was a rejection of this seamless verisimilitude of realism, and sought to 'lay bare the device', or to make manifest the process of producing meaning-construction in film. For example, the director John Cassavetes used to offer 'close-up' sound of a conversation in a scene too distant to hear realistically; or in Jean-Luc Godard's film *Une Femme est une Femme* (1961, *A Woman is a Woman*), there is the absurd gag in which an actress flips an egg in the air and catches it a few minutes later, after taking a telephone call. Modernist cinema included the work of the avant-garde (surrealist, counter-cinema and underground cinema), and explored and exposed the formal concerns of the medium by placing them at the forefront of consciousness. Modernist cinema questioned and made visible the meaning-production practices of film: it interrogated the technology it used, the power of its gaze, and its power to represent; and through an exploration of the plasticity of its spatial and temporal qualities, it turned the gaze of the camera back on itself as a critical tool, questioning *how* and *what* it represented. For example, this might manifest itself in a shot of a conversation without 'cross-cutting' so that the camera 'whizzes' from speaker to speaker.

Hence, in the light of these formal innovations, it might appear that cinema was always a 'proto-postmodern' form. However, one can gradually distinguish a 'postmodernist' cinema from a 'modernist' cinema; although John Orr in *Cinema and Modernity* has persuasively argued that many of the characteristics of postmodernist film – pastiche, self-conscious narrative, game-playing, polyvalence – are no more than 'neo-modern inventions' (Orr, *Cinema and Modernity* (Cambridge, Polity Press, 1993), p. 3). In constructing a distinction between modernist and postmodernist cinema, Tony Wilson has suggested that 'To investigate the transparency of the image is modernist but to undermine its reference to reality is to engage with the aesthetics of postmodernism' (Wilson, 'Reading the Postmodernist Image: A "Cognitive Mapping"', *Screen*, 31:4 (Winter 1990): 396). Investigating the 'transparency of the image' might be seen in the 'scientific' camera experiments of Sergei Eisenstein, Alfred Hitchcock or Godard, while the undermining of the image's reference to reality might be evident in the work of directors like Quentin Tarrantino, Derek Jarman or Peter Greenaway.

Fredric Jameson has argued that modernist cinema, like modernist painting, literature and music, consists of the construction of a personal style, based on an insistence upon the agonised expression of the alienated individual, most visibly captured in Edvard Munch's painting *The Scream:*

> The great modernisms were . . . predicated on the invention of a personal, private style, as unmistakable as your fingerprint, as incomparable as your own body. But this means that the modernist aesthetic is in some way organically linked to the conception of a unique self and private identity, a unique personality and individuality, which can be expected to generate its own unique vision of the world and to forge its own unique, unmistakable style. (Jameson,

'Postmodernism in Consumer Society', in Hal Foster (ed.), *Postmodern Culture* (London, Pluto Press, 1985), p. 114)

Jameson does not elaborate upon how this 'fingerprinting' style manifests itself specifically with relation to the field of film in this essay; but one might conceive of the *auteur* theory of the 1960s as one way in which film was constructed based upon the powerful originating style and figure of the author-director. *Auteur* refers to the way in which a director's discernible style is evident in the *mise-en-scène* of the film or to the director's signature in the final film itself. Well-known exemplars of auteurism are Orson Welles and Hitchcock in the United States, Godard and Jean Renoir in France, and Rainer Werner Fassbinder and Wim Wenders in Germany. Postmodernist film departs from this by uncoupling style from the author-director, which opens up the arena for a plurality of styles and voices which circulate within a flattened, dehistoricised space. For example, *Pulp Fiction* (1994) borrows its styles and sequences from a variety of other films: the dance competition is clearly influenced by Godard's *Bande à parte* (1964), after which Tarantino has named his production company. Other homages to Hitchcock's *Psycho* (1960), John Boorman's *Deliverance* (1972), François Truffaut's *Jules et Jim* (1961), Luc Besson's *La Femme Nikita* (1990), and the films of John Woo, Sam Peckinpah, Brian De Palma and Don Siegel are also evident.

Jameson's work has set much of the tone for discussion concerning what constitutes postmodern film. His terms are largely derived from his conviction that postmodern culture ushers in a new 'depthlessness', celebrating 'surfaces' in a denial of material history and an effacement of the historical past. He suggests that postmodern film is governed by 'nostalgia' or *la mode rétro* ('retrospective styling'), and he treats this as the postmodern cultural paradigm of film, 'an alarming and pathological symptom of a society that has become incapable of dealing with time and history' ('Postmodernism', p. 117). 'Nostalgia films' fall into three types:

1. films which are about the past and take place in the past (*Chinatown* (1974), *American Graffiti* (1973));
2. films that 'reinvent' the past (the *Star Wars* series, *Raiders of the Lost Ark* (1981));

3. films which are set in the present which evoke the past (*Body Heat* (1981)).

Body Heat, for example, alludes to America in the 1930s, but is actually set in contemporary small-town Florida. The film's narrative and its art direction confuse the temporal sense, as all these films work with a pastiche of the past, suggesting that 'we seem condemned to seek the historical past through our own pop images and stereotypes about that past, which itself remains forever out of reach' ('Postmodernism', p. 118).

Vehemently rejecting Jameson's attempts to suggest that there is an objective reality outside texts, and his derision of popular culture in his analysis of postmodernism, Norman Denzin has attempted to formulate a critique of postmodern social theory partly by attempting to learn from postmodern cinema. In particular, his analysis of the film *Blue Velvet* (1986) sets out what he regards as the quintessential features of a postmodern film from 'that contemporary postmodern phenomenon called David Lynch' (Denzin, *The Cinematic Society: The Voyeur's Gaze* (London, Sage, 1995), p. 65). A disquieting exploration of the way people avoid the sinister side of life, *Blue Velvet* concerns a college student who finds a mysterious ear in a field. He then seeks the body to which it belongs; this eventually leads him to meet a nightclub singer, whose husband and child are being held hostage. Eventually he meets the demoniacal hostage-taker who is involved in sexually tormenting the singer in exchange for the safety of her family. Based upon his analysis of the film, Denzin argues that postmodern film demonstrates several principal features:

1. an effacement of the boundaries between the past and the present and a treatment of time which locates the viewing subject in a perpetual present;
2. a manifestation of the unpresentable in front of the viewer which challenges the boundaries that ordinarily separate private and public life;
3. the introduction of a wild sexuality and violence which signify modes of freedom and self-expression, which are at one and the same time abhorred and attractive;
4. the unreal and hyperreal as always real and not just possibilities.

Denzin perceives *Blue Velvet* and other postmodern cultural texts as echoes and reproductions of the turmoils and contradictions that define the late 1980s and early 1990s. For Denzin, such films:

> locate strange, eclectic, violent, timeless worlds in the present. They make fun of the past as they keep it alive. They search for new ways to present the unpresentable, so as to break down the barriers that keep the profane out of the everyday. However, they take conservative political stances, while they valorize and exploit the radical social margins of society ... The postmodern eye looks fearfully into the future and it sees technology, uncontrolled sexual violence, universally corrupt political systems. Confronting this vision, it attempts to find safe regions of escape in the fantasies and nostalgia of the past. Dreams are the postmodern solution to life in the present. (*Cinematic*, p. 79).

Consequently, he regards postmodern films like Lynch's work as 'dangerous texts' (p. 80), since 'Politically barren, they reproduce the very cultural conditions they seek to criticize. While superficially calling for a culture of resistance, they "ARE pop culture" ... They contribute to the creation of "a culture of indifference"' (*Cinematic*, p. 80). In the end, Denzin finds the postmodernism reflected in *Blue Velvet*, as well as in others such as *sex, lies and videotape* (1989), *Wall Street* (1987), *When Harry Met Sally* (1989) and *Paris, Texas* (1984) to be examples of an insidious and iniquitous culture, the ideological logic of which is conservative to the core. 'Cinematic representations of postmodernism also fail to offer anything more than superficial solutions to the present conditions' (*Cinematic*, p. 150). Instead of those narratives which offer simplistic, ideological answers to complex questions, Denzin wishes to promote interrogative, transgressive and formally challenging postmodern films which critically explore the postmodern condition and all its contradictions.

Pied pipers playing the postmodern tune have caused film studios to emerge with a host of other films which make use of the mystique and cachet of the term 'postmodern' as a sales pitch. Many of these films demonstrate all the postmodern characteristics of a pastiche of styles, a nostalgia for a lost past, and a flattening out of history: the *Back To The Future* series (1985–90), the *Indiana Jones* trilogy, the James Bond movie *Goldeneye* (1995), as well as a whole host of other movies which have been widely discussed, like *Blade Runner* (1982) and films from directors such as Jarman, Greenaway and David Cronenberg.

If there is one cinematic event that rivals *Blade Runner* for supreme postmodern status, it has been the Wachowski brothers' *The Matrix Trilogy*, comprising *The Matrix* (1999), *The Matrix Reloaded* (2003) and *The Matrix Revolutions* (2003). Having spawned a franchise in its own right by storming popular culture with websites, computer games, blogs, animation, comics, and also producing a plethora of academic studies, such as Matt Lawrence's *Like a Splinter in Your Mind: The Philosophy Behind the Matrix Trilogy* (Oxford, Wiley-Blackwell, 2004), Christopher Grau's edition of essays in *Philosophers Explore 'The Matrix'* (Oxford, Oxford University Press, 2005) and Stacy Gillis' *The Matrix Trilogy: Cyberpunk Reloaded* (London, Wallflower Press, 2005) among others. The films clearly wear their postmodern credentials on their sleeves: 'Welcome to the desert of the real', says the character Morpheus in *The Matrix*, offering the whole trilogy as working explicitly within a paradigm derived in part from the postmodern theory of Jean Baudrillard, whose *Simulacra and Simulation* makes its appearance in *The Matrix* in the 'Follow Instructions' scene. Thomas Anderson (a.k.a. Neo, played by Keanu Reeves) opens a copy of Baudrillard's *Simulacra and Simulation* at a chapter entitled 'On Nihilism', which acts as a hollow hardcover book in which Neo hides black market software. Many discussions have taken off from this instance of 'intellectual placement', concerning many key postmodern preoccupations, such as the film's relation to cyberpunk, its handling of Baudrillardian ideas on simulacra, the politics of gender and race, cyberculture and the body, appearances and virtual realities, the characters' dress style, the music score, and its intertextuality and theological allusions. Derided and applauded in equal measure for its teasing and often opaque narrative, the film has nevertheless generated a hugely dedicated fan base which has meticulously probed and analysed every detail of the films for clues, traces and evidence to support their archetypal postmodern status.

STOP and THINK

General

- To what extent are all films in some sense 'postmodern', in so far as they partake of similar stylistic features (jump cuts, montage, allusions to other genres, etc.)? Are films therefore only 'postmodern' as a consequence of the era in which they are made?

Specific

- Jameson's 'nostalgia' appears to be improperly analysed. Exactly what is it that modern audiences wish to feel nostalgic about? When he discusses nostalgia in relation to adventure serials like *Star Wars,* he seems to ignore the issue of gender: does this nostalgia differ for men and women? Do men and women desire the same past?
- Watch a film like *Batman* (1989). Make a list of the images, scenes and characteristics which you regard as postmodern. How do these compare with a similar list derived from watching high modernist films like Lang's *Metropolis* (1926) or Eisenstein's *The Battleship Potemkin* (1925)?

Key characteristics of postmodern film

1. A pastiche of other genres and styles, not just imitating their look but alluding to famous scenes or cinematic styles. Examples include the imitation of the western in *Blazing Saddles* (1974), or the allusions to Arthurian literature in *Monty Python and the Holy Grail* (1974). *Thelma and Louise* (1991) can be seen as a pastiche of American road movies, as well as of 'buddy' films like *Butch Cassidy and the Sundance Kid* (1969).

2. A 'flattening' of history, a style which presents the past in the present; or a 'retro' cinema, or nostalgia film, e.g. *Batman*, or the *Back to the Future* series, or *Goldeneye*. The *Indiana Jones* trilogy incorporates instances of intertextuality, referring either to other genres or to earlier episodes in the series.

3. Self-reflexivity of technique: Greenaway's films, for instance, such as *The Draughtsman's Contract* (1982), *The Belly of an*

Architect (1987), *Drowning by Numbers* (1987) or *Prospero's Books* (1991) are heavily structured by self-reflexive scenes. Tilda Swinton's *Orlando* (1993) breaks the frame by having the actress turn her attention to the audience directly. The cartoon series *The Simpsons* works with a knowing, ironic self-conscious referentiality, as when episodes introduce cartoon versions of real people into the plot-lines, or when episodes are based upon famous American texts, as when Edgar Allan Poe's poem 'The Raven' forms the basis for a ghost story in which Homer and Bart figure as characters.

4. A celebration of the collapse of the distinction between high and low cultural styles and techniques (*Pulp Fiction*). The cartoon images pasted into live performances in *Who Framed Roger Rabbit?* (1988) is another example of the fusion of genres.

Postmodern film: an example

Perhaps the most widely discussed film with respect to the context of postmodernism (and now almost a cliché) is Ridley Scott's cult movie, *Blade Runner* (1982; director's cut, 1992). It has spawned thousands of articles about its content, its relation to contemporary culture, and its use of technological special effects, as well as two fictional sequels by H.W. Jeter, a book about its production by Paul Sammon *(Future Noir: The Making of 'Blade Runner'* (New York, HarperCollins, 1996)), comic adaptations, fanzines, a controversial release of the original uncut version in *Blade Runner: The Director's Cut*, and even a sophisticated website produced by '2019 Off-World' <http://scribble.com/uwi/br/>. There are numerous articles by those who perceive *Blade Runner* and Philip K. Dick's sci-fi novels as forerunners of cyberculture (see the discussion later in this chapter) and the novels of authors like William Gibson and Bruce Sterling. In other words, *Blade Runner* has become part of a whole culture in itself, which has evolved alongside the advent of virtual reality technology and posthuman cyborg theory (see the discussion in relation to Donna Haraway's ideas later in this chapter).

As we have noted, Jameson argues that the modernist film is one in which an eminent style is cultivated, which he argues is the agonised expression of the individual, speaking in the uniqueness of his or her personal idiom simultaneously of potency and alienated helplessness. What replaces such an outlook in postmodernist culture is not so much the absence of style as its relativisation, its detachment from the concept of a powerful originating author. We have multiple styles, which are juxtaposed with one another, creating a polyphony of voices. This in turn brings about the flattening of historical origins, so what are circulated are not only pastiches, but also dislocated histories. It is precisely this mode of 'retro' cinema or nostalgia and pastiche of past styles that one can see in *Blade Runner*, especially in the cityscape. This is not the clean, ultramodern city of films like *Logan's Run* (1976) or *Things to Come* (1936), but a postindustrial, recycled city. As Giuliana Bruno describes it, 'The postmodern aesthetic of *Blade Runner* is thus the result of recycling, fusion of levels, discontinuous signifiers, explosion of boundaries, and erosion. The disconnected temporality of the replicants and the pastiche of the city are all an effect of a postmodern, postindustrial condition: wearing out, waste' (Bruno, 'Ramble City: Postmodernism and *Blade Runner*', *October*, 41 (1987): 61–74). This is a hybrid city in a number of respects. The design for the film's cityscapes emerged from a collage of historical images: the designers drew upon Jacob Riis's 1890s photographs of New York's Lower East Side, many of which are reproduced in the 1998 paperback reprint of his classic exposé of urban squalor, *How the Other Half Lives*; the tense urban night scenes of the American painter Edward Hopper, such as 'Night Birds', which shows a dysfunctional couple sitting over coffee in an all-night diner; the ornate and detailed sketches of the sci-fi comic *Heavy Metal*; engravings and pictures by William Hogarth (such as the famous 'Gin Lane') and Jan Vermeer; and Lang's film *Metropolis*. This hybridity is also evident in the fact that although the city is Los Angeles, it looks in parts like Hong Kong, New York and Tokyo. In other words, the film presents an imaginary city, a synthesis of images quoted from a variety of cultural sources.

This fusion of signifiers and levelling of hierarchies is also evident in the construction of the film's fashion. This is a future built upon the detritus of a retrofitted past (our present), in which the city exists as a spectacular site; a future in which the nostalgia for a simulacrum of history in the forms of the *film noir* and forties fashion dominates; a future in which the only visible monument is a ziggurat for a corporate headquarters. The futuristic set and action mingle with drab 1940s clothes and offices, punk rock hairstyles, pop Egyptian styles and oriental culture. The population are singularly multicultural and the language they speak is an agglomeration of English, Japanese, German and Spanish. The film alludes to the private-eye genre of Raymond Chandler and the characteristics of *film noir*, as well as Biblical motifs and images.

This pastiche and intensification of the visual spectacle in the film derive from postmodernism's effacement of the referent and its celebration of the signifier. The film is overtly preoccupied with the logics of representation and visuality at every turn: in its dominant image of the eye; in its bold exhibition of the advertisements for various commodities; in its concern with televisual technology and photography; in its metanarrative about the breakdown of the real and the unreal, copies and originals, authenticity and inauthenticity. Nowhere is this more clearly evident than in the replicants. As Baudrillard argues, the 'society of the spectacle' is the society of the simulation. The concept of the simulation goes right to the postmodern heart of the film, with its exploration of the boundaries between the human and the inhuman/cyborg. Replicants after all are 'simulations' of humans; and while the film is based upon Deckard's task of hunting down the rogue 'non-human' cyborgs, it gradually becomes evident that qualitative or other distinctions between replicant and human are blurred and even effaced. It comes as no surprise to learn that the replicants are known as 'Nexus' models: for the replicants form a matrix of concerns with history, memory, the visual and simulation, in the film's main investigation into what constitutes the identity of an authentic human.

Televisual prosthetics and postmodern cyberbodies

Televisual technology has undergone a tremendous revolution in the twentieth century. From the cinema screen through the television screen to the video screen, we have constantly been subjected to an increasingly Orwellian screen culture. In recent years, this televisual culture has been revolutionised by the development of the microprocessor and advanced computer networking, to form what we now call cyberspace. Virtual reality has been the popularised form of this new 'telespace' which has come to dominate many of our contemporary techno-fantasies about extending the capacities of human control. With the exploitation of such techniques in video games, Mario the Plumber or Lara Croft are probably better-known characters than Mickey Mouse or Superman! To this extent, any exploration of postmodernity needs a viable discussion of its relation to new technologies and modes of communication.

A huge euphoria has attached itself to technophiles' accounts of the revolution of cyberspace technology and it has often been expressed in a singularly 'mystical' and transcendental manner. Howard Rheingold, a populist champion of virtual reality, has made some astonishing claims for new culture and societies emerging from this technology (Rheingold, *The Virtual Community: Homesteading on the Electronic Frontier* (New York, HarperPerennial, 1994)). In addition, the new postmodern centrality of the image and technoculture has motivated an urgent reassessment of the function and competence of the human body. Claims that the body has disappeared, that the body no longer exists, that the mind/body split can be transcended, that the body is no longer 'human', all circulate in a number of debates about postmodernism. Arthur and Marielouise Kroker have been at the forefront of this debate ever since the publication of their books *The Postmodern Scene* (1988) and *The Panic Encyclopaedia* (Basingstoke, Macmillan, 1989). Their argument has largely been that the body is no longer *here*: that it has been superseded by the new technology and by the decentring effects of post-Enlightenment philosophies. Often sounding a note of apocalypticism, the Krokers evoke an era in which bodies have ceased to possess a power independent of various circuits:

> For we live under the dark sign of Foucault's prophecy that the bourgeois body is a descent into the empty site of a dissociated ego, a 'volume in disintegration', traced by language, lacerated by ideology, and invaded by the relational circuitry of the field of postmodern power. (Arthur Kroker and Marielouise Kroker, 'Theses on the Disappearing Body in the Hyper-Modern Condition', in Kroker and Kroker (eds), *Body Invaders: Panic Sex in America* (Montreal, New World Perspectives, 1987), pp. 20–34; p. 20)

This is largely a theory of the body derived from the theories of the French *philosophes* Baudrillard, Georges Bataille, and Deleuze and Guattari. These theorists largely perceive the body to be dissolving into a stream of floating parts, a 'body-without-organs', which reveals that it has been processed by the media, and that we experience our bodies only as 'fantastic simulacra of body rhetorics' (Kroker and Kroker (eds), *Body Invaders*, p. iv). Indeed, the capacity for technology to alter what is regarded as uniquely human is being explored practically as well as conceptually. The Australian performance artist Stelarc pushes at all the human body's limitations and states: 'Today technology is no longer exploding out from the body, in an external fashion, but is imploding and sticking to the skin. It is imploding and entering into the interior of the body' (Stelarc, quoted in Howard Caygill, 'Stelarc and the Chimera', *Art Journal* (Spring 1997): 46 51). His explorations of the limits of the body and its potential extension by technology have led him to prosthetic experiments (substitute or additional limbs) in the 1980s and 1990s. With performances like *The Third Hand* (Tokyo, 1981) (see Figure 11) and *Amplified Body, Laser Eyes, and Third Hand* (Tokyo, 1986), he has interacted with technology no longer as a supplement to the body, but as integral to the body's organisation and as a potential for its reorganisation.

Virtual reality is another site for the exploration of ways in which bodies and their capacities can be extended. Alongside the provocative technological prophecies of cyber-gurus like Jaron Lanier and Manuel de Landa, the excitement generated by the cyberpunk fiction of novelists like Bruce Sterling and William Gibson, and the titillations of popular cultural representations in films like *Johnny Mnemonic* (1995), *The Lawnmower Man* (1992) and *Disclosure* (1994), every day sees new and sensationalist extensions of the capacity of the internet to broadcast globally: a performance by the virtual rock band MONDO Vanilli, a woman giving birth, a couple losing their virginity. New interests and developments in computer technology have opened up the relationship of technology to the body in a multitude of ways. Cyberspace, cyborgs and cybernetics are a significant part of postmodern culture, and have led to prolific speculation about the emergence of a posthuman body. This posthuman body is

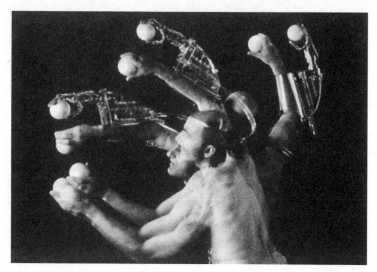

Figure 11 Stelarc, *The Third Hand*, Tokyo (8 May 1981)

partly the consequence of postmodern relations of power and pleasure, virtuality and reality, sex and its consequences. The posthuman
body is a techno-body, a screen, a hybridised version of pluralities:
a cyborg, a hybrid, a body-without-organs, a virtual body, a body-
in-process. Some theorists have been quite emphatic in their enunciation of a new posthuman body, a body which does not necessitate
the domestic routines of a human body. These theories verge on
the fantastic, often modelling themselves on more popular ideas
like those seen in the films *Robocop* (1987) and *Terminator* (1984),
but then many do not concur with the separation of the real from
the fantastic in the first place.

   The cyborg is a notional body, an ideal which has been appropriated by various feminists like Donna Haraway, who have expressed
particular interest in the possibilities of the posthuman. They feel
that it offers ways in which to escape the hitherto restrictive physical
differences upon which cultural gender hierarchies (like woman/
nature, man/culture) have been built. Contrary to the model of the
cyborg as a 'superman', Donna Haraway's notion of the cyborg is
an entity which is specifically conceived to be a 'creature in a

post-gender world' (Haraway, *Simians, Cyborgs and Women: The Reinvention of Nature* (London, Free Association, 1991), pp. 150–1). This cyborg becomes a symbol of the transgression of the boundaries between human and animal, organism and machine, the physical and the non-physical. As an offspring of a *feminist* science fiction, this cyborg is part of a feminist exploration of ways to restructure traditional gender oppositions; and as such, it features all the characteristics of partiality, hybridity, pastiche and playful irony one expects in models of postmodern subjectivity. Some feminist performance artists are equally concerned with the potential to alter the body in order to raise questions about gender construction. Orlan, a provocative French performance artist, has embarked on a life-long project entitled 'The Reincarnation of Saint Orlan'. To compare her work to that of Stelarc, this has involved her in having her facial physical features gradually changed by various operations, in order to critique the ideal of feminine beauty by fitting her face to a digital image culled from mythic icons of feminine beauty. Videos of her 'performances' show surgeons dressed in designer outfits by Paco Rabanne, Orlan on the operating table, reading from psycho-analytical texts, with the surgeon steadily going about her business. Not only turning heads, this frequently turns stomachs as well; and her work has elicited as much negative criticism from feminists as positive support for her project.

This debate about a new postmodern subjectivity in relation to technological developments has largely been spurred on by sociological arguments about the 'postindustrial' society and the 'information society', which capture an air of social and utopian promise. Some theorists argue that these new technologies redefine textuality and our textual practice, and that these new technologies form part of a wider restructuring of our subjectivity and cultural organisation. The work of Mark Poster in a poststructuralist form suggests that this new mode of information reconfigures communication as symbolic exchange and, by extension, affects subjectivity and the matrix of social relations (Poster, *The Mode of Information: Poststructuralism and Social Context* (Cambridge, Polity Press, 1990)). George Landow argues in a similar vein that 'we must abandon conceptual systems founded upon ideas of center, margin, hierarchy, and linearity, and replace them with ones of multi–linearity, nodes, links and networks' (Landow, *Hypertext: The Convergence of Contemporary Critical Theory and Technology* (Baltimore, Johns Hopkins University Press, 1992), p. 2). Landow perceives computer technology as heralding a new era in reading and writing practices, and as a consequence, a whole new cultural revolution.

One can readily identify three themes which characterise this 'reshaping' of culture as a series of 'links' and 'networks':

1. *The 'severing' of body and subject*. The social spaces of multi-media and cyberspace enable subjects to re-examine, play and experiment with, and ultimately transform their own multiple subjectivity. In *Imagologies*, Mark C. Taylor and Esa Saarinen celebrate this new-found fluidity of subjectivity: 'In cyberspace I change myself as easily as I change my clothes. Identity becomes infinitely plastic in a play of images that knows no end. Consistency is no longer a virtue but becomes a vice; integration is limitation. With everything always shifting, every one is no one' (Taylor and Saarinen, *Imagologies: Media Philosophy* (London, Routledge, 1994), p. 1). See also Donna Haraway's accounts of the collapse of subject categories and boundaries of the body through the interventions of twentieth-century technology. The popular fantasy is that cyberspace is the rhizomatic space of Deleuze and Guattari (see Chapter 2 for the discussion of this concept) made concrete, where everything is connected to everything else, and where all trajectories are nomadic and rootless, and all space is deterritorialised.

2. *Democratisation and the virtual community*. Marshall McLuhan was the first to announce the concept of a 'global village' based upon the democratisation of information. It ignores questions of ownership, information barriers and rules, and precipitates the collapse of national boundaries and the territoriality of the sovereign nation-state. Yet it does introduce a question about the extent to which information is the privilege of the wealthy and powerful, since one can only log into this 'virtual community' if one has access to a networked PC.

3. *The contiguity of language-use with larger social and cultural practices*. In the shift from the book to the screen, a new interactive

reader emerges. The limitations of the book are radically opened up by digital information systems, ushering in a new, thoroughly fluid, dynamic, networked space. Consequently, as Landow argues, there is a need for new educational and pedagogical practices.

Ever since Jean-François Lyotard introduced postmodernism within the context of advances in communication and the 'information age' as long ago as 1979 when he wrote his path-breaking book *The Postmodern Condition*, numerous investigations have taken place on the impact of the new technologies that have come to dominate our lives, and many arguments have been put forward about the ways in which they are an intricate part of the postmodern environment. The impact of these technologies has been felt in a whole host of areas: for example, upon writing and communication; upon ideas of the body and the human; upon notions of the global economy; upon surveillance culture and the formation of communities. 'Cybercultures', as this field of study has come to be defined and known in recent years, has become inextricably associated with the postmodern, with its emphases on the post-human, the post-national, the post-sexual, and with questions to do with locating popular cybercultures and cyber-subcultures, defining cyberfeminism and the cybersexual. In *An Introduction to Cybercultures* (London, Routledge, 2001), David Bell explores the wide variety of concerns of cyberculture, and argues persuasively that cyberspace exists as a story, a narrative that we tell ourselves. Consequently, Bell argues that there is no cyberspace, but rather cyberspaces (plural). The emphasis is always on the ideas, metaphors, images and modes of representing cyberspace and cyberculture; 'computers don't just give shape to metaphors, but are themselves shaped by metaphors' (*An Introduction to Cybercultures*, p. 8). Furthermore, the politics of cyberculture should always be considered. Bell demonstrates how the emergence of cyberspace is dependent upon the histories of the development of the computer, the Internet and the World Wide Web, all of which are implicated in military developments and requirements. Similarly, there is also the emergence of Virtual Reality, which has developed in parallel – and which also has a military research dimension to its birth, as well as being indebted to the entertainment industry, with 3D movies, Senso-rama, and the IMAX cinema system: 'VR remains a key component of cyberculture, since it offers the promise of immersive and inter-active environments that mirror cyberpunk's imaginings more closely than the Internet' (*An Introduction to Cybercultures*, p. 15). Bell is concerned with the political economy of the Internet, increasingly the site where technology and society are implicated with capitalist modes of production, and the associated political, economic and social relations that underpin capitalism. He quotes Saskia Sassen: 'Electronic space has emerged not simply as a means for communicating, but as a major new theatre for capital accumula-tion and the operations of global actors' (Sassen, 'Digital Networks and Power', in M. Featherstone and S. Lash (eds), *Spaces of Culture: City, Nation, World* (London, Sage, 1999), p. 49). Another critic, Timothy Luke, argues a similar case in 'Simulated sover-eignty, telematic territory: the political economy of cyberspace' (*Spaces of Culture*, pp. 27ff). Highlighting the political economy of cyberspace, Luke defines what he terms 'dromoeconomics' – a new political-economic realm defined by the speed of economic and information relations. Pointing to digital sweatshops and virtual alienated labour in the Third World, these new economies under-mine the familiar notion of democracy that has underpinned the hype about the Internet since its inception. Jonathan Bignell sounds a further cautious note about the democratisation in computer tech-nology. Noting that computers have been popularised as progressive (in magazines like *Wired* and *Mondo 2000*), as tools for extending democracy and humanistic understanding, the popularisers them-selves seem to be wrapped up in Western-controlled industries and the diffusion of goods and markets. For example, citing the work of Leslie Haddon on 'Interactive Games' (in Philip Haywood and Tana Wollen (eds), *Future Visions: New Technologies of the Screen* (London, BFI, 1993), pp. 123–47), Bignell observes that narrative histories of computer games establish clear connections with the American military and space industries, reinforcing Fredric Jame-son's view that postmodernism reflects the global ambitions of late capitalism and the domination of Western powers (see Jonathan Bignell, *Postmodern Media Culture* (Edinburgh, Edinburgh University Press, 2000).

Cybercultures have also added impetus in recent years to the discussions of the post-human, or inhuman, issues largely driven by the convergence of information technology and the body. Continuing the questions raised by people like Stelarc and Orlan, a variety of recent studies have addressed themselves to the 'post-human', such as N. Katherine Hayles's *How We Became Posthuman: Virtual Bodies in Cybernetics, Literature, and Informatics* (Chicago, University of Chicago Press, 1999); Scott Brewster's *Inhuman Reflections: Rethinking the Limits of the Human* (Manchester, Manchester University Press, 2000), and Robert Pepperell's *The Posthuman Condition: Consciousness Beyond the Brain* (Bristel, Intellect, 2003). Many of these issues about what makes a human *human* cross over with issues raised about the state of digital technology, visual culture, and sexual identity. This has been consolidated in studies of visual culture (see, for example, Nicholas Mirzoeff (ed.), *The Visual Culture Reader* (1998; 2nd edition, London, Routledge, 2002)), where the discussions about changing modes of perception, virtual communities, new cyber-identities, cyber-subcultures and countercultures, and the politics of technological changes, all point to the way in which cyberculture is forcing new configurations of postmodern and post-human concerns. In addition, increasing attention has been given to the ways in which language and code have grown more entangled, so that the lines that once separated humans from machines, analog from digital, and old technologies from new ones, have become blurred. Key studies such as N. Katharine Hayles's *My Mother Was a Computer* (Chicago, University of Chicago Press, 2005) and Mark Poster's *Information Please: Culture and Politics in the Age of Digital Machines* (Durham NC, Duke University Press, 2006) consider the new relation of humans to information machines, a relation that avoids privileging either the human or the machine but instead focuses on the structures of their interactions.

Cyberculture and televisual technological developments clearly dovetail with a number of postmodern concerns, such as the construction of the body, the organisation of space, the engendering of humans, and the possibility of newly emergent forms of consciousness and identity. Unable to prophesy the future completely but nevertheless seduced by the prospect of post-symbolic communication, cyberculture oscillates between acting as a vanguard of

conceptual revolution, and the most traditional, apocalyptic, mil-
lennial anxieties of a culture which sees itself doomed to perpetual
repetition.

Selected reading

Bell, David, *An Introduction to Cybercultures* (London, Routledge, 2001).
    A very accessible and thorough introduction to the major forms,
    practices and meanings of cyberculture.
Bell, David and Barbara Kennedy (eds), *The Cybercultures Reader* (2000;
    2nd Edition, London, Routledge, 2007).
    An excellent sourcebook for this new interdisciplinary field of cybercul-
    ture studies, providing articles by leading critics and theorists on subjects
    as diverse as popular cybercultures, cyberfeminisms, cybersexualities,
    post(cyber)bodies and cybercolonisation.
Bukatman, Scott, *Blade Runner* (London, British Film Institute, 1997).
    An excellent short introduction to all aspects of the film, with good visual
    examples and a useful brief bibliography.
Collins, J., 'Postmodernism and Television', in R.C. Allen (ed.), *Channels of
    Discourse, Reassembled* (London, Routledge, 1992), pp. 327–53.
    An excellent introductory essay, focusing on signs, irony, intertextuality,
    subjectivity and bricolage, with examples from *Twin Peaks* and other
    TV shows. A good annotated bibliography.
Featherstone, Mike, and Roger Burrows, *Cyberspace / Cyberbodies / Cyber-
    punk* (London, Sage, 1995).
    An innovative collection of essays by many of the leading theorists
    of cyberculture on such topics as: technological extensions to bodies,
    cyberprosthetics, bodies in cyberspace, virtual environments, and cyber-
    punk fiction as prefigurative social and cultural theory.
Fiske, John, 'Postmodernism and Television', in J. Curran and M. Gurevitch
    (eds), *Mass Media and Society* (London, Edward Arnold, 1991), pp. 55–67.
    A good introductory essay, which sets out the issues clearly and accessibly.
Goodwin, Andrew, 'Music Video in the (Post)modern World', *Screen*, 28:3
    (1987): 6–23.
    An excellent introductory essay, with a useful analysis of postmodern
    criticism and its weaknesses, and a critique of E. Ann Kaplan's position.
    Examples include Madonna, Bruce Springsteen and Tina Turner.
Grossberg, Lawrence, 'The In-Difference of Television, or, Mapping
    TV's Popular (Affective) Economy', *Screen*, 28:2 (Spring 1987): 28–45,

reprinted in *Dancing in Spite of Myself: Essays on Popular Culture* (Durham NC, Duke University Press, 1997), pp. 125–44.

A good argumentative piece, which provides an interesting materialist analysis of television in the postmodern era.

Kroker, Arthur, and David Cook, *The Postmodern Scene: Excremental Culture and Hyperaesthetics* (Macmillan, Basingstoke, 1988).

A series of manifesto statements and saturnalian observations concerning the 'panic site' of postmodernism, characterised by the double-signs of 'decay/ecstasy, hyper-pessimism/hyper-optimism, memory/amnesia'. The book is conceived of as a guide to 'the ecstatic implosion of post-modern culture into excess, waste and disaccumulation' that constitutes fin-de-millennium culture.

Mirzoeff, Nicholas (ed.), *The Visual Culture Reader* (1998; 2nd edition, London, Routledge, 2002).

With rapid changes in the field of visual culture, this book examines the consequences in fields as diverse as visual art, television, film, advertising, surveillance, digital cultures and fashion.

Orlan, Bernard Blistene, Deke Dusinberre and Caroline Cros, *Orlan: Carnal Art,* translated by Deke Dusinberre (Paris, Flammarion, 2004).

Real, Michael, 'Postmodern Aesthetics: MTV, David Lynch and the Olympics', in *Exploring Media Culture* (London, Sage, 1996), pp. 237–66.

A useful introductory chapter, which focuses on a number of different televisual media within the general context of postmodernism.

Robins, Kevin, *Into the Image: Culture and Politics in the Field of Vision* (London, Routledge, 1996).

A fascinating introductory study of the politics of cyberspace and the new technological developments in televisual communications. Recommended reading.

Smith, Marquard, Julie Joy Clarke, William Gibson and Julie Clarke (eds), *Stelarc: The Monograph* (Cambridge MA, MIT Press, 2006).

The first comprehensive study of Stelarc's work practice, this gathers a range of writers who approach the work from a variety of perspectives, including William Gibson, Arthur and Marilouise Kroker, and Stelarc himself in conversation with Marquard Smith.

Wollen, Peter, 'Ways of Thinking About Music Video (and Post-modernism)', *Critical Quarterly*, 28:1–2 (Spring–Summer 1986): 167–70.

A useful critical introduction to contemporary culture and music videos.

Wyver, John, 'Television and Postmodernism', in Lisa Appignanesi (ed.), *Postmodernism:ICA Documents 4* (London, ICA 1986), pp. 52–4.

A very good introductory discussion of television and postmodernism.

There are a number of interesting websites related to the material discussed
in this chapter.

- Stelarc's Homepage: <http://www.stelarc.va.com.au/>
- MTV Online: <http://www.mtv.com/>
- The Internet Movie Database: <http://uk.imdb.com/>
- *The Panic Encyclopaedia:* <http://www.freedonia.com/panic/>
- The Cyberpunk Website <http://project.cyberpunk.ru/>
- *CTheory* (an online journal of cyberculture and theory): <http://
  eserver.org/ctheory/>

Postmodernism and the social sciences

Hugely dominated by a positivist, scientific paradigm of understanding the world, that is, a belief in the effectiveness of rational inquiry and logical/empirical investigation, the social sciences have sometimes lagged behind other intellectual subjects in embracing the implications of postmodernist ideas. Owing to their different paradigms of exploration, the artistic and literary spheres do not always offer an easy analogy for discourses in the social sciences, and consequently the new discourses for postmodernity are not as fully worked out in the social sciences. Unlike the visual or literary arts, in the social sciences new styles or techniques are barely evident, and the extent to which postmodernism can be identified as a new mode of representing things in the social sciences is still uncertain. As the editors of *Postmodernism and the Social Sciences* readily admit, *'new* ways of doing are sometimes characterised as postmodern mainly because they are new' (Joe Doherty, Elspeth Graham and Mo Malek (eds), *Postmodernism and the Social Sciences* (Basingstoke, Macmillan, 1992), p. 12). Yet although new questions are emerging in the social sciences, it must be stressed that there is no coherent project at work in this 'postmodern' challenge to dominant discourses in the social sciences; rather, it has emerged as a set of plural discourses and motivations which are prompted by a dissatisfaction with the prevailing structures and patterns in these areas of knowledge. The implications of 'postmodern' ideas and interrogations have yet to be realised and thought through fully in the social sciences, although there are areas where the ideas have gained a stronger grip and intellectual following than others. This chapter will move more quickly than previous ones, ranging more generally across a whole range of social sciences without specific attention to each and every subject. It will consider the influences that postmodernist theories are beginning to have on the social sciences in general, and will then focus on two areas in particular – social psychology and international relations theory – as 'case-studies' where the ideas have been theorised quite substantially.

Positivism and the social sciences

The social sciences have been intimately tied up with the Enlightenment and modernisation, part of a massive attempt to demythologise society and to wrest it from the grip of the arbitrary power of church and monarchy, which based its legitimacy in theology. This has occurred through a rationalisation of social structures, for example, by explaining the origins of social structures in terms of such things as economic competition and the establishment of power bases which protect privilege, rather than seeing them as 'natural' or 'god-given', and a differentiation of branches of knowledge into discrete disciplines, allowing humans to build up bodies of knowledge of specific areas in great detail. Central to this manoeuvre was the claim of the exclusive truth-producing capacity of science in contrast to religion, metaphysics and folk traditions: that science was better able to analyse and consequently predict accurately the course of life events. Theories of objective knowledge and of social evolution were key to this project. Steve Smith's essay 'Positivism and Beyond', an excellent exploration of the role and grip of positivism within the social sciences and international relations (IR) theory in particular, argues that there are four clear characteristics at work in the positivist approach: (a) *logicism*: this is the belief that deductive logic ought to act as the verification for objectivity in scientific theory; (b) *empirical verificationism*: the belief that only empirically verifiable statements, that is, those which can be proved to be accurate by practical experiment and demonstration, are scientific; (c) *theory and observation distinction*: the view that there is a strict separation between observations and theories, with observations being construed as theoretically neutral; (d) *the theory of causation*: the belief in a causal relationship allows social scientists to make deductive inferences from an abstract model, or to posit the existence of regularities in unobserved phenomena. For example, one can extrapolate certain production and consumption relationships from a supply-and-demand model of economics, without having to observe all physical instances of its action empirically (Smith, 'Positivism and Beyond', in Steve Smith, Ken Booth and Marysia Zalewski (eds), *International Theory: Positivism and Beyond* (Cambridge, Cambridge University Press, 1996), pp. 11–44; p. 15). Concerned at the lack of reflection in positivist IR theory, Smith is keen to challenge the pre-eminence that positivistic social science has enjoyed in IR theory since the 1950s, because he believes that it has four fundamental fallacies:

1.   a conviction in the concept of a unified science;
2.   that there is a distinction to be drawn between objective facts and social values, where facts are considered to be unmediated by any theoretical framework;
3.   a belief in the regularities of the social as well as the natural world;
4.   a belief that it is empirical validation or falsification that is the stamp of 'real' inquiry (Smith, 'Positivism and Beyond', p. 16).

In a nutshell, positivism believes that facts are out there waiting to be discovered and that the only reliable way to achieve this knowledge is to follow methods based on the natural sciences.

Yet qualms and anxieties about the shortcomings and failures of modernist social science emerged in the 1960s. Despite its ambitions, social theory constantly failed to provide adequate scientific 'foundations' for itself: the attempt to demarcate science from non-science persistently foundered. Time and again science proved to be deeply entrammelled with the dynamics of social control and domination. The model of natural science as a paradigm for knowledge began to be rejected because people increasingly saw it as part of a larger, corrupting, techno-scientific cultural imperative. Consequently, a crisis of methodology and representation emerged, as the aims and goals of modernist social analysis gradually fell into disrepute. Offering indeterminacy instead of determinacy, diversity instead of unity, difference over synthesis, complexity in place of simplification, and intertextual relations rather then causality, postmodernist social sciences appear to 'locate' meaning rather than 'discover' it. In this respect, the French poststructuralist philosophers have had a profound effect on analyses of the weaknesses, contradictions, excesses and abuses in modern social sciences: Jean-François Lyotard's investigations into the state of knowledge in the postmodern age; Michel Foucault's analyses of the webs of institutional power and sexuality; Jean Baudrillard's exploration of the effects of the media, seduction and hyperreality; Jacques Derrida's deconstruction of language and the claims of philosophy; Jacques Lacan's work on the psychoanalytic unconscious – all these have dramatically altered the terrain of the 'human sciences' like psychology, sociology, ethnography, international relations, education and law.

The law, of course, has always been closely bound up with language and representation: the very discourse of justice is studded with terms concerning limits, boundaries, precedents, precision, analogy and transgression. Consequently, because law is everywhere, it comes as no surprise that it has become a site of postmodern theoretical debate, albeit relatively late in the day, in the mid-1980s. For some time, people outside the realm of jurisprudence have written extensively about the implications of poststructuralist thought for legal theory (for example, Derrida, Drucilla Cornell, Gillian Rose, Lyotard); in recent years, jurists have themselves begun to get in on the act. Costas Douzinas and Ronnie Warrington have produced some of the more sustained accounts of the implications of postmodern thought for jurisprudence, particularly in their book *Postmodern Jurisprudence: The Law of the Text in the Texts of Law* (1994). They take orthodox jurisprudence to task for its attempted exclusivity, its semblance of purity, and its blindness to the grounds of its own constitution: 'Jurisprudence interprets texts of law to discover their meaning and reason. Postmodern critical theory reads all types of texts to discover their law' (Douzinas and Warrington, *Postmodern Jurisprudence*, p. ix). Jurispridence attempts to fabricate legal texts into a monological, seamless thread, in which authorised and uniform structures are endlessly invoked and repeated. That is, the law is a field in which the ultimate deciding factor is precedence – how a similar case was decided in the past – and in which it is possible to escape conviction on a 'legal technicality' even though guilt might have been otherwise established. These are aspects of jurisprudence which look 'inwards' to its own body of texts and practices, rather than 'outwards' to the world beyond the court. Postmodern theory opposes this 'inwardness' by seeking to question 'the "reason" of the law'. In particular, working with the ethical ideas of Derrida and Emmanel Levinas (the French phenomenologist who has inspired such contemporary philosophers as Lyotard, Hélène Cixous and Maurice Blanchot), postmodern jurists envision a legal theory which is a 'jurisprudence of alterity', in which they are concerned to recognise explicitly the power structures in abstract theories of the law and to meet the ethical demands of otherness. Other legal theorists are equally concerned with demystifying the positivist mentality of the neutrality of the law: Mary Joe Frug uses postmodern theoretical ideas to uncover a gendered politics of the law (*Postmodern Legal Feminism* (New York, Routledge, 1992)), while Anthony Carty sees poststructuralist ideas as a way to challenge the law's foundationalist illusions (*Post-modern Law* (Edinburgh, Edinburgh University Press, 1990)). In all cases, postmodern legal theorists are concerned to subvert the modernist notion of the law as a grand narrative of impartiality and objectivity, demonstrating that it is deeply imbricated in textual representations and linguistic rhetoric.

Many of the postmodern challenges to modernist scientific theories are concerned with progressively problematising the issues of representation, objectivity and the author–reader relationship. For example, in ethnography, or the study of the customs and cultures of nations and races, James Clifford and Stephen Tyler have targeted their critiques at the model of the lone interpreter who places emphasis on observational technique aided by powerful theoretical abstractions (the positivist subject–object dichotomy once again). They argue that such a modernist organisational interpretative model covertly embeds within it a *monologic* neo-colonial narrative of foreign cultures, which effectively protects authorial priority in the production of meaning. In other words, modernist anthropology is still committed to a model of knowledge in which the author-observer's knowledge of the 'other' culture results from a one-way interpretation, which maintains a colonialist hierarchy of power in the interpretative model. Postmodern anthropology seeks therefore to erode and subvert this tyrannical perspective, offering instead *dialogic* forms which enable the communication of ambiguity, discord and heterogeneity that has been censored, suppressed or denied by monologic forms. In what it perceives to be a committed ethical strategy, by aiming to empower the indigenous voice, a postmodern anthropology opens up the contingency of cultural interpretation, raising questions like (a) who is speaking for any group's identity and authenticity, (b) what are the essential elements or boundaries of any culture, (c) how do 'self' and the 'other' clash in the encounters of interethnic relations? For example, in a study which owes much to deconstructive ideas, Stephen A. Tyler trenchantly opens his book on postmodern anthropology with what is often regarded as a key theme for many postmodern theorists: 'These essays . . . deny that theory is the enabling condition for rational life, and they overturn the notion that knowing is the necessary means and precondition of doing, saying, and feeling. They thus express the mood of postmodern sentiment' (Tyler, *The Unspeakable: Discourse, Dialogue, and Rhetoric in the Postmodern World* (Madison WI, University of Wisconsin Press, 1987), p. xi). Tyler attempts to show how our discourses of cultural anthropology are riddled with key metaphors, narratives and allegories that constitute it and make it possible (for example, the privilege accorded to the visual in our sensory lexicon, as in 'seeing is believing' or 'I see what you mean'); and Tyler goes on to show how these systemic repetitions make an identity between what is known and the structures of knowledge.

Yet despite the alliance with the theoretical ideas of postmodernism evident in some of these challenges, there are just as many social scientists who are wary of the general, all-embracing faddishness of the term 'postmodernism'. Consequently, there is an understandable reluctance among some in the social sciences to define postmodernity explicitly as a distinctive period. Some of the most influential economic and social scientists – among them Anthony Giddens, Scott Lash, John Urry and Ulrich Beck – are convinced that important and far-reaching social changes are occurring in contemporary societies, yet refrain from describing them in terms of postmodernity. Rather, they call it 'reflexive modernisation', a term that they explicitly devised to break 'the stranglehold which [debates about modernity versus postmodernity] have tended to place on conceptual innovation' (Beck, Giddens and Lash, *Reflexive Modernization* (Cambridge, Polity Press, 1994), p. vi). Lash and Urry have argued elsewhere that not all cultural forms in disorganised capitalism are 'postmodern', but that they do have an 'elective affinity' (see Lash and Urry, *The End of Organized Capitalism* (Cambridge, Polity Press, 1987)). Postmodernism for these sociologists tends to be characterised by a matter of economic mode rather than formal style: they juxtapose modern 'organised' capitalism with postmodern 'disorganised' capitalism. In their socio-economic studies, they conclude (similar to Baudrillard) that analysis of contemporary 'disorganised' capitalism is important not because we are a consuming society, but because we consume *signs* and *images*. Agreeing that the traditional concept of 'exchange-value' has been transformed into 'sign-value', and that signs float free of their referents, they read postmodern culture as the logical manifestation of capital as described by Marx, in which 'all fast-fixed frozen relations melt into air'.

Socio-economic analyses of late twentieth-century industrialised societies tend to dovetail with concepts within organisation theory. For example, Scott Lash's concept of 'dedifferentiation' to describe postmodern forms of production (Lash, 'Postmodernism as a Regime of Signification', *Theory, Culture and Society*, 5:2–3 (1988): 311–36) has overlapped with investigations into the connection between concepts of postmodernity and the realities of organisational structures and contexts. 'Dedifferentiation' refers to a reversal of that process of differentiation which people like Max Weber, the influential twentieth-century German sociologist and economist, discerned as a central characteristic of the 'Fordist' organisational processes of modernity. Postmodern organisation theory gestures to a more organic, less differentiated enclave of organisation than those dominated by the huge bureaucratic structures of modernity. Against the rigid job classifications, the mass form of assembly-line production system, the deskilled jobs and adversarial labour relations that characterise modernist/'Fordist' business organisation, postmodern organisation theorists pose the alternative post-Fordist or Japanese 'Fujitsuist' structures, of workforce participation schemes, production centred upon team co-operation, flexible, niche markets and a multiskilled labour force.

Elsewhere, in education theory for example, there are attempts to think through the implications of a postmodern reaction to the domination of abstract theory and claims for an objective practice in modernity. A critical debate which frequently occurs in education is the extent to which pedagogical practices are neutral in terms of their theoretical underpinnings: the extent to which teaching is a matter of possessing skills and tools. Postmodern pedagogy is a search for practices which enact a democratic use of knowledge, texts and cultural practices. Henry A. Giroux has made an extensive case for cultural studies as the postmodern political and ethical project to understand the 'contemporary' and confront dominant culture as a praxis of theory. In his essay 'Is There a Place for Cultural Studies in Colleges of Education?' (in Henry A. Giroux, Colin Lankshear, Peter McLaren and Michael Peters (eds), *Counternarratives: Cultural Studies and Critical Pedagogies in Postmodern Spaces* (London, Routledge, 1996), pp. 41–58), Giroux outlines six ways in which cultural studies might be conceived of as shaping new pedagogical practices:

1. Cultural studies centres upon issues relating to cultural difference, power and history, unpacking their multiplicity.
2. Cultural studies places a significant emphasis on studying language and power and how language is used to fashion social identities and legitimate specific forms of authority. Language is no longer treated as a technical and expressive device, but as a site of social contestation in which historical and contingent practices actively engage in the formation, production, organisation and circulation of texts and institutional powers.
3. Cultural studies links the curriculum to the experiences that students bring to their encounter with institutionally legitimated knowledge.
4. Cultural studies explores the production, reception and situated use of all forms of the culture of print.
5. Cultural studies questions history as a linear narrative unproblematically linked to progress, rethinking it in terms of a series of ruptures and displacements, forcing self-reflection about

one's own historical location amid relations of power, privilege and subordination.

6. Cultural studies forces self-reflection about pedagogical practice.

In tandem with Giroux's work, Peter McLaren has also developed a wide-ranging critical pedagogy as a strategy to alter educational practices as part of a project of social and cultural transformation, in his book *Critical Pedagogy and Predatory Culture: Oppositional Politics in a Postmodern Era* (London, Routledge, 1995). Grounded in 'a politics of ethics, difference and democracy', McLaren criticises Enlightenment epistemology and economic liberalism in favour of 'a new socialist imaginary grounded not in specific forms of rationality but in forms of detotalised agency and the expansion of the sphere of radical democracy to new forms of social life' (*Critical Pedagogy*, p. 24). One sphere which is frequently construed as a new form of social life in pedagogical theories is the advent and impact of computer information technology. Indeed, large claims are made for the ways in which learning and teaching practices are set to be altered by computer technology. In particular, computer hypertext has been championed by George Landow as an example of the fundamental features of text-based computing which are shaping the emergent world of digitised and networked information. In *Hypertext: The Convergence of Contemporary Critical Theory and Technology* (Baltimore, Johns Hopkins University Press, 1992), Landow uses poststructuralist theory to demonstrate the ways in which hypertext and computer-based information systems are altering the ways in which reading and knowledge retrieval take place. He makes a strong case for hypertext operating as a postmodern form of 'lateral' knowledge as opposed to modernism's model of knowledge as 'depth'.

In other fields in the social sciences, though, very little in terms of a developed form of postmodern inquiry has emerged. In economics, for example, although there have been attempts to problematise modernist economics, such as Donald McCloskey's *The Rhetoric of Economics* (1986), which analyses the way in which economic writing is couched in persuasive discursive rhetoric, there is no sustained postmodern economic theory. As one commentator puts it, 'Indeed, while one would tend to look to non-mainstream economics for evidence of postmodernism, a leading critic of modernism (and implicit advocate of postmodernism) is McCloskey who works in the neoclassical or mainstream tradition' (Sheila Dow, 'Postmodernism and Economics', in Doherty *et al.* (eds), *Postmodernism and the Social Sciences*, pp. 148–61). Elsewhere, Peter Midmore in 'Towards a postmodern agricultural economics' (Aberystwyth, UWA, 1995) has explored the feasibility of postmodernism in relation to rural economics, and although the appeal of a set of ideas which stresses the local and the diverse may seem appropriate, Midmore is less certain about the ethical value of a relativist postmodernism for a discipline which has traditionally cared about spatial inequalities. This is an interesting manifestation of how the debate in economics is in its infancy, since the debate about postmodernism and ethics is already at an advanced stage in literary, philosophical and cultural studies, especially under the large influence of Levinas's phenomenological ethics.

The issue of relativism is crucial for the social sciences, and others debate the very validity of postmodern ideas entering the social sciences. John Haldane argues that the notion of a postmodern social science is philosophically contradictory and self-refuting. According to Haldane, the acceptance of postmodernism would lead to the demise of social science, and the retention of social science inevitably means the rejection of postmodernism: *'if relativism is true then social science is impossible'* (Haldane, 'Cultural Theory, Philosophy, and the Study of Human Affairs: Hot Heads and Cold Feet', in Doherty *et al.* (eds), *Postmodernism and the Social Sciences*, pp. 179–95; p. 192). The upshot of Haldane's argument is that postmodernism in the social sciences is a confusing and at times bewildering array of different positions, some of which appear to be well established in some disciplines, whilst others seem tangential, marginal and a cry in the wilderness.

Social psychology

Social psychology focuses upon how social and cultural norms and values are translated into individual thoughts and actions. It focuses on our behavioural decisions about the competing options that confront us all in complex societies, and might be understood as the 'psychology of everyday life'. According to Ian Parker, during the 1960s and 1970s the field of social psychology was beset by a crisis

(Parker, 'Discourse Discourse: Social Psychology and Postmodernity', in J. Doherty, pp. 80–94; p. 80). This crisis was largely the consequence of complaints about the dominant paradigm of research into social behaviour, which was grounded in laboratory experiment. It was felt that this approach ignored or was blind to the terminology which defined the way the experiments were described, understood and explained. Therefore, it was felt that a 'linguistic turn' was needed to get out of some of the problems associated with this lack of linguistic self-reflection. This 'turn to discourse' drew attention to the ways in which social psychology constructed its own theoretical position and its 'data'. Parker argues that social psychology has been obsessed with trying to establish universal truths about social interaction, based upon a disarmingly naive belief in the power of facts. 'Discourse analysis' allowed social psychologists to be reflexive about the area's truth-claims. In his essay 'Toward a Postmodern Psychology' (in Steinar Kvale (ed.), *Psychology and Postmodernism* (London, Sage, 1992), pp. 17–30), Kenneth Gergen has mapped out modernist psychology in the following points:

1. It argued for the existence of a basic, knowable subject matter of psychology.
2. It believed in universal psychological processes.
3. It held to the view that method was a guarantee of truth.
4. It was convinced that research was progressive.
5. It was behaviourist as well as humanist.

Various characterisations of the postmodernist reaction to these tendencies have been explored. Some have argued that postmodern social psychology is a move from modernist positivism to an interpretative, value-constituting science; that it is an acknowledgement that subjectivity is decentred and multi-sited; and that what was previously held to be an autonomous agent of power is now dispersed into anonymous fields of language structures and matrices of power relations. Others have criticised modernist psychology for treating subjects as manipulable objects, rather than as collaborators with whom one negotiates appropriate explanations for behaviour.

So far, claims Parker, the word 'postmodern' has been 'used to buttress existing (albeit marginal) approaches' ('Discourse Discourse', p. 88). Although poststructuralist and deconstructionist lines of inquiry have met with stern resistance, discourse analysis in a more Foucauldian form has found an easier way into psychology. This has meant situating social psychology within discourses of surveillance and notions of selfhood. Discourse analysis 'provides techniques which build on content analysis up to higher levels of meaning, and these techniques *appear* to be systematic' ('Discourse Discourse', p. 83). The leading exponents of discourse analysis in social psychology are Jonathan Potter and Margaret Wetherell, in *Discourse and Social Psychology* (London, Sage, 1987). Deliberately self-reflexive about its own truth-claims and hence eschewing any universalist, totalising perspective, discourse analysis in psychology draws attention to the discursive construction of the subject's own theoretical position. In other words, the power relationships in which the psychologist finds himself or herself with regard to the object of analysis, the nature of the terminology used in carrying out and reporting the experiments, and the methods of experimentation themselves, all now become part of the experimental research. Discourse analysis struggles to resist the closure of much social psychology, and corrodes the truth-claims of other supposedly scientific 'discoveries', drawing attention to the power invested in certain lines of inquiry.

This approach left psychologists pondering the problem of whether to open their arms to postmodernism and act as if it is the 'true' state of things, or whether they ought to treat it as a social phenomenon which needs understanding. The consequence of the postmodernist intervention, Parker argues, has been that two ways forward in social psychology have emerged: (a) to make a study of the phenomenon of postmodernism, analysing the way in which the postmodern has entered various sectors of society (which would keep postmodernism at bay from social psychology); or (b) to provide a postmodern study of social behaviour, which would be based upon radicalised descriptions of accountability and subjectivity.

STOP and THINK

- Are there conflicts between the liberatory aspects of modern *thought* and the conservative nature of modern *institutions*?

- Is there a difference between types of reflexivity, i.e. between a reflexivity which merely dissolves our experiences into a fragmentation of different perspectives, and a reflection that situates our activities in a wider context by taking into account historical and social influences?
- To what extent is modern social psychology impaled upon its own paradox of being a discipline that constitutes the individual – psychology – and a discipline that studies society – sociology?

A fundamental task of the new social psychology is to rescue the subject from on the one hand the social management theories emerging from 'Fordism' and on the other the 'deskilling' contributed by the oppressive practices of psychology ('Discourse Discourse', p. 91). Social psychology has always seen its role as bridging the gulf between the social and the individual: now radical psychology *is* joining the two. Reflexivity is one solution to the crisis in which the discipline has found itself. Yet connecting the social and the individual through reflexivity effectively *depoliticises* the activity: it does not really disturb traditional approaches to psychology. Many of the postmodern challenges have sought to import the issue of politics into social psychology – only then will it be radicalised. Ian Parker notes: 'Discourse analysis can be put to progressive uses, but only because we also hold to narratives about progress which are more important than social psychology' ('Discourse Discourse', p. 93). So Parker, it would appear, does firmly believe in the political validity and necessity of grand narratives.

A significant debate has opened up within social psychology as to the best way of developing a psychology which will meet these new demands. One influential voice in the development of a 'postmodern intervention' in modern psychology is John Shotter. In an essay entitled '"Getting in Touch": The Metamethodology of Postmodern Sciences of Mental Life' (in Shotter, *Cultural Politics of Everyday Life: Social Constructionism, Rhetoric and Knowing of the Third Kind* (Buckingham, Open University Press, 1993), pp. 19–35), Shotter argues that psychology has to move from the modernist paradigm of a detached, theory-testing observer to a 'postmodern', involved, participatory engager: 'a shift from a way of knowing by "looking at" to a way of knowing by being "in contact, or in touch with" . . . the adoption of an involved rather than an external, uninvolved *standpoint*' ('Getting', p. 20). Arising from this shift are several other changes of attitude and aims in investigative procedure: there is a shift from the dominance of the abstract and theoretical knowledge to the practical and everyday; a shift from an interest in *things* to an interest in *activities* and *uses*; a shift away from individuals' thought processes to a focus on the social environment and what this 'allows' or 'permits'; from isolated observational procedures to those negotiated with others; from starting points in reflection to local ones embedded within the historical flow of social activity in everyday life; from language primarily treated as a representation of reality to language as constituting a set of social relations; from operating with received structures and paradigms, which are already accepted as authoritative, towards pragmatic modes, which allow for spontaneous error-correction and find their warrants in locally constituted situations or circumstances ('Getting', p. 20). Shotter's call for a postmodern social psychology is based on a rejection of the metanarrative of objectivity and progressive development in modernist scientific theories, which he argues get in the way of practice. His attempt to get at the 'cultural politics of everyday life' carries echoes of the cultural critic and sociologist Michel de Certeau, whose work on 'the practices of everyday life' has been widely influential in reconfiguring common social practices and rethinking the ways in which abstract theories have all but obscured the object of study.

International relations theory

It is perhaps fitting that this book on 'beginning postmodernism' should conclude with a section dealing with world politics. For if there is any agreement about the subject of postmodernism across the various disciplines, then it centres upon the function and the nature of politics, power, hierarchy and domination. It is somewhat surprising in this context that postmodernism has reared its head relatively recently in the fields of politics and international studies, during the late 1980s. International relations (IR) theory, which forms a subset of international politics, had fallen under the sway of the social sciences during its development as a field of study and knowledge, with the emphasis on the 'science' more than the 'social'. The challenge mounted by postmodern theorists to the dominant paradigms of IR theory has been directed principally at the positivists within IR. If modernist international relations centred primarily upon a politics of state boundaries and how to maintain them, then a postmodern international relations has been more globally oriented, challenging the belief that boundaries are fixed and static. As Paul Virilio, the twentieth-century French analyst of the influence of technology and mechanisms of speed on society, has demonstrated, the postwar world is one where speed and space have become intricately interconnected. A critic of the art of technology, Paul Virilio has keenly observed that media images are often part of a strategy of war and that mistake is becoming indistinguishable from attack. For more than fifty years Virilio has continued to produce criticism on technology and its moral, political and cultural implications. Having coined the term 'dromology' (meaning the logic of speed that underpins society), in such books as *Speed and Politics* (1977; New York, Semiotext(e), 1986), *War and Cinema* (London, Verso, 1989) and *The Information Bomb* (London, Verso, 2000), Paul Virilio is noted for his assertion that the logic of ever-increasing acceleration lies at the heart of the organisation and transformation of the contemporary world. Postmodern theorists have felt that in this age, IR theory is far too serious a matter to be left to the positivists.

Realism has been the most widely influential theoretical tradition in IR since the 1940s. Although defining Realist theory is itself a controversial subject, nevertheless one might argue that the key orthodox Realist theorists were the historian E.H. Carr (1892–1982) and the influential post-war political theorist Hans Morgenthau (1904–80). Emerging largely as a reaction to the political, social and economic calamity of the Second World War and the newly emergent political formations, such Realist theorists incorporated a positivist scientific basis into IR theory. In general, they maintained that an objective scientific epistemology is sufficient to know and order the world. Derived from modernist concerns, the positivist stance espouses the positions that there are universal laws which govern social behaviour and that these are objectively discernible through empirical investigation. As Morgenthau has put it, 'there exists an *objective* and *universally valid truth* about matters political . . . [which] is accessible to human reason' (Morgenthau, Preface to the third edition, *Politics Among Nations: The Struggle for Power and Peace* (1948; New York, Alfred Knopf, 1964), n.p.). Discriminating between 'facts' and 'values', these objective truths then form the basis for manipulating and controlling the international environment. This causal understanding of the world and its actions is a central characterisation of the positivist approach. Furthermore, the positivists adhered to the belief that there are universal human characteristics and that these are unchanging qualities. Finally, positivists generally operated with a state-centric view of the world, in which international politics is construed as a set of relations between individual states, each with its own internal domestic boundaries demarcating it from what lay beyond its territorial sovereignty. Politics, according to the Realists, is possible on the inside (where power can be tamed and the state of nature transformed into civil society), but anarchy or 'the state of war' (as Jean-Jacques Rousseau, the French eighteenth-century philosopher of social politics and individual freedom, called it) is the perpetual condition on the outside. This political discourse of binary opposition, of what was inside and outside the state, had been established during the mid-seventeenth century and had defined the language of politics for three centuries. The sovereignty of states and this binary discourse of inside/outside determined the limits of politics, focusing on democracy, justice and identity.

Morgenthau has left the most lasting political Realist legacy to IR, as set out in his 'Six Principles of Political Realism' in *Politics Among Nations*. Morgenthau derives his political position from the English seventeenth-century philosopher Thomas Hobbes (1588–1679), who argued in his book *Leviathan* (1651) that humans are naturally selfish and that they have escaped anarchy by entering into a social contract, by which they submit to a sovereign. Morgenthau takes as his starting point the Hobbesian argument that in the absence of an all-powerful 'leviathan' or 'government', there can be no social order. Therefore, Hobbes' understanding of the state of nature is translated by the Realist political theorist into a view of the international system as anarchic because of the absence of legitmate authority. Thus, all foreign policy for Morgenthau is any means of which the ends are the protection and preservation of the state's power status. As a sphere of action, the political is an autonomous space in which political success is to be judged in terms of its preservation of the integrity of common good that is the state. There can be no room for moral values, in a state's pursuit of power. For a rational state's interest is inevitably power, and for Morgenthau, this principle is universally valid. The state is perceived as a container for domestic values, and foreign power politics as the only way to preserve those values. In order to exist in the maelstrom of international anarchy, all states are involved in a permanent battle for power: acquiring it, augmenting it, utilising it. Morgenthau's depiction of international relations is an ideal tableau in which circumspect diplomats carefully and realistically evaluate the consequences of various objective policies and act accordingly. It is not difficult to see how the logic of this theory of the international system leads inevitably to the escalation of military power and a political confrontation like the Cold War, in which a precarious 'balance of power' existed between the great powers and their alliances (i.e. NATO and the 'Eastern bloc').

One might conveniently summarise the Realist position as follows:

1. The maintenance of the national interest is the 'prime directive' of all nation-states. This is the procurement of power and the desire to dominate and subjugate other states.
2. There can be no political position which is 'neutral'.
3. All states have an ethics of responsibility – state leaders must maintain the security of the state at *all* costs, even if this means threatening or using force.
4. The anarchical state of international relations forces the escalation of military strength sufficient to act as a deterrent against attack.
5. Economics is subordinate to military might, the former only being useful in promoting the latter.
6. The state is the source (communitarianism) and condition of all values.

STOP and THINK

- Steve Smith and others charge positivism with lacking self-reflection and failing to scrutinise its own epistemological blind spots. Where does positivism take into account the effects of language/discourse in its understanding of political phenomena?

- Positivism is also described as a legacy of modernist social science. To what degree do positivist theories rely on a set of modernist dichotomies and an inherent hierarchy erected upon only one element? What sort of power–knowledge relationship does positivism's distinction between 'facts' and 'values' construct?

- Many critics of positivism argue that it leaves out of consideration other factors. What sorts of marginalised or ignored areas might these be? Does this limit the understanding of what constitutes the political in positivist theories?

- With specific relation to Realism, critics question its *descriptive* power, as well as its ability to account for the contemporary cleavages and fissures that define global politics – i.e. how 'real' is the political picture sketched out by Realism? Can Realism actually be conceived of in the singular, or are there *realisms*? To what extent is the agenda for contemporary politics set by warfare rather than welfare? In the light of the collapse of the perceived threat from the Eastern bloc, how much are the rules of international politics dictated by ozone-layer holes and ecological disasters rather than foreign missiles and hostile hegemonies?

- Finally, how good a *predictive* theory is Realism? What is its track-record at analysing and predicting the future of global relations? Morgenthau argues that the forces inherent in human nature in the realm of politics are the will to dominate and the struggle for power. How is it that the state is not then construed as the expression of the interests of the ruling class? How is it that the state diplomats escape those inherent forces, i.e. do not struggle with one another for power? Why are there different logics at work in domestic and international politics? Does not

Morgenthau's argument ignore the power politics *between* domestic institutions?

___

The postmodernist challenge: textualising IR theory

The calm of the postwar Realist and positivist hegemony in IR theory was upset by the advent of various post-positivist interventions in the late 1980s and early 1990s, among which was the challenge posed by postmodernism. Like feminists, critical theorists and others, postmodern theorists in IR have largely been motivated by challenging many of the assumptions of realist-cum-positivist ideas. One of the principal books on the subject is that edited by James Der Derian and Michael Shapiro, entitled *International/ Intertextual Relations: Postmodern Readings of World Politics* (New York, Lexington Books, 1989). This book incorporates a number of readings in postmodern international relations, and although it denies a unitary approach, it nevertheless demonstrates an emerging consensus among the contributors that there is a need to question the fallacies and aporiae (or sites of acute textual indeterminacy or self-contradiction) of rationalist empiricism that has held sway for so long in the field. Der Derian, a principal figure in the postmodern challenge to mainstream IR theory, aims 'to interrogate present knowledge of international relations through past practices, to search out the margins of political theory, to listen for the critical voices drowned out by official discourses, to conduct an inquiry into the encounter of the given text with the reacting text' (Der Derian, 'The Boundaries of Knowledge and Power in International Relations', in Der Derian and Shapiro (eds), *International/Intertextual Relations: Postmodern Readings of World Politics*, p. 6). Der Derian then issues a summons to a new form of critical thought:

> International relations requires an intertextual approach, in the sense of a critical inquiry into an area of thought where there is no final arbiter of truth, where meaning is derived from an interrelationship of texts, and power is implicated by the problem of language and other signifying practices. . . . an intertextual strategy attempts to understand the placement and displacement of theories, how one theory comes to stand above and silence other theories, but also

how theory as a knowledge practice has been historically and often arbitrarily separated from 'events', that is, the materially inspired practices comprising the international society. This is to challenge the given boundaries of the battlefield, both the geopolitical lines between the states and within systems, and the theory/practice divisions inscribed by the discipline. ('Boundaries of Knowledge', p. 6)

Much of this position derives from Derridean theories of 'textual supplementarity'. This means that no text stands alone, since something always has to be added to it in order for meaning to be constructed. Consequently, all texts are constantly gesturing or drawing attention to their 'margins' or their peripheral contexts. Der Derian's postmodern conviction is that politics also does not lie *behind* texts, but is *intrinsic* to the way they are structured and written. The reality of power politics is not divorced from its representations, but is constituted and inscribed in them. Consequently, Der Derian contests the Realist's separation of the subject from the object of knowledge, as well as the 'pure' autonomy of the 'discipline' of international relations theory.

In his influential analysis of intelligence, Der Derian makes the following statement:

What I suggest, then, is that for this textual moment we leave causation to the political scientists and the promulgation of monologic truths to the national security state courtiers, in favor of an intertextual approach which investigates how these two discourses – the fictive literature of international intrigue and the 'factive' literature of national security and espionage – produce meaning and legitimate particular forms of *power* and espionage. (Der Derian, *Antidiplomacy: Spies, Speed, Terror, and War* (Oxford, Blackwell, 1992), p. 46)

Der Derian's analyses go on to blend characteristically all the elements of low culture and pastiche with CIA reports, IR theory and James Bond movies, 'dedifferentiating' the separation of genres. This highly aesthetic dimension flies in the face of the carefully abstract arguments generated by Realist-positivist science. His writing challenges the simple division between objective theory and subjective representation. Like Derrida's injunctions, Der Derian's work constantly reminds one how IR theory has operated upon a 'forgetting' of the *inscription* or *rhetoric* of the documents of political relations. Following such a call, postmodern theorists of IR have studied the 'intertexts' of contemporary politics: the relationship between events and their textual representation. This has taken the shape of a study of spies and their textual representation (Der Derian), the rhetoric of sports as a structuring discourse for international relations (Shapiro), a semiotic analysis of the major theorists of deterrence (Timothy Luke), and the deconstruction of the boundaries which constitute states (R.B.J. Walker).

This thoroughgoing textualisation of IR theory has amounted to nothing less than a subversion of many of the most deeply held convictions in the discipline. For example, Walker and Richard Ashley have argued in several essays that IR has historically been based upon a sophisticated binary opposition of international–domestic politics, where the representation of international relations as the domain of violent, hostile and anarchic activity relies upon the opposite picture of the domestic arena as one of peace, domesticity and orderly progress. Walker in particular has been instrumental in deconstructing that shibboleth of IR theory, the principle of state sovereignty, in *Inside/Outside: International Relations as Political Theory* (Cambridge, Cambridge University Press, 1993). State sovereignty has had a special status within IR theory because it has been so important in founding modern concepts of political identity, as we have seen with Realist theory. Often defined as the exercise of power within a delimited territory, state sovereignty implies an oppositional model of an inside/outside for political government. Consequently, the state on the 'inside' is seen as a stable community and is given a positive priority over the anarchical, unruly and turbulent international 'outside'. 'Inside' is regarded as the sphere of steady electoral politics, while the 'outside' is construed as the disturbance of politics. Although this model has been a powerful idea in providing us with political identities by erecting borders between 'us' and 'them', Walker is concerned to deconstruct this illusory dichotomy and move beyond state sovereignty. Yet he poses no simple alternative to the modern state, since he argues that the opposition of time–space is so deeply rooted within the modern state that this dichotomy would itself have to be deconstructed before a new conception of the state might emerge.

Walker's and Ashley's characterisations of IR are of a discursive arena that establishes boundaries and legitimates certain responses to problems. Consequently, such postmodern theorists are just as interested (if not more so) in the power invested in the different discourses of IR as a discipline (itself establishing an inside/outside hierarchy) as they are in the power invested in the world political stage: 'Theories of international relations are more interesting as aspects of contemporary world politics that need to be explained than as explanations of contemporary world politics' (Walker, *Inside/Outside*, p. 6). Consequently, in the light of the critique of solving international relations based upon a model of inside/outside, Walker is just as critical of the discipline of IR, which, he argues, utilises the same conceptual structure. Without self-reflexive attention to its own constitution and epistemological limitations, the very rationale for IR is brought into question. Featuring prominently among the postmodern challenges to IR theory is the attempt to get the discipline to rethink its structures of constituting itself as a discipline. In an article entitled 'The Achievements of Post-structuralism' (in Smith *et al., International Theory*, pp. 245–6), Ashley has tentatively offered an inventory of what 'poststructuralist accomplishments' might include, from which one might select the following points to describe what postmodern IR theorists seek to do:

1. to raise the centrality of the problems and crises of representation in modern political life;
2. to sensitise theory to the importance and functions of paradox and ambiguity in political life;
3. to provide new ways of rethinking the questions of agency, power and resistance;
4. to invite radical rethinkings of questions of the political functions of knowledge, memory and history;
5. to provide new approaches to relations of time and space, pace and place, boundaries and transgressions; and to offer distinctive interpretations of the relations between part and whole, localities and totalities, nationalities and internationalities;
6. to demonstrate the importance and possibility of taking seriously the manifold subaltern voices of modern political life

(see the earlier discussion of the 'subaltern' in Chapter 2), coupled with raising awareness of the implications of constructs
of race, gender, ethnicity, nativity, exile, needs and rights in
practices of statecraft; but with a painstaking attention to the
difficulties, dangers and paradoxes involved in any attempt to
theorise and speak a radical alterity;

7. to explore the dependence of modern statecraft upon practices
   that work to tame resistances, domesticate or exteriorise excess,
   and constitute some resemblance of an exclusionary space of
   subjectivity that the state can be claimed to represent;

8. to reinterpret and restructure traditional practices of international law and diplomacy, which have hitherto taken for granted
   stable communities with fixed identities.

Taking stock in the new millennium

The first decade of the new millennium has seen International
Relations, like most other disciplines, continuing to debate the value
and feasible contribution of postmodern theory to the discipline. In
the face of a petering out of the energy of poststructuralist theory,
Nick Rengger and Ben Thirkell-White weighed up the trajectories
and positions of current IR theory in *Critical International Relations
Theory after Twenty-five Years* (Cambridge, Cambridge University
Press, 2007). Apart from James Der Derian's *Virtuous War* (New
York, Westview Press, 2001), which considers the conditions of
'postmodern war', and some significant contributions to feminist
IR theory with Christine Sylvester's *Feminist International Relations*
(Cambridge, Cambridge University Press, 2001), Jenny Edkins'
Trauma and the Memory of Politics (Cambridge, Cambridge Univer-
sity Press, 2003), and Cindy Weber's *Imagining America at War*
(London, Routledge, 2005), Rengger and Thirkell-White are not
able to point to any specific developments in this field during
the 2000s.

Arguably, the discipline has had its attention forcibly redirected
to other issues by the consequences of 9/11. A flurry of political
analyses followed the event, many of considerable interest for their
intervention in debates about some conventional and well trodden
ideas in IR theory, such as the challenge to international order and

justice posed by transnational actors who violently reject the secular liberal commitment of western elites and institutions. Seeking to contextualise the event and its aftermath, *Worlds in Collision: Terror and the Future of Global Order*, edited by Ken Booth and Tim Dunne (Basingstoke, Palgrave Macmillan, 2002), contains essays and reflections by leading intellectuals. While there are many disagreements between the authors, the book nevertheless positions the 'war on terror' as a defining paradigm in the struggle for global order, and many of the essays are at pains to unpick potentially explosive oppositional binaries such as the West/the rest, Islam/ United States and terrorism/democracy. Saturated with a host of associations, paranoias, illusions, fictions and 'New Ageist coincidences', debates about 9/11 can sometimes feel mired in populist hyperbole and prejudice. David Simpson's *9/11: The Culture of Commemoration* (Chicago, University of Chicago Press, 2006) examines the ways in which 9/11 has been aestheticised, exploited and appropriated, even as Ground Zero remains a contested site of commemoration. The debates that have been spawned by the events of 9/11 (the publications are too numerous to mention here), and subsequently 7/7, and the invasions of Afghanistan and Iraq are multiple and varied; some argue that the events are part and parcel of the consequences of a virulent late capitalism, while others argue that the attacks marked the very decisive end of postmodernism, since it was theoretically unequipped to deal with the political and ethical consequences. Unsurprisingly, the field of international relations has been drawn to explaining the use of violence by terrorist groups – previously, terrorism studies had been on the margins of several disciplinary areas, including criminology, comparative politics and anthropology. What had been unclear in the work of those associated with terrorism studies was the extent to which various cases were interrelated: comparability between the causes and consequences of terrorism studies in, for example, Ireland, Spain and Sri Lanka was assumed rather than demonstrated. Today a focus on terrorism has suddenly became a major force in IR debates and one can barely open a book with seeing some debate on terror and international law. Many of the issues about political representation, agency, surveillance and moral contestation that preoccupied postmodern IR theory seem to have been picked up in this area.

The commonplace suggestion that the 'turn' towards postmodern thinking has run its course is one that needs to be scrutinised. When it comes to sophisticated work on the post-9/11 order, postmodern-inspired work has arguably shaped International Relations more than its other competing paradigms. James Der Derian's essay '*In Terrorem*: Before and After 9/11' (in Booth and Dunne (eds), *Worlds in Collision: Terror and the Future of Global Order* (Basingstoke, Palgrave Macmillan, 2002), pp. 101–17) is one such example. Indeed, postmodernists have been at the forefront in showing that jihadists are not reactionary anti-moderns. Quite the opposite: Al Qaeda has skilfully exploited globalised technologies to maximise its support. Moreover, writers such as Faisal Devji (see *Landscapes of the Jihad: Militancy, Morality, Modernity* (Crises in World Politics) (Ithaca NY, Cornell University Press, 2005), point out that Islam does not belong *there* but is deeply entwined *here* in terms of the history and cultural practices of large parts of the 'West', a view also articulated in cultural studies and post-colonial theory by writers like Ziauddin Sardar, who urges the importance of the interchange and dialogue between Islam and the modern world.

Looking at the response of 9/11 by leading states in the international system, it is clear that postmodern ideas and methods have a great deal of explanatory value. The lessons of asymmetric warfare are being relearned, and in the process the paradox of political power has been revealed: as the former Czech playwright and President observed, in politics the powerless are often the most powerful. The other key contribution by postmoderns to understanding the dynamics of world order in the early twenty-first century concerns their unrelenting critique of the claims by western states that they act ethically in their international conduct. The mistreatment of prisoners and suspected terrorists in detention centres such as Guantanamo and Bagram has called into question the superiority of liberal political institutions. Such a levelling of the ethical landscape effectively re-states the arguments advanced by the earlier generation of postmoderns: all states, as Nietzsche argued, are 'cold monsters'. Efforts to claim moral superiority are simply a technique that masks deeper structural logics of power politics grounded in exclusionary notions of identity and community.

STOP and THINK

- Postmodern IR theorists like Walker and Ashley contend that international politics is constructed by our discursive concepts. Consider the way in which different concepts like 'community', 'state' and 'international system' structure our thinking about political entities. Do these correspond to 'actual' entities, or are they merely linguistic constructs?

- When thinking about identity politics, are the 'state' and 'nation' the same thing? (For example, think about the different sites of political machinery and political ideology.) If not, does this act as a weakness in Walker's ideas?

- A further issue to consider in relation to Walker's ideas is the extent to which the question of sovereignty is defined more or less exclusively as a consequence of territorial location. Consider the relationship between the Palestinians and Israelis, or the Kurds and Iraqis, or the Catalans and the Spanish. Are these debates about identity solely about territory? What other issues are involved? (For example, consider culture, language and race.)

- There are other forms of IR theory which are equally motivated by a challenge to positivist assumptions, yet which do not take up the poststructuralist mantle. Andrew Linklater and the Critical Theorists, for example, take a far more materialist stance, which would certainly be disavowed by the likes of Der Derian and Walker. To what degree does the postmodernist attack on the ideals of the Enlightenment, particularly the concept of rationality as an emancipatory mechanism, disable the subject as agent in politics? Can the anti-foundationalist and relativist postmodernist position accommodate the notion of political dialogue between ethical subjects, especially if it regards subjectivity as merely the *effect* of textual representation? Does the poststructuralist textualist approach ignore the material conditions in which international relations function in favour of subverting forms and structures in something of an historical vacuum?

Selected reading

Davies, Margaret, *Delimiting the Law: 'Postmodernism' and the Politics of Law* (London, Pluto Press, 1996).
A good introductory book, although it does require some knowledge of deconstruction.

Doherty, Joe, Elspeth Graham and Mo Malek (eds), *Postmodernism and the Social Sciences* (Basingstoke, Macmillan, 1992).
This book contains a variety of very good introductory essays to various fields of social scientific inquiry, including social psychology, geography, developmental psychology, IR, economics, anthropology, sociology and cultural theory.

Freeman, M.D.A. (ed.), Chapter 14, *Lloyd's Introduction to Jursiprudence* (6th edn, London, Sweet and Maxwell, 1994).
A very general overview of law and postmodernism, including a series of key extracts which discuss the main issues. A good introduction.

Kvale, Steinar, *Psychology and Postmodernism* (London, Sage, 1992).
An exploration of the intersection between postmodern ideas and their implication from the standpoint of psychology. Examines the key current debates about the nature of the self, knowledge in social life, and practice as knowledge, in an approachable and useful fashion.

Shotter, John, *Cultural Politics of Everyday Life: Social Constructionism, Rhetoric and Knowing of the Third Kind* (Buckingham, Open University Press, 1993).
Contains Shotter's essay '"Getting in Touch": The Metamethodology of Postmodern Sciences of Mental Life', which argues for a postmodern social psychology. Also contains other essays which are germane to the issue of how social psychology ought to reconfigure itself as a postmodern practice.

International relations theory

Burchill, Scott, 'Realism and Neo-realism', in Scott Burchill and Andrew Linklater (eds), *Theories of International Politics* (Basingstoke, Macmillan, 1996), pp. 67–92.
A very good introduction to the strengths and weaknesses of Realism, Hans Morgenthau and E.H. Carr, and their legacy to IR theory.

Der Derian, James, and Michael Shapiro (eds), *International/Intertextual Relations: Postmodern Readings of World Politics* (New York, Lexington Books, 1989).
A highly influential book of essays on the subject of postmodernist IR theory. Written by the foremost postmodern theorists, like Der Derian, Robert Ashley and R.B.J. Walker, this book demonstrates the variety of

the postmodern approach, but is principally concerned with arguing the necessity for a textualised understanding of political relations. Tends to be addressed to the more advanced student.

Devetak, Richard, 'Postmodernism', in Scott Burchill and Andrew Linklater (eds), *Theories of International Politics* (Basingstoke, Macmillan, 1996), pp. 179–209.

An excellent and comprehensive introduction to the key thinkers, concepts and relations in the debate about the postmodern challenge to IR theory.

Dunne, Timothy, 'Realism', in Steve Smith and John Baylis (eds), *The Globalization of World Politics: An Introduction to International Relations* (Oxford, Oxford University Press, 1997), pp. 109–24.

An excellent introductory summary of the main principles and key thinkers in the debate about political Realism, as well as a good critique of its premises.

Rengger, Nick, and Mark Hoffman, 'Modernity, Postmodernism and International Relations', in Joe Doherty, Elspeth Graham and Mo Malek, (eds), *Postmodernism and the Social Sciences* (Basingstoke, Macmillan, 1992), pp. 127–47.

An excellent introduction to the arguments proposed by postmodern IR theory, particularly for students who are not specialists in the discipline.

Rosenau, Pauline, 'Once Again Into the Fray: International Relations Confronts the Humanities', *Millennium: Journal of International Studies*, 19:1 (1990): 83–110.

A somewhat generalised introduction, but does position the postmodern challenge to positivist IR theory quite well.

Smith, Steve, 'New Approaches to International Relations', in Steve Smith and John Baylis (eds), *The Globalization of World Politics: An Introduction to International Relations* (Oxford, Oxford University Press, 1997), pp. 165–90.

A very approachable introduction to reflexivist theories of IR, with an informative section on postmodern ideas.

Smith; Steve, Ken Booth and Marysia Zalewski (eds), *International Theory: Positivism and Beyond* (Cambridge, Cambridge University Press, 1996). A collection of essays which look at the various challenges posed to IR theory by post-positivist approaches. In particular, Steve Smith's essay offers an excellent analysis of the hegemony of positivism in the social sciences and how this has dominated IR until the 1980s. Other chapters by significant theorists within the post-positivist debate deal specifically with the multiplicity of theories, like feminist, poststructuralist, hermeneutic, critical theory and scientific realist perspectives, which seek to question the assumptions embedded within a positivist stance.

9

Conclusion: whither postmodernism?

The trouble with reality is that it isn't realistic any more. (Norman Mailer)

It would appear that concluding a book on postmodernism with a discussion of notions of 'nationhood' is a suitable culmination point. For nationhood, national identity and the state of the nation are significant sites for contemporary debate about the effects of postmodernism on our daily lives. After the dissolution of the Cold War, the collapse of the Berlin Wall, the emergence of new and faster means of electronic communication, and the entrenchment of capitalism on a global scale, it has been increasingly felt that social and political communities in the geopolitical sphere need significant reconceptualisation. State sovereignty can no longer rely on modernist static processes of classification and spatial separations. Indeed, the very concept of state 'sovereignty' is no longer reflected in empirical reality (if in fact it ever was), as capital is stretched across the globe, causing new problems of locating and policing financial operations, and electronic media such as the World Wide Web (which respects no state boundaries) pose new problems of regulation and legislation to national governments. For instance, political sanctions in the late 1990s against Iraq include the denial of internet access, which was effectively a denial of (postmodern) world citizenship. The necessity of articulating a credible construction of identity, democracy, community, responsibility or security without the presupposition of the presence of territorial space, a distinct boundary of demarcation between here and there, has become one of the most imperative considerations of the late twentieth century.

It is in this rapidly changing political and social climate that postmodernism has intervened with its various critiques of modernist elitism. As a populist, one might view postmodernism as an attack on the elitism of modernism; as a radical, one might support modernism as the site of an emancipatory consciousness and attack postmodernism as mere superficial kitsch. In its escape from what it perceived as the logical excesses of rationality, postmodernism can be seen to be an intellectual recoil from Hiroshima and the Holocaust; and these in turn were understood as the end to which western civilisation was doomed, of which the effects of the regimentation and standardisation of consciousness in the assembly line, the Somme and Guernica were but the fatal phantoms. In its denunciation of metanarratives and promotion of a world of simulation, postmodernism emerges as a discourse which naturalises and apologises for the social and economic status quo of advanced capitalist countries and their continuing exploitation of natural resources and human labour. These different narratives lead to conflicting views of postmodernism, what Hal Foster has described as a 'postmodernism of resistance and a postmodernism of reaction' (in *Postmodern Cultures* (London, Pluto Press, 1985), p. xii). Foster urges the necessity of a postmodernism of resistance which acts as a counter-practice to the '"false normativity" of a reactionary postmodernism':

> In opposition (but not *only* in opposition), a resistant postmodernism is concerned with a critical deconstruction of tradition, not an instrumental pastiche of pop- or pseudo-historical forms, with a critique of origins, not a return to them. In short, it seeks to *question* rather than *exploit* cultural codes, to *explore* rather than *conceal* social and political affiliations. (*Postmodern Cultures*, p. xii, my italics)

Foster's appeal to a postmodernism which lays bare the discursive strategies of late capitalism is not justified by a parallel attempt to seek the authentic essence of social and subjective forms hidden in mystifying and obscuring representations. He resists the moralising exhortation to recover authenticity in the past or to transcend an inadequate present. Instead he aims at a mode of inquiry that continually disrupts the structures of intelligibility that provide both individual and collective identities for persons and communities, as well as the assumptions of social order within which people are defined and confined.

The mode of representation continues therefore to be the key issue. It is often difficult to decide whether one is reading a book about postmodernism, or a postmodern book; whether one is watching a film about postmodernism, or a postmodern film. The history of the debate over the politics of postmodernism began as a debate over the way to deal with representation. Conservatives advocated a 'return' to representation, which they understood as an intimate correlation between the existence of things and the techniques of expressing them. More radical forms of postmodernism, such as poststructuralism, shunned this mimetic or verificationist approach to representation, and have concentrated upon the spheres of power and authority invested in various modes of representation. This has meant that discourses are scrutinised for being resistant or complicit with the predominant forms of intelligibility. The difficulty occurs in deciding whether such analytical consciousness can operate without the aid of the benefit of metanarrative critiques – economic awareness, multicultural awareness, alertness to problems of sexuality. Society needs to work out a form of cultural analysis which can yoke the positive elements of an ambivalent cultural politics with a narrative of greater freedoms, of greater self-reflexivity about our situations within cultural and economic power, and of a greater social responsibility, a responsibility which moves beyond a complacent extension of the franchise of fragile and weakened economic ideologies and organisations.

It is not possible, nor is it the intention here, to offer a 'summing up' of the characteristics of postmodernism in such vast areas as those covered in this book. Nevertheless, it is possible to note the pattern of certain ideas, preoccupations, cultural obsessions, concerns or procedures that repeat themselves throughout the different subjects. Some are as follows:

- History is taken as a crucial site of debate and contest. In a context where the art world sees the past as a supermarket which the artist raids for whatever goodies he or she wants,

arguments about the use, abuse, popularisation, aesthetici-
sation and dehistoricisation of the past recur with unerring
regularity, as differing camps attempt to claim the theoretical
high ground concerning the significance of different models of
pastness.

• The role of the aesthetic or of ornamentation has always been a
fractious issue. Postmodernism has ushered in a new penchant
for ornamentation, especially evident in music, visual art and
architecture. This has provoked further political debate as to
whether style over content has become an end in itself.

• The body, just like the nation, has always been the site of political contention. Under postmodernism, this debate has inten-
sified, as people are increasingly conscious of the techniques
of physical and psychological control. The body has never
simply been one's own: yet now, under highly technologically
proficient and efficient mechanisms, it is scrutinised, surveilled,
regularised, sanitised and corralled by systems and forces in
ways hitherto unparalleled. In the rhetoric of the techno-
utopians, one can also see a fixation with immortality, a neuro-
sis which permeates whole sectors of contemporary culture in
its efforts and belief that one can transcend one's body through
technological accomplishments.

• This obsession goes hand in hand with the new preoccupation
with space and metaphors of space, cyberspace being one
obvious experimental site. It is increasingly recognised that a
politics of discourse is tied to a politics of space. A central argument of the radical nature of postmodernism is its production
of new spaces, e.g. an atrium, which is space as spectacle (an
atrium isn't much *use*, even for promenading), opposing the
institutionalised existing spaces which have reinforced existing
forms of power. Others accuse postmodernism of focusing on
space to the exclusion of time, and once again returning to the
debate about the absence or expulsion of history from cultural
analysis.

• It is impossible not to recognise how our lives are inextricably
bound up with signs and texts, and this too is a recurrent theme
in postmodernist writing: information systems, textual representations, visual and electronic media, and advertising cultures

surround us at every turn. Everything is constantly and insistently *mediated* to us by all types of print and visual media, to the extent that people have begun to theorise the disappearance of the *world* and the appearance of the *word* and *image*. This has led some to urge the necessity of rematerialising the word (showing the material processes that go into making meanings and values), while others have described the world in which our consciousnesses are trapped in an arena of simulations, forgeries and fabrications.

Despite the constant injunctions and demands by contemporary culture to think laterally and in an interdisciplinary fashion, disciplines still seem so closed, segregated and sequestered from one another. Yet it is clear that many of these disciplines are struggling with the same problems and issues; and it might be that closer interaction between these subject areas might *enable* rather than *inhibit* a better understanding of contemporary culture and its problems. Literary analysis can learn about the politics of power and ideas of nationhood from international relations theory; visual art and sculpture can learn about manipulating their audience from the professionalisation of popular culture in the music business; and the social sciences can learn the pitfalls and strengths of textual and interpretative strategies from literary analysis.

On 1–3 December 1986, the *Guardian* ran a survey of the condition of modern and postmodern culture, printing the reports of various arts analysts on the state of British culture. With the surrounding pages swirling with reports about Oliver North and the Irangate scandal in the United States and the Guinness scandal breaking in London, it is not too surprising that the *Guardian* analysts perceived postmodernism to be the consequence of a culture going down the tubes, a state of decadence as Britain approached cultural burnout. Their reports stress the trivialisation of culture, the collapse of content into style, and the random amalgamation of bits of the past in a desperate attempt to shore up the present as exciting, innovative and radical.

Yet, just over a decade later, with a 'New' Labour government and 'Cool Britannia' resonating in every soundbite, postmodernism has not delivered the apocalyptic crises that the *Guardian* columnists predicted on the eve of Christmas in 1986. Although the concern for style continues to saturate and dominate popular consciousness, it would seem that traditional culture nevertheless appears to be thriving in Britain, Europe and the rest of the world. However, in the process of mapping out the 'modernisation' of the Labour Party, Tony Blair reaffirmed even New Labour's commitment to postmodern beliefs. Writing in the *Guardian* on 27 May 1996, Tony Blair urged people to accept that 'The spirit of the times has changed beyond recognition since 1964. The *totalising ideologies* of left and right no longer hold much purchase.' This appears to be a rhetoric of political capitulation rather than political initiative. It signals a retreat from the notion that politicians and people can *change the world*. It accepts the postmodern state of affairs (metanarratives no longer exist) rather than treating it as a strategy for dealing with contemporary society (a suspicion of the power of metanarratives). We can see here how so much of the postmodern rhetoric of finality and integrity, of the desperate need for authenticity or sincerity in the face of wholesale simulation, has permeated the very fabric of everyday consciousness.

The fact that postmodern rhetoric structures so much of daily life is perhaps not that surprising when one considers that postmodernism has now been around as a concept and in debate since roughly the mid-1970s, and it is retrospectively possible to see that postmodernism has developed a history. That history is an uneven and irregular one. On the one hand, it shows postmodernism declining as a serious contender for the historical periodisation of culture during the last twenty-five years of the millennium, as it appears to be losing much of its intellectual *kudos* and power in some disciplines (literature, cultural theory). On the other hand, it is quite clearly becoming a major issue in other disciplines (international relations theory, history, some of the social sciences), as positivism and modernist scientism lose their hold. If redefinitions of postmodernism have occurred over the past twenty-five years, then it is perhaps evident that there seems to be an increasing concern for the politics of everyday life. If everything was a question of economics in the 1980s, then everything seems to be a question of ethics in the 1990s. This has raised an increasing awareness of the responsibilities involved in representation and communication, and broadened the scope of debate about political and ethical responsibility.

Although a thirteen-letter word, 'postmodernism' continues to be treated as a four-letter word in many quarters. Anxieties about its conservative political complicity, its reactionary aesthetic ideology, and its philosophical contradictions continue to dog its diagnostic or forensic utility in analysing contemporary culture. Unable to shrug off a residual connotation of decadence and degeneration, postmodernism nevertheless remains a hotly contested concept, a concept in which many people are still trying to look for the stigmata of the new consciousness in contemporary cultural production.

The *Guardian Weekend* (20 June 1998) advertised a website at Monash University in Australia, called 'The Post-modern Generator': <http://www.cs.monash.cdu.au/links/postmodcrn/html>. Claiming to allow you to vent your anger at the turgid nature of postmodernist texts, it is a computer program that lets one produce 'completely meaningless ... randomly generated' postmodern essays. By amalgamating prominent names, notable popular figures and jargon words, the Generator emerges with essays which ape intelligence yet which are completely meaningless phrases strung together with mock plausibility. It is hoped that after reading this book, instead of drowning by 'isms', students may be able to detect and measure the vacuous quality of such 'mock seriousness' of 'imitation postmodernism'. Who knows: perhaps it will initiate the construction of a similar computer program in Britain or the United States.

Select bibliography

This bibliography is mainly designed to provide further details of books relevant to the discussions in various chapters. Owing to the massive list of publications in all these areas, this is not intended to be a definitive list. Nor does it include the bibliographical details already cited in the text of the chapters, or in the short selected reading sections appended at the end of each chapter, except in certain instances where an appraisal of the book's value has not been fully made in the text. Apart from the works in the anthologies, this is an annotated list of *secondary* material, varying from introductory to more sophisticated discussions.

General introductions to postmodernism

Appignanesi, Richard, and Chris Garratt, *Postmodernism for Beginners* (Cambridge, Icon Books, 1995).
   With its familiar cartoon style and excellent text, this book covers postmodernism across art, theory and history in an approachable and humorous fashion.
Brooks, Neil and Josh Toth (eds), *The Mourning After: Attending the Wake of Postmodernism* (Amsterdam and New York, Rodopi, 2007).
   Through a series of essays by key theorists, it addresses the issue of whether we have moved beyond postmodernism, arguing that a postmodern inheritance and a certain vigour persist in the debates.
Connor, Steven, *Postmodern Culture* (Oxford, Blackwell, 1989).
   A good, thought-provoking introduction to the subject of postmodernism in the humanities. Covers a wide range of material and contains a useful bibliography.

Connor, Steven (ed.), *The Cambridge Companion to Postmodernism* (Cambridge, Cambridge University Press, 2004).

A useful companion that offers essays written by specialists in different aspects of postmodernist thought that have had significant impact upon contemporary cultural production and debate, covering areas such as film, literature, art and performance, religion and law.

Eagleton, Terry, *The Illusions of Postmodernism* (Oxford, Blackwell, 1996).

A stimulating, approachable and polemical critique of postmodernism's strengths and failings, its ambivalences, contradictions and cultural *milieu*.

Featherstone, Mike (ed.), Special issue on postmodernism, *Theory, Culture, Society*, 5 (June 1988).

A good introduction, with essays on postmodernism and sociology, philosophy, architecture, feminism, film, urbanism and the city, politics and popular culture.

Hebdige, Dick, 'Staking out the Posts', in *Hiding in the Light: On Images and Things* (London, Routledge, 1988), pp. 181–207.

A sophisticated essay which sceptically lays out the territory of the relation of Marxism to postmodernism, focusing especially upon the constitutive role of negation throughout discourses of postmodernism – what he terms 'the three negations': 'Against Totalitariansim', 'Against Teleology' and 'Against Utopia'.

Lopez, José and Gary Potter (eds), *After Postmodernism: An Introduction to Critical Realism* (London and New York, Athlone Press, 2001).

Examining what comes 'after' postmodernism, this book considers the increasing interest in 'critical realism' as a possible alternative way of moving forward. The flexibility of critical realism as a methodology is illustrated by a range of essays that address such diverse areas as quantum mechanics, literary theory, cyberspace, nature, the unconscious, postmodernism, and theory itself.

Lyon, David, *Postmodernity* (Buckingham, Open University Press, 1994).

A good and accessible introduction, charting the lineage of the concept of postmodernity as idea, critique, cultural experience and social condition, with a broad range of cultural reference.

Malpas, Simon, *The Postmodern* (London, Routledge, 2005).

A useful introductory guidebook that investigates the theories and definitions of postmodernism and postmodernity, and explores their impact in such areas as identity, history, art, literature and culture.

McGuigan, Jim, *Modernity and Postmodern Culture* (1999; 2nd Edition, Buckingham: Open University Press, 2006).

Critically assesses claims made about the 'postmodernisation' of culture and society, and explores the complex interplay between the modern and the postmodern in an increasingly 'globalised' world. Maintains that although culture may be 'postmodern' in terms of art, entertainment and everyday life, modernity exists and is pervasive.

Rose, Margaret A., *The Post-modern and the Post-industrial: A Critical Analysis* (Cambridge, Cambridge University Press, 1991).
This is a useful text for an introduction to the history of the term and its use across a broad range of subjects. Contains a useful bibliography.

Silverman, Hugh J. (ed.), *Postmodernism – Philosophy and the Arts* (New York, Routledge, 1990).
A range of readable essays, in which the first half raises general theoretical questions about the language and politics of postmodernism, and the second part focuses on some particular 'sites' – architecture, painting, literature, theatre, photography, film, television, dance, fashion. Contains a helpful bibliography of books, articles and journals on postmodernism.

Wheale, Nigel (ed.), *The Postmodern Arts: An Introductory Reader* (London, Routledge, 1995).
Another good introductory book, which combines general arguments with individual case-studies.

Philosophy and cultural theory

Baudrillard, Jean, *Selected Writings,* ed. Mark Poster (Stanford CA, Stanford University Press, 1988).
A good collection of the writings of Baudrillard, with useful commentaries.

Bauman, Zygmunt, *Intimations of Postmodernity* (London, Routledge, 1991).
A sophisticated study of postmodernism: for the advanced student, with discussions of sociology and Baudrillard.

Brodribb, Somer, *Nothing Mat(t)ers: A Feminist Critique of Postmodernism* (2nd edn, North Melbourne, Spinifex Press, 1993).
A useful feminist polemic against postmodernism, which offers incisive critiques of a number of leading theorists.

Brooker, Peter (ed.), *Modernism/Postmodernism* (London, Longman, 1992).
A useful collection of extracts from the leading thinkers in this debate, exploring various ways in which to think about the relationship between modernism and postmodernism. Good for beginners.

Callinicos, Alex, *Against Postmodernism: A Marxist Critique* (Cambridge, Polity Press, 1990).

A good, thoroughly argued polemic against postmodernism from a Marxist perspective. Offers critiques of all the leading thinkers and their ideas.

Caputo, John D. and Michael J. Scanlon (eds), *God, the Gift and Postmodernism* (Bloomington IN, Indiana University Press, 1999).

Including contributions from key theorists, this book questions the authority and limits of 'the modern' in the call to religious experience, and explores areas where philosophy and religion have become increasingly and surprisingly convergent.

Crowther, Paul, *Philosophy After Postmodernism* (London, Routledge, 2003).

Instead of simply rejecting postmodern thought, Crowther tries to assimilate some of its main features, identifying conceptual links between value, knowledge, personal identity and civilisation, understood as a process of cumulative advance.

Flax, Jane, *Thinking Fragments: Psychoanalysis, Feminism, and Postmodernism in the Contemporary West* (London, Routledge, 1990).

A stimulating feminist interrogation of the utility of postmodern ideas for feminism. More suitable for the advanced student.

Fulkerson, Mary McClintock, *Changing the Subject: Women's Discourses and Feminist Theology* (Minneapolis MN, Fortress Press, 1994).

Investigates the many ways in which women's scriptural 'performances' are liberating, offering three sample readings of 'emancipatory discourses' from diverse social locations that display the variety of ways in which women are oppressed and resistant.

Hart, Kevin, *The Trespass of the Sign: Deconstruction, Theology and Philosophy* (New York, Fordham University Press, 1989).

Contrary to popular thought on the topic, Hart demonstrates that deconstruction does not have an antitheological agenda and offers a clear and thorough account of the relations between deconstruction and theology.

Harvey, David, *The Condition of Postmodernity* (Oxford, Blackwell, 1990).

One of the central books in the definition of postmodernism, this is an excellent, wide-ranging and easily approachable book on postmodernism across cultural arenas. Interesting on film, geography, economics, architecture and cultural theory.

Jameson, Fredric, *Postmodernism, or the Cultural Logic of Late Capitalism* (London, Verso, 1991).

Another landmark text in the debate concerning postmodernism, this is the result of several earlier essays. Deals provocatively with film, architecture, video, art, economics, space, ideology and cultural theory. For the more advanced reader.

Norris, Christopher, *The Truth About Postmodernism* (Oxford, Blackwell, 1993).
An advanced and sophisticated critique of philosophical appropriations by postmodern theorists, which challenges their various apocalyptic tones.

Tester, Keith, *The Life and Times of Postmodernity* (London, Routledge, 1993).
This book offers an introductory albeit sceptical appraisal of postmodernism as a 'great transformation'. It regards postmodernism as a reflection of the problems of modernism, focusing on issues of identity, nostalgia, technology, responsibility and the other.

Ward, Graham, *Barth, Derrida and the Language of Theology* (Cambridge, Cambridge University Press, 1995).
This book reveals Karl Barth's closeness to postmodern thinking and underlines his relevance to current debates on the language of theology.

Wright, Elizabeth, and Edmond Wright (eds), *The Žižek Reader* (Oxford, Blackwell, 1999).
Divided into three parts – Culture, Woman and Philosophy – this provides a comprehensive and accessible introduction to Žižek's work.

Wyschogrod, Edith, *Crossover Queries: Dwelling with Negatives, Embodying Philosophy's Others* (New York, Fordham University Press, 2006).
From an important theorist, this book probes both the desire for God and an ethics grounded in the interests of the other person, seeing these as moments both of crossing over and of negation, commenting on philosophical and theological issues that have shaped the recent past as well as scientific and technological questions that will preoccupy us in the near future.

Literary arts

Adam, Ian, and Helen Tiffin (eds), *Past the Last Post: Theorizing Post-Colonialism and Post-Modernism* (Brighton, Harvester Wheatsheaf, 1991).
Useful introductory essays on the nature of the 'post' in postcolonial literature and theory.

Alexander, Marguerite, *Flights from Realism* (London, Edward Arnold, 1990).
Investigates the historical impulses that have driven postmodernism, and its dialogical relationship with realism. Introductory essays on Thomas Pynchon, Kurt Vonnegut, Salman Rushdie, E.L. Doctorow, John Fowles, Joseph Heller and Paul Auster.

Barker, Francis, Peter Hulme and Margaret Iverson (eds), *Postmodernism and the Re-reading of Modernity* (Manchester, Manchester University Press, 1992).

Very good essays ranging across science fiction, detective fiction, art, history, critical and cultural theory.

Bukatman, Scott, *Terminal Identity: The Virtual Subject in Postmodern Science Fiction* (Durham NC, Duke University Press, 1993).

An excellent discussion of cyberculture, cyberspace and science fiction. Good on science fiction in film and literature, new concepts of subjectivity, popular culture and cultural theory. With a comprehensive bibliography and filmography, this is probably better for the more advanced student.

D'haen, Theo, and Hans Bertens (eds), *British Postmodern Fiction* (Amsterdam, Rodopi, 1993).

Good introductory essays on contemporary fictional styles, including realism, magic realism, historiographic fiction and metafiction, as well as such novelists as Samuel Beckett, Martin Amis, Christine Brooke-Rose, Peter Ackroyd and Graham Swift.

Eaglestone, Robert, *The Holocaust and the Postmodern* (Oxford, Oxford University Press, 2004).

This book argues that postmodernism, especially understood in the light of the work of Emmanuel Levinas and Jacques Derrida, is a response to the Holocaust.

Gilbert, Alan, *Another Future: Poetry and Art in a Postmodern Twilight* (Middletown CT, Wesleyan University Press, 2006).

A collection of critical essays on contemporary poetry, art, culture, and politics that investigate the current state of these fields and seek a new discourse for thinking beyond postmodernism.

Gregson, Ian, *Contemporary Poetry and Postmodernism: Dialogue and Estrangement* (Basingstoke, Macmillan, 1996).

A collection of detailed essays which chart the development of experimental poetic techniques of estrangement out of modernist dialogic practices. Essays on Edwin Morgan, John Ashbery, Denise Riley, Roy Fisher and others.

Lee, Alison, *Realism and Power: Postmodern British Fiction* (London, Routledge, 1990).

Focuses on the subversive techniques of British postmodern fiction, examining its challenge to realist traditions. Discussions of Alasdair Gray, John Fowles, Salman Rushdie and Graham Swift. A good introduction accompanied by a useful bibliography.

Niall, Lucy, *Postmodern Literary Theory: An Introduction* (Oxford, Blackwell, 1997).
A provocative discussion of how postmodern literary theory derives from a late eighteenth-century romantic tradition. Explores a range of theorists and writers touching on issues such as reason, ethics, reading, interpretation and history in relation to Acker, Auster, Barth and Pynchon.

Waugh, Patricia, *Practising Postmodernism Reading Modernism* (London, Edward Arnold, 1992).
A good discussion of the relationship between modernism and post-modernism. Focuses on modernist writers from the perspective of postmodern theory.

Wolmark, Jenny, *Aliens and Others: Science Fiction, Feminism and Postmodernism* (Brighton, Harvester Wheatsheaf, 1993).
Considers feminist science fiction and its intersection with postmodernist ideas, with writers like Octavia Butler, Gwyneth Jones, Pat Cadigan, Vonda McIntyre and C.J. Cherryh providing the main textual focus.

Zurbrugg, Nicholas, *The Parameters of Postmodernism* (London, Routledge, 1993).
Concerned with outlining the relationship of postmodern cultural practices with those of the avant-garde. For the more advanced student.

Architecture and concepts of space

Carter, E., J. Donald and J. Squires (eds), *Space and Place: Theories of Identity and Location* (London, Lawrence and Wishart, 1993).
Through the diverse prisms of colonialism, national identity and urban experience, essays by prominent theorists explore the themes of home and exile, Englishness and imperialism, and city space. For more advanced students.

Davis, Mike, *City of Quartz* (London, Verso, 1990).
A study of the culture, urban planning and architecture of Los Angeles. Very good on all aspects of popular culture and contemporary theories of urban planning.

Duncan, J.S. and D. Ley (eds), *Place/Culture/Representation* (London and New York, Routledge, 1993).
Examines the interconnections of spatial and cultural analysis, with particular attention to cultural geography, landscape and the politics of place and space, from the perspective of theoretical ideas about discourse, intertextuality, metaphors and rhetorical structures.

Ellin, Nan, *Postmodern Urbanism* (Oxford, Blackwell, 1996).

Explores urban design, and what postmodernism means for the design of large-scale environments. Examines the contemporary crises beleaguering the built environment and the architectural and planning professions.

Frampton, Kenneth, 'Towards a Critical Regionalism', in Hal Foster (ed.), *Postmodern Culture* (London, Pluto Press, 1985), pp. 16–30.

A key document in the debate about urban planning and postmodern architectural practices.

Ghirardo, Diane, *Architecture After Modernism* (London, Thames and Hudson, 1994).

A good, easily accessible, introductory book on developments within architecture after the decline of modernism. Focuses on the reconfigurations of public, domestic and urban space.

Jencks, Charles, *Free–style Classicism* (London, Architectural Design, 1982).

A specific focus on the classical revival and its manifestations in postmodern architects like Arata Isozaki, Takefumi Aida, O.M. Ungers, Robert Stern, James Stirling and Michael Graves.

Jencks, Charles, *The Language of Post-Modern Architecture* (London, Academy Editions, 6th edition, 1991).

An influential analysis of how architecture can be treated as a language. Final chapter shows the emergence of a postmodern language with its emphasis on hybridity, mixed materials and eclectic pluralism.

Jencks, Charles, *The Prince, the Architects, and New Wave Monarchy* (London, Academy Editions, 1988).

A useful collection of the Prince of Wales' speeches on architecture, contextualised with responses by various architects and journalists.

Jencks, Charles, *The Architecture of the Jumping Universe* (1995; rev. edn London, Academy Editions, 1997).

A study of morphogenesis in architecture, focusing particularly on how the science of complexity is affecting architectural practice and contemporary culture. Looks at the architecture based upon fractals, waves and twists by people like Peter Eisenman, Frank O. Gehry and Daniel Libeskind.

Klotz, Heinrich, *The History of Postmodern Architecture*, trans. Radka Donnell (Cambridge MA, MIT Press, 1984).

A monumental study of the phenomena of postmodern architecture. Lavishly illustrated, this is an essential book focusing upon all aspects of postmodern architecture and its leading practitioners in a readable and provocative manner.

Larson, Magali Sarfatti, *Behind the Postmodern Façade* (Berkeley CA, University of California Press, 1993).

Explores the evolution of architecture in the postmodern era. Analyses the complex tensions that exist between economic interest, professional status and architectural product.

Olalquiaga, Celeste, *Megalopolis: Contemporary Cultural Sensibilities* (Minneapolis, University of Minnesota Press, 1992).

Analysing the diverse articulations of the hybrid forms of contemporary metropolitan culture, this book focuses on the benefits and disadvantages of subjectivity being shaped by and engaging with the city.

Soja, Edward W., *Thirdspace: Journeys to Los Angeles and Other Real-and-Imagined Places* (Oxford, Blackwell, 1996).

A sophisticated extension of the discussion of space in postmodern theory from his first book, *Postmodern Geographies* (1989), and includes within it extensive discussions of contemporary geographical and spatial theory. For the more advanced student.

Soja, Edward W., *Postmetropolis: Critical Studies of Cities and Regions* (Oxford, Blackwell, 2000).

The third volume of Soja's trilogy on urban studies, this book focuses upon the dramatically restructured megacities – here called postmetropolises – that have emerged since the 1960s all over the world, presenting six discourses on the postmetropolis that have developed, locally and globally, to make sense of the new urbanisation processes.

Stern, Robert A.M., *New Directions in American Architecture* (New York, George Braziller, 1969).

Seminal focus on postmodern architects like Peter Eisenman, Robert Venturi, Louis Kahn, Philip Johnson, Charles Moore, and the new urbanism.

Taylor, Mark C., *Disfiguring: Art, Architecture, Religion* (Chicago, University of Chicago Press, 1992).

This book considers the relationship of modernist art and architecture to postmodernist art and architecture through the trope of 'disfigurement'. Good on Anlsem Kiefer, Robert Rauschenberg, Andy Warhol and Peter Eisenman, Michael Graves and Bernard Tschumi.

Watson, Sophie, and Keith Gibson (eds), *Postmodern Cities and Spaces* (Oxford, Blackwell, 1994).

An excellent collection of essays by leading people on the politics of postmodern space and cities. Considers such issues as feminism and space, urban walking, and sexuality.

Visual art, sculpture and the design arts

Berger, Maurice (ed.), *Postmodernism: A Virtual Discussion* (New York, Distributed Art Publishers, 2003).

An online symposium's posted discussion that addresses itself to a range of issues surrounding the validity, usefulness, and complexities of the term 'postmodernism' in relation to art.

Britt, David (ed.), *Modern Art: Impressionism to Post-Modernism* (London, Thames and Hudson, 1989).

A very helpful set of essays on twentieth-century art movements and styles, with a particularly good introductory essay on postmodern art by Marco Livingstone.

Broude, Norma, and Mary D. Garrard (eds), *The Power of Feminist Art: The American Movement of the 1970s; History and Impact* (New York, Abrams, 1994).

An excellent series of essays which discuss the role of feminism in art since the 1970s, looking at social protest, feminist performance art, constructions of the body, collaborative projects and anti-essentialism. Lavishly illustrated.

Brunette, Peter, and David Wills (eds), *Deconstruction and the Visual Arts* (Cambridge, Cambridge University Press, 1994).

A variety of essays on aesthetics, art history and criticism, film, television and architecture, offering creative and experimental readings of visual 'texts' derived from the ideas of Jacques Derrida.

Collins, Michael, *Towards Post-modernism: Design Since 1851* (London, British Museum Publications, 1987).

An introductory book whose last chapter is most useful on developments from pop to postmodern design.

Collins, Michael, *Post-Modern Design* (London, Academy Editions, 1989).

A lavishly illustrated book which covers the area of postmodern design in Italy, the United States, Japan and elsewhere. It is cautious about distinguishing between 'Late-Modern' design and 'Postmodern' design.

Crimp, Douglas, *On the Museum's Ruins* (Cambridge MA, MIT Press, 1993).

Studies the shift from the autonomous modernist artwork to the discursive contexts of postmodernism. Good on photography, site sculpture and history. For more advanced study.

Crowther, Paul, *Critical Aesthetics and Postmodernism* (Oxford, Oxford University Press, 1993).

An advanced attempt to theorise postmodern art in relation to poststructuralist theories of sublimity, often involving sophisticated philosophical argument. Nevertheless, this is one of the more serious examples of post-modernist art criticism which deals with recent debates within theories of representation.

Erjavec, Aleš, Martin Jay and Boris Groïs (eds), *Postmodernism and the Postsocialist Condition: Politicized Art Under Late Socialism* (Berkeley, University of California Press, 2003).

Examines the way artists registered the exhaustion of the socialist vision and absorbed the influence of art movements such as constructivism, pop art, and conceptual art, as well as the provocations of Western pop culture in a unique version of postsocialist postmodernism.

Foster, Hal, Rosalind Krauss, Yve-Alain Bois, and Benjamin H.D. Buchloh, *Art Since 1900: Modernism, Antimodernism, Postmodernism* (London, Thames and Hudson, 2005).

Destined to become the standard history for the foreseeable future, the book is uniquely arranged so that there are one or two essays per year. Often undervalued movements are given as much respect as the well-established.

Harrison, Charles, and Paul Wood (eds), *Art in Theory: 1900–1990* (Oxford, Blackwell, 1992).

A monumental collection of essays and statements on art history during the twentieth century. Excellent sections on critical theory, the politics of art, modernist art, originality and postmodernism. An exceptional resource for beginners and more advanced students.

Hertz, Richard (ed.), *Theories of Contemporary Art* (Englewood Cliffs NJ, Prentice-Hall, 1985).

Contains a variety of seminal essays by people like Kim Levin, Barbara Rose, Joseph Kosuth, Donald Kuspit, Craig Owens, Thomas Lawson, Douglas Crimp, Allan Sekula, Hal Foster, Lucy Lippard, Rosalind Krauss, Benjamin Buchloh and Douglas Davies, which discuss the end of modernism and the advent of innovative styles and techniques in the 1970s and 1980s. The essays cover a wide range of development within visual art, sculpture and performance art.

Krauss, Rosalind E., *The Originality of the Avant-Garde and Other Modernist Myths* (Cambridge MA and London, MIT Press, 1985).

Contains several key discussions of postmodern art, especially relating developments within poststructuralist theory to postmodernism and sculpture.

Pollock, Griselda (ed.), *Generations and Geographies in the Visual Arts: Feminist Readings* (London, Routledge, 1996).

Although explicitly concerned with feminist art and aesthetic theory, this nevertheless engages with many terms and issues that preoccupy

postmodern theory. An excellent and provocative collection of essays
on feminist art, Cindy Sherman, Jenny Saville and Orlan, as well as the
body, regional identity, the maternal and art history.

Roberts, John, *Postmodernism, Politics and Art* (Manchester, Manchester
University Press, 1990).
An advanced discussion of modernism, realism and postmodernism.
Considers the politics of visual art under Thatcherism, ethnicity and art,
and history and art, although it remains critical of 'postmodernism' as an
obfuscating term.

Taylor, Brandon, *The Art of Today* (London, Weidenfeld and Nicolson, 1995).
An excellent and comprehensive survey of art movements since the
mid-1970s, with several sections explicitly dealing with postmodern art,
performance, sculpture and gender.

Wood, Paul, Francis Frascina, Jonathan Harris and Charles Harrison,
Modernism in Dispute: Art since the Forties (London and New Haven CT,
Open University Press, 1993).
Particularly helpful discussions of art in recent decades, attempting to
put the developments within the context of the 'break' with modernism,
and with several sections dealing explicitly with 'The idea of the
postmodern'.

Popular culture and music

Brooks, Ann, *Postfeminisms: Feminism, Cultural Theory and Cultural Forms*
(London, Routledge, 1997).
An excellent discussion of what constitutes recent theoretical debates
in feminist theory. Touches upon cultural theory, postmodernity and
popular culture.

Docker, John, *Postmodernism and Popular Culture: A Cultural History*
(Cambridge, Cambridge University Press, 1994).
Accessible discussion of popular culture and the theories of the principal
figures, touching on the relationship of modernism to postmodernism,
structuralism and poststructuralism, and soap operas.

Korsyn, Kevin, *Decentering Music* (New York and Oxford, Oxford University Press, 2003).
Recalling Foucault, Hayden White, Žižek and others, this book examines
the problems of arrogating authority for speaking about music in a time
of crisis for the humanities.

Lipsitz, George, *Dangerous Crossroads: Popular Music, Postmodernism and
the Poetics of Place* (London, Verso, 1994).
An exploration of the cultural politics of music culture in Los Angeles.

McClary, Susan, 'Terminal Prestige: The Case of Avant-Garde Music Composition', *Cultural Critique,* 12 (Spring 1989): 57–81.
Good discussions of Laurie Anderson and Philip Glass, and a persuasive attempt to contextualise the cultural reasons for why composers produce 'difficult' music.

Nyman, Michael, *Experimental Music, Cage and Beyond* (New York, Schirmer Books, 1974).
An essential book for any understanding of debates in contemporary music.

Polin, Claire, 'Why Minimalism Now?', in Christopher Norris (ed.), *Music and the Politics of Culture* (London, Lawrence and Wishart, 1989), pp. 226–39.
A very clear and good introductory essay on the politics of minimalist music.

Ross, Andrew (ed.), *Universal Abandon?: The Politics of Postmodernism* (Minneapolis, University of Minnesota Press, 1988).
A range of interviews and essays by leading figures, on such subjects as literature, theory, popular culture art, film and politics.

Ross, Andrew, and Tricia Rose (eds), *Microphone Fiends: Youth Music and Youth Culture* (New York and London, Routledge, 1994).
Looks at the ways in which youth culture is constantly reinvented and the various meanings with which youth music is invested.

Storey, John, *An Introductory Guide to Cultural Theory and Popular Culture* (Brighton, Harvester Wheatsheaf, 1993).
An excellent, introductory, chronological history of cultural studies and its intersection with critical and cultural theories.

Stratton, Jon, 'Beyond Art: Postmodernism and the Case of Popular Music', *Theory, Culture and Society,* 6:1 (February 1989): 31–57.
On the basis of a study of romantic notions of the sublime, Stratton establishes a three-stage historical development of popular music, arguing that the third stage is a postmodern aesthetic, in which pop music has operated 'within a concern with emotion and involvement, . . . based on excess'.

Swiss, Thomas, John Sloop and Andrew Herman (eds), *Mapping the Beat: Popular Music and Contemporary Theory* (Oxford, Blackwell, 1998).
Issues of power, identity, politics and space are combined with a series of detailed analyses of popular music in a theoretically sophisticated, historically contextualised and politically engaged collection of essays.

Film, video and televisual culture

Bignell, Jonathan, *Postmodern Media Culture* (Edinburgh, Edinburgh University Press, 2000).

Examines the relationships between theories of the postmodern and contemporary media institutions, products and consumers, and analyses the function of media examples in the work of key theorists.

Bordo, Susan, *Unbearable Weight: Feminism, Western Culture and the Body* (Berkeley CA, University of California Press, 1993).

Part Three of this book is entitled 'Postmodern Bodies', and provides an interesting critique of postmodernity and its cultural effects on women's bodies.

Degli-Esposti, Cristina (ed.), *Postmodernism in the Cinema* (New York, Berghahn, 1998).

This anthology offers sophisticated and multi-faceted discussions of a number of key issues in relation to cinema such as auteurism, national cinemas, metacinema, the parodic, history, and colonisation.

Dery, Mark (ed.), *Flame Wars: The Discourse of Cyberculture* (Durham NC, Duke University Press, 1994).

An excellent range of essays by key theorists investigating cybercultures across a variety of subjects.

Friedberg, Anne, *Window Shopping: Cinema and the Postmodern* (Berkeley CA, University of California Press, 1993).

Develops an account of cinema's role in postmodern culture. Shows how nineteenth-century visual experiences anticipate contemporary cinematic pleasures. Good on Fredric Jameson, Walter Benjamin and MTV.

Gillis, Stacy, *The Matrix Trilogy: Cyberpunk Reloaded* (London, Wallflower Press, 2005)

A collection of critical essays on the massive phenomenon that is the three Matrix films, including the subsequent Websites, computer games and *The Animatrix* films. Among the topics considered are the new cyberpunk, Baudrillardian simulacra, the politics of gender and race, the femme fatale, costume, cyberculture and the body, virtual realities and special effects.

Grebowicz, Margret, *Gender after Lyotard* (Albany NY, SUNY Press, 2007).

Examines Lyotard's writings on the posthuman in light of contemporary feminist theory.

Halberstam, Judith, and Ira Livingston (eds), *Posthuman Bodies* (Bloomington IN, Indiana University Press, 1995).

An interesting collection of essays which focus upon new ways of conceiving and constructing the human body.

Massumi, Brian, *Parables for the Virtual: Movement, Affect, Sensation* (Durham NC, Duke University Press, 2002).

This book views the body and media such as television, film and the Internet as cultural formations that operate on multiple registers of sensation beyond the reach of the reading techniques founded on the standard rhetorical and semiotic models. It tackles related theoretical issues by applying them to cultural mediums as diverse as architecture, body art, the digital art of Stelarc and Ronald Reagan's acting career.

Mazierska, Ewa, and Laura Rascaroli, *Crossing New Europe: Postmodern Travel and the European Road Movie* (London, Wallflower Press, 2006). Examines the ways in which European films have mirrored and explored complex different modes of travel and movement during the past thirty years, and the changing socio-political space of Europe which has in turn produced new forms of political and national identity.

Mitchell, William J., *City of Bits: Space, Place, and the Infobahn* (Cambridge MA, MIT Press, 1995). An interesting book exploring architecture and urbanism in the context of digital telecommunications, speculating about the emergent cities, social practices, art and new communities of cyberspace in the twenty-first century.

Nayar, Pramod K., *Virtual Worlds: Culture and Politics in the Age of Cybertechnology* (London, Sage, 2004). Considers a range of key writers, theorists and issues within the debates of cyberculture.

O'Bryan, C. Jill, *Carnal Art: Orlan's Refacing* (Minneapolis MN, University of Minnesota Press, 2005). Considers how the artist's ever-fluctuating reconstructions of her face question idealised beauty and female identity, persuasively arguing that Orlan's surgically reinvented face succeeds in both reinforcing and breaking apart corporeal subjectivity and representation.

Stallabrass, Julian, *Gargantua: Manufactured Mass Culture* (London, Verso, 1996). Scrutinising amateur photography, computer games, cyberspace, shopping and television, this book focuses on contemporary culture and its Gargantuan proportions and character, challenging postmodernism's attachment to subjectivity and indeterminacy.

Tetzlaff, David J., 'MTV and the Politics of Postmodern Pop', *Journal of Communication Inquiry*, 10:1 (1986): 80–91. A good, introductory article on the phenomenon of MTV and postmodern analyses.

Trend, David (ed.), *Reading Digital Culture* (Oxford, Blackwell, 2001). A comprehensive collection of the most influential essays on digital media written in recent years.

Ziaddin, Sardar, and Jerome Ravetz (eds), *Cyberfutures: Culture and Politics on the Information Superhighway* (London, Pluto Press, 1996).

Useful and interesting essays reflecting upon the cultural and political
dimensions of the colonisation of cyberspace.

Social sciences

Anthropology and ethnography

Clifford, James, *The Predicament of Culture* (Cambridge MA, Harvard
University Press, 1988).
Uses many postmodern ideas about identity, space and representation in
defining what constitutes a postmodern ethnography.
Hine, Christine, *Virtual Ethnography* (London, Sage, 2000).
Considers the challenges that new technologies pose to traditional ways
of studying culture and society.

Economics

Cullenberg, Stephen, Jack Amariglio and David F. Ruccio (eds), *Postmod-
ernism, Economics and Knowledge* (London, Routledge, 2001).
Brings together major theorists of economics including Arjo Klamer,
Deirdre McCloskey, Julie Nelson, Shaun Hargreaves Heap and Philip
Mirowski, on diverse areas of postmodernism and economics.
Ruccio, David F. and Jack Amariglio, *Postmodern Moments in Modern
Economics* (Princeton NJ, Princeton University Press, 2003).
Investigates a range of key subjects such as gender, Marxism and uncer-
tainty in relation to postmodern economic theory.

Education theory

Fischman, Gustavo, Peter McLaren, Heinz Sunker and Colin Lankshear
(eds), *Critical Theories, Radical Pedagogies, and Global Conflicts* (Lanham
MD, Rowman and Littlefield, 2005).
Responding to some oppressive and challenging conditions, a group of
committed educators and activists seek to link educational transformation to the larger struggle to transform oppressive social relations.
Hill, Dave, Peter McLaren, Mike Cole and Glenn Rikowski (eds), *Marxism
Against Postmodernism in Educational Theory* (1999; Lanham MD, Lexington Books, 2002).
Written by renowned British and American educational theorists, this
book examines the infusion of theories of postmodernity into educational
theory, policy, and research.
Orr, David W., *Ecological Literacy: Education and the Transition to a Postmodern World* (New York, SUNY Press, 1992).

Argues for the necessity of finding a postmodern 'connective education' which is 'life-centred' to overcome the pernicious effects of education in the modern world.

Usher, Robin and Richard Edwards, *Postmodernism and Education* (London, Routledge, 1994).

Responding to the interest in postmodernism as a way of understanding social, cultural and economic trends, this book explores the impact that postmodernism has had upon the theory and practice of education.

International relations and politics

Ashley, R.K., 'Living on Border Lines: Man, Poststructuralism and War', in J. Der Derian and M.J. Shapiro (eds), *International/Intertextual Relations: Postmodern Readings of World Politics* (New York, Lexington Books, 1989), pp. 259–321.

A long, seminal essay on what issues ought to preoccupy a postmodern international relations theory. Focuses on anti-humanism, textuality, poststructuralism and history, and the sovereignty debate. Essential reading, yet advanced.

Der Derian, James, 'The Boundaries of Knowledge and Power in International Relations', in J. Der Derian and M.J. Shapiro (eds), *International/Intertextual Relations: Postmodern Readings of World Politics* (New York, Lexington Books, 1989), pp. 3–10.

A brief yet useful introduction to postmodern international relations and poststructuralism.

Gray, Chris Hables, *Postmodern War: The New Politics of Conflict* (London, Routledge, 1997).

Discusses how computerisation and other scientific advances have affected warfare, and how rhetoric disguises the destructive potential of increasingly powerful weapons.

Jarvis, D.S.L., *International Relations and the Challenge of Postmodernism* (Columbia SC, University of South Carolina Press, 2000).

Explores the critical terms and motifs of postmodernism in international relations, exploring the work of Richard Ashley and feminist revisions in particular.

Rengger, N.J., *Political Theory, Modernity and Postmodernity* (Oxford, Blackwell, 1995).

Attempts to relate the debates about modernity and postmodernity to political theory. Understanding postmodernity 'as a description of the current state of modernity as a socio-cultural form and what follows from that', Rengger is neither wholehearted in his defence of modernity nor offering a full acceptance of a 'postmodern turn'. Instead, he argues that one has to abandon the increasingly sterile dichotomous structure of the 'modernity debate' (modern versus postmodern), since it obstructs the ethico-political implications of modernity for political theory.

Shapiro, Michael J., *Reading the Postmodern Polity: Political Theory as Textual Practice* (Minneapolis MN, University of Minnesota Press, 1992).

Incorporates a wide range of ideas from poststructuralist theorists, analysing power, authority and the distribution of resources. Contains several essays on Don DeLillo's fiction, as well as other contemporary cultural practices and experiences.

Sylvester, Christine, *Feminist Theory and International Relations in a Post-modern Era* (Cambridge, Cambridge University Press, 1992).

Relates feminism to discussions of international relations and postmodernism. For more advanced students.

White, Stephen K., *Political Theory and Postmodern* (Cambridge, Cambridge University Press, 1991).

A sophisticated book on the philosophy of responsibility, especially how postmodernism can inform 'ethico-political' reflection.

Law

Carty, Anthony (ed.), *Post-modern Law: Enlightenment, Revolution and the Death of Man* (Edinburgh, Edinburgh University Press, 1990).

An advanced philosophical argument about the anti-foundationalism of postmodern law.

Douzinas, Costas, Peter Goodrich and Yifat Hachamovitch (eds), *Politics, Postmodernity and Critical Legal Studies: The Legality of the Contingent* (London, Routledge, 1994).

In analysing the cultural significance of law, the contributors show how critical jurisprudential analysis undermines positivistic attempts to support a normative viewpoint of the legal order.

Douzinas, Costas and Adam Gearey, *Critical Jurisprudence: The Political Philosophy of Justice* (Oxford, Hart Publishing, 2005).

Provocative and insightful, this book challenges readers to question dominant readings of the law, tracing a tradition of critical thought that has always haunted the orthodoxy.

Edgeworth, Brendan, *Law, Modernity, Postmodernity: Legal Change in the Contracting State* (Aldershot, Ashgate, 2003).

This book examines the interrelationship between the unravelling of the post-war welfare state and legal change and by reference to theorists of postmodernity such as Zygmunt Bauman, Scott Lash and John Urry, and David Harvey, argues that contemporary law and legal institutions have changed in ways that mirror the transformation of the interventionist welfare state and its Keynesian economic infrastructure.

Frug, Mary Joe, *Postmodern Legal Feminism* (New York, Routledge, 1992).
Utilises postmodern ideas to uncover the gendered politics of the law.

Goodrich, Peter, *Oedipus Lex: Psychoanalysis, History, Law* (Berkeley, University of California Press, 1995).
Offers an original and evocative reading of legal history and institutional practice in the light of psychoanalysis and aesthetics, keenly attuned to the discontinuities, silences, and gaps in the cultural tradition of the law.

Goodrich, Peter and David Gray Carlson (eds), *Law and the Postmodern Mind: Essays on Psychoanalysis and Jurisprudence* (Ann Arbor MI, University of Michigan Press, 1998).
This book argues that the postmodern legal mind has introduced a series of 'minor jurisprudences' or partial forms of legal knowledge, which both compete with and subvert the modernist conception of a unitary system of law.

Litowitz, Douglas E., *Postmodern Philosophy and Law* (Lawrence KA, University Press of Kansas, 1999).
This book offers a critical introduction to writings on law by key post-modern philosophers – Nietzsche, Foucault, Derrida, Lyotard, and Rorty – and articulates the strengths and weaknesses of postmodern legal theory.

Minda, Gary, *Postmodern Legal Movements: Law and Jurisprudence at Century's End* (New York, New York University Press, 1995).
Focuses on the ways that the study and practice of law have been profoundly influenced by a number of powerful new movements that rethink the interaction between law and society, focusing more on the tangible effects of law than on its procedural elements.

Patterson, Dennis (ed.), *Postmodernism and Law* (Aldershot, Dartmouth Publishing, 1994).
A collection of leading articles on justice, feminism, subjectivity and constitutionalism.

Stacy, Helen, *Postmodernism and Law: Jurisprudence in a Fragmenting World* (Aldershot, Ashgate, 2001).
Considers the ethical questions that postmodernism raises for the legitimation of legal rules and legal judgments, arguing that strands of postmodernism offer legal reasoning and adjudication elements of liberal promise that foster and protect individual agency.

Organisation theory

Clegg, Stewart R., *Modern Organizations: Organization Studies in the Post-modern World* (London, Sage, 1990).

Produces a sophisticated argument about the connection between post-modernity and new organisational structures.

Hassard, John, and Martin Parker (eds), *Postmodernism and Organizations* (London, Sage, 1993).

A good introduction to postmodernism, outlining the concepts under-pinning a postmodern organisational analysis. Suceeding essays focus on deconstruction, desire, pluralism and relativism. Worthwhile reading.

Hancock, Philip and Melissa Tyler, *Work, Postmodernism and Organization* (London, Sage, 2001).

The book provides a critical review of the debates that have shaped organisation theory during the 1990s, making clear the meaning and significance of postmodern ideas for contemporary organisation theory and practice.

Hatch, Mary Jo, *Organization Theory: Modern Symbolic and Postmodern Perspectives* (Oxford, Oxford University Press, 1997).

A clear and comprehensive introduction to the study of organisations, charting the changing models from modern to postmodern theories.

Linstead, Stephen, *Organization Theory and Postmodern Thought* (London, Sage, 2003).

This book provides an excellent reference for students and academics alike for understanding the key elements of postmodern thinking with reference to organisation studies.

Psychology and psychotherapy

Frie, Roger (ed.), *Understanding Experience: Psychotherapy and Postmodernism* (London, Routledge, 2003).

The authors address the postmodern debate in contemporary psycho-therapy and psychoanalysis through clinical case discussion and theoretical exegesis.

Holzman, Lois and John R. Morss (eds), *Postmodern Psychologies* (New York and London, Routledge, 2000).

Gathering essays from such eminent people as Gergen, Shotter and Parker, this book reflects on the achievements and limitations of attempts to develop postmodern analyses in psychology research and practice.

Sociology

Agger, Ben, *Postponing the Postmodern: Sociological Practices, Selves, and Theories* (Lanham MD, Rowman and Littlefield, 2002).

Examines conceptions and theories of the self in a post-9/11 world.

Ashley, David, *History without a Subject: The Postmodern Condition* (Boulder CO, Westview Press, 1997).

Beginning with an analysis of how changes in the global economy are affecting the lives of ordinary Americans, this book suggests that the postmodern condition can be likened to the balkanisation of culture and society and the 'Brazilianisation' of politics and the economy.

Best, Steven and Douglas Kellner, *The Postmodern Adventure: Science, Technology, and Cultural Studies at the Third Millennium* (New York, Guilford Press, 2001).

In the face of massive geopolitical shifts and dramatic developments in computerisation and biotechnology heralding the transformation from the modern to the postmodern age, this book explores the challenges to theory, politics, and human identity that we face on the threshold of the third millennium, confronted as we are by altered modes of work, communication, and entertainment; new postindustrial and political networks; novel approaches to warfare, genetic engineering, and even cloning.

Choi, Jongryul, *Postmodern American Sociology: A Response to the Aesthetic Challenge* (Lanham MD, University Press of America, 2004).

Explores the modern, the postmodern, and the relationship between the two in terms of three paradigms of knowledge: science, morality and aesthetics.

Cooke, Philip, *Back to the Future* (London, Unwin Hyman, 1990).

The first half explores modernity and its characteristic modes and practices; the second half examines those discourses ranged against or countering the project of modernity, although Cooke argues that they renew it. A readable and accessible discussion, it maps out the sociology of social transformation clearly.

Crook, Stephen, Jan Pakulski, and Malcolm Waters, *Postmodernization: Change in Advanced Society* (London, Sage, 1992).

A lucid and engaging theoretical analysis of the changes in contemporary society, which traces the impact of societal transformation in six areas: culture and style; the state and monopoly capitalism; race, class and gender; the emergence of new societal movements; flexible manufacturing systems; and the decline in authority of scientific explanation.

Gottdiener, M., *Postmodern Semiotics: Material Culture and the Forms of Postmodern Life* (Oxford, Blackwell, 1995).

Considers the role of semiotics and symbols in postmodern society.

Mestrovic, Stjepan G., *The Barbarian Temperament: Toward a Postmodern Critical Theory* (London and New York, Routledge, 1993).

Arguing that the fundamental basis of contemporary society is non-rational, this is a sophisticated study of the definitions of what it is to be 'civilised'. Considers the repackaging of barbarianism and the idea of progress in the debates about civilisation in modernity and postmodernity.

Nicholson, Linda, and Steven Seidman (eds), *Social Postmodernism: Beyond Identity Politics* (Cambridge, Cambridge University Press, 1995).

Essays by leading figures focusing on gender, sexuality, politics, economics and social movements. Defends social postmodernism by blending microsocial concerns with a cultural analysis of their broader political vision.

Owen, David (ed.), *Sociology After Postmodernism* (London, Sage, 1997).

Considers the challenge postmodernism poses to class, gender, law, race and ethnicity, culture and media, sexuality and the body.

Powell, Jason L. and Tim Owen (eds), *Reconstructing Postmodernism: Critical Debates* (Hauppauge NY, Nova Publishers, 2007).

This book focuses on three continuing areas of debate in social science: debunking the central theoretical postmodern tenets of identity, methodology, governance and modernist theory; engaging with current social issues and events in popular culture; rethinking postmodernism in light of under-researched analyses of time and ageing, the 'body', 'biology' and 'choice'.

Rosenau, Pauline Marie, *Post-modernism and the Social Sciences: Insights, Inroads and Instructions* (Princeton NJ, Princeton University Press, 1995).

Offers a good introduction to the debates and terminologies originating in the humanities and their transformation in restructuring the social sciences. Also provides a useful glossary of postmodern terms to assist the uninitiated reader with special meanings not found in standard dictionaries.

Seidman, Steven (ed.), *The Postmodern Turn: New Perspectives on Social Theory* (Cambridge, Cambridge University Press, 1994).

Gathers some of the most important statements on postmodern approaches to human studies by people like Jean-François Lyotard, Michael Foucault, Donna Haraway, Richard Rorty and Cornel West.

Smart, Barry, *Modern Conditions, Postmodern Controversies* (London, Routledge, 1991).

Focuses on modernity and its consequences, anxiety about the project of modernity and its postmodern conditions. Discussions of all the seminal thinkers, and good on Marxism, postindustrialism, technology and postmodernism. For the more advanced student.

Other postmodernisms

History

Breisach, Ernst, *On the Future of History: The Postmodernist Challenge and Its Aftermath* (Chicago, University of Chicago Press, 2003).
Provides a comprehensive overview of postmodernism and its complex relationship to history and historiography, placing postmodern theories in their intellectual and historical contexts.

Jenkins, Keith, *Re-thinking History* (London, Routledge, 1991).
A polemical introductory guide to an understanding of what constitutes historical research in postmodern conditions.

Jenkins, Keith (ed.), *The Postmodern History Reader* (London, Routledge, 1997).
Reproduces many of the key contributions to recent debates.

Jenkins, Keith, *Refiguring History: New Thoughts on an Old Discipline* (London, Routledge, 2003).
Arguing for a re-figuration of historical study, this book presents the past and questions about the nature of history as interminably open to new and disobedient approaches.

Southgate, Beverley C., *History: What and Why?: Ancient, Modern, and Postmodern Perspectives* (London, Routledge, 1996).
A good introductory guide to historiography, including a short but accessible discussion of postmodern history and the viability of its challenges to orthodox practices.

Southgate, Beverley C., *Postmodernism in History: Fear or Freedom?* (London, Routledge, 2003).
With her main concern to counter 'pomophobia' and to assert a positive future for historical study in a postmodern world, Southgate describes the core constituents of postmodernism and provides a lucid and profound analysis of the current state of the debate.

Southgate, Beverley C., *What is History For?* (London, Routledge, 2005).
With traditional notions of truth and historical representation under question, Southgate rethinks the function of history and renegotiates its uses for the postmodern age.

Thompson, Willie, *Postmodernism and History* (Basingstoke, Palgrave Macmillan, 2004).
In a clear, jargon-free introduction to postmodernist theory and its significant impact on the study of history, Thompson presents key ideas in a straightforward way.

Museology

Walsh, Kevin, *The Representation of the Past: Museums and Heritage in the Post-modern World* (London, Routledge, 1988).
This book examines the 1980s' boom in preserving the past, the 'heritage industry', as part of the experience of living in the postmodern world.

Anthologies/readers

Boyne, Roy, and Ali Rattansi (eds), *Postmodernism and Society* (Basingstoke, Macmillan, 1990).
A good, wide-ranging collection of essays on the subject of postmodernism across disciplines, including art, architecture, fashion, feminism, theory and language.

Docherty, Thomas (ed.), *Postmodernism: A Reader* (Brighton, Harvester Wheatsheaf, 1993).
An excellent collection of principal documents in the debate about postmodernism, organised into useful subsections. Theorists include Jürgen Habermas, Fredric Jameson and Jean Baudrillard, and sections are prefaced by helpful and interesting commentaries. One of the better anthologies for students, with a wide-ranging bibliography.

Jencks, Charles (ed.), *The Post-modern Reader* (London, Academy Editions, 1992).
Contains many of the usual central pieces by leading theorists, like Jürgen Habermas, Andreas Huyssen, Linda Hutcheon, Jean-François Lyotard, Jean Baudrillard and Charles Jencks. Wide-ranging in its focus, it also has an unusual and interesting section on science and religion.

Taylor, Victor E. and Charles E. Winquist (eds), *Postmodernism: Critical Concepts* (1998; London, Routledge, 2001).
This major four-volume encyclopedia attempts broad coverage, attempting to present the reader with historically significant foundational texts charting the development of postmodernism as a critical concept through the works of the key thinkers, postmodernism's reception, and then demonstrating postmodernism's impact in virtually every intellectual discipline.

Waugh, Patricia (ed.), *Postmodernism: A Reader* (London, Edward Arnold, 1992).
Includes the central and now canonical essays by Jürgen Habermas, Jean-François Lyotard, Jean Baudrillard and Fredric Jameson, but also a useful section on philosophical predecessors and a select bibliography. In contrast to others, this anthology is weighted towards the literary critical.

Index

Note: Page numbers given in *italic* refer to illustrations.

403450